KETTENHUND!

KETTENHUND!

The German Military Police in the Second World War

GORDON WILLIAMSON

Frontispece above: Having removed his cap, note the clean head of the *Feldgendarmerie Hauptmann* compared with the rest of his dust caked face during the advance into Russia, summer 1941.

Frontispece below: A *Feldgendarmerie* NCO escorting a large column of Soviet prisoners.

Fonthill Media Limited
Fonthill Media LLC
www.fonthill.media
books@fonthill.media

First published in the United Kingdom and the United States of America 2014
Reprinted 2021

British Library Cataloguing in Publication Data:
A catalogue record for this book is available from the British Library

ISBN 978-1-78155-332-9

Typeset in 10 pt on 13 pt Gill Sans
Printed and bound in England

Contents

A *Feldgendarmerie Unteroffizier* carrying out a check on the rear lights of a naval staff car. (*Josef Charita*)

Unit mechanics service the motorcycles of a *Feldgendarmerie Trupp*.

Acknowledgements

My father served with the Provost Company of the famed Scottish unit 51 (Highland) Division, seeing service in North Africa and Italy and landed with the Division in Normandy in June 1944.

Having developed a passionate interest in history and in particular military history at an early age, the fact that my father had served throughout World War Two with the Corps of Military Police no doubt influenced my taking a particular interest in that branch of the military. Eventually, having moved to a city with a local Military Police unit of the Territorial Army, I took the opportunity to join and spent most of the 1980s with the Royal Military Police.

This gave me the opportunity not only to experience life as a military policeman, albeit on a part-time basis, but also to travel to Europe during military exercises and meet the military police personnel from our Nato allies. These experiences included a highly enjoyable attachment to a unit of the *Feldjäger*, the military police of the German *Bundeswehr*. During that attachment I was particularly interested in the attitude of some of these modern German military policemen to their wartime predecessors. Despite the fact that it was not "politically correct" to show to much interest in the Third Reich, most were fascinated to see photos of some of the *Feldgendarmerie* artefacts in my collection.

Unfortunately, at that time very little had been published on then subject and I thus began to collect information for myself from a wide variety of sources.

Study of published sources such as the *Heeresverordnungsblätter* (Army Regulation Sheets) and their airforce and naval equivalents, *Heeresdienstvorschrift* (Army Service Regulations) and *Allgemeine Heeresmitteilungen* German Army Gazette all provided detailed information on regulations relating to the military police whilst surviving copies of the *Feldgendarmerie Vorschrift* (Military Police Regulations) revealed the duties and tasks which these troops were expected to perform.

Even trade periodicals for uniform outfitters, such as *Uniformenmarkt*, reveal announcements regarding insignia being introduced.

Documents known as the *Kriegsstärkenachweisung* were consulted for the authorised tables of equipment and manpower for each type of unit whilst existing databases of the *Feldpost* (field post) numbers allocated to military units, though not complete, were a useful tool for cross referencing *Feldgendarmerie* units which existed.

It addition, study of original examples of the *Wehrpass* (Military Pass) and *Soldbuch* (Paybook) belonging to *Feldgendarmen* proved to be a mine of information.

Last but not least, I am grateful to members of the militaria collecting community for making available so many photographs, both wartime shots and those of surviving examples of *Ordnungstruppe* ephemera.

I am also grateful to a number of German veterans who contributed information on their experiences in, and encounters with, the *Feldgendarmerie*. Without all of their help, this book would not have been possible.

Erwin Bartmann +
David Bunch
Gary Chambers
Josef Charita
Clyde R. Davis
Ludwig Dinger +
Sebastian Golawski
Heinz Heuer +
Kevin Huckfield
Ian Jewison
Herbert E. Kail
Henner Lindlar
Oskar Lösel +
Peter von Lukacs
Robert Noss
George Peterson
Scott Pritchett
Bill Shea
Brecht Schotte
Walter Spiller
Wim Saris
Christoph Schultz
Willi Schumacher
Gottfried Schwittalla +
Otto Spronk
Hans Sturm +
Jan Arne Straete
Bart Verstraeten
Peter Whamond
Helmut Weitze
Gary Wood

Introduction

It is probably true to say that in almost any of the World's armies, the least popular troops in the eyes of the regular soldier will be that nation's military police. Many servicemen seem to feel that the military police serve no other purpose than to make life difficult for them, conveniently forgetting that without the military police to plan and sign supply routes, defend vulnerable points, provide convoy escorts and a myriad of other essential tasks, the soldier's life would be far more difficult and dangerous.

Many of the greatest soldiers of all time have been quoted complimenting the service provided by these little loved troops. Perhaps one of the most telling of such comments was made by Field Marshal Bernard L. Montgomery in 1945 when, talking of the momentous battle for Normandy in the summer of 1944 he said:

> The Battle of Normandy and subsequent battles would not have been won but for the work and co-operation of the Provost on the traffic routes.

But what of Germany's military police? Like Great Britain and other countries, Germany's military police have had a long history, much of it perfectly honourable. It must be said however, that whatever the military achievements of the *Feldgendarmerie*, from 1939 to 1945 they, along of course with every other German soldier, served the Nazi regime. Along with every other branch of the military, there would have been those who served with honour, whilst others who fully believed in the ideals of the Third Reich were certainly less hesitant to become involved in war crimes and instances are documented of *Feldgendarmerie* units assisting *SS* and security troops in atrocities, particularly during 'anti-partisan' actions.

The study of the operational activities of individual units however is beyond the scope of this work the purpose of which is to describe the organisational structure of the many military police type units best described as *Ordnungstruppe*—or troops whose primary duty was to maintain order, of which the *Feldgendarmerie* was but one, and the uniforms and insignia that they wore. This book covers only the *Ordnungstruppe* of the military. The German police including the civil *Gendarmerie* maintained its own field units, but the *Gendarmerie* operating in the field were entirely different to the *Feldgendarmerie*, or military police proper, which of course was a branch of the German *Wehrmacht*, not the police.

If any reader has additional information they would wish to share, the author has created a website which the reader is invited to visit, at http://www.feldgendarmerie.net where additional additional information and images in support of this book will be provided. Any contributions of additional information will be gratefully received and added to the databases which will ultimately be added to this site.

Historical Perspective

In ancient times the task of maintaining order and discipline within Germanic armies tended to be carried out by a designated '*marschall*'(marshal). The term itself derives from two Germanic words *marah* meaning horse, and *schalk* meaning servant, as that individual was primarily responsible for ensuring measures were taken for the care, stabling and provisioning of the army's horses, something essential for efficient movement of large armies at that time. The position was also sometimes referred to as the *oberstallmeister*.

The position of marshal was one of great responsibility and soon grew to encompass not just the care of the horses but general administration and policing of the armies. A royal edict of 1312 apparently also gave the marshal absolute legal power which made him a figure that generated considerable fear.

The title '*profos*' (provost) entered German usage from France in the sixteenth century with a later document from the seventeenth century describing the provost's tasks as punishing disobedient soldiers and dealing with 'freebooters, robbers, vagabonds those who carried forbidden weapons' and what were termed 'lazy rogues'. The provost became, in effect, judge jury and executioner in one, with his mounted knights as his 'enforcers'.

In 1577, the *Reichspolizeiordnung* was issued and in the various individual Germanic lands mounted police units were formed bearing a variety of designations, such as police dragoons (*polizei-dragonen*), police hussars (*polizei-husaren*) and police rifles (*polizei-jäger*)

These were turbulent times and through the sixteenth and seventeenth centuries, military discipline was brutal in the extreme. Although this changed in time, the terms remain to this day. In the British Army, military police are organised into 'provost' companies and the senior ranking military police officer is the provost marshal (a term also recently reintroduced into use in the US armed forces).

Back in the eighteenth century, Friedrich Wilhelm I used his Prussian hussars not as combat cavalry, but for apprehending deserters and other similar tasks of a police type nature. In 1740 they were officially established with the title *Feldjägertruppe*. By the middle of that century, such troops were also being used for tasks which would become common for military police in the future but were unusual for police type units at the time such as route planning and investigation, courier services and escort duties.

By the early nineteenth century things were beginning to change and in 1810 the Prussian Army received a new formation, the *Armeegendarmerie* which took over many of the tasks which had been performed by the previous Hussar units.

Leibgendarmes who were effectively police charged with close-protection duties for royalty, and were carefully selected from the best quality cavalry NCOs, were now part of the retinue of the king. To this day, the military police of many countries maintain sections that are trained in close-protection duties to maintain the safety of VIPs.

There also existed at this time, the Prussian *Landgendarmerie*, which would be under the command of an army general, and thus in both disciplinary and administrative terms a military unit, but whilst acting on civil policing type duties, would be under the control of the district authorities. Moves were beginning however, to differentiate between those police units with solely military functions and those which related to policing the civilian populace.

One can already see the beginnings of what would grow to be a bewilderingly complex German police structure by the twentieth century.

Bavaria too, joined Prussia in creating a distinct military police formation and in 1813 the *Gendarmerie im Felde* (literally field-police or 'police in the field') was formed.

On the outbreak of the Franco-Prussian war in 1870, orders were issued for the raising of *Feldgendarmerie* units. The purpose of these troops included—maintaining order in the areas around troop billets and garrisons, searching buildings, villages etc. for weapons, enemy soldiers, spies etc.—preventing the looting of villages along the army's route of march—patrolling the battlefield, prevention of looting of the dead and wounded—support of requisitioning—serving with field courts martial—transport of condemned individuals—bringing prisoners to collecting points—collecting and passing on of stragglers—fighting against fifth columnists—keeping free the roads to the rear of advancing troops by patroling—protection of supply columns from looting and theft, particularly in the forest-rich areas of the Vosges and traffic control at bridges.

Following the successful conclusion of the short Franco-Prussian war, the various military police type units were disbanded and this situation remained until the outbreak of the First World War.

Germany entered the First World War in 1914 having formed a total of 33 *Feldgendarmerie-Truppen*, each with a strength of around 60 NCOs and men, usually built around a core of members of the *Landgendarmerie* drafted into the army and led by selected personnel from other branches of the army in particular officers and experienced NCOs from the cavalry. By the end of the war, the total number of *Feldgendarmerie* units had increased to 115.

Above left: Two *Feldgendarmerie* NCOs in the peacetime dark green uniform, later replaced by field grey.

Above right: The details of the gorgets worn by these *Feldgendarmen* show them to belong to *VIII Armeekorps*. Above the Roman numeral of the *Armeekorps* is the individual number of the *Feldgendarm*.

A later wartime gorget with grey painted finish. The Arabic numeral without Roman numeral below shows this to be a gorget worn in a Prussian *Gardekorps*.

Approximately 35 per cent of *Feldgendarmen* were former senior NCOs from the civil police with the remainder evenly divided between junior NCOs and enlisted men transferred from the cavalry. *Feldgendarmen* normally operated in three-man patrols or *Streifen* consisting of one man from each of the rank groups.

In the late stages of the war *Feldgendarmeriekorps z.b.V.* was formed on the Western Front and by the end of hostilities, this had grown in strength to the size of a full Regiment, and was renamed *Gendarmerie-Regiment* 9.

Following Germany's defeat in 1918, the *Feldgendarmerie* was once gain disbanded and from 1918 until mobilisation in 1939 Germany had no dedicated military police branch for its armed forces.

A disarmed *Feldgendarm*, but still in full uniform, assisting US Military Police with traffic control in the American zone. (*US Signal Corps Photo*)

Not *Feldgendarmerie per se*, but many former *Feldgendarm*en and police personnel such as this individual were trained and supervised by the British Corps of Military Police in the British zone of occupation. The armband text reads 'M.G. Police' (M.G.='Military Government')

1
The Feldgendarmerie

(i) Feldgendarmerie des Heeres

After the end of the First World War, the Germany army lost its *Feldgendarmerie* units and this situation remained unchanged throughout period of the Weimar Republic and its *Reichswehr* and indeed also for the early years after the creation of the new *Wehrmacht*.

Unlike most nations which maintained military police units even during peacetime, the *Wehrmacht* formed such units only on a temporary basis, by drafting personnel from the civil police, most often the *Motorisierte Gendarmerie*. Other nations of course, including the British, had reinforced their military police during times of need, by drafting civilian policemen, but for a nation which was rapidly expanding its military forces it was a somewhat unusual situation for the Germans to create only temporary military police units. Such units were formed for major military exercises and major troop movements such as those which occurred during the so-called 'Flower-Wars' (the *Anschluss* with Austria and the occupation of the Sudetenland). These units however were disbanded again soon afterwards.

Only with the mobilisation of the Army in the lead up to the Second World War did the serious creation of permanent military police units begin. In fact the *Feldgendarmerie* units were some of the first to be created, orders specifying that they had to begin forming up within 12 hours of the mobilisation orders, a perfectly logical move as units concerned with order and discipline and the movement of large bodies of troops needed to be in place before the remainder of the army began to form.

Of course the *Wehrmacht* already had access to a small cadre of troops who had served in the previous temporary units and so the rapid creation of these new permanent units was made easier. Some 280 officers and just under 7,900 NCOs and men were transferred from the civil police in the weeks before the outbreak of war.

The tasks that were to be performed by the *Feldgendarmerie* fell into three basic categories.

Maintaining order and discipline

i) Monitoring of order and discipline amongst service personnel.

ii) Collection of prisoners of war and formation of collecting points at the front, both for prisoners and for German stragglers.

iii) Investigation of crimes committed by military personnel.

iv) Apprehension of deserters.

v) Monitoring movement of troops in transit to and from leave, (in co-operation with the Army Patrol Service (*Streifendienst*).

Motorisierte Gendarmerie NCO wears the *Feld=Gendarmerie* armband over his police sleeve eagle.

This *Motorisierte Gendarmerie* NCO wears the *Deutsche Wehrmacht* armband over his sleeve eagle and the *Feld=Gendarmerie* armband just above the cuff.

— 4 —

Lichtbild des Inhabers:

Din A 9. 37×52 mm.

(Eigenhändige Unterschrift des Inhabers.)

— 1 —

Dienstausweis

Nr. 211

Friedrich Willuweit

(Name des Inhabers.)

Gend.-Wachtmeister

(Amtsbezeichnung.)

Din A 6. 105×148 mm. Vordr. R. Pol. Nr. 1.

Polizei Ausweis of Friedrich Willuweit, a police NCO who also served with the *Feldgendarmerie.*

Above left: Feldgendarmerie troops at drill practice with the Kar98k.

Above right: A *Gendarmerie* NCO wears the *Deutsche Wehrmacht* armband below the sleeve eagle and the *Feld=Gendarmerie* armband above the cuff.

Oberkdo. 6. Armee

<u>In der Brusttasche zu tragen!</u>

Gleichzeitig Ausweis

(Nur gültig in Verbindung m. d. Soldbuch!)

Dem Feldgendarm erie-Offz. Leutnant Kurt Schulte-Berge der in meinem persönlichen Auftrag seinen Dienst erfüllt und durch Ringkragen sichtbar herausgehoben wird, ist von allen Wehrmachtsangehörigen, wer er auch sei, in Ausübung seines Dienstes Gehorsam entgegenzubringen. Wer einem Feldgendarm in seiner Dienstaufsicht den Gehorsam verweigert oder nicht gehorcht, wird von mir genau so bestraft, als ob mir der Gehorsam verweigert worden ist.

Insbesondere haben die Feldgendarmen zu überwachen:

Haltung und Disziplin aller Wehrmachtsangehörigen,
Verkehrsdisziplin und Straßenordnung,
Verdunkelung und Tarnung.

Andererseits verlange ich vom Feldgendarm:

Äußerste Zuverlässigkeit,
Höchsten Einsatz seiner Person,
Vorbildliche militärische Haltung,
Taktvolles militärisches Benehmen Vorgesetzten gegenüber bei Ausständen.

Balck
General d. Panzertruppe

Ausweis issued by 6th Army to be used in conjunction with the *Soldbuch*, confirming the authority of the *Feldgendarm*. (*Ian Jewison*)

Feldgendarmerie NCOs prepare food at a POW collecting point as Soviet prisoners look on. (*Sebastian Golawski*)

Above left: The *Feldgendarmerie Oberfeldwebel* at left wears the marksmanship lanyard as well as the trade badge for a *Waffenfeldwebel* (Ordnance NCO).

Above right: Feldgendarm guarding a Soviet prisoner. The Kgf patch on the prisoner's tunic is for '*Kriegsgefangener*'. (*Henner Lindlar*)

Traffic control

i) Planning and marking of military routes.
ii) Traffic control and direction.
iii) Control of traffic at water crossings.
iv) Monitoring of military traffic.
v) Ensuring priority of movement for certain traffic.

Security

i) Prevention of sabotage and espionage
ii) Protection of headquarter locations
iii) General police tasks in occupied areas where no indigenous police functions are available.
iv) Protection of lines of communication in rear areas
v) Combating partisans and *Francs Tireurs*.

Above left: An iconic image of the typical *Feldgendarm* on traffic control duty. (*Clyde R. Davis*)

Above right: Feldgendarmerie dog handler with a muzzled Boxer dog. This is the same soldier pictured in the photo showing the *Waffenrock* (note the Panzer Assault Badge—rarely seen worn by a *Feldgendarm*).

20

noch **IV. Aktiver**

Ausbildung

Mit der Waffe

Karabiner 98 k,

M.G. 08,

Pistole 08

22

21

Wehrdienst

Ausbildung

Sonstige Ausbildung, Lehrgänge

Nachrichtenmann

W.K.F. Kl. III, M.K.F. Kl. I W.K.F. Kl. II

Schreiber-Uffz.

Lehrgang für Schutzhundeführer

bei der Hunde-Staffel Nachr. A.A.

82.- Magdeburg v. 23.8.-26.10.43

Abzeichen usw.

An entry from the Stanitz *Wehrpass* previously illustrated showing his attendance at a dog-handler's course.

Above left: A *Feldwebel* and *Hauptfeldwebel* of *Feldgendarmerie* with their German Shepherd dog.

Above right: The German Shepherd was immensely popular, both as a pet and as a working dog with the *Feldgendarmerie*.

Allocation of Feldgendarmerie Units

Although, eventually all branches of the armed forces would have their own military police units, most of these had limited areas of responsibility, whereas the *Feldgendarmerie* of the army had far greater authority and more widely ranging tasks. Not surprisingly then, the breakdown of the *Feldgendarmerie* of the army is fairly complex.

Feldgendarmerie troops were allocated at the following levels.

Army / Army Corps

Each army or army corps (usually a grouping of several divisions) was to be allocated a *Feldgendarmerie Abteilung* with a strength of three companies. These larger units were generally under the control of the commander of the rear areas or *Kommandeur rückwärtiges Armeegebiet*, usually abbreviated to '*Korück*'.

After the beginning of Operation Barbarossa, a *Feldgendarmerie Abteilung* was also allocated to the *Korück* for each army corps.

Feldgendarm on traffic control duty.

Feldgendarmerie Unteroffizier with French Colonial prisoners.

Corps

Each corps (normally formed from two or more divisions) was allocated a *Feldgendarmerietrupp* (mot).

Divisions

Each division was allocated a *Feldgendarmerietrupp*, the type of *trupp* allocated depended on the type of division, e.g. infantry divisions: *Feldgendarmerietrupp* a (mot), panzer divisions: *Feldgendarmerietrupp* b (mot).

Garrison divisions: initially, no *Feldgendarmerie* elements were allocated but later in the war partially motorised *Feldgendarmerietrupp* c (teilmot.) or *Feldgendarmerietrupp* d (teilmot.)

Security divisions: none allocated, any *Feldgendarmerie* function would be provided by *Feldgendarmerie* from the local *Feldkommandantur* to which the security division was subordinated.

Exceptions occurred, and some large, elite units such as *Grossdeutschland* had a full *Feldgendarmerie Kompanie* of three platoons or *Züge*.

Brigades

Many independently operating brigades were allocated a *Feldgendarmerietrupp* a (mot.) or *Feldgendarmerietrupp* b (mot.)

Kommandanturen

Many (but not all) command posts, be it at local, district or field level were provided with a partially motorised *Feldgendarmerie* unit, a *Feldgendarmerietrupp* c (teilmot.) or *Feldgendarmerietrupp* d (teilmot).

Many large cities, both in Germany and in the occupied countries, had their own *Feldgendarmerie Kompanie* (teilmot.) subordinated to the local *Wehrmachtkommandantur*.

Equipment Levels

Every German military unit was equipped according to a very specific scale, referred to as the *Kriegsstärkenachweisung* (KStN) which dictated the strength in men and equipment that was approved for that type of unit. These KStN were not necessarily permanent and could be altered over time, so the details below should be considered as 'typical' rather than absolute, and at various times units may carry supernumerary personnel or be under strength. Units being undermanned was certainly a common occurrence in wartime.

Traffic post on the Eastern Front near Charkow in March 1943.

From the earliest days of the war, guarding prisoners was an important and common function for the *Feldgendarmerie*. Here French prisoners are marched into captivity in 1940.

Feldgendarmerie in greatcoats on a winter training exercise in Schirgiswalde.

Feldgendarmerie Gefreiter travelling by train enjoys a sumptuous meal.

Feldgendarmerie Abteilung

Headquarters

Command Group

3 officers, 3 NCOs and 3 men (i.e. company commander, radio/telephone crew, company sergeant, medical NCO, company clerk.)

1 × staff car.

1 × small bus.

Repair/Maintemance Troop:

1 NCO and 3 men (*Schirrmeister NCO, mechanics).*

1 × motorcycle/sidecar combination.

1 × 2 ton truck.

Transport/Supply Element:

4 NCOs and 8 men (paymaster NCO, transport NCOs, QM NCOs, drivers, cooks).

2 × 2 ton trucks.

2 × 3 ton trucks.]

Total Weapons Allocation for the above

8 × pistols.

19 × carbines.

4 × machine pistols.

1 × light machine gun.

Plus 3 or 4 × *Feldgendarmerie Kompanien* each comprising 3 × *Feldgendarmerietruppen.* Allocations for *Truppe* and *Kompanien* are given below.

Feldgendarmerie section equipped with motorcycles and a light four seat car.

This Opel Olympia was just one of many civilian automobile models pressed into military service, here with *Feldgendarmerie Trupp* 468.

Feldgendarmerie with their Mercedes 170 staff car. The emblem on the front fender is the tactical sign for a *Feldgendarmerie* unit. (*Sebastian Golawski*)

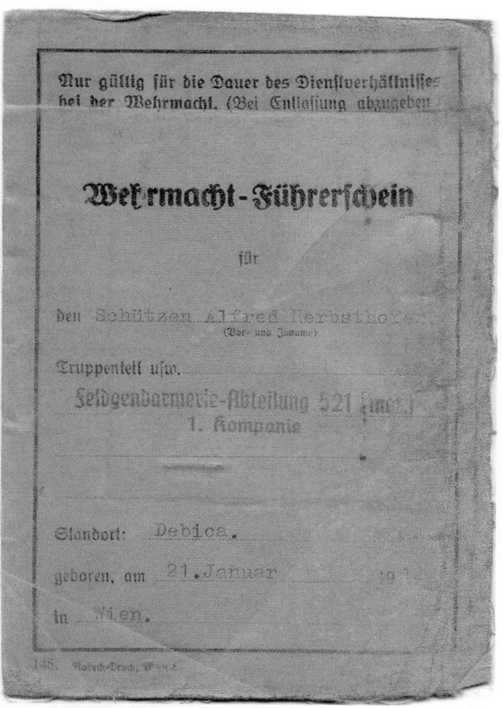

Nur gültig für die Dauer des Dienstverhältnisses
bei der Wehrmacht. (Bei Entlassung abzugeben)

Wehrmacht-Führerschein

für

den Schützen Alfred Herbsthofer
(Vor- und Zuname)

Truppenteil usw.

Feldgendarmerie-Abteilung 521
1. Kompanie

Standort: Debica.

geboren, am 21.Januar 19

in Wien.

Cover of the military driving licence.

Schütze Alfred Herbsthofer
(Vor- und Zuname)

erhält die Erlaubnis, nach Ablegung der Prüfung
ein Kraftfahrzeug mit Antrieb

Verbrennungsmaschine

führen.

Debica , den 17.April 19 40

Feldgendarmerie-Abtlg.
(Verwaltungsbehörde) 521 (mot.)
(Unterschrift)
Der amtlich anerkannte
Hilfs-Kraftfahrsachverständige

Nr. 16 1940 W.K.S. Liste 1

Herbsthofer Alfred
(Eigenhändige Unterschrift des Inhabers)

Driving licence for a *Feldgendarmerie* NCO.

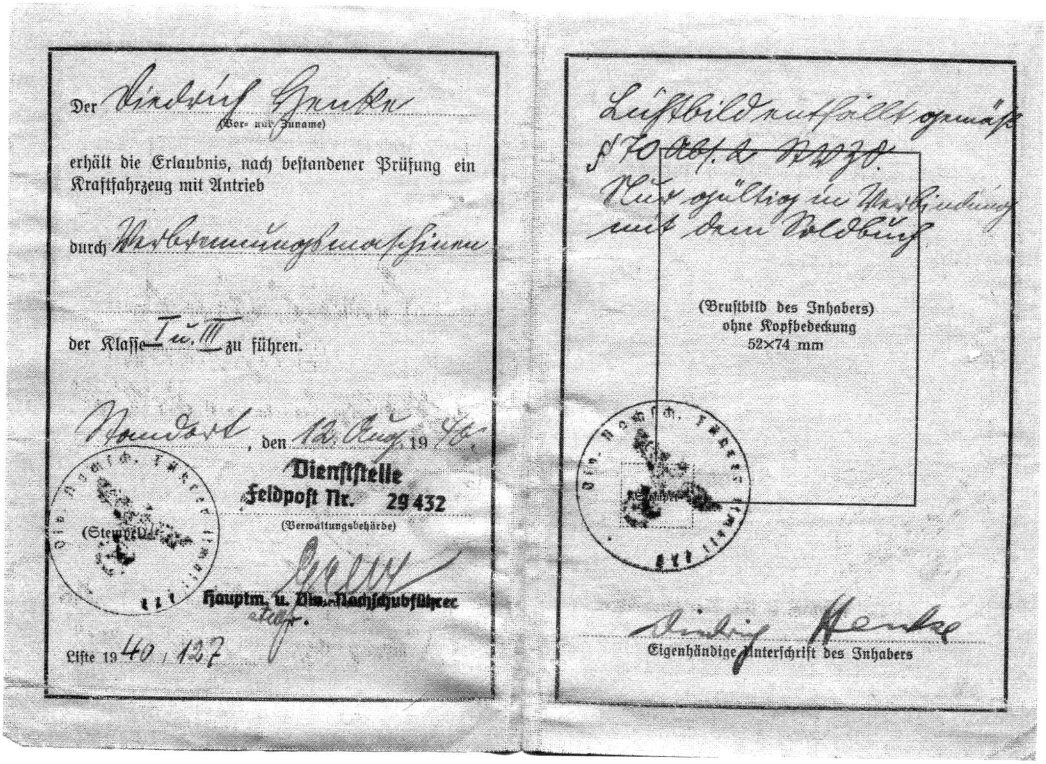
Der
(Vor- und Zuname)
erhält die Erlaubnis, nach bestandener Prüfung ein Kraftfahrzeug mit Antrieb
durch
der Klasse I u. III zu führen.
, den 12. Aug. 1940
Dienststelle
Feldpost Nr. 29432
(Verwaltungsbehörde)
(Stempel)
Hauptm. u. Div.-Nachschubführer
Liste 1940 / 127

Nur gültig in Verbindung mit dem Soldbuch
(Brustbild des Inhabers)
ohne Kopfbedeckung
52×74 mm
Eigenhändige Unterschrift des Inhabers

Driving licence without photograph, valid only when used in conjunction with a *Soldbuch* which has a photograph.

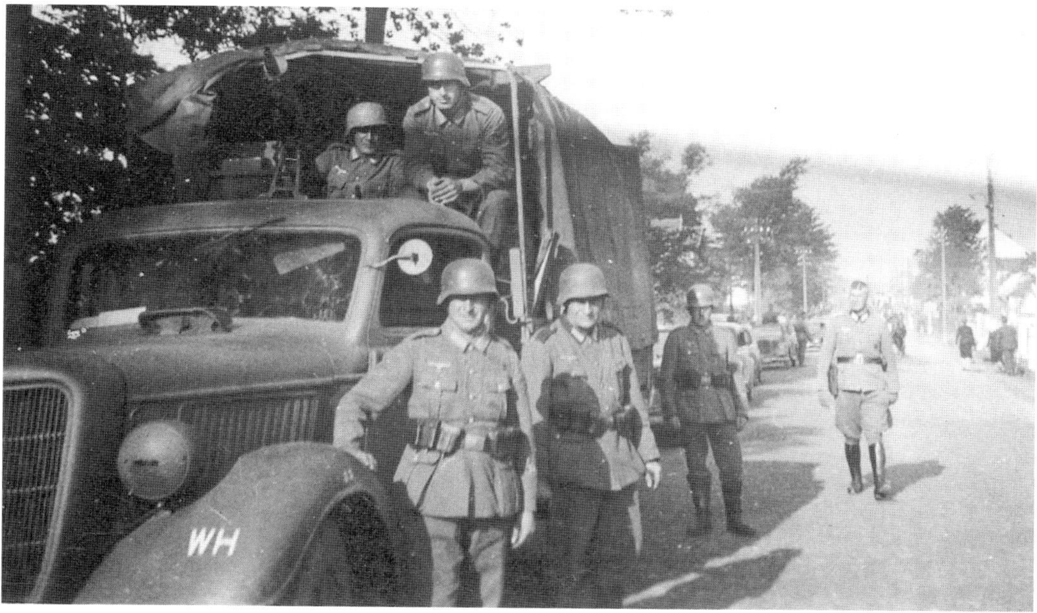

Typical 3 ton truck from a *Feldgendarmerie* unit on the border with Russia, July 1941.

The P.08 Luger pistol (*Robert Adams-adamsguns.com*)

The Walther P38 never fully replaced the P.08 Luger (*Robert Adams- adamsguns.com*)

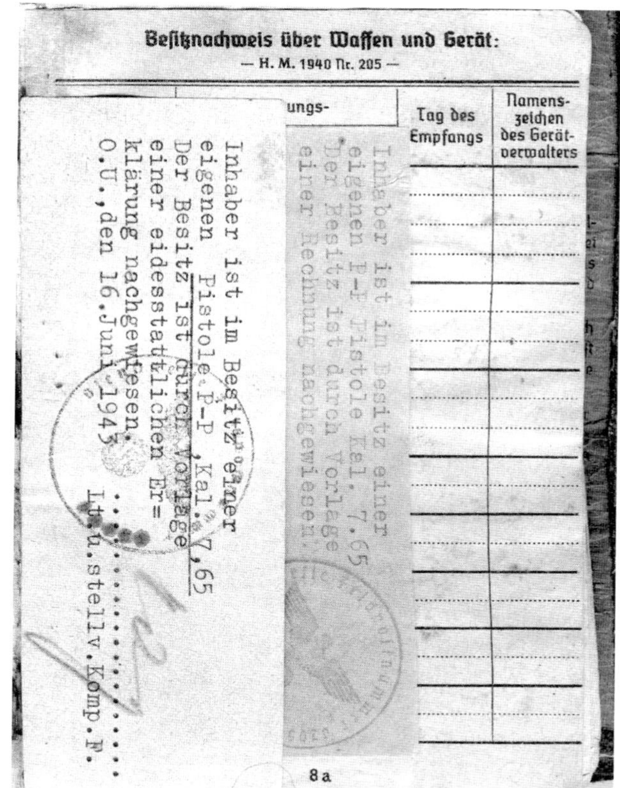

Besitznachweis über Waffen und Gerät:
— H. M. 1940 Nr. 205 —

...ungs-	Tag des Empfangs	Namenszeichen des Gerätverwalters

Inhaber ist im Besitz einer
eigenen Pistole P-P ,Kal. 7,65
Der Besitz ist durch Vorlage
einer eidesstattlichen Er=
klärung nachgewiesen.
O.U.,den 16.Juni 1943
Lt.u.stellv.Komp.F.

8a

Soldiers were occasionally permitted to carry their own personal firearms in place of the army issue pieces. In such cases a certification was added to the *Soldbuch* confirming the weapon was the soldier's personal property.

Feldgendarmerie Kompanie

7 officers, 114 NCOs and 55 men.

Command group

1 officer, 4 NCOs and 6 men (company commander, radio/telephone crew, company sergeant, medical NCO, company clerk.

1 × kubelwagen.
1 × bus.
4 × carbines.
3 × pistols.
1 × machine pistol.

Repair/maintemance troop :

1 NCO and 3 men (*Schirrmeister NCO, Mechanics).*

1 × motorcycle/sidecar combination.
1 × 2 ton truck.
3 × carbines.
1 × pistol.

Notice all the traffic post signs stored around the spare wheel on the bonnet of this *Feldgendarmerie* Volkswagen Kubelwagen.

Pre-war Opel Olympia 2 door model 13237 in the service of the *Feldgendarmerie*.

Rather than military type jeeps, the majority of vehicles used by the *Feldgendarmerie* appear to be civilian cars impressed into military service.

Captured Russian GAZ 1.5 ton light truck pressed into service with the *Feldgendarmerie*.

Two *Feldgendarm*en from *Feldgendarmerie-Trupp* 468 with their motorcycle combination.

Feldgendarmerie with Zundapp motorcycle combination on the Eastern Front.

Transport/supply element :
4 NCOs and 8 men (paymaster NCO, transport NCOs, QM NCOs, drivers, cooks).
2 × 2 ton trucks.
2 × 3 ton trucks
11 × carbines.
1 × pistol.

Feldgendarmerie Zug (×3)
1 officer, 20 NCOs and 10 men.
3 × motorcycles.
2 × motorcycle combinations.
8 × kubelwagen.
20 × carbines.
11 × pistols.
4 × machine pistols.
3 × light machine guns.

Feldgendarmerietrupp a (mot)
2 officers, 21 NCOs and 10 men.
6 × motorcycles.
2 × motorcycle combinations.
7 × kubelwagen.
1 × 3 ton truck.
17 × carbines.
12 × pistols.
6 × machine pistols.
3 × light machine guns.

Feldgendarmerietrupp b (mot)
3 officers, 41 NCOs and 20 men.
2 × motorcycles.
4 × motorcycle combinations.
17 × kubelwagens.
3 × 2 ton truck.
1 × 3 ton truck.
45 × carbines.
13 × pistols.
9 × machine pistols.
5 × light machine guns.

20

noch **IV. Aktiver** Wehrdienst

21

Ausbildung (auch im Kriege)

Mit der Waffe Gewehr 98
Pistole 08

22

Ausbildung (auch im Kriege)

Sonstige Ausbildung, Lehrgänge

Abzeichen usw. (auch im Kriege)

The weapons training page from the Hahnel *Wehrpass*. Note that even for a senior NCO, he has been trained only in the use of rifle and pistol.

A *Feldgendarm* uses a Kettenkrad tracked motorcycle to pull a light truck out of the mud on the Russian Front. (*Josef Charita*)

A group of *Feldgendarmerie* NCOs with a captured French Citroen Traction Avant.

Zundapp heavy motorcycle combination of the *Feldgendarmerie* parked under a tree as its rider takes a rest.

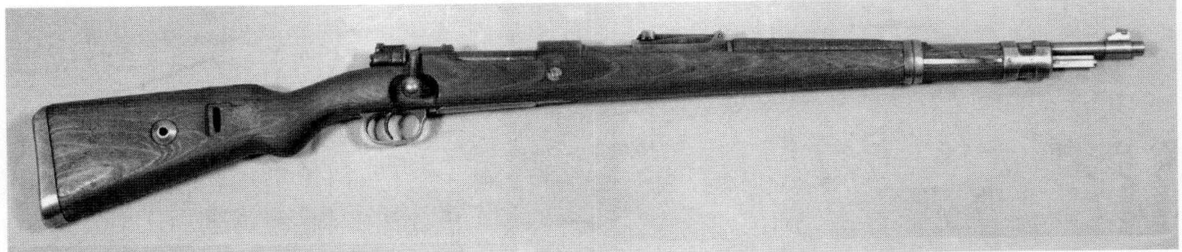

The basic weapon for most German soldiers, including the *Feldgendarmerie*, was the Kar98k Carbine. (*Armémuseum Stockholm*)

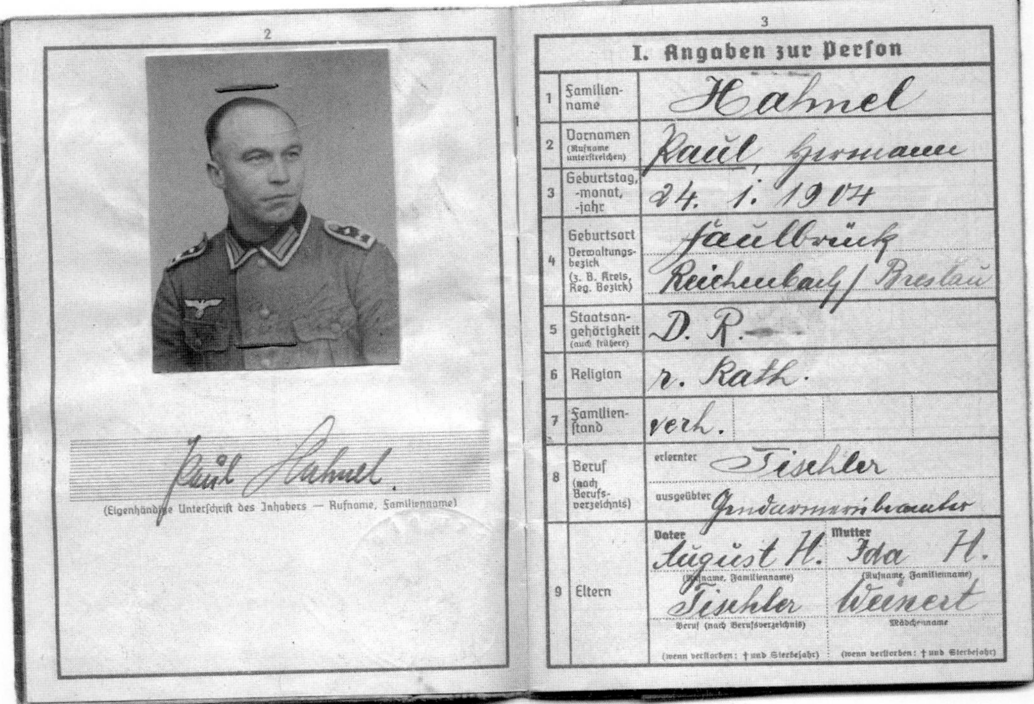

2

Paul Hahnel

(Eigenhändige Unterschrift des Inhabers — Rufname, Familienname)

3

I. Angaben zur Person

1	Familienname	Hahnel
2	Vornamen (Rufname unterstreichen)	Paul, Hermann
3	Geburtstag, -monat, -jahr	24. 1. 1904
4	Geburtsort Verwaltungsbezirk (z. B. Kreis, Reg. Bezirk)	Faulbrück Reichenbach / Breslau
5	Staatsangehörigkeit (auch frühere)	D. R.
6	Religion	r. kath.
7	Familienstand	verh.
8	Beruf (nach Berufsverzeichnis)	erlernter Tischler ausgeübter Gendarmeriebeamter
9	Eltern	Vater: August H. (Rufname, Familienname); Tischler (Beruf (nach Berufsverzeichnis)); (wenn verstorben: † und Sterbejahr) Mutter: Ida H. (Rufname, Familienname); Weinert (Mädchenname); (wenn verstorben: † und Sterbejahr)

The *Wehrpass* of *Stabsfeldwebel* Paul Hahnel from *Feldgendarmerie Trupp* 833.

Opposite above: Service with the *Feldgendarmerie* of the German Army is also recorded in the *Polizei Dienstpass* of Willuweit.

Opposite below: Entries from the *Polizei Dienstpass* of Walter Tronnier whose *Wehrpass* is shown elsewhere indicating his service with the army as a temporary *Feldgendarm* pre-war during the occupation of the Sudetenland followed by full time army service with the *Feldgendarmerie* during the Second World War.

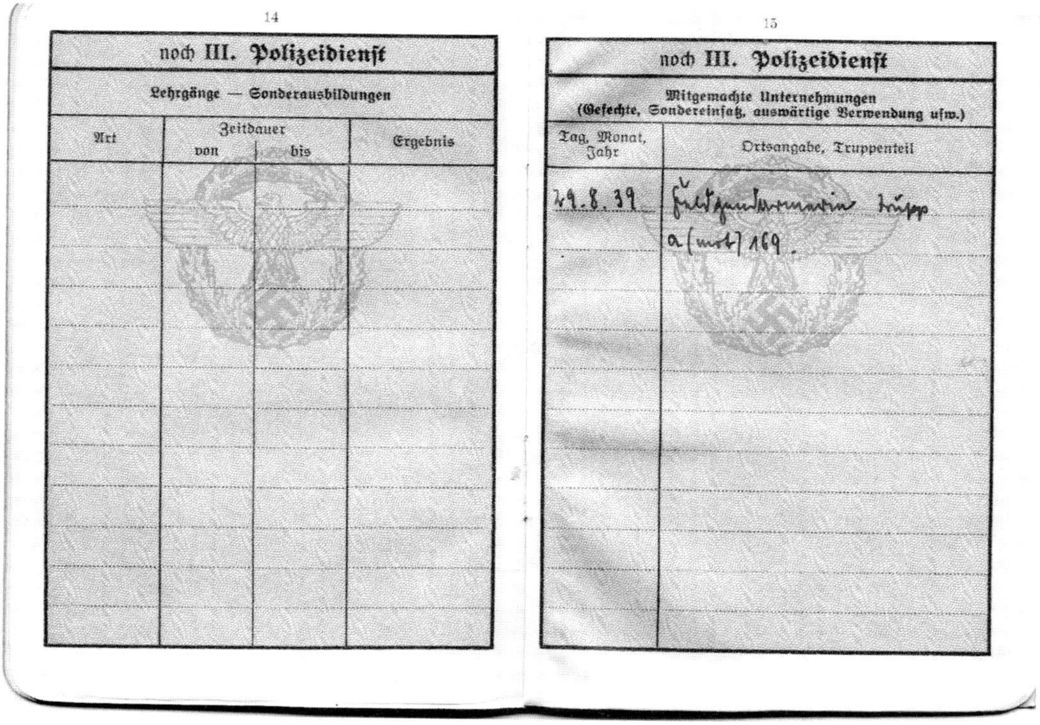

14

noch III. Polizeidienst

Lehrgänge — Sonderausbildungen

Art	Zeitdauer von	Zeitdauer bis	Ergebnis

15

noch III. Polizeidienst

Mitgemachte Unternehmungen (Gefechte, Sondereinsatz, auswärtige Verwendung usw.)

Tag, Monat, Jahr	Ortsangabe, Truppenteil
29.8.39	Feldgendarmerie Trupp a (mot) 169.

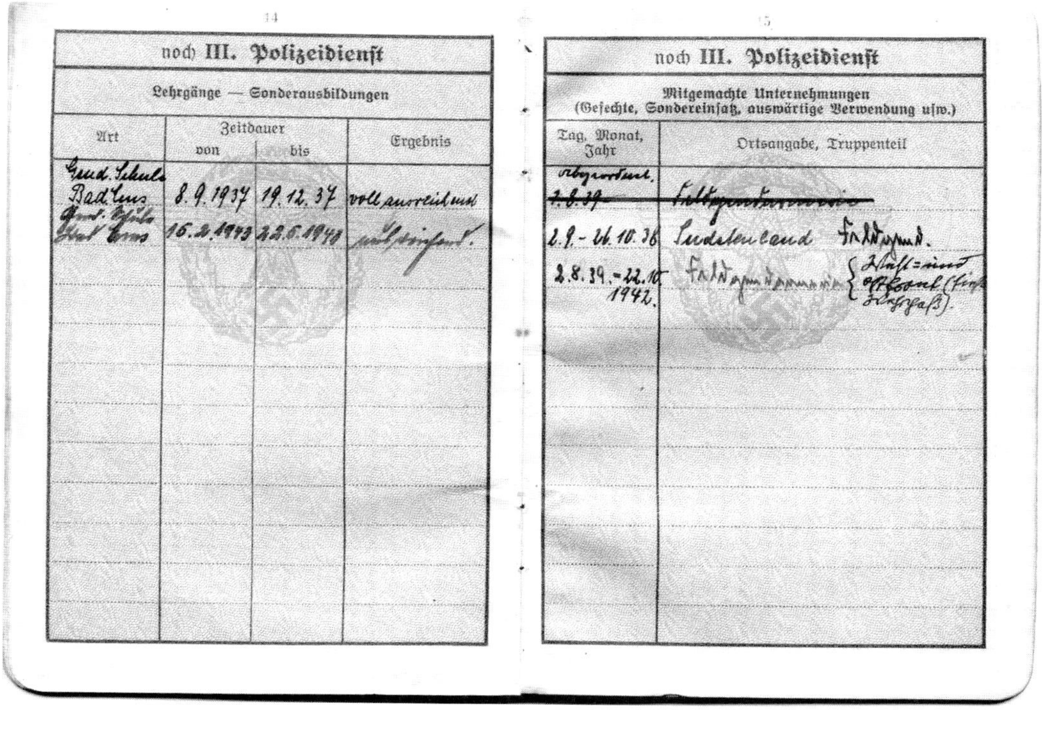

14

noch III. Polizeidienst

Lehrgänge — Sonderausbildungen

Art	Zeitdauer von	Zeitdauer bis	Ergebnis
Gend. Schule Bad Ems	8.9.1937	19.12.37	voll ausreichend
Gend. Schule Bad Ems	16.2.1943	22.5.1943	[illegible]

15

noch III. Polizeidienst

Mitgemachte Unternehmungen (Gefechte, Sondereinsatz, auswärtige Verwendung usw.)

Tag, Monat, Jahr	Ortsangabe, Truppenteil
abgeordnet. ~~2.8.39~~	~~Feldgendarmerie~~
2.9.–26.10.38	Sudetenland Feldgend.
2.8.39.–22.10. 1942.	Feldgendarmerie { Kraft=rad [illegible] ([illegible])

Feldgendarmerie motorcycle combination with the bullet shaped 'Steib' sidecar.

Above left: Motorcycle combination from *Feldgendarmerie-Trupp* 468, the bracket on the front of the sidecar is the mount for a storage container.

Above right: Feldgendarmerie Unteroffizier. Note the 'F.Gend' painted on the front mudguard. The motorcycle is an NSU, less commonly seen than BMW or Zundapp models.

Feldgendarmerie motorcycles. Note that the two at left still bear their civilian licence plates whilst the two at right have their military plates with 'WH' (*Wehrmacht Heer*) prefix.

Not every *Feldgendarm* had the luxury of travelling in a Mercedes like this *Unteroffizier*. (*Sebastian Golwaski*)

Obsolescent weapons such as the Bergmann MPI8 were also used by the *Feldgendarmerie*. (*Quickload at en.wikipedia*)

Feldgendarmerietrupp c (Teilmot)

I officer, 25 NCOs and 7 men.

- 18 × bicycles.
- 4 × kubelwagens.
- 1 × 3 ton truck.
- 19 × carbines.
- 10 × pistols.
- 5 × machine pistols.
- 3 × light machine guns.

Feldgendarmerietrupp d (Teilmot)

I officer, 20 NCOs and 6 men.

- 3 × motorcycles.
- 6 × bicycles.
- 4 × staff cars.
- 15 × pistols.
- 12 × carbines.
- 2 × machine pistols.
- 1 × light machine gun.

A commonly held perception regarding the typical *Feldgendarm*, probably fuelled by to some degree by movie images of such troops is that they were usually armed with MP40 type machine pistols. As can be seen from the above however, the standard weapon for the *Feldgendarmerie* was the infantry carbine, usually the Mauser Kar98k with only a handful of machine pistols per unit. In fact in many units, especially those on occupation duty, armament often comprised captured and obsolete enemy weapons.

Feldgendarmerie from Sonderverband 287 with their Volkswagen Kubelwagen light field car.

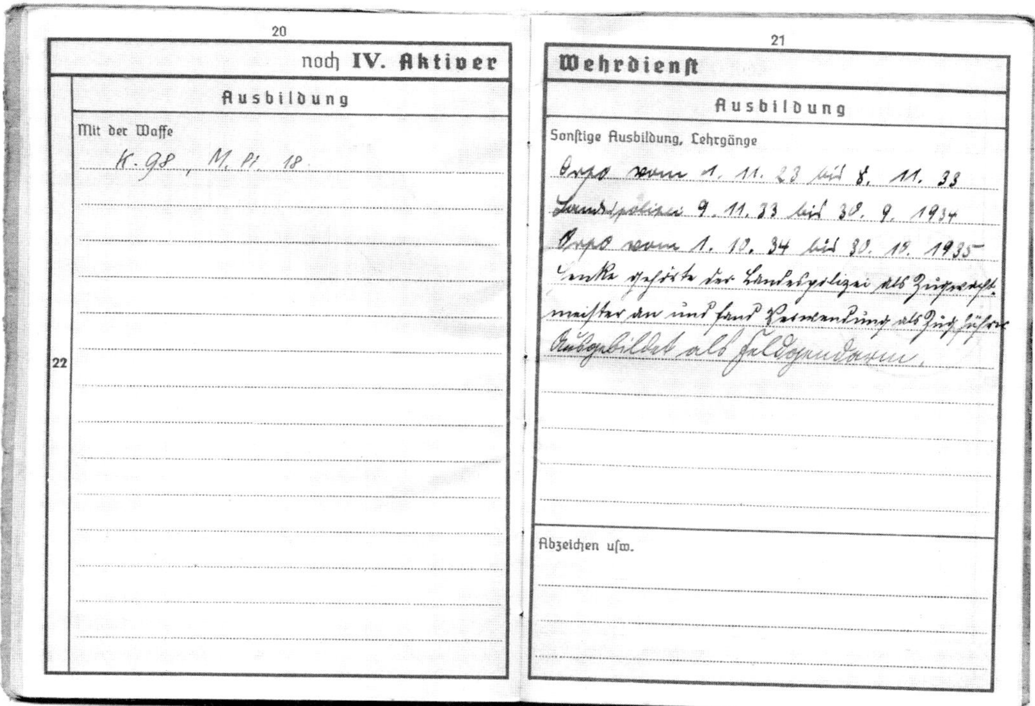

20

noch IV. Aktiver

Ausbildung

Mit der Waffe

K. 98, M. Pi. 18

22

21

Wehrdienst

Ausbildung

Sonstige Ausbildung, Lehrgänge

Orpo vom 1. 11. 33 bis 8. 11. 33

Landespolizei 9. 11. 33 bis 30. 9. 1934

Orpo vom 1. 10. 34 bis 30. 10. 1935

Abzeichen usw.

Weapons training page from the *Wehrpass* of Diedrich Henke seen previously shows that as well as being trained on the Kar98k, he has also been familiarised with the MP l8 machine pistol.

Above left: The bicycle was a perfect sensible mode of transport for navigating narrow country lanes in some rear areas.

Above right: Apart from a new paint job, most civilian vehicles in military service were unmodified, but a special hooded 'Notek' lamp was usually fitted to the left fender as here.

The humble bicycle was also an important part of *Feldgendarmerie* equipment.

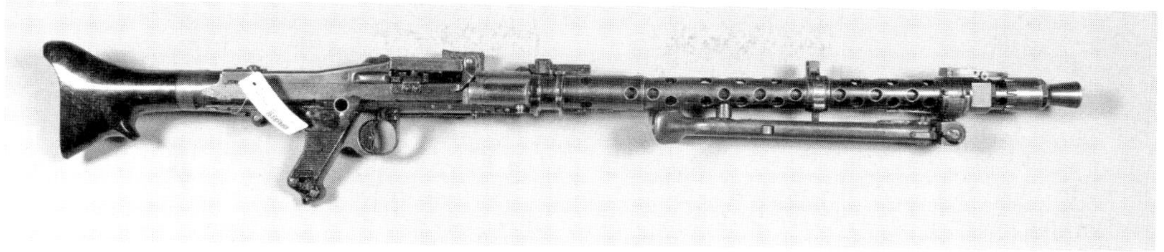

The highly effective MG34 was standard issue in small numbers to each *Feldgendarmerie Trupp and Abteilung* . (*Armémuseum Stockholm*)

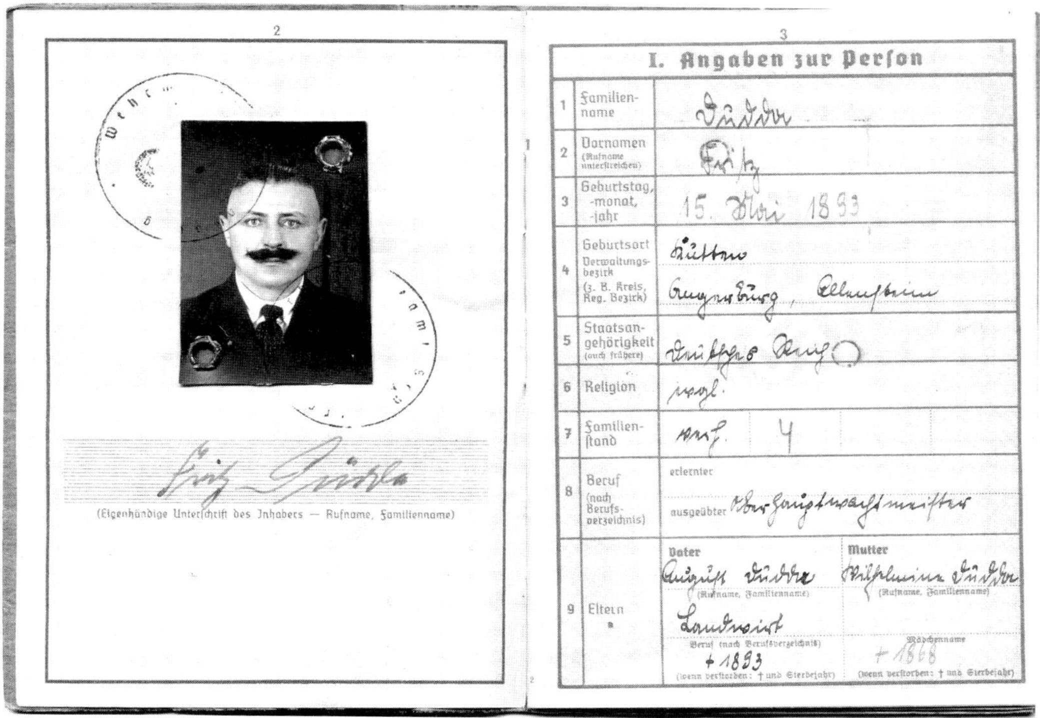

2

Fritz Dudde

(Eigenhändige Unterschrift des Inhabers — Rufname, Familienname)

3

I. Angaben zur Person

1	Familienname	Dudde
2	Vornamen (Rufname unterstreichen)	Fritz
3	Geburtstag, -monat, -jahr	15. Mai 1893
4	Geburtsort Verwaltungsbezirk (z. B. Kreis, Reg. Bezirk)	
5	Staatsangehörigkeit (auch frühere)	
6	Religion	
7	Familienstand	
8	Beruf (nach Berufsverzeichnis)	erlernter / ausgeübter
9	Eltern	Vater: (Rufname, Familienname); Beruf (nach Berufsverzeichnis); (wenn verstorben: † und Sterbejahr) — Mutter: (Rufname, Familienname); Mädchenname; (wenn verstorben: † und Sterbejahr)

Wehrpass for *Stabsfeldwebel* Fritz Dudde of *Feldgendarmerie-Trupp* 463.

20

noch **IV. Aktiver**

Ausbildung (auch im Kriege)

Mit der Waffe

Karabiner 98, Gewehr 98, Pistole 08, l.M.G. und s.M.G.

22

21

Wehrdienst

Ausbildung (auch im Kriege)

Sonstige Ausbildung, Lehrgänge

Abzeichen usw. (auch im Kriege)

At the opposite end of the training scale, Dudde has been trained in the Kar98k Carbine, the older G98 rifle, the P.08 Pistol, the l.M.G. (light machine gun) and s.M.G. (heavy machine gun).

A two man *Feldgendarmerie* patrol with their Opel staff car.

The use of civilian vehicles had its problems as few could cope as well as heavier military vehicles in bad weather.

The machine pistol MP40 was used by the *Feldgendarmerie* in limited numbers. (*Quickload at en.wikipedia*)

Uniforms

All branches of the German armed forces were allocated a specific *Waffenfarbe* or branch of service colour. In the case of the *Feldgendarmerie* this was orange-red or *orangerot*. This choice was almost certainly because of the use of this same colour by the civil *Gendarmerie*.

This colour was worn in various ways. It was used as piping to the crown and cap band of the visor cap. It was also used as a Russia braid 'soutache' or inverted vee around the national cockade on both the field grey field cap and the tropical field cap for officers and other ranks until mid 1942 when this feature was removed.

The *Waffenfarbe* was also used as piping to the shoulder straps of NCOs and enlisted men and underlay to the shoulder straps of officers. It was featured as a coloured strip to the centre of each bar of '*Litzen*' on the collar tabs of officers and also on the early issue collar tabs for NCOs and enlisted men.

On the subject of *Waffenfarbe* it is perhaps worth mentioning that the *Feldgendarmerie* was not the only branch to use orange-red *Waffenfarbe*. The army's recruiting branch also used this colour until 1942 after which it changed to white. Other smaller branches such as the ordnance and engineering branches also used orange-red *Waffenfarbe*. However, these other branches also featured identifying devices on their shoulder straps—in the case of the recruiting branch a roman numeral designating the *Wehrkreis* or military district was featured and for ordnance troops, the letters Fz (for *Feldzeug*) for supplementary officers, crossed canon for ordnance officers and a cogwheel for engineering officers. A strap with only orange *Waffenfarbe* and no other identifying device therefore is most likely *Feldgendarmerie*.

Early Uniforms

During the earliest operations which involved the *Feldgendarmerie*, many of those who transferred either temporarily or permanently from the *Gendarmerie* continued to wear their original police uniforms, including where appropriate, the *Motorisierte Gendarmerie* cuffband.

In period photos, these grey green uniforms can be easily identified by the contrasting dark brown cuffs. The collar was also dark brown as opposed to the dark green collar worn on army uniforms of the period.

The lack of an army pattern national emblem (eagle and swastika) over the right breast pocket is also an instant indicator that the uniform is of the police and not the army.

In order to identify them as carrying out Military as opposed to civil police duties, they were issued with a green cloth armband on which was machine woven the legend '*Feld=Gendarmerie*' in two lines of yellow Gothic text. A variant is also known with the legend machine embroidered in yellow thread rather than woven.

This was worn on the left sleeve of the tunic as well as the greatcoat or the protective motorcyclists coat if worn. This armband was often, but not always worn in such a manner as to cover the police version of the national emblem on the left sleeve.

It should also be noted that on occasion this armband was worn by other *Wehrmacht* troops acting as temporary *Feldgendarmen*, though its greatest use was certainly by members of the civil police acting as military police.

The regulation cuffbands used by the police (i.e. *Motorisierte Gendarmerie*, *Deutsche Wehrmacht* etc) were machine or hand embroidered on a mid/dark brown wool base.

The same NCO is seen here first as a civilian policeman and as a *Feldgendarmerie Unteroffizier*. Many came from the police to serve a term of duty with the *Feldgendarmerie* and then return to the police.

These transitional police uniforms have been amended by having an army breast eagle added along with army style shoulder straps and army style NCO braid around the collar.

Above: Cufftitle for the *Motorisierte Gendarmerie* which supplied so many of its personnel for duty in the *Feldgendarmerie*.

Left: This transitional police uniform has the *Feld=Gendarmerie* armband placed over the sleeve eagle and also has an army national emblem added to the right breast.

Above left: A junior NCO from the *Motorisierte Gendarmerie*, which provided a large portion of the first personnel to serve in the *Feldgendarmerie*.

Above right: A rare shot of cloth sides with the embroidered unit number being worn on the shoulder strap, highly unusual for the *Feldgendarmerie*.

A *Feldgendarmerie* cuffband also exists manufactured in the same style as the police cuffbands, both in machine embroidered and hand embroidered form. It seems logical to assume that these were the first *Feldgendarmerie* cuffbands to be introduced and were first worn during this transitional phase when elements of the original police uniform were still being used. Photographic evidence of the occasional use of this early type *Feldgendarmerie* cuffband well into the war does exist however.

Uniforms

No special trousers, footwear etc. were used by the *Feldgendarmerie*, only the tunic or field blouse bearing the appropriate insignia would be identifiable as being for the military police.

The cut and style of the tunic was absolutely generic with no special features relevant to the wearer's position as a military policeman other than the attached insignia.

All of the standard uniforms used by the army were utilised by the *Feldgendarmerie*, those most commonly encountered on period photographs include:

M38 Officers Tunic

A field grey tunic with dark green collar having four pleated pockets with scalloped flaps and fastened with five buttons. The sleeves featured turned back cuffs. It was similar to the M36 tunic for other ranks but in much finer quality material.

Some officers, for field use, had their own tunics made in similar cut to the M36 other ranks tunic without turned back cuffs, but usually from better quality wool.

M36 Field Blouse

A field grey tunic with dark green collar having four pleated pockets with scalloped flaps and fastened with five buttons.

M40 Field Blouse

As M36 but with field grey collar.

M41 Field Blouse

As M40 but with six-button fastening.

M42 Field Blouse

As M40/41 but with non-pleated pockets.

M43 Field Blouse

As M42 but with straight cut pocket flaps.

There were also some minor internal changes but the above are the main features which may be identified from period photos. It should also be noted that soldiers admired the contrasting dark green collars of the M36 tunics so much that many later issue types had the field grey collars replaced by dark green collars.

It is also worth noting that the M36 etc nomenclature is not the original German terminology but one which has been created by collectors and militaria enthusiasts in order to standardise descriptions and is now almost universally used.

Above left: Feldgendarmerie in winter dress. Note that, unusually, the soldier at right has added the metal insignia from the visor cap to his M43 field cap.

Above right: An unusual instance of mixed dress. This NCO wears the regulation Feldgendarmerie tunic, but with a civil Gendarmerie visor cap.

The officer tunic worn here with full insignia including the cufftitle and a hand embroidered bullion wire sleeve eagle.

Above left: A *Feldgendarmerie Hauptmann* wears the sleeve eagle but no cufftitle whilst his Adjutant following behind can be seen to wear both the sleeve eagle and cufftitle.

Above right: The *leutnant* at right wears a fine example of the officers' service tunic with bullion police pattern sleeve eagle and standard woven cufftitle.

Feldgendarmerie Trupp on parade with its officers. Note how the bullion sleeve eagles worn by the officers stand out.

Another example of the officer's tunic cut from wool in the enlisted style, here worn with the cufftitle but no sleeve eagle.

Mounted *Feldgendarmerie* Officer. Horses were often used by the *Feldgendarmerie* on the Eastern Front.

The basic early 'M36' type field blouse with dark green collar and pleated pockets with scalloped flaps worn by a *Feldgendarmerie* enlisted man.

Junior NCOs from *Feldgendarmerie Trupp* 468 in service dress with the visor cap.

The small size of this soldier's holster suggests that he is carrying a smaller weapon than the common P.08 or P.38, most likely a Walther PP or Mauser HSc.

Above left: An off-duty *Stabsfeldwebel* tries out a pair of sunglasses in a local Bazaar. (*Josef Charita*)

Above right: A *Feldgendarmerie Oberfeldwebel* in service dress with visor cap, armed with a pistol the holster of which is just visible under his left arm.

On leave and in walking out dress, a *Feldgendarmerie Geferiter* poses for a snap with two lady friends

The 'M40' field blouse. Now with a field grey collar but still retaining the pleated pockets and scalloped flaps, is worn here by a *Feldgendarmerie Gefreiter*.

Captured Russian light trucks being used by *Feldgendarmerie Trupp* 468.

Two rather tough looking *Feldgendarmerie* NCOs interrogate a female suspect.

Feldgendarmerie in Kiev, 1943. Note that the *Unteroffizier* at right wears neither the arm eagle or cufftitle.

Two *Feldgendarm*en relax on the shores of the Adriatic.

Note the mix of field grey and dark green for collars and shoulder straps in this group of rankers and junior NCOs.

The M43 *Einheitsfeldmütze* dates this photo to after 1943, but the arm eagle and cufftitle still being used indicates that it is prior to March 1944.

Above left: The taller *Feldgendarm* here wears the 'M41' field blouse, being basically similar to the 'M40' but with six button fastening.

Above right: An 'M42' field blouse still having the scalloped pocket flaps but no pleats, and with six button fastening worn by a *Feldgendarmerie Obergefreiter*.

Waffenrock

Given that the *Feldgendarmerie* was only formed during mobilisation just prior to the outbreak of war, and that use of the *Waffenrock* or dress tunic was soon to be withdrawn for the duration, it is unsurprising that very little evidence has emerged to show the use of this particular style of tunic by the *Feldgendarmerie*.

Wartime photographs do exist however, which undeniably show the *Waffenrock* being worn by *Feldgendarmerie* troops complete with sleeve eagle and cuffband.

This author has as yet been unable to track down any surviving example of such a tunic however, and given the relatively small size of the *Feldgendarmerie* as a proportion of the German army during the early period when the *Waffenrock* may have been worn, it unlikely that many authentic examples have survived.

During research for this book, an interesting photograph was discovered showing a *Feldgendarmerie* senior NCO wearing a converted *Gendarmerie* tunic as a dress uniform. At first glance this may have appeared as a converted *Waffenrock* but on closer examination, details of the tunic reveal it is most certainly a police pattern tunic complete with contrasting cuffs. The cut of police and army *Waffenrock* tunics is completely different.

It is impossible to know from the monochrome image whether the collar and cuffs remain in the original brown of the *Gendarmerie* have been re-tailored with green cloth but this seems

Above left: The parade dress *Waffenrock* tunic is rarely encountered for *Feldgendarmerie* troops but it certainly existed. The *Feldgendarmerie* sleeve eagle is visible on this example.

Above right: Another fine and rare shot of the *Waffenrock* being worn by a *Feldgendarm*. In this case both the sleeve eagle and cufftitle are evident.

Pictured on his wedding day, this *Oberfeldwebel* wears an embroidered version of the *Feldgendarmerie* cufftitle on a brown wool base.

unlikely as converted *Waffenrock* tunics would normally have the contrasting dark cuffs removed. It is also interesting to note that this tunic bears an embroidered *Feldgendarmerie* cuffband in the police style.

It seems therefore that this tunic is an example of one of the transitional period tunics, where the former *Gendarmerie* NCO has simply added the appropriate *Feldgendarmerie* insignia, including the army breast eagle, to his *Gendarmerie* tunic.

What makes this rather unusual, is that the medal ribbons he wears include that for the East Front Medal, meaning that this photograph was not taken until at least 1942. It would appear that this NCO pulled his old transitional *Polizei/Heer* tunic out of storage to wear for his wedding day. He also carries a police NCO Sword!

Tropical Tunics

As *Feldgendarmerie* operated in all the areas where such uniforms were used, it can be safely assumed that the full range of tropical pattern tunics may be found being worn by *Feldgendarmerie* personnel. It seems however that the police pattern national emblem worn on the left sleeve of field grey dress until 1944 was rarely featured on the tropical tunic or tropical shirt though the cuffband was widely used.

Above left: Two *Feldgendarmerie* NCOs in tropical uniform. Note that, typically, only the cufftitle is worn on the left sleeve.

Above right: This photograph of a *Feldgendarmerie* NCO proves that at least sometimes, the sleeve eagle was indeed worn on the tropical uniform.

This photograph of two *Feldgendarm*en is a perfect example of how much difference there was in the appearance of tropical clothing due to the bleaching effect of the sun.

Oberleutnant Hans Hausser in tropical dress while serving with *Feldgendarmerie-Trupp* 498. On the original photo the orange *Waffenfarbe soutache* over the cockade on his cap can just be seen. Hausser later won the Knight's Cross whilst serving in the *Waffen-SS*.

Men from the *Feldgendarmerie Trupp* of *Sonderverband* 287 relax with some music.

Feldgendarmerie on Crete the stooping figure at right showing the very rare use of the *Feldgendarmerie* sleeve eagle on the tropical shirt.

Feldgendarmerie from *Sonderverband* 287 in tropical dress, typically, without the use of the sleeve eagle.

Greatcoats

The full range of army pattern greatcoats was used by the *Feldgendarmerie*. The cuffband was normally featured though the police pattern national emblem was not featured on the left sleeve.

Motorcycle Coats

One form of dress widely used by the *Feldgendarmerie* was the waterproof rubberised coat. This was an ankle length double breasted coat in grey green waterproof material, but with normal field grey cloth collar. It could be buttoned up between the legs for comfort when riding a motorcycle. The only insignia on this coat were the shoulder straps.

Army Feldgendarmerie Headgear

There were no special headgear designs for the *Feldgendarmerie* but various types of headgear were manufactured using the orange-red *Waffenfarbe* colour allocated to these troops.

From wartime photographs at least the following forms of head wear with orange-red *Waffenfarbe* are know to have been worn by *Feldgendarmerie*.

Visor Cap for Officers.

A pair of very hard looking *Feldgendarmen* wearing the greatcoat one with dark green and one with field grey collar. Note that the arm eagle is not worn on the greatcoat, but the cufftitle is featured.

A group of *Feldgendarmerie* officers and Senior NCOs wearing the regulation greatcoat.

Left: Feldgendarm on guard duty in Stalino on the Russian Front. Note that on the heavy duty winter greatcoat (*Wachmantel*), no insignia is being worn.

Below: Feldgendarmerie troops in Schirgiswalde, 1941. Note the Kar98k Carbines being carried.

Above left: Feldgendarm on guard duty. The fact that he has no ammunition pouches on his belt and would only have the five rounds in the weapon's magazine suggests that the area is considered safe.

Above right: Keeping warm on the Eastern Front during winter was extremely difficult especially on static police duty. Note the huge felt overboots worn on top of the jackboots by this *Feldgendarm*. (*Photo courtesy Brian L. Davis*)

Right: Rare shot of a *Feldgendarmerie Feldwebel* from the so-called Spanish Blue Division on the Eastern Front. Note the 'España' sleeve shield. (*Otto Spronk Photo Files*)

Two of the *Feldgendarm*en in this shot are wearing the loose fitting waterproof motorcyclist coat.

Motorcycle patrol in winter, struggling to progress through deep snow.

Above left: In cold weather, this *Feldgendarm* wears the woollen balaclava like toque to protect his neck and head. (*Photo courtesy Brian L. Davis*)

Above right: The motorcyclists protective waterproof coat was never the most stylish of garments!

Visor Cap for NCOs/Enlisted Men.
Feldmütze altere Art (so called Crush Cap).
Feldmütze for Officers.
Feldmütze for NCOs/Enlisted Men.
Tropical M40 *Feldmütze*.

Study of wartime photographs will show that virtually every type of generic headgear that was worn by the majority of army personnel was also used by the *Feldgendarmerie* (i.e. M35 and M42 Steel Helmets, M43 *Feldmütze* etc.)

Although the regular army steel helmet was used by *Feldgendarmerie* troops, occasional photos emerge showing *Feldgendarmerie* troops wearing steel helmets with the police national insignia decals. As there was no '*Feldgendarmerie* Helmet' *per se*, it is safe to assume that those troops wearing these helmets are some of the former civil police personnel who were drafted into the army to serve with the *Feldgendarmerie* and retained their original police helmets.

Above left: This photo shows to good effect the M38 Feldmütze with the inverted 'V' of orange *Waffenfarbe* over the national colours cockade.

Above right: The officers' version of the *Feldmütze* had silver piping around the flap and crown. The example worn here also features the orange *Waffenfarbe soutache* over the cockade.

This fine portrait study shows the visor cap for NCOs and enlisted ranks to good effect. It has orange piping around the crown and band.

This shot shows a fine range of *Feldgendarmerie* headgear being worn including the M38 Feldmütze, the officers and enlisted ranks visor caps and in the centre, the old style field cap (the so-called crusher cap).

Above left: Feldgendarm on guard duty armed with the standard Mauser Kar98k Carbine. Dnjepropetrovsk.

Above right: Feldgendarmerie NCOs will also often be seen, as here, carrying a map/document case from the waist belt. (*Barry Smith*)

Insignia

Collar Patches

Collar Patches for officers were in the regular style, with matt silver grey braid *Litzen* on a dark green badge-cloth base. In the centre of each Litze was a strip of orange *Waffenfarbe* either as a single strand cord or woven in a Russia braid 'V' style. In 1944 the use of fully machine woven collar tabs for officers became widespread.

For Dress uniforms such as the *Waffenrock*, the *Litzen* were hand embroidered in bright silver braid on an orange base.

Collar Patches for junior ranks were machine woven in a matt grey artificial silk with a dark green strip between the two bars of *Litze*. The centre of each bar carried a stripe in the orange colour of the *Feldgendarmerie*. Early collar tabs with *Waffenfarbe* were usually machine sewn onto a dark green patch before attachment to the collar.

From 1938, new '*Einheitslitzen*' began to be used which lacked the *Waffenfarbe* stripe down the centre of each bar of *Litze*, the central strip between the bars and the stripe down the centre of each bar all being in dark green.

In 1940, a new version of the collar patch was introduced in which the central strip and the stripe down the centre of each bar were no longer in dark green but mouse grey. These later patterns were often machine sewn directly to the collar without the use of a backing patch.

Despite the fact that the version with *Waffenfarbe* colours was being phased out before the creation of the *Feldgendarmerie*, original tunics with the *Waffenfarbe* to the collar patches are well enough known to suggest that these troops were able to obtain patches with the appropriate *Waffenfarbe*.

Lower ranks patches for *Waffenrock* dress tunics normally featured machine woven bright aluminium thread *Litzen* with the space between the bars open so that when mounted on the orange base patch the *Waffenfarbe* colour would also be visible in this space between the bars.

Feldgendarmerie tropical tunics used the same collar tabs as those worn by all other troops, with blue grey artificial silk bars featuring a rust brown strip between each bar and a similarly coloured stripe down the centre of each bar. These were machined directly to the collar without a backing patch. Officers would often wear the collar patches from their field grey uniform in lieu of these tropical patches.

Shoulder Straps

Shoulder straps for senior officers for the field uniform were made from intertwined matt silver grey braid. The braid itself was made by attaching two 5 mm strips of Russia type Soutache braid side by side so that the weave of the threads on the braid formed opposing 'V' shapes.

The braid was then sewn to a base of orange coloured wool, stiffened internally with a strip of stiff board.

Straps for all ranks were made in two styles, either fixed, which were sewn directly into the shoulder seam of the uniform, or removable in which case a small understrap was attached to the base of the strap, this passing through a loop on the tunic shoulder seam, to allow the strap to be buttoned in place.

Officer's straps for dress uniforms were identical in style to those for the field uniform, but made from bright aluminium braid. The straps as above had two gilt rank stars for *Oberst*, one

Above left: A *Feldgendarmerie* Leutnant wearing the hand embroidered aluminium thread version of the cuffband. Note that he also carries the Army dress dagger.

Above right: The large size holster carried by this soldier suggests he is equipped with the P.08 Pistol.

As we can see here, height was not really a factor for serving in the *Feldgendarmerie*!

for *Oberstleutnant* and none for *Major*. Straps for these grades were usually approximately 3.8 cm wide.

Junior officer shoulder straps were manufactured in a similar manner with matt silver grey braid for the field uniform and bright aluminium for the dress uniform. In the case of junior officers the braid was made from two 4–5 mm wide twin strips of soutache type braid sewn together side by side to give the impression of four strands. This was then laid along the strap, around the curved end and back down giving the overall impression of eight strands.

This style strap was worn with two gilt stars for the rank of *Hauptmann*, one for *Oberleutnant* and without stars for *Leutnant*.

NCO / Enlisted straps were originally made from dark green badge cloth for the upper surface and usually field grey for the undersurface. They were around 4.5 cm wide with the buttonhole end rounded and featured an understrap with buttonhole fitting to allow it to be removable from the field blouse. Examples without an understrap were also made, these being intended for sewing permanently into the shoulder seam of dress or private purchase tunics.

The edge of the strap featured a 2 mm wide strip of piping in the orange *Waffenfarbe* colour. This piping could be wool but in later straps was usually in woven rayon.

From May 1940, straps began to be made with the top surface in field grey cloth rather than dark blue green and from around 1944 as an economy measure straps began to be made with no underlay, only the top surface. In such cases a reinforcing strip of rayon was sewn to the undersurface.

NCOs wore edging to their shoulder straps consisting of 9 mm wide aluminium braid with a diamond weave pattern. In 1940 subdued braid was introduced made from field grey coloured rayon with a similar weave pattern. The aluminium braid was never actually replaced by the new style, and both aluminium and subdued braid can be found on straps used right through to the end of the war.

Straps with braid around the entire edge of the strap were worn with three white metal rank stars for *Stabsfeldwebel*, two stars for *Oberfeldwebel*, one for *Feldwebel*, and no stars for *Unterfeldwebel*.

Straps for *Unteroffizier* had braid only around the sides and curved end of the strap, the lower (shoulder) end being bare.

Lower ranks, from *Schutze* to *Stabsgefreiter* had no braid on the shoulder straps.

Shoulder straps for the tropical field blouse were of identical design to those for the field grey uniforms but were made from olive green cotton material with the artificial silk braid in rust brown colour where appropriate.

Early tropical straps as worn in North Africa predominantly had a brown wool underlay whilst later straps tend to have field grey wool underlay. Piping on tropical straps is generally in orange coloured artificial silk weave.

Units which carried their own special insignia of the shoulder strap (i.e. the GD cipher worn by *Grossdeutschland* units) featured these as gilt metal emblems for officer straps, silvered white metal for NCOs and embroidered for enlisted ranks. In the case of embroidered versions these were to be in the same colour as the *Waffenfarbe* colour in which the straps were piped, in the case of *Feldgendarmerie* straps—*orangerot*.

As can be seen by the example of a *Grossdeutschland Feldgendarm* shown in this book, although a black and white image, it can be seen that the GD cipher indeed appears to be in the same colour as the piping.

A *Feldgendarmerie Oberfeldwebel* relaxes in his personal quarters.

Presentation of awards to *Feldgendarmerie* troops in August 1941.

This 'Spiess', a *Stabsfeldwebel*, wears the *Feldgendarmerie* cufftitle above the sleeve rings.

A *Feldgendarmerie Oberfeldwebel* poses with his proud family.

Sleeve Eagle

Members of the *Feldgendarmerie* wore, in addition to the regular national emblem over the right breast pocket, the police version of the national emblem on the left sleeve as follows:

Officers

For officers the sleeve eagle consisting of an eagle grasping the usual wreathed swastika in its talons, all on an oval wreath of oakleaves, was hand embroidered in silver aluminium wire, with the exception of the swastika which was normally embroidered in black thread. The insignia was worked on a field grey coloured wool base.

Lower Ranks

For lower ranks the arm eagle was the same as that for the civil *Gendarmerie*, having the design (again with the exception of the swastika) machine embroidered in orange thread on a field grey base. Unlike the civil *Gendarmerie* however, the military police emblem did not show the name of the wearer's home base town at the top of the badge.

Early examples of the sleeve eagle tend to be found worked on to a circular field grey wool patch, whilst later examples had the backing cloth trimmed closely around the outline of the insignia.

On most examples, the outer portion of the eagle's wings will be found to have six segments. A rarer variant however with only three segments is known and photographic evidence of its wear by *Feldgendarmerie* troops exists.

The *Feldgendarmerie* sleeve eagle was withdrawn from use by an order of 10 March 1944 (*Heeresmiteilungsblatt 44, Nr 158*). How quickly this order was implemented is not known but given the *Feldgendarmerie*'s task of ensuring order and discipline it seems logical that they would be amongst the first troops to comply with the new order so it might seem logical that the lack of this feature would be an indicator of a photograph having been taken after March 1944.

Occasional photos known to have been taken before this date and showing no sleeve eagle are known, so although using the lack of sleeve eagle as a general rule of thumb to date a photograph is not unreasonable, it should not be relied on absolutely, especially for officers whose use of the regulation sleeve eagle prior to March 1944 seems to have been sporadic at best.

This extremely rare portrait study of a *Feldgendarm* from the *Grossdeutschland* Division clearly shows the GD monogram on the shoulder straps is embroidered in the same colour as the piping to the strap. (*Photo courtesy Sebastian Golawski)*

Note the concurrent use of both types on sleeve eagle, on circular and on shaped backing.

The officer's version of the sleeve eagle was a high quality item, hand- embroidered in silvered wire thread.

Above left: This portrait shot shows the wear of the early style sleeve eagle on circular backing.

Above right: This *Feldgendarmerie Unteroffizier* wears the later style eagle where the backing is cut to the outline shape of the embroidery.

Right: A relatively uncommon version of the sleeve eagle with only three segments to the outer wing instead of the normal six is worn by this *Stabsfeldwebel*.

158. Feldgendarmerie.

Das Hoheitsabzeichen der Ordnungspolizei an der Uniform der Feldgend. fällt mit sofortiger Wirkung weg. Ziff. 32 der H. Dv. 275 ist entsprechend zu berichtigen.

O. K. H. (Ch H Rüst u. BdE), 10. 3. 44
— 6473/44 — AHA/Stab III.

The Army Service Regulations bulletin entry regarding the removal of the sleeve eagle.

After the armistice with France in 1940, the *Feldgendarmerie* worked closely with the French Civil *Gendarmerie*.

Cuffbands

A special cuffband was introduced for members of the military police. It was the same for all ranks and consisted of a machine woven rayon band some 3.2 cm wide in mid-brown colour (exact shades will vary with some significantly darker than others) with a pale grey edge and in pale grey gothic lettering the inscription '*Feldgendarmerie*'.

It was worn on the lower left sleeve by all ranks, by regulation 14.5 cm from the cuff though this varied in practice.

So far, three very distinct weave patterns have been noted on original examples of this cuffband indicating that more than one firm was involved in their manufacture.

The obverse of all three types is virtually identical with just minor spacing differences between some of the letters.

The most common reverse pattern shows a mass of loose threads running across the width of the band, a common feature of so called 'BeVo' woven insignia.

A second type has a much more tightly woven reverse with no loose threads whilst the third and rarest pattern has the reverse face show the brown base weave as on the obverse with a ghosted reverse image of the lettering. This exact style of weave is also known on a few of the rarer *Waffen-SS* unit titles, suggesting that this pattern was made by the same firm.

Whilst wartime photographs of *Feldgendarmerie* NCOs and lower ranks generally show the correct, regulation insignia being worn, where officers are concerned usage of insignia seems to have been less well adhered to.

Photographs will be noted where the sleeve eagle is worn with no cuffband, a cuffband with no sleeve eagle, both insignia or indeed no insignia!

As previously mentioned, the early machine or hand embroidered *Feldgendarmerie* cuffbands in the *Polizei* style (on a dark brown wool band) may also be encountered on wartime photographs. The cuffband was withdrawn from use in 1944.

It should be noted that where a unit already wore a cuffband of its own, i.e. *Grossdeutschland, Feldherrnhalle* etc then the *Feldgendarmerie* cuffband was worn in addition to the unit cuffband. In some cases, i.e. *Grossdeutschland*, the unit and *Feldgendarmerie* cuffbands were worn on different sleeves. Where both bands were to be worn on the same sleeve (i.e. *Feldherrnhalle*, or campaign bands such as *Afrika* or *Kreta*), the *Feldgendarmerie* band was worn immediately below the other

Gorget

The most iconic piece of *Wehrmacht* military police insignia was without doubt the special gorget was introduced for the *Feldgendarmerie* and which closely followed the style of those used in the First World War. It consisted of a curved plate which was stamped from thin sheet steel with a turned edge. In the centre was a national emblem affixed by prongs on its reverse, over a dark grey painted scroll with the inscription '*Feldgendarmerie*' in Latin script, also affixed by prongs. At either top corner was a stippled button similar to those used on the tunic. The buttons, national emblem and lettering on the scroll were painted in a yellowish-cream coloured luminous paint. The face of the plate was finished initially in a matt silver colour though some later wartime pieces (particularly those manufactured by the Assmann firm) had a dark grey finish.

The gorget was suspended around the neck by a simple steel chain. The chain was affixed to the right hand side of the reverse face, and attached by simply slipping one of the links of the chain over a flat prong mounted behind the left hand button. A further flat prong is mounted just to the left of centre. This was intended to slip into the buttonhole of the wearer's tunic and prevent the gorget swinging around if the wearer leaned forward.

The reverse face of the gorget was normally covered either with stiff lacquered card or field grey wool.

Mention should also be made of the unique pattern of gorget worn by *Feldgendarmerie* from the *Grossdeutschland* Division. Locally modified by the unit, a thin sheet metal plate was affixed across the concave top edge of the Gorget plate and painted black with a white edge. In the centre of the plate, the GD cipher was featured, either painted, or formed by attaching one of the white metal NCO grade GD shoulder strap ciphers.

Until recently only a couple of extremely badly worn and rusted examples were known to have survived. Recently however, an example in fine condition emerged from the estate of a deceased former member of the GD *Feldgendarmerie*, *Feldwebel* Hugo Misamer. This is, at the time of writing, the only intact example known and the author is profoundly grateful to the owner, Sebastian Golawski for permission to show this incredibly rare piece in this work.

From 10 March 1944, use of the sleeve eagle was discontinued as shown here, only the cufftitle was worn though this ultimately would also be deleted.

Three junior NCOs in winter service dress. Going by the design of the holster being used, they are armed with the P.08 Luger pistol.

Members of *Feldgendarmerie Trupp* 468 pose for a group shot in duty order.

Above left: This fine, clear shot shows the standard machine woven all ranks version of the *Feldgendarmerie* cufftitle being worn.

Above right: A rare version of the cufftitle embroidered in Latin script rather than Gothic is worn by this *Unteroffizier*.

The *leutnant* on the left of this shot wears a hand embroidered aluminium thread version of the cufftitle.

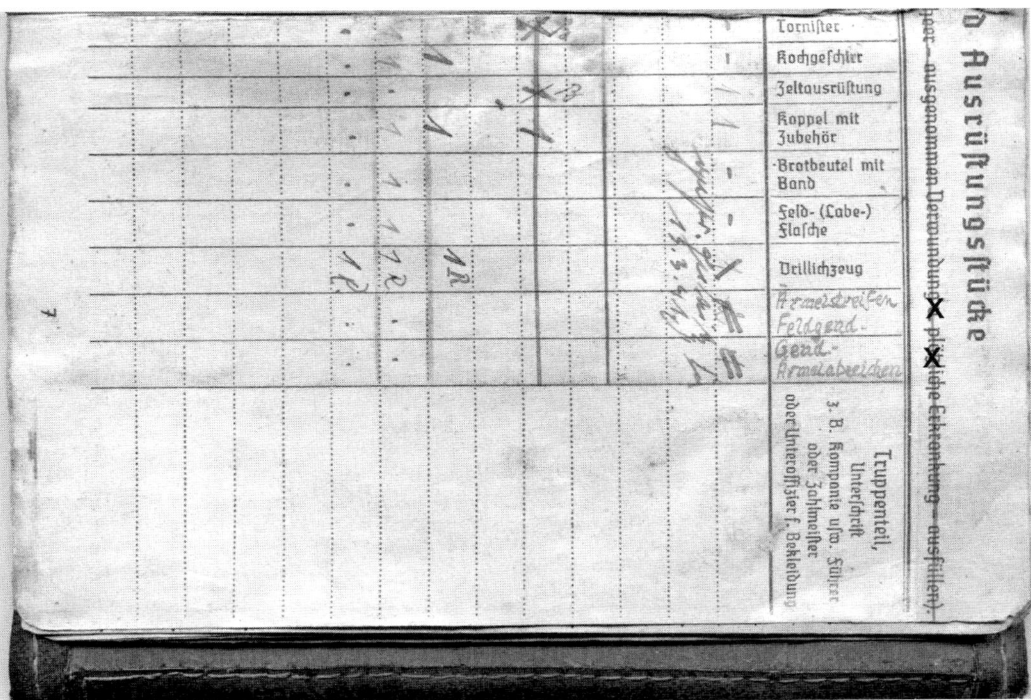

Ausrüstungsstücke

Tornister
Kochgeschirr
Zeltausrüstung
Koppel mit Zubehör
Brotbeutel mit Band
Feld- (Labe-) Flasche
Drillichzeug
Ärmelstreifen Feldgend.
Gend.-Ärmelabzeichen
Truppenteil, Unterschrift d. B. Kompanie usw. Führer oder Zahlmeister oder Unteroffizier f. Bekleidung

The uniform issue page from a *Feldgendarmerie Soldbuch* showing entries for the sleeve eagle (*Gend. Ärmelabzeichen*) and cufftitle (*Ärmelstreifen Feldgend*).

An 'M43' field blouse, with straight pocket flaps, no pleats and six button fastening. Note that the unit cufftitle '*Feldherrnhalle*' is worn above the *Feldgendarmerie* band.

In this fine portrait, the *Feldgendarm* is wearing the M43 *Einheitsfeldmütze*. This universal field cap no longer sported any feature that would identify its wearer as *Feldgendarmerie*. (*Photo courtesy Jan Arne Straete*)

The gorget worn by this *Obergefreiter* is a good example of how quickly the finish on these items was worn away by constant use.

An unusual gorget, probably locally made. Its purpose is unknown but the soldier is almost certainly not *Feldgendarmerie* but is fulfilling some form of police type duty within the unit.

A young admirer examines this *Stabsfeldwebel's* gorget.

Was trägt die Feldgendarmerie? Uebergangsuniform ist die graugrüne Gendarmerie-Uniform, aber mit Rangabzeichen des Heeres und Brust-

Hoheitsabzeichen des Heeres; am linken Oberarm Polizeihoheitszeichen, jedoch ohne Standortbezeichnung. — Im übrigen ist für die Soldaten der Feldgendarmerie die Felduniform des Heeres vorgesehen, Waffenfarbe orangerot, linker Oberarm mit besonderem Hoheitsabzeichen (dem der bewaffneten Verbände der Schutzstaffeln entsprechend). Am linken Unterarm ein braunes Band mit Inschrift „Feldgendarmerie". Wir zeigen den dazugehörigen Ringkragen im Bilde und gleichzeitig den Ringkragen „Bahnhofswache".

An extract from the publication '*Uniformen Markt*' describing the gorget and insignia used by the *Feldgendarmerie*.

Note the distinctive unique gorget with its 'GD' symbol worn by the *Feldgendarm* in the centre of this shot. (*Sebastian Golawski*)

This shot of exhausted *Feldgendarm*en from the *Grossdeutschland* Division shows the special gorget to good advantage. (*Sebastian Golawski*)

Even *Feldgendarmerie* from elite motorised units like *Grossdeutschland* utilised horses as a mode of transport on the Eastern Front. (*Sebastian Golawski*)

Awards and Decorations

Whilst eligibility for awards to members of the *Feldgendarmerie* and related units was no different to that for other branches of the *Wehrmacht*, the types of duty and tasks they were required to perform naturally restricted the number of awards to which they would be able to aspire.

The following list covers those that are known from primary evidence to have been awarded to *Feldgendarmen* and may be seen worn by them in wartime photographs. Where relevant, for example with campaign awards, some specific units of the *Feldgendarmerie* whose members may have qualified for these awards are noted.

Sports Awards

DRL Sports Badge

The DRL (*Deutsche Reichsbund für Leibesübungen*) Sports Badge was introduced in 1937 and replaced the earlier DRA (*Deutscher Reichs-Ausschuss*) Sports Badge. It was issued as a general incentive for physical fitness for both men and women and featured an oval wreath of oakleaves tied with a bow at its base and with a swastika superimposed over this bow. In the centre was an intertwined monogram comprised of the initials DRL. The badge came in three grades, bronze, silver and gold dependant on the level of physical fitness achieved.

SA Sports Badge

Instituted in 1933 for members of the SA and SS, the SA Sports badge was similar in concept to the DRL badge, being awarded in three grades, bronze, silver and gold dependant on the level of physical fitness achieved. For this badge however, the recipient had to show that he fully agreed with the Nazi philosophy and the training exercises which had to be passed included field craft and military training as well as regular physical fitness training. In addition the tests had to be re-taken every year in order to avoid forfeiture of the award.

This *Stabsfeldwebel* wears the DRL Sports Badge on his tunic pocket.

Above left: The DRL Sports Badge.

Above right: The SA Sports Badge.

Both the DRL (above) and SA (below) Sports Badges are worn by this *Unteroffizier.*

Service Awards

Police Service Awards

The series of awards was instituted by Hitler on 30 January 1938 to recognise long and loyal service in the German police. It was awarded in three grades:

8 Years: A silver coloured medal 38 mm in diameter with on its obverse the Polizei national emblem in relief. The reverse features a large numeral '8' with, around the rim, the inscription *Für Treue Dienst in der Polizei*. It was worn on a plain cornflower blue ribbon.

18 Years: A silver coloured cross 'Pattée', measuring 42 mm × 42 mm with the Police pattern national emblem in the centre. The reverse centre featured an oval medallion with the legend *Für Treue Dienst in der Polizei*. The award was suspended from a cornflower blue ribbon onto which was embroidered the police national emblem in white thread.

25 Years: A Gold coloured cross ' Pattée' measuring 42 mm × 42 mm with the police pattern national emblem in the centre. The reverse centre featured an oval medallion with the legend *Für Treue Dienst in der Polizei*. The award was suspended from a cornflower blue ribbon onto which was embroidered the police national emblem in golden yellow coloured thread.

With many members of the *Feldgendarmerie* having transferred directly from the civil police, particularly in the early years of the war it is not uncommon to find *Feldgendarmen* with both *Wehrmacht* and *Polizei* long service awards.

As many were considered simply on detached duty from the police to the army, service time with the army could also be counted towards the award of police long service awards.

Wehrmacht Service Awards—Dienstauszeichnung der Wehrmacht

On 16 March 1936 a series of awards was instituted to recognise long and loyal service in the Armed Forces. New awards of the *Wehrmacht* long service award were halted for the duration of the war in 1940. Those who had already received the 18 or 25 year awards by that time were predominantly senior officers so it is unlikely that awards of anything greater than the 4 and 12 year awards will be encountered as awarded to soldiers during their service in the *Feldgendarmerie*.

These awards were as follows:

4th Class (4 Years): A 30 mm diameter silvered medal with the *Wehrmacht* style national emblem in the centre. Around the rim, in Gothic style *Frakturschrift*, is the legend *Treue Dienst in der Wehrmach*'. On the reverse is a circular wreath of oakleaves surrounding the numeral '4'.

The award was worn from a plain cornflower blue ribbon onto which is pinned a small silvered metal national emblem with outspread wings.

3rd Class (12 Years): A similar medal but gold coloured and with the numeral '12' contained within the wreath on the reverse face.

On awards to Luftwaffe personnel the small national emblem worn on the ribbon was of the unique Luftwaffe style. The awards were worn when appropriate in combination as follows:

For 4 Years—the 4 year medal

For 12 Years—both the 4 and 12 year medals

Campaign Awards

A series of awards were created to commemorate the so-called 'Flower Wars' of 1938–39, so called because of Germany successfully annexing Austria, Czechoslovakia and the port of Memel without military opposition. Many of the members of the *Motorisierte Gendarmerie* who formed the initial manpower cadres of the *Feldgendarmerie* were to earn these awards while serving as temporary military police during these large scale troop movements.

Medals

The Commemorative Medal of 13 March 1938—*Die Medaille zur Erinnerung an den 13. März 1938*

Instituted on 1 May 1938 to commemorate the *Anschluss* whereby Austria lost its independence and was absorbed into the greater German *Reich*.

The 34 mm diameter silvered medal, whose design was based on that of the 1938 Party Day badge, showed on its obverse a naked figure bearing a swastika banner, leading a smaller naked figure, whose chains had been broken (representing the annexed nation being 'rescued' and brought home into the *Reich* by Germany), onto a podium bearing the eagle and swastika. Around the edge of the reverse face was the slogan *Ein Volk, Ein Reich, Ein Führer* the gap between each phrase punctuated by small swastikas. In the centre was the date *13. März 1938*.

The medal was suspended from a red ribbon with white/black/white edges. Over 318,000 were awarded.

The Commemorative Medal of 1 October 1938—*Die Medaille zur Erinnering an den 1 Oktober 1938*

This award was instituted on 18 October 1938 to commemorate the annexation of the Sudetenland.

Its design followed that of the *Anschluss* medal and had an identical obverse design. On the reverse, only the date was altered to *1 Oktober 1938*. In this case the colour of the award was changed to a matt bronze finish. The medal was suspended from a black ribbon with narrow white edges and a red central stripe.

The annexation of the Sudetenland was soon followed by the occupation of the whole of Czechoslovakia and to celebrate this on 1 May 1939 a clasp was instituted for wear on the ribbon of the medal of 1 October 1938 by those holders of the medal who had subsequently taken part in the occupation of the remainder of Czechoslovakia. The bronze clasp depicted Prague castle. Well over one million 1 October 1938 medals were issued, with in excess of 130,000 Clasps.

The Medal Commemorating the Return of Memel—*Die Medaille zur Erinnerung an die Heimkerhr des Memellandes*

The last, and rarest of the 'Flower Wars' medals to be introduced the Memel medal was instituted on 1 May 1939 to commemorate the seizure of the district of Memel from Lithuania which had taken place on 22 March 1939. The obverse design followed that of its predecessors, and the medal was once again finished in a bronze colour. The reverse this time was showed the legend *Zur Erinnerung an die Heimkerhr des Memellandes 22 März 1939*. The slogan surrounding the reverse edge was replaced on this award by a border of oakleaves.

The Police Long Service Medal for 8 years service.

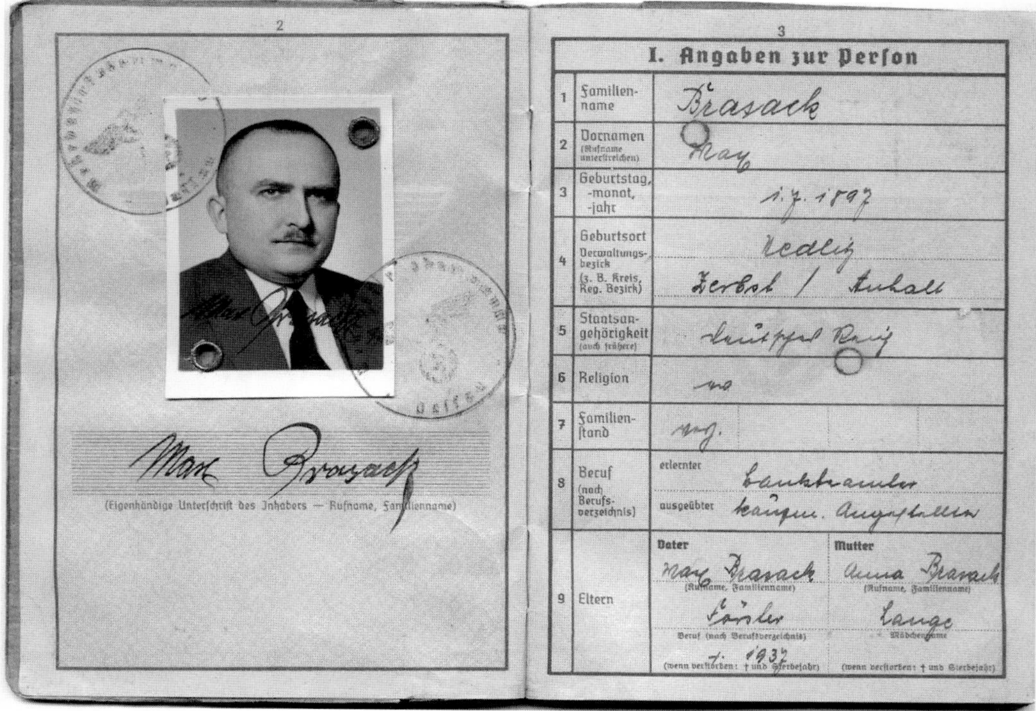

2

(Eigenhändige Unterschrift des Inhabers — Rufname, Familienname)

3

I. Angaben zur Person

1	Familienname	Brasack
2	Vornamen (Rufname unterstreichen)	
3	Geburtstag, -monat, -jahr	
4	Geburtsort Verwaltungsbezirk (z. B. Kreis, Reg. Bezirk)	
5	Staatsangehörigkeit (auch frühere)	
6	Religion	
7	Familienstand	
8	Beruf (nach Berufsverzeichnis)	erlernter / ausgeübter
9	Eltern	Vater (Rufname, Familienname) Beruf (nach Berufsverzeichnis) (wenn verstorben: † und Sterbejahr) / Mutter (Rufname, Familienname) Mädchenname (wenn verstorben: † und Sterbejahr)

Wehrpass to *Leutnant* Max Brasack, a former policeman who served in the *Feldgendarmerie*.

38

noch V. Wehrdienst im

Beförderungen und Ernennungen *)

Mit Wirkung vom	Befördert oder ernannt zum

noch 34

Orden und Ehrenzeichen *)

35 [illegible] Medaille z. Erinnerung an d. 1. Oktober 1938, Polizeidienstauszeichnung Stufe II.

*) Bestätigung der Beförderungen, Ernennungen und Verleihungen nach Abschluß von Übungen durch den Entlassungstruppenteil usw. mit Dienststelle, Unterschrift, Dienstgrad, Dienststellung und Dienststempel.

39

Beurlaubtenstande

Wehrversammlungen, dabei Belehrung über Spionage, Spionageabwehr, Landesverrat u. Wahrung des Dienstgeheimnisses

36

Dienststempel Tag, Monat, Jahr	Dienststempel Tag, Monat, Jahr
Dienststempel Tag, Monat, Jahr	Dienststempel Tag, Monat, Jahr
Dienststempel Tag, Monat, Jahr	Dienststempel Tag, Monat, Jahr
Dienststempel Tag, Monat, Jahr	Dienststempel Tag, Monat, Jahr

The final entry is for a Police Long Service award. (*Polizei dienstauszeichung*)

Armed Forces Long Service Medal for 4 years.

Soldbuch
zugleich Personalausweis
Nr. 10
für
den Oberfeldwebel d. Feldgend.
(Dienstgrad)
ab (Datum) (neuer Dienstgrad)
ab
ab
Erich Wolter
(Vor- und Zuname)
Beschriftung und Nummer der Erkennungsmarke 3. Pz. Ers. Komp. Pi. Ers. Btl. 24, 174
Blutgruppe 0
Gasmaskengröße 2
Wehrnummer 15/34/7

Soldbuch for *Oberfeldwebel* Erich Wolter, from *Feldgendarmerie*.

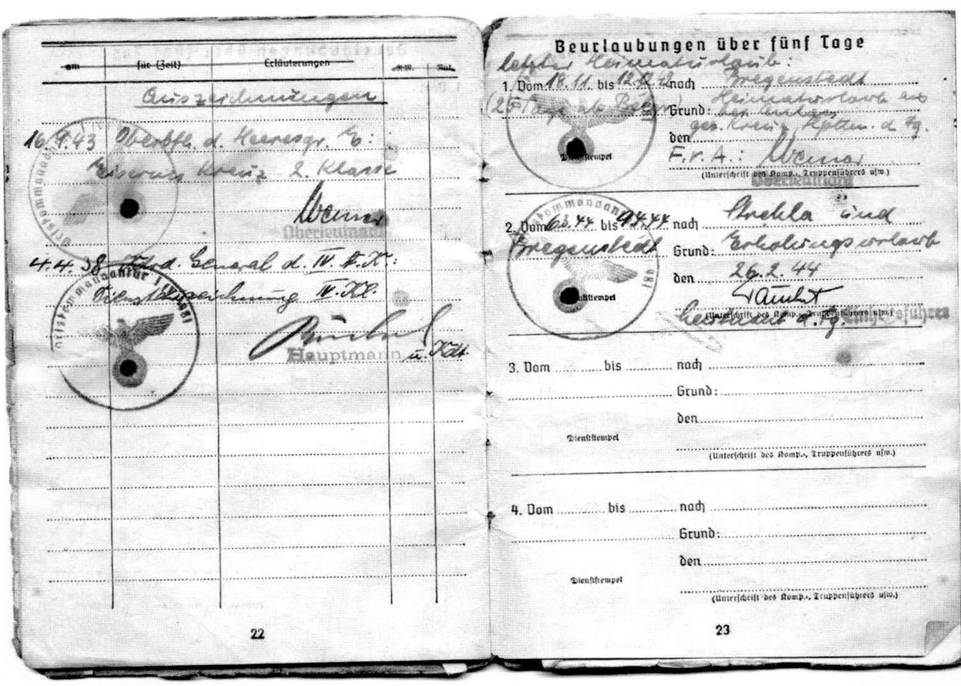

Auszeichnungen
16.7.43 Oberbfh. d. Heeresgr. E: Eisernes Kreuz 2. Klasse
Oberleutnant
4.4.38 Kdr. General d. IV. A.K.: Dienstauszeichnung IV. Kl.
Hauptmann u. Kdt.

22

Beurlaubungen über fünf Tage
1. Vom 18.11. bis 12.12.42 nach
Grund:
den
Dienststempel
(Unterschrift des Komp.-, Truppenführers usw.)
2. Vom 6.3.44 bis 9.4.44 nach
Grund: Erholungsurlaub
den 26.2.44
Dienststempel
(Unterschrift des Komp.-, Truppenführers usw.)
3. Vom bis nach
Grund:
den
Dienststempel
(Unterschrift des Komp.-, Truppenführers usw.)
4. Vom bis nach
Grund:
den
Dienststempel
(Unterschrift des Komp.-, Truppenführers usw.)

23

The awards entries from the Wolter *Soldbuch*, the second entry being for the Army 4 year Long Service medal (*Dienstauszeichnung* IV. Kl.)

Above: The medal for the *Anschluss* with Austria.

Right: Award document for the *Anschluss* Medal to Police, later *Feldgendarmerie*, NCO Willi Haas.

Der Führer und Reichskanzler

hat aus Anlaß der Wiedervereinigung
Österreichs mit dem Deutschen Reich

dem Polizeiwachtmeister

Willi H a a s
in Pforzheim

die

**Medaille zur Erinnerung
an den 13. März 1938**

verliehen.

Berlin, den 31. M ä r z 1939

Der Staatsminister
und Chef der Präsidialkanzlei
des Führers und Reichskanzlers

Meissner

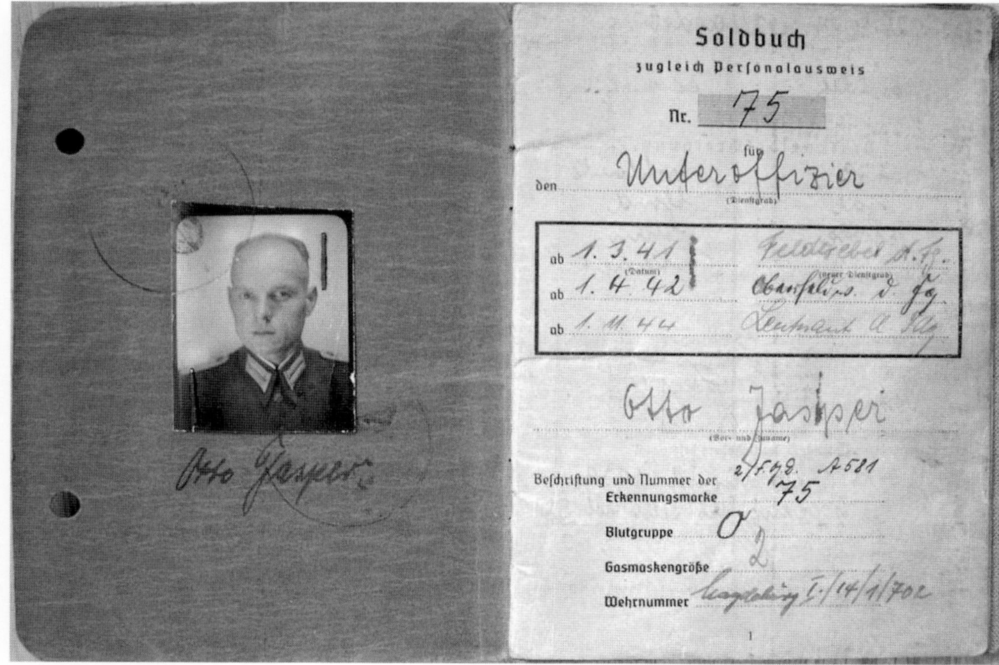

Soldbuch
zugleich Personalausweis
Nr. 75
für
den Unteroffizier
(Dienstgrad)
ab 1.3.41
ab 1.4.42
ab 1.11.44 Leutnant
Otto Jasper
(Vor- und Zuname)
Beschriftung und Nummer der Erkennungsmarke 2/F.G.A. 581 75
Blutgruppe O
Gasmaskengröße 2
Wehrnummer Magdeburg I/14/1/702
1

Soldbuch for *Leutnant* Otto Jasper of *Feldgendarmerie Abteilung* 581.

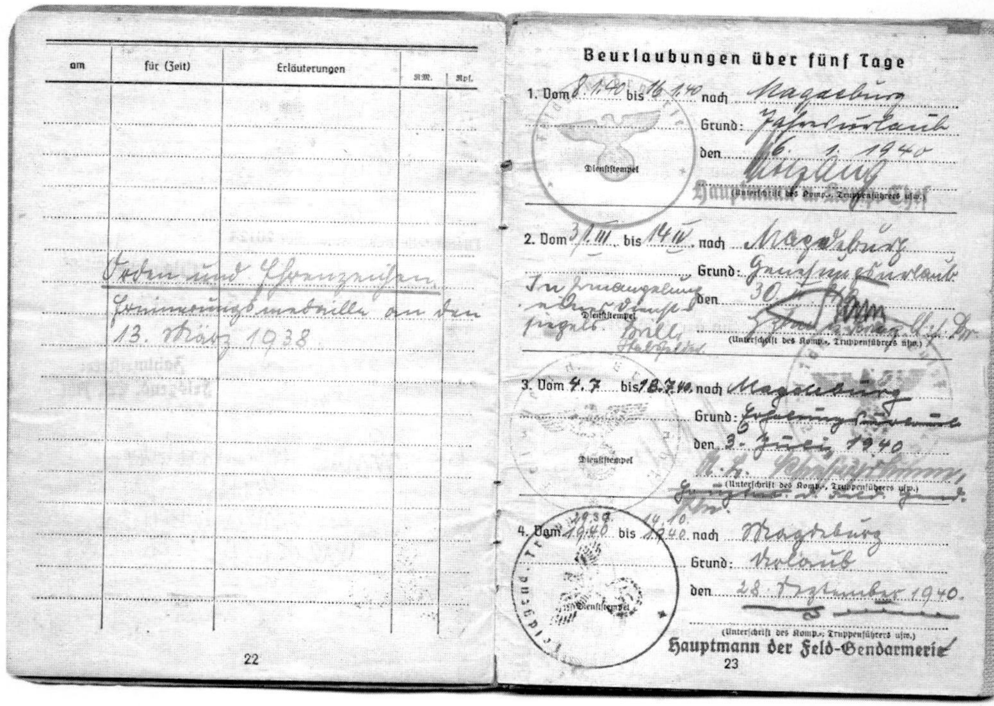

am	für (Zeit)	Erläuterungen	RM.	Rpf.
	Orden und Ehrenzeichen			
	Erinnerungsmedaille an den 13. März 1938.			

22

Beurlaubungen über fünf Tage

1. Vom ... bis ... nach Magdeburg
Grund: ...
den 16. 1. 1940
(Unterschrift des Komp.-, Truppenführers usw.)

2. Vom ... bis ... nach Magdeburg
Grund: ...
den 30. ...
(Unterschrift des Komp.-, Truppenführers usw.)

3. Vom 4.7. bis 18.7.40 nach Magdeburg
Grund: ...
den 3. Juni 1940
(Unterschrift des Komp.-, Truppenführers usw.)

4. Vom ... bis 14.10.40 nach Magdeburg
Grund: Urlaub
den 28. September 1940.
(Unterschrift des Komp.-, Truppenführers usw.)
Hauptmann der Feld-Gendarmerie

23

Awards page from the Jasper *Soldbuch* showing the entry for the *Anschluss* Medal. (*Erinnerungsmedaille* 13.3.1938).

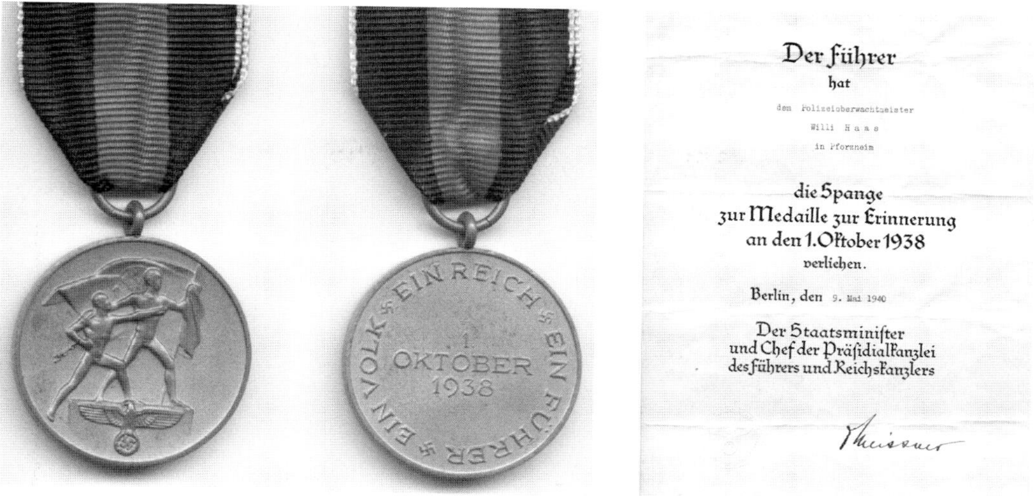

Der Führer
hat
dem Polizeioberwachtmeister
Willi Haas
in Pforzheim
die Spange
zur Medaille zur Erinnerung
an den 1. Oktober 1938
verliehen.

Berlin, den 9. Mai 1940

Der Staatsminister
und Chef der Präsidialkanzlei
des Führers und Reichskanzlers

Meissner

Above left: The medal for the occupation of the Sudetenland.

Above right: Award document for the Prague Clasp to the Sudetenland Medal to a Police NCO serving with the *Feldgendarmerie*.

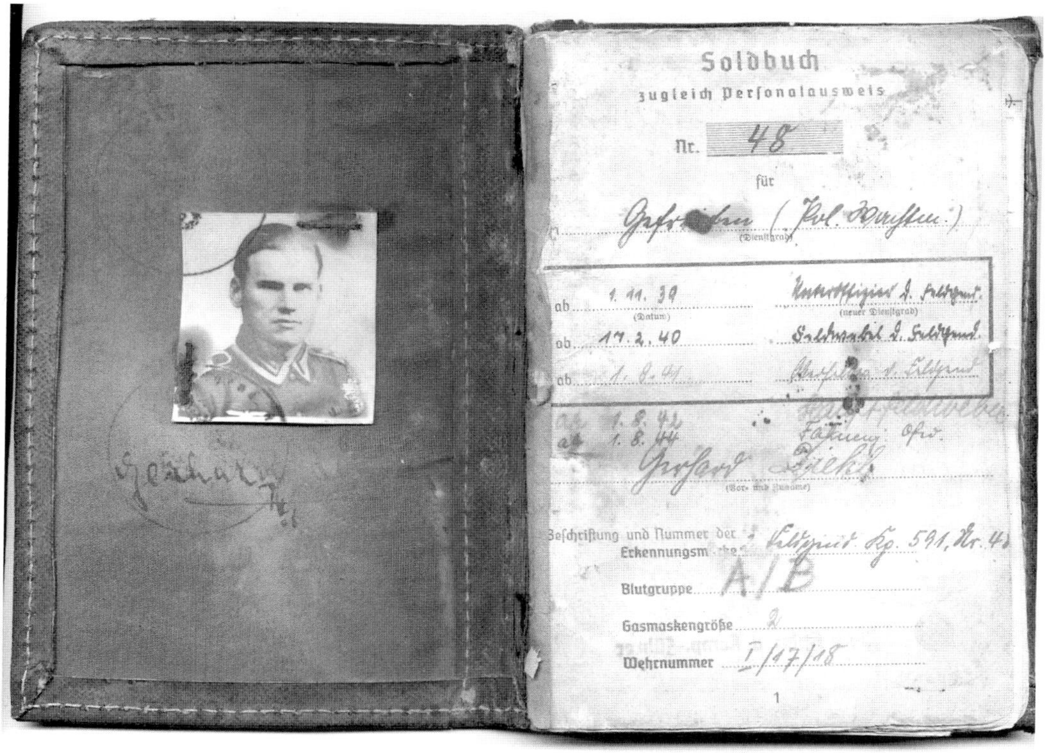

Soldbuch for *Fahnenjuncker-Feldwebel* Gerhard Diehl of *Feldgendarmerie-Trupp* 780.

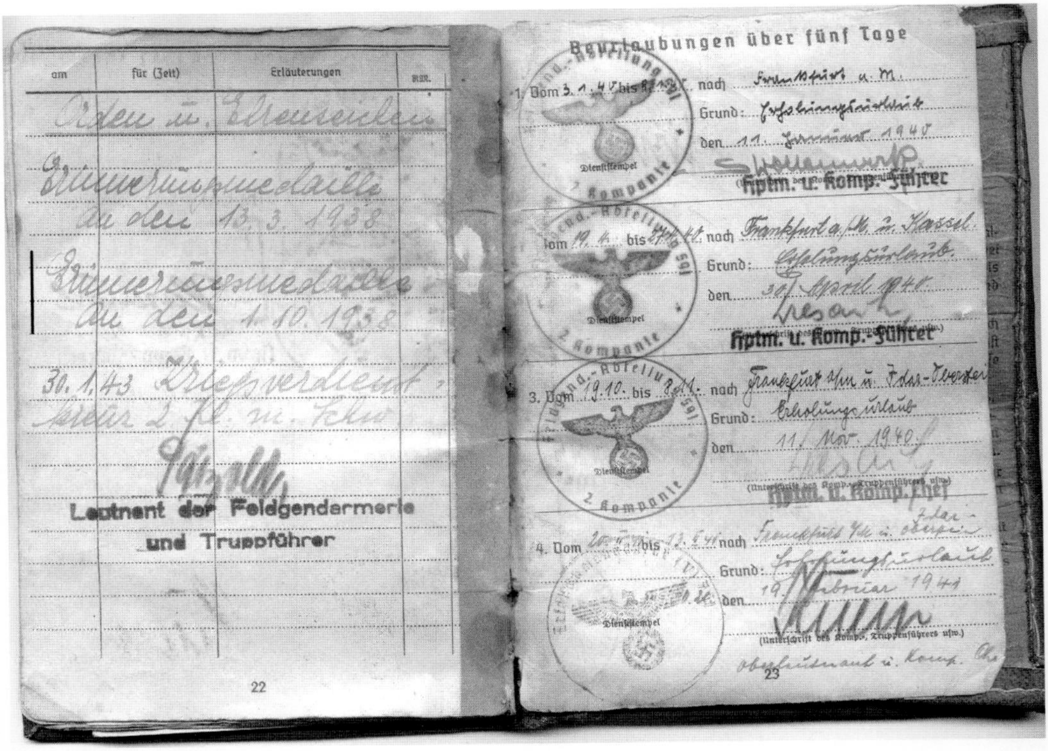

Awards page from the Diehl *Soldbuch* showing the entry for the Sudetenland Medal. (*Erinnerungsmedaille* 1.10.1938).

Medal for the return of Memel.

East Front Medal—*Medaille 'Winterschlacht in Osten'/Ostmedaille*

Based on a design concept by a front line Waffen-SS combat soldier, *SS-Unterscharführer* Ernst Krauss, the *Ostmedaille* was instituted on 26 May 1942, and was intended to recognise those soldiers who had endured the first winter of the war on the eastern front. Over 3 million were issued. The circular medal, some 3.6 cm in diameter, had a gunmetal coloured centre with silvered rim and topped by a silvered steel helmet sitting on a stick grenade.

In the obverse central field was a *Wehrmacht* style eagle and swastika over a laurel branch, and on the reverse, the legend *Winterschlacht im Osten 1941-42, over a laurel branch crossed with a sword. The medal was suspended from a red ribbon featuring a narrow central black stripe bordered in white.*

The medal was to be awarded to those who had served on the eastern front between 15 November 1941 and 26 April 1942, and had fulfilled the following conditions:

a) Having completed fourteen days of combat service

b) Having completed sixty days of non-combatant service

c) Having been wounded in action or having suffered frostbite serious enough in nature to have warranted the award of the wound badge.

Those who were killed in action during this period were awarded the medal posthumously.

IM NAMEN DES FÜHRERS
UND
OBERSTEN BEFEHLSHABERS
DER WEHRMACHT
IST DEM

Feldwebel Fritz M e s s e r
1./Feldgend. Abt. 561 (mot.)

AM 8. August 1942

DIE MEDAILLE
WINTERSCHLACHT IM OSTEN
1941/42
(OSTMEDAILLE)
VERLIEHEN WORDEN.

Feldgend. Abt. 561

FÜR DIE RICHTIGKEIT:

Major u. Abt.- Kdr.

Award document for the Eastern Front Medal to *Feldwebel* Fritz Messer of *Feldgendarmerie Abteilung* 561 (mot.)

The Eastern Front Medal (*Ostmedaille*).

Soldbuch = Zweitschrift
zugleich Personalausweis

Nr. 81

für

den Unteroffizier
(Dienstgrad)

ab .... (Datum) .... (neuer Dienstgrad)
ab
ab

Alfred Beck
(Vor- und Zuname)

Beschriftung und Nummer der Erkennungsmarke 1. Gen./Feldgend. Ers. Abt. Nr. 62

Blutgruppe A B

Gasmaskengröße 2

Wehrnummer Mettmann 98/286/9

1

Soldbuch for *Unteroffizier* Alfred Beck of the *Feldgendarmerie Ersatz Abteilung*.

Auszeichnungen

Datum	Art der Auszeichnung	Verleihungsurkunde	Bestätigung des Komp.- usw. Führers Dienstgrad
9.8.42	Medaille Winterschlacht im Osten 1941/42		

Dienststempel

Oberleutnant u. Komp.-Führer

22

Beurlaubungen über fünf Tage

(Vor Urlaubsantritt auszufüllen)

1. Vom ... bis ... nach ...
Grund: ...
den ... Januar 1944
Dienststempel
Oberleutnant u. Komp.-Führer

2. Vom ... bis ... nach ...
Grund: ...
den 17. Dez. 1944
Dienststempel
Oberleutnant u. Komp. Fhr.

3. Vom ... bis ... nach ...
Grund: ...
den ...
Dienststempel
(Unterschrift des Komp.-, Truppenführers usw.)

4. Vom ... bis ... nach ...
Grund: ...
den ...
Dienststempel
(Unterschrift des Komp.-, Truppenführers usw.)

23

Above: Award page from the Beck *Soldbuch* showing the entry for the Eastern Front Medal.

Right: Feldgendarmerie Obergefreiter on his wedding day. The ribbon in his buttonhole is for the East Front Medal.

IM NAMEN DES FÜHRERS
UND
OBERSTEN BEFEHLSHABERS
DER WEHRMACHT
IST DEM

Feldwebel der Feldgendarmerie
Christian Kreussel
Feldg.Komp. (mot) 757

AM 15.8.42

DIE MEDAILLE
WINTERSCHLACHT IM OSTEN
1941/42
(OSTMEDAILLE)
VERLIEHEN WORDEN.

FÜR DIE RICHTIGKEIT:

Major u. Kommandeur der
Feldgend.

Award Document for the Wound Badge in Black to *Feldwebel* Christian Kreussel of *Feldgendarmerie Leutnant* 757.

IM NAMEN DES FÜHRERS
UND
OBERSTEN BEFEHLSHABERS
DER WEHRMACHT
IST DEM

Feldwebel Fritz Messer
1./Feldgend. Abt. 561 (mot.)

AM 8. August 1942

DIE MEDAILLE
WINTERSCHLACHT IM OSTEN
1941/42
(OSTMEDAILLE)
VERLIEHEN WORDEN.

FÜR DIE RICHTIGKEIT:

Major u. Abt.- Kdr.

Award Document for the Wound Badge in Black to *Feldwebel* Fritz Messer of *Feldgendarmerie Abteilung* 561.

Campaign Shields

Krim Shield

Instituted by Adolf Hitler on 25 July 1942, the *Krim* shield was intended to reward those who had honourably taken part in the fighting in the Crimea between 21 September 1941 and 4 July 1942 and in particular in the following battles:

Breakthrough at Perekop between 21 and 30 September 1941
Breakthrough at Juschun between 18 and 27 October 1941
Advance leading to the breakthrough at Kertsch between 28 October and 16 November 1941.
Initial attack on Sevastopol between 17 and 31 December 1941
Combat at Feodosia between 15 and 18 January 1942
Defensive actions at Parpatsch between 19 January and 7 May 1942
Recapture of Kertsch peninsula between 8 May and 21 May 1942
Capture of Sevastopol between 7 June and 4 July 1942

Otherwise, a total of three months unbroken service between the above dates was required though this condition could be waived if the recipient had been wounded.

The award consisted of a typical heraldic style shield with the eagle and swastika national emblem over a field showing a map of the Crimea with the word *'Krim'* embossed over the representation of the peninsula. At top left of the main field is the date 1941 and at top right 1942.

The shield was stamped from sheet metal, was bronze in colour and was mounted on a piece of appropriate coloured wool cloth which was then stitched to the left upper arm of the tunic. Each soldier was awarded up to five examples for attaching to various garments.

Feldgendarmerie units which were involved in the fighting in the Crimea and some of whose members would have been eligible for the award of the Krim shield include the following:

Feldgendarmerie Trupp (mot) 22.
Feldgendarmerie Trupp a (mot) 315.
Feldgendarmerie Trupp 170.
Feldgendarmerie Trupp 46.
Feldgendarmerie Trupp (mot) 173.
Feldgendarmerie Trupp a (mot) 312.
Feldgendarmerie Trupp 132.
Feldgendarmerie Trupp (mot) 24.
Feldgendarmerie Trupp 30.
Feldgendarmerie Trupp (mot) 154.
Feldgendarmerie Trupp (mot) 42.
Feldgendarmerie Trupp 442.
Feldgendarmerie Trupp 756.
Feldgendarmerie Abt. 683.

Cholm

Instituted by Adolf Hitler on 1 July 1942, the Cholm shield was based on design proposals submitted by one of the soldiers actually involved in the battle, *Polizei-Rottwachtmeister* Schlimm with the support of the commander of German troops in the pocket, *Generalmajor* Scherer. The shield was authorised

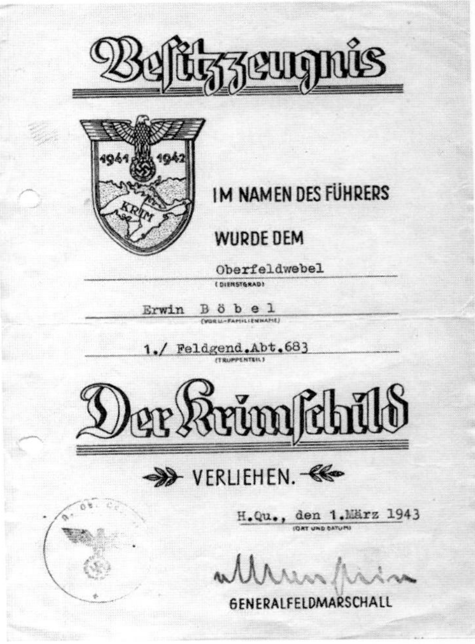

Besitzzeugnis

IM NAMEN DES FÜHRERS

WURDE DEM

Oberfeldwebel
(DIENSTGRAD)

Erwin Böbel
(VOR- U. FAMILIENNAME)

1./ Feldgend.Abt.683
(TRUPPENTEIL)

Der Krimschild

VERLIEHEN.

H.Qu., den 1.März 1943
(ORT UND DATUM)

GENERALFELDMARSCHALL

Above left: The Krim Shield.

Above right: Award document for the Krim Shield to *Oberfeldwebel* Erwin Böbel of *Feldgendarmerie Abteilung* 683.

2

D. Henke

Diedrich Henke

(Eigenhändige Unterschrift des Inhabers — Rufname, Familienname)

3

I. Angaben zur Person

1	Familienname	Henke
2	Vornamen (Rufname unterstreichen)	Heinrich Georg Friedrich
3	Geburtstag, -monat, -jahr	6. Januar 1904
4	Geburtsort Verwaltungsbezirk (z. B. Kreis, Reg. Bezirk)	Eversten Oldenburg
5	Staatsangehörigkeit	Deutsch. Reich
6	Religion	evgl
7	Familienstand	verheir. 11.5.31
8	Beruf (nach Berufsverzeichnis)	erlernter: Maschinenschlosser; ausgeübter: Landessparkassen-Inspektor
9	Eltern	Vater: Diedrich Henke (Rufname, Familienname); Arbeiter, Beruf (nach Berufsverzeichnis); (wenn verstorben: † und Sterbejahr) — Mutter: Helene Henke (Rufname, Familienname); Ahlers, Mädchenname; (wenn verstorben: † und Sterbejahr)

Wehrpass for Dietrich Henke of *Feldgendarmerie-Trupp* 240.

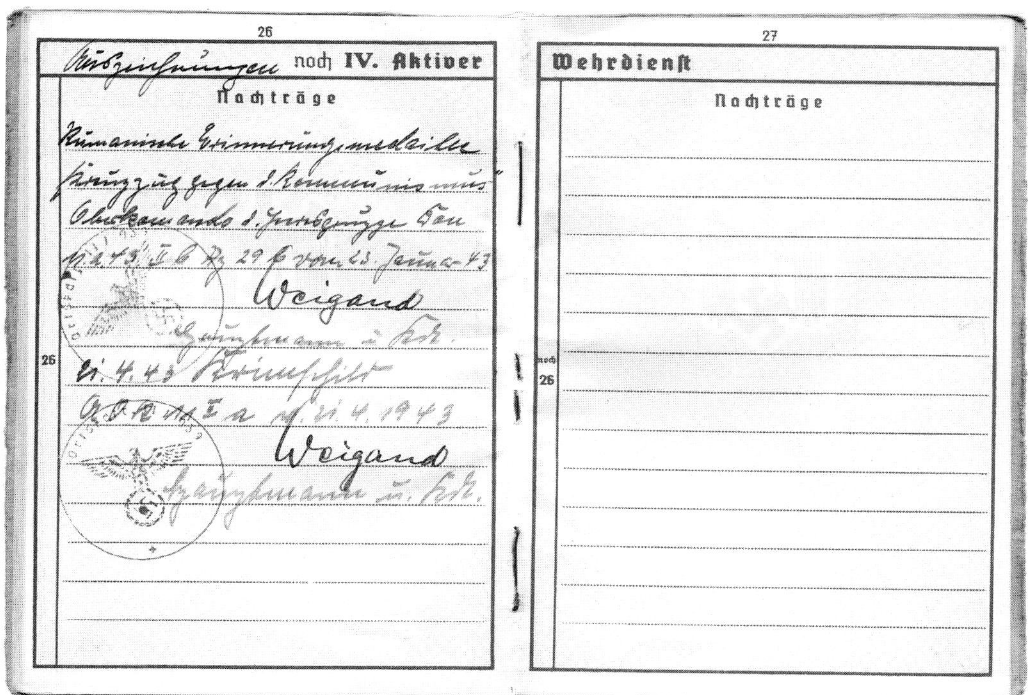

26

Auszeichnungen noch IV. Aktiver

Nachträge

Rumänische Erinnerungsmedaille
„Kreuzzug gegen d. Kommunismus"
Oberkommando d. Heeresgruppe Don
Nr. 43 II b Az. 29 b vom 23. Januar 43
Weigand
Hauptmann u. Kdt.
21.4.43 Krimschild
O.K.H. II a v. 21.4.1943
Weigand
Hauptmann u. Kdt.

26

27

Wehrdienst

Nachträge

noch 26

Above left: Entry from the Henke *Wehrpass* showing the award of the Krim Shield in April 1943.

Above right: Feldgendarmerie Oberfeldwebel wearing the Krim shield immediately above the sleeve eagle.

The Cholm Shield

for all of those who were honourably engaged in the defence of the Cholm pocket.

The shield portrays a large closed-winged *Wehrmacht* style eagle grasping an Iron Cross with swastika centre in its talons, over the word 'Cholm' and the year 1942. It was matt silver coloured and was manufactured first in stamped steel and later also in zinc. The shield was worn on the upper left sleeve.

Various elements of several units were encircled within the pocket, and although it has not been possible at this time to identify with certainty the involvement of *Feldgendarmerie* troops, the fact that two regiments from *123 Infanterie Division* as well as elements of *218 Infanterie Division* were in the pocket suggests that at least some personnel from *Feldgendarmerie Trupp 123* and *Feldgendarmerie Trupp a (mot) 218* would have been eligible for the award as the movement of such large numbers of troops would certainly have necessitated *Feldgendarmerie* involvement.

Kuban Shield

Instituted on 20 September 1943 by Adolf Hitler, the Kuban shield recognised the determined defensive actions in the Kuban bridgehead from February to October 1943, following the collapse of the 6th Army at Stalingrad.

The shield was available to all those who had been honourably engaged in the fighting for a period of at least 60 days, or had been wounded whilst serving in the bridgehead or had been engaged in at least one major action.

The shield was similar in design to the *Krim* shield but with the main field topped by a banner with the word 'KUBAN' over a stylistic representation of the bridgehead with a number of the main battle sites identified, i.e. Krymskaja, Noworossijsk, Lagunen.

Like the *Krim* shield, the Kuban was also stamped from sheet metal, bronze in colour and worn

The Kuban Shield

on the upper left sleeve, mounted via a piece of appropriately coloured cloth.

Feldgendarmerie units which were involved in the fighting in the bridgehead area and some of whose members would have been eligible for the award of the Kuban Shield include the following:

Feldgendarmerie Trupp (mot) 198.
Feldgendarmerie Trupp 140.
Feldgendarmerie Trupp a (mot) 150.
Feldgendarmerie Trupp a (mot) 370.
Feldgendarmerie Trupp a (mot) 101.
Feldgendarmerie Trupp 13.
Feldgendarmerie Trupp (mot) 97.
Feldgendarmerie Trupp a (mot) 173.
Feldgendarmerie Trupp 94.
Feldgendarmerie Trupp (mot) 444.
Feldgendarmerie Trupp a (mot) 418.
Feldgendarmerie Abt. 685.

Demjansk Shield

During early February 1942, II Armeekorps under *General der Infanterie* Graf Brockdorff-Ahlefeld was surrounded by Soviet forces around the small town of Demjansk. Supported by *Luftwaffe* supply drops the German troops in the pocket held out until April when it eventually broke out of the encirclement. On 25 April 1943, Hitler approved a campaign shield for those involved in the defence of the Demjansk pocket.

At the top of the matt silver-grey colored shield, which in the majority of cases was stamped from sheet steel, sat the eagle and swastika flanked either side by log bunkers. Below this was a panel bearing the title 'Demjansk' and in the centre field a stylised aircraft, representing the *Luftwaffe,* over crossed swords, representing the ground forces. At the bottom of the shield was the year 1942.

The shield was to be awarded to those who had:

a) served honourably in the pocket for at least 60 days
b) had been wounded in action in the pocket
c) had been awarded a gallantry awards whilst serving in the pocket.

Feldgendarmerie units active in the pocket included:

Feldgendarmerie Trupp c 12.
Feldgendarmerie Trupp 30.
Feldgendarmerie Trupp 32.
Feldgendarmerie Trupp 123.
Feldgendarmerie Trupp 290.
SS-Feldgendarmerie Trupp 3.

Lappland Shield

The Demjansk Shield

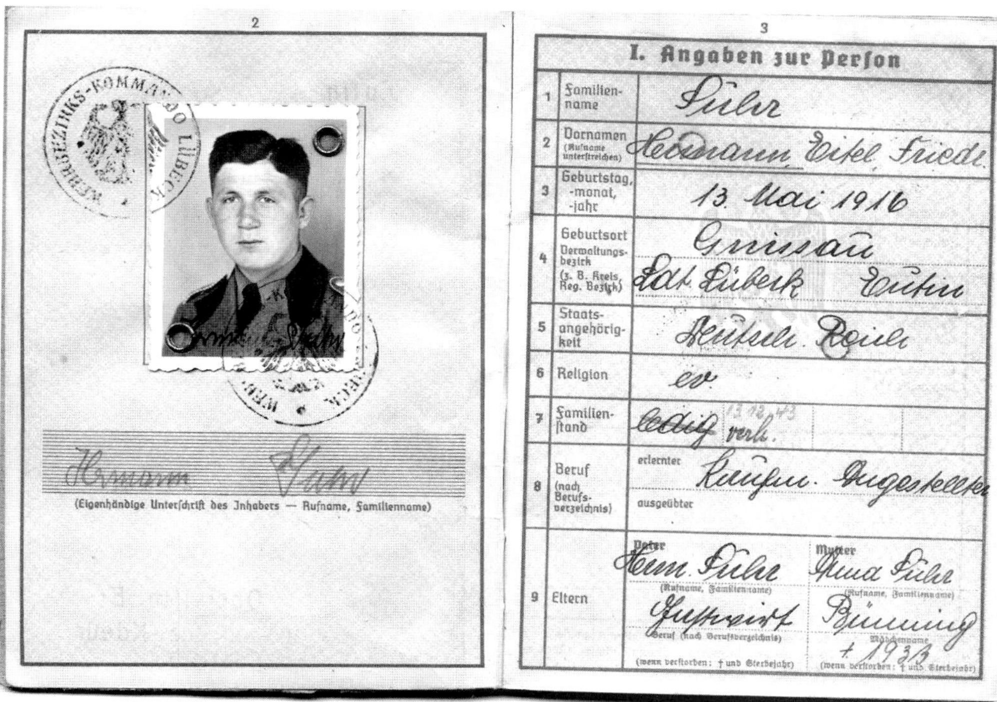

2

Wehrbezirks-Kommando Lübeck

Hermann Sühr

(Eigenhändige Unterschrift des Inhabers — Rufname, Familienname)

3

I. Angaben zur Person

1	Familienname	Sühr
2	Vornamen (Rufname unterstreichen)	Hermann Eitel Friedr.
3	Geburtstag, -monat, -jahr	13. Mai 1916
4	Geburtsort Verwaltungsbezirk (z. B. Kreis, Reg. Bezirk)	Gnissau Ldt. Lübeck Eutin
5	Staatsangehörigkeit	Deutsches Reich
6	Religion	ev.
7	Familienstand	ledig 13.12.43 verh.
8	Beruf (nach Berufsverzeichnis)	erlernter: Kaufm. Angestellter ausgeübter:
9	Eltern	Vater: Herm. Sühr (Rufname, Familienname) Gastwirt (Beruf nach Berufsverzeichnis) (wenn verstorben: † und Sterbejahr) Mutter: Anna Sühr (Rufname, Familienname) Bünning (Mädchenname) + 1933 (wenn verstorben: † und Sterbejahr)

Wehrpass to *Unteroffizier* Hermann Sühr of *Feldgendarmerie-Trupp* 30.

38

noch **V. Wehrdienst im**

Beförderungen und Ernennungen *)

	Mit Wirkung vom	Befördert oder ernannt zum
noch 34		

Orden und Ehrenzeichen *)

35
22.7.43 Kraftfahrbewährungsabzeichen Gold
31.12.43 Demjanskschild

*) Bestätigung der Beförderungen, Ernennungen und Verleihungen nach Abschluß von Übungen durch den Entlassungstruppenteil usw. mit Dienststelle, Unterschrift, Dienstgrad, Dienststellung und Dienststempel.

39

Beurlaubtenstande

Wehrversammlungen, dabei Belehrung über Spionage, Spionageabwehr, Landesverrat u. Wahrung des Dienstgeheimnisses

36	Dienststempel Tag, Monat, Jahr	Dienststempel Tag, Monat, Jahr
	Dienststempel Tag, Monat, Jahr	Dienststempel Tag, Monat, Jahr
	Dienststempel Tag, Monat, Jahr	Dienststempel Tag, Monat, Jahr
	Dienststempel Tag, Monat, Jahr	Dienststempel Tag, Monat, Jahr

Awards page from the Sühr *Wehrpass* showing the award of the *Demjanskschild*.

The last of the shield awards to be officially approved, the Lappland shield was designed in February 1945, to recognize the efforts of *20 Gebirgsarmee* under General Boehme. Not officially approved until 1 May 1945, one day after Hitler's death, the shield is only known in crude locally made form, produced some time after *20 Gebirgsarmee* surrendered to the British on 8 May 1945.

Not surprisingly in the circumstances, the eagle represented at the top of the shield does not carry the swastika. It sits over a field with a map of the region surmounted by the title Lappland. The lack of the offending swastika resulted in the British taking a relaxed view of the production of the shield as a commemorative piece for the men of *20 Gebirgsarmee*.

Entries were made into the *Soldbuch* of recipients and award documents were produced but the shield itself was never intended for wear and the majority of those original examples which are known do not feature a cloth backing for attachment to the sleeve and indeed many do not even feature a method of attachment to a cloth patch.

Those *Feldgendarmerie* units which would have qualified for the award of the shield include:

Feldgendarmerie Trupp c (mot) 462.
Feldgendarmerie Trupp (mot) 99.
Feldgendarmerie Trupp d 1114.
Feldgendarmerie Trupp c (tmot) 702.
Feldgendarmerie Trupp 210.
Feldgendarmerie Trupp 295.
Feldgendarmerie Trupp 280.
Feldgendarmerie Trupp c (tmot) 274.
Feldgendarmerie Trupp 436.
Feldgendarmerie Trupp 433.
Feldgendarmerie Trupp 470.

The Lappland Shield

Im Namen und im Auftrag des
Oberbefehlshabers der 2o. (Geb.) Armee
General der Gebirgstruppe Böhme

wurde dem

Stabsfeldwebel W i l l i . E n d e r s
der Feldgendarmerie Ersatz Abteilung I

der L A P P L A N D S CH I L D
verliehen.

Horsteumes , den 12. August 1945

Richter.

Leutnant und Stellvertr. Truppführer
Feldgendarmerie Ers. Abt. I

Right: Award document for the Lappland Shield to a *Stabsfeldwebel* of *Feldgendarmerie Ersatz Abteilung* I.

Below: Soldbuch for *Stabsfeldwebel* Willi Enders. Note his rank on transferring from the civil police as *Gendarmerie Wachtmeister*. (*Ian Jewison*)

Soldbuch
zugleich Personalausweis 3659
Nr. 15
für
den Gend. Wachtmstr.
(Dienstgrad)
ab 17. XI. 1939 Feldwebel
(Datum) (neuer Dienstgrad)
ab 1. I. 1940 Oberfeldwebel z.
ab 1. 2. 1945 Stabsfeldwebel
Willi Enders
(Vor- und Zuname)
Beschriftung und Nummer der
Erkennungsmarke 15 Feldg. Tr. 67
Blutgruppe 0
Gasmaskengröße 2
Innsbruck
Wehrnummer 10/1/65/2
1

A. Zuletzt zuständige Wehrersatzdienststelle: Innsbruck

B. Zum Feldheer abgesandt von:¹)

	Ersatztruppenteil	Kompanie	Nr. der Truppenstammrolle
a	~~2./Feldgend. Ers. Abtlg. 1~~		~~X/1005~~
b			
c			

C.

	Feldtruppenteil²)	Kompanie	Nr. der Kriegsstammrolle
a	~~Feldgendarmerie Trupp 62~~		
b	~~Feldgendarmerie Trupp 67~~		~~22~~
c	Feldgendarmerie-Trupp 210		46

D.

Jetzt zuständiger Ersatztruppenteil²)	Standort
~~Pz. Abw. Ers. Abt. 48~~	~~Graz~~
~~Feldgend. Ers. Abtlg. 1~~	~~Litzmannstadt~~
Feldgend. Ers. Abt.	Litzmannstadt

(Meldung dortselbst nach Rückkehr vom Feldheer oder Lazarett, zuständig für Ersatz an Bekleidung und Ausrüstung)

¹) Vom Ersatztruppenteil einzutragen, von dem der Soldbuchinhaber zum Feldheer abgesandt wird.
²) Vom Feldtruppenteil einzutragen und bei Versetzungen von einem zum anderen Feldtruppenteil derart abzuändern, daß die alten Angaben nur durchstrichen werden, also leserlich bleiben.

Weiterer Raum für Eintragungen auf Seite 17.

4

Anschriften der nächsten lebenden Angehörigen

des Willi Enders (Vor- und Zuname)

1. Ehefrau: Vor- und Mädchenname Olga, Johanna geb. Klodek

(ggf. Vermerk „ledig")

Wohnort (Kreis) Meerane / Sa.

Straße, Haus-Nr. Schillerstr. 6

2. Eltern: des Vaters, Vor- und Zuname August Enders

Stand oder Gewerbe

der Mutter, Vor- u. Mädchenname

Wohnort (Kreis) Herdorf / Sieg

Straße, Haus-Nr.

3. Verwandte oder Braut:*) Olga Klodek

Vor- und Zuname

Stand oder Gewerbe

Wohnort (Kreis) Meerane / Sa.

Straße, Haus-Nr. Schillerstr. 6

*) Ausfüllung nur, wenn weder 1. noch 2. ausgefüllt sind.

5

Soldbuch entries show that Enders served with *Feldgendarmerie-Trupp* 67 and 210. (*Ian Jewison*)

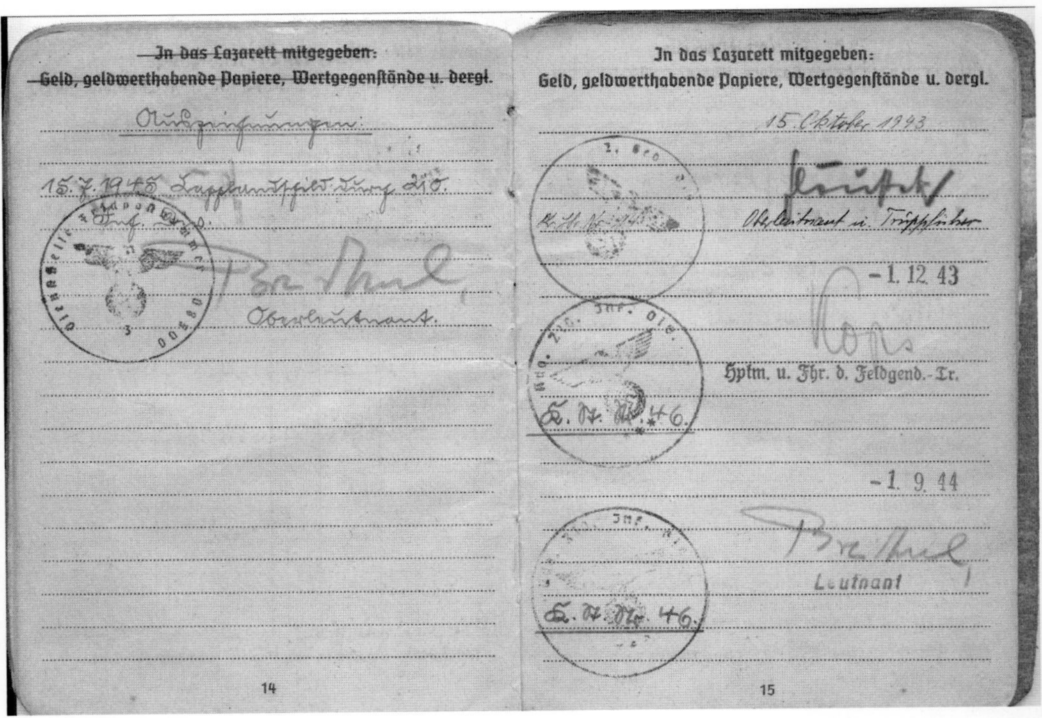

~~In das Lazarett mitgegeben:~~
~~Geld, geldwerthabende Papiere, Wertgegenstände u. dergl.~~

Auszeichnungen:

15.7.1945 Lapplandschild Trupp 210

Obeleutnant.

14

In das Lazarett mitgegeben:
Geld, geldwerthabende Papiere, Wertgegenstände u. dergl.

15. Oktober 1943

Oberleutnant u. Truppführer

−1. 12. 43

Hptm. u. Fhr. d. Feldgend.-Tr.

−1. 9. 44

Leutnant

15

Note the entry for the award of the *Lapplandschild* dated 15 July 1945, after the end of the war.

Cuffbands

Afrika Cuffband

The *Afrika* cuffband was instituted on 15 January 1943 and formally announced via *Allgemeine Heeresmitteilungen Nr. 60*, of 27 January 1943. The band was to be awarded to those who had served in North Africa for at least six months, though this time qualification could be waived if an individual had been wounded in action and the time qualification was reduced to three months if the recipient had contracted a disease during his service.

The time qualification was also waived if the individual had only arrived in theatre towards the end of the campaign and thus had not be able to complete six months service in which case the time qualification could be reduced to four months.

The band was 3.2 cm wide, and made from a mid brown camelhair material (*Kamelhaarstoff*) with an edging in silver-grey rayon Russia braid. On the band is embroidered the word *AFRIKA*, flanked either side by a palm tree, also in silver grey rayon thread. The band was worn on the lower left sleeve.

Feldgendarmerie units which had served in North Africa included:
Feldgendarmerie Trupp (mot) 33c.
Feldgendarmerie Trupp (mot) 200c.
Feldgendarmerie Trupp 90 le. Div.
Feldgendarmerie Trupp (mot) 999.
Feldgendarmerie Trupp (mot) 613.
Feldgendarmerie Trupp (mot) 498.

Kreta Cuffband

The *Kreta* cuffband was instituted by Adolf Hitler on 16 October 1942, (*Heeres Verordnungs Blatt* 1942, directive 23, page 457, No. 874) and was intended to recognise the wearer's participation in the invasion of Crete from 20 to 27 May 1942. The award consisted of a white cotton cloth band 3.2 cm wide, with an edging in golden yellow rayon Russia braid. On the band was embroidered the word *KRETA, bracketed by an acanthus leaf design, all also executed in golden yellow rayon thread. The band was to be worn on the lower left sleeve.*

It was awarded to those who:

a) took part in the assault on Crete between 20 and 27 March 1942 by parachute or landing by glider.
b) took part in air operations over Crete.
c) took part in operations in the waters around Crete prior to 28 May 1942. This latter condition also included army personnel who were transported to the island by sea on 19 May 1942.

Due to the relatively small size of the invasion force, it is thought that the only Feldgendarmerie units likely to have qualified for the Kreta cuffband were:
Feldgendarmerie Trupp 95.
Feldgendarmerie Trupp 7 Flieger Div.

Kurland Cuffband

The final campaign cuffband to be instituted during World War two, the *Kurland* cuffband was created at the request of *Generaloberst* von Vietinghoff, the commander of *Heeresgruppe Kurland and instituted on 12 March 1945.*

The *Afrika* cufftitle.

Above left: The *Oberfeldwebel* at right is wearing the *Afrika* cufftitle immediately above his *Feldgendarmerie* band.

Above right: Oberfeldwebel of *Feldgendarmerie* wearing both the Kreta and *Feldgendarmerie* cufftitles.

The Kreta cufftitle.

The Kurland cufftitle.

In order to qualify for the award, the individual simply had to:

a) take part in three combat engagements.

b) be wounded in action.

c) If neither a) or b) applied, then to serve for three months in the theatre.

Due to the difficulties faced in producing this band so late in the war, several formats exist depending on whether the band was produced in Germany, or locally 'in theatre' using whatever methods were available. The silver-white cloth band shows the word KURLAND in black between the a shield bearing the coat of arms of the *Hochmeister* (Grand Master) of the Teutonic Knights on the left and one bearing the stag's head coat of arms of the city of Mitau on the right. As with other campaign cuffbands, the *Kurland* band was to be worn on the lower left sleeve.

Due to the large number of troops serving in the *Kurland* area in the final stages of the war, it is not surprising that there were several *Feldgendarmerie* units which would qualify. These included:

Feldgendarmerie Trupp (mot) 121.
Feldgendarmerie Trupp 30.
Feldgendarmerie Trupp 132.
Feldgendarmerie Trupp a (mot) 225.
Feldgendarmerie Trupp a (mot) 187.
Feldgendarmerie Trupp a (mot) 263.
Feldgendarmerie Trupp 126.
Feldgendarmerie Trupp (mot) 121.
Feldgendarmerie Trupp 290.
Feldgendarmerie Trupp (mot) 11.
Feldgendarmerie Trupp a (mot) 900.
Feldgendarmerie Trupp 122.
SS-Feldgendarmerie Trupp 15.
SS-Feldgendarmerie Trupp 19.
Feldgendarmerie Trupp (mot) 24.
Feldgendarmerie Trupp b (mot) 2.
Feldgendarmerie Trupp a (mot) 218.
Feldgendarmerie Trupp 1121.
Feldgendarmerie Trupp 205.
Feldgendarmerie Trupp 181.
Feldgendarmerie Trupp a (mot) 410.
Feldgendarmerie Trupp 421.
Feldgendarmerie Trupp 450.
Feldgendarmerie Trupp 438.
Feldgendarmerie Trupp (mot) 473.

It should be noted that although *Soldbuch* and *Wehrpass* entries for the *Kurland* band are not particularly rare, examples of the band itself or the certificate of possession relating to it are extremely scarce. This suggests that many awards may have been made purely 'on paper' with an entry made into the individuals documents, but with the actual cuffband not being received do to production difficulties.

Gallantry Awards

Iron Cross

One of the best known military awards of all time, the Iron Cross was reinstituted on 1 September 1939, in four initial grades, the second class, first class, Knight's Cross and Grand Cross, with 1939 clasps to the 1914 second and first classes also being introduced.

The basic traditional design, of a blackened iron core held within a silvered frame, was retained. In the new version however, the obverse centre contained the swastika emblem of the Third Reich with the new institution date of 1939 in the lower arm. The reverse core design was plain, apart from the original institution date of 1813 in the lower arm.

As was the case with the Imperial predecessors of this award, the basic grade was the second class, suspended from a ribbon in the national colours, now changed from black and white to black, white and red.

The award itself was normally only worn on the day it was awarded, or later on the medal bar with parade dress. For normal service only the ribbon was worn, from the tunic buttonhole.

The 1939 clasp to the 1914 second class consisted of an eagle grasping a wreathed swastika in its talons, over a plaque with the year 1939. It was worn affixed to the 1914 second class ribbon in the buttonhole. The clasp measured 30 mm × 30 mm.

The 1939 first class had the same obverse design as the second class, but had a plain flat reverse to which was attached a hinged pin fitting by which the award was pinned to the left breast of the uniform.

The 1939 clasp to the 1914 first class was of similar design to the second class clasp but with longer wingspan at 45 mm and with a hinged pin fitting on the reverse. It was pinned to the left breast of the tunic above the 1914 first class.

The only other grade which is of interest to a study of the *Feldgendarmerie* is the Knight's Cross, as there is a single claimed *Feldgendarmerie* recipient.

The Knight's Cross was similar in design to the second class but larger, at 48 mm × 48 mm and with the frame in solid silver. An eyelet was affixed to the top edge of the cross to accept a silver wire loop through which a 50 mm wide neck ribbon was passed.

Heinz Heuer

Heinz Heuer was born in Berlin in March 1918. After completing his schooling he attended a course of further education, studying economics, before joining the cadet preparatory school in Potsdam.

On 1 November 1936, Heuer joined the Brandenburg Police School, but his training here was interrupted by his having to complete his two-year term of compulsory military service. On completion of his national service, he returned to police training at the various training establishments in Potsdam, Eiche, Berlin and at the Police Technical School in Berlin. He was then posted to *Ordnungspolizei* headquarters in the *Reichsinnenministerium* in Berlin. Heuer also served with the *Abwehr* and the *Oberkommando der Wehrmacht* overseas department. He became a courier to the *Polizei Division* and other police leadership staffs and later served with all of the armed services and on temporary attachments to various embassies overseas.

Heuer's war service included duty with the elite *Brandenburg* division and he also saw service in Africa, Asia and Turkey. For his courier duties, Heuer became the first police recipient of the *Kraftfahtbewährungsabzeichen* in Gold.

During the Battle of Berlin in 1945, Heuer served as an *Oberfeldwebel* of the *Feldgendarmerie* in command of a small combat group. According to Heuer's own testimony, he was summoned to Hitler's headquarters one day and tasked by General Krebs with a special mission. He and his small band of men were to locate a suspected Soviet command post. Heuer had already carried out several dangerous missions and quickly set off on his new task with a small force of 28 men. On the night of 21 April, Heuer located the enemy command post and after a short fight, captured it along with all the documents and maps it contained.

On his return trip, Heuer and his *Kampfgruppe* ran into trouble when they met a strong Soviet tank force. During the battle which ensued, 27 enemy tanks were destroyed. Heuer's personal claim was an amazing 13 tanks. Considering that his small unit had no anti-tank guns and had to destroy all these tanks at point-blank range with satchel charges, stick grenades and single-shot *Panzerfausts*, their achievement was all the more impressive.

Krebs was delighted with Heuer's success and the information and maps he captured. For his achievement, Heuer was awarded the Knight's Cross on the 22 April and given a battlefield promotion to *Leutnant.*

Heuer was taken into Soviet captivity in Berlin when the Third Reich finally crumbled. He was held in Soviet camps in Berlin, then in Siberia and then in a punishment camp in Oms. Heuer ultimately ended up in the hands of the GPU in east Berlin, but escaped with the help of a sympathetic Soviet officer.

After the war, Heuer became a consultant with the British military police in Berlin. In 1947, he moved to West Germany and again became an active police officer up until his retirement in 1967 through disability caused by his wounds

No records exist confirming the award of the Knight's Cross to Heuer, perhaps unsurprisingly considering the chaotic situation in Berlin in the closing weeks of the war. This fact however, has led some to suggest that the award was never made, or that if made because it was never formally recorded through the regulation award process, is invalid.

As Herr Heuer is now deceased it is probably unlikely in the extreme that positive proof either way of the award of the Knight's Cross to him will ever be established.

There are however, other undoubted examples of former *Feldgendarmen* going on to win the Knight's Cross, or Knight's Cross winners serving in the *Feldgendarmerie* if only temporarily.

Johannes Hauser

A fine example of a former *Feldgendarm* winning the Knight's Cross is the case of Johannes 'Hans' Hauser.

Hans Hauser was born in Innsbruck on 31 January 1916 and was commissioned as a *Leutnant* in the police in 1938 at the age of 22, remaining with the police until 1942 when he was assigned to the army and served as a *Leutnant* in the military police, eventually commanding *Feldgendarmerie Trupp 498 b (mot.)* He served in Lybia and Sicily with the *Feldgendarmerie*, ultimately reaching the rank of *Hauptmann der Feldgendarmerie* in April 1943. Recalled from the army in 1943, he was promoted to *SS-Hauptsturmführer* in the *SS-Polizei Division* as company commander of *3/. SS-Polizei Schutzen Regiment 3.*

Hauser served on the Eastern Front during 1943/44 winning the Iron Cross second and first classes. He was promoted to *SS-Sturmbannführer und Major der Schutzpolizei* in November 1944.

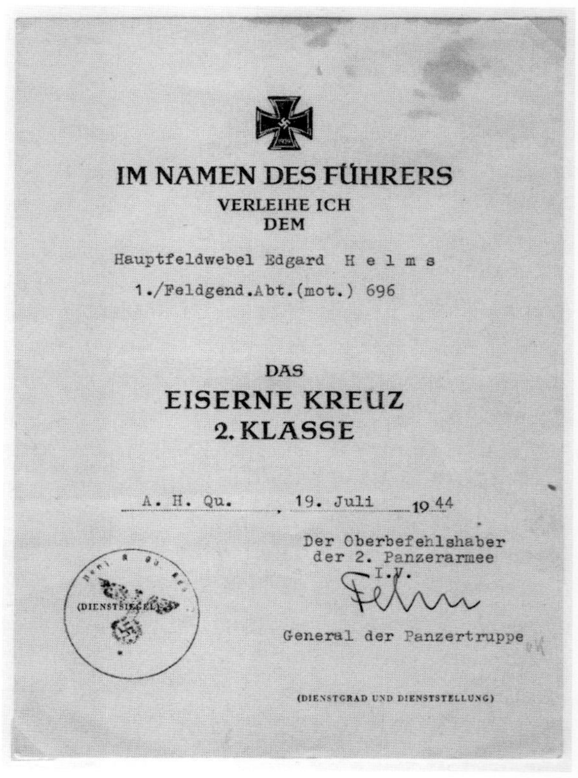

IM NAMEN DES FÜHRERS
VERLEIHE ICH
DEM

Hauptfeldwebel Edgard H e l m s
1./Feldgend.Abt.(mot.) 696

DAS
EISERNE KREUZ
2. KLASSE

A. H. Qu., 19. Juli 1944

Der Oberbefehlshaber
der 2. Panzerarmee
I.V.

General der Panzertruppe

(DIENSTSIEGEL)

(DIENSTGRAD UND DIENSTSTELLUNG)

Above left: The Iron Cross Second Class.

Above right: Award document for the Iron Cross Second Class to a *Feldgendarmerie* Hauptfeldwebel. (*Walter Spiller Collection*)

Opposite above: Wehrpass for Stabsfeldwebel Walter Tronnier of *Feldgendarmerie Abteilung* 531.

Opposite below: Awards page from the Tronnier *Wehrpass* showing the entry for the Iron Cross Second Class.

2

Walther Frommer

(Eigenhändige Unterschrift des Inhabers — Rufname, Familienname)

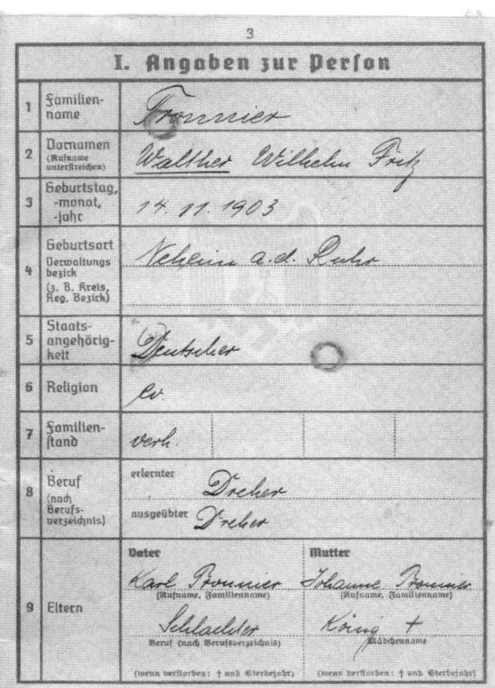

3

I. Angaben zur Person

1	Familienname	Frommer
2	Vornamen (Rufname unterstreichen)	Walther Wilhelm Fritz
3	Geburtstag, -monat, -jahr	14. 11. 1903
4	Geburtsort Verwaltungsbezirk (z. B. Kreis, Reg. Bezirk)	Mülheim a.d. Ruhr
5	Staatsangehörigkeit	Deutscher
6	Religion	ev.
7	Familienstand	verh.
8	Beruf (nach Berufsverzeichnis)	erlernter Dreher ausgeübter Dreher
9	Eltern	Vater: Karl Frommer (Rufname, Familienname); Schlachter, Beruf (nach Berufsverzeichnis); (wenn verstorben: † und Sterbejahr) Mutter: Johanne Frommer (Rufname, Familienname); König + Mädchenname; (wenn verstorben: † und Sterbejahr)

46

Größenangaben

Gasmaske 2

Stahlhelm 57 ½

38 Mütze 56 ½

Stiefel 28

Blutgruppe: A

Nachträge

Eisernes Kreuz II. Klasse am 3.10.41

Hauptmann der Feldgendarmerie und Komp. Chef

39 15.8.42 Ostmedaille verliehen

Hptm. u. Komp.-Chef

47

Entlassungstag am 22.10.42

Abgefunden nach A. H. M./41 Ziffer 601

Wehrsold	vom 23.10. bis 5.11.	RM.	28.00
Verpflegungsgeld	vom 23.10. bis 5.11.	RM.	16.80
Unterkunftsverg.	vom — bis —	RM.	—
Entlassungsgeld		RM.	—
insgesamt:		RM.	44.80

Marschverpflegung für den [illegible]

21.10.42

Ausgezahlt: Festgestellt:

Uffz. u. Rechnungsf. Zahlmeister.

1939 Clasp to the 1914 Iron Cross Second Class.

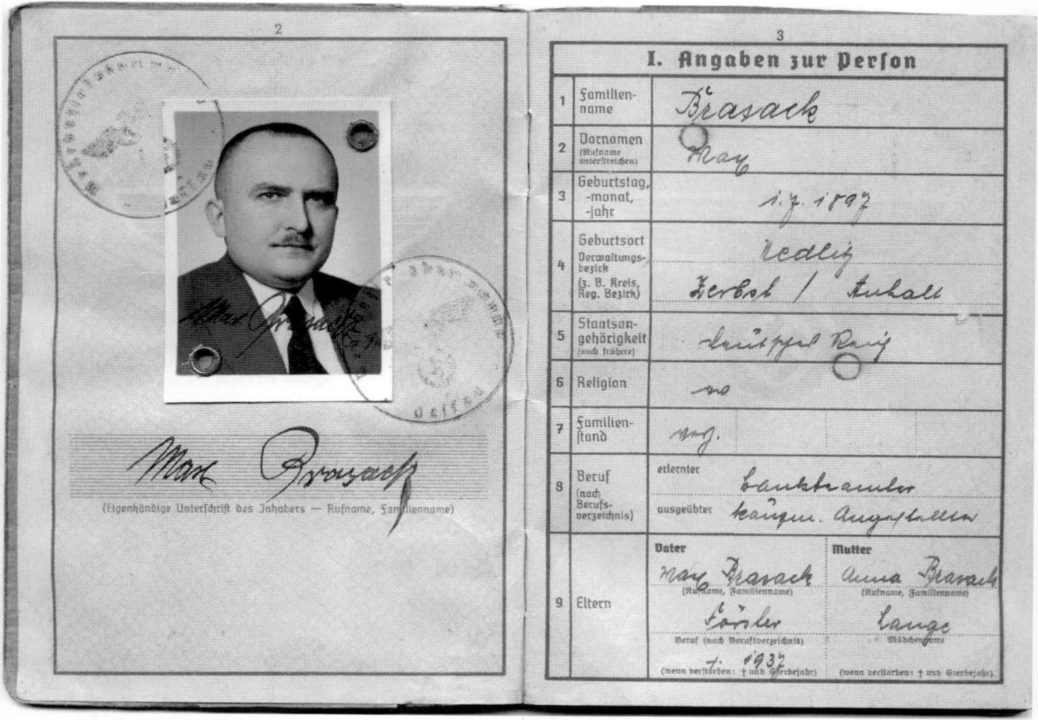

2

Max Brasack

(Eigenhändige Unterschrift des Inhabers — Rufname, Familienname)

3

I. Angaben zur Person		
1	Familien-name	Brasack
2	Vornamen (Rufname unterstreichen)	Max
3	Geburtstag, -monat, -jahr	1.7.1897
4	Geburtsort Verwaltungsbezirk (z. B. Kreis, Reg. Bezirk)	Zerbst / Anhalt
5	Staatsangehörigkeit (auch frühere)	Deutsches Reich
6	Religion	ev
7	Familienstand	verh.
8	Beruf (nach Berufsverzeichnis)	erlernter: Bankbeamter; ausgeübter: kaufm. Angestellter
9	Eltern	Vater: Max Brasack (Rufname, Familienname); Beruf (nach Berufsverzeichnis); (wenn verstorben: † und Sterbejahr) † 1937 — Mutter: Anna Brasack (Rufname, Familienname); Lange (Mädchenname); (wenn verstorben: † und Sterbejahr)

Wehrpass for *Oberfeldwebel* Max Brasack of *Feldgendarmerie-Trupp* a (mot) 183.

26

noch **IV. Aktiver**

Nachträge

Orden u. Ehrenzeichen

Spange zum E.K. II. Klasse

(verliehen lt. Urkunde am 22.III.42.)

Oberleutnant u. Einheitsführer

26 Verleihung der Ostmedaille: "Winterschlacht im Osten 1941/42" gemäß Schreiben d. 83. Inf. Div. Abt. IIa Nr. 29 vom 4. 6. 1943.

Major u. Ortskommandant

27

Wehrdienst

Nachträge

2.6.42 Verw. Abzeichen i. schwarz durch Res. Laz. Wernigerode

Major u. Ortskommandant

noch 26

Awards page from the Brasack *Wehrpass* showing the entry for the 1939 Clasp to the 1914 Iron Cross Second Class.

This elderly *Feldgendarmerie Leutnant* wears the 1939 Clasp to the 1914 Iron Cross Second Clasp in his buttonhole.

Iron Cross First Class.

SS-Hauptsturmführer Oskar Lösel, commander of *SS-Feldgendarmerie Kompanie* 17 in 17 *SS-Panzergrenadier* Division Götz von Berlichingen.

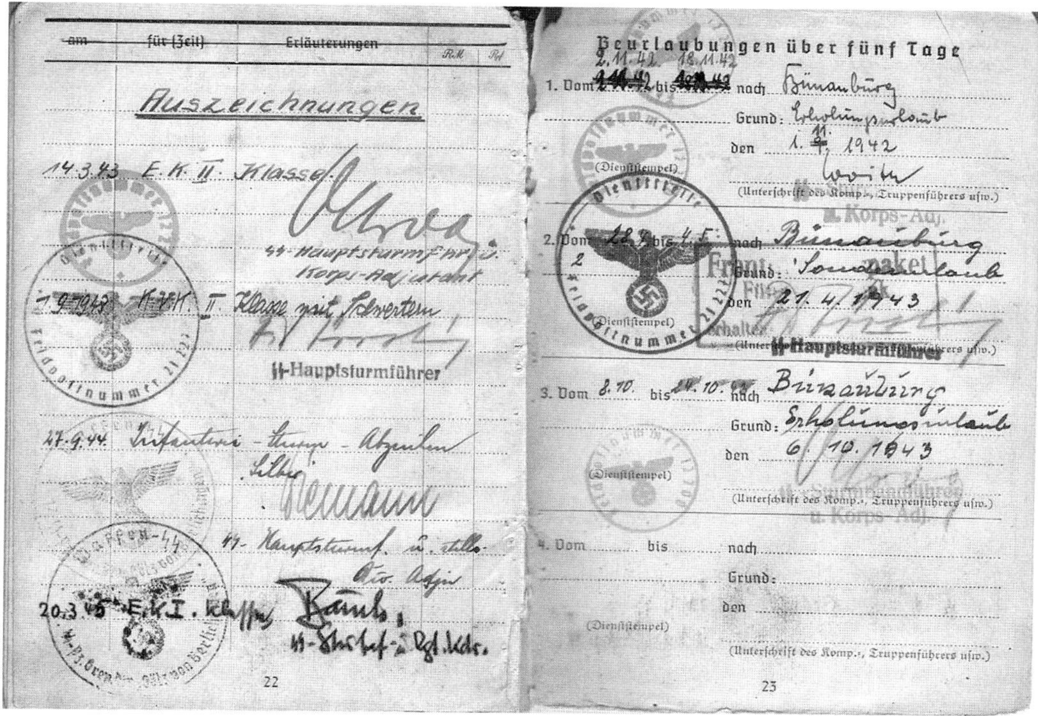

am	für (Zeit)	Erläuterungen	RM	Rpf

Auszeichnungen

14.3.43 E.K. II. Klasse

SS-Hauptsturmführer u. Korps-Adjutant

1.9.1943 K.V.K. II. Klasse mit Schwertern

SS-Hauptsturmführer

27.9.44 Infanterie-Sturm-Abzeichen Silber

SS-Hauptsturmf. u. stellv. Div. Adju.

20.3.45 E.K.I. Klasse

SS-Stubaf. u. Rgt. Kdr.

22

Beurlaubungen über fünf Tage

1. Vom 2.11.42 bis 18.11.42 nach Lüneburg
Grund: Erholungsurlaub
den 1.11.1942
(Dienststempel)
(Unterschrift des Komp.-, Truppenführers usw.)

2. Vom 22.4. bis 4.5. nach Lüneburg
Grund: Sonderurlaub
den 21.4.1943
(Dienststempel)
SS-Hauptsturmführer
(Unterschrift des Komp.-, Truppenführers usw.)

3. Vom 8.10. bis 24.10.43 nach Lüneburg
Grund: Erholungsurlaub
den 6.10.1943
(Dienststempel)
(Unterschrift des Komp.-, Truppenführers usw.)

4. Vom bis nach
Grund:
den
(Dienststempel)
(Unterschrift des Komp.-, Truppenführers usw.)

23

Entry from the Lösel *Soldbuch* showing the award of the Iron Cross First Class in March 1945.

The 1939 Clasp to the 1914 Iron Cross First Class.

Above left: The Knight's Cross of the Iron Cross.

Above right: Oberfeldwebel Heinz Heuer, reputed to have been decorated with the Knight's Cross in Berlin in the closing days of the war. The badge on his left sleeve is the *Kraftfahrbewährungsabzeichen.*

Hauser subsequently served for a brief spell of time with *13 SS-Gebirgs Division Handschar* before being appointed to command a *Kampfgruppe* which had been hurriedly assembled from soldiers returning from leave and those recovering from wounds. This *Kampfgruppe* was attached to *2 SS-Panzer Division Das Reich* for the defence of Vienna and absorbed into the *SS-Regiment Der Führer*. After seeing some ferocious combat during the fighting for the Florisdorfer Bridge before being rushed to the area around Dresden where it repelled attacks from Polish troops serving in the Red Army.

The regiment ended the war in Prague combatting the Czech uprising there before retreating westwards to surrender to US Forces. Just before the war ended, on 6 May 1945, Hauser was decorated with the Knight's Cross of the Iron Cross for his actions during these final battles of the war.

It was not uncommon during the Second World War for decorated German soldiers recovering from wounds who had rejoined their unit but were still restricted to 'light duties', to be temporarily attached to the divisional *Feldgendarmerie* element. Here they could carry out useful duties with the benefit of their status as decorated combat soldiers adding a certain extra degree of 'moral authority' when dealing with other soldiers.

A case in point is that of Gefreiter Helmut Valtiner from *Gebirgsjäger Regiment 143*. Awarded the Knight's Cross of the Iron Cross on 13 June 1941, whilst recovering from wounds he was attached to *Feldgendarmerie Trupp 91* giving a photographer the chance to capture the rare sight of a *Feldgendarm* wearing the Knight's Cross at his neck.

Johannes Hauser, seen here when serving with *Feldgendarmerie Trupp* 498 b (mot.), would win the Knight's Cross in the closing days of the war as an *SS-Sturmbannführer* with the *Der Führer* Regiment.

Unteroffizier Helmut Valtiner of *Gebirgsjäger Regiment* 143, serving with the *Feldgendarmerie* of his parent Division whilst recuperating from wounds after winning the Knight's Cross.

German Cross in Gold

The German Cross (the title refers to the swastika in the centre, this of course being a form of 'hooked cross') was instituted by Adolf Hitler on 28 September 1941 in an attempt to bridge the considerable gap which existed between the Iron Cross first class and the Knight's Cross of the Iron Cross.

The award was generally bestowed upon these who had carried out *several* notable military exploits none of which in themselves would attract the award of the Knight's Cross but for which the Iron Cross first class already held was insufficient recognition.

The award consisted of a large (63 mm diameter) sunburst radiant star in a matt silver colour over which was laid a thinner, slightly smaller, blackened inner radiant star. In the centre was a matt silver disc bearing a gilt metal laurel wreath around its border and with a black enamelled swastika (the 'German Cross') in its centre. This complex piece was of multi-part constriction held together with prongs and rivets and featured a strong vertical hinged pin fitting on the reverse. It was worn on the right breast of the tunic.

In view of the significant weight of the original award and the likelihood of the enamelling to the central swastika being damaged, a cloth embroidered version was also produced for wear in the field, though many preferred to wear the original metal award.

Only three recipients of the German Cross in Gold are known from the *Feldgendarmerie*, plus one from the *Bahnhofswache*. These are as follows:

Major Werner Weber—*Feldgendarmerie Abteilung 682.*

Leutnant d.R. Peter Scholz—*Feldgendarmerietrupp 1544 (544 V.G.D.).*

Oberleutnant d.R. Johannes Kandziora—*2./ Feldgendarmerie Abteilung 531.*

Obergefreiter Hans Schlotter—*Bahnhofswachabteilung 2.*

Kandziora was awarded the German Cross on 14 November 1944, his achievements probably being crowned by his actions during the final battles for the Cherkassy pocket on the eastern front in February 1944. Approximately 60,000 German troops including the elite *5 SS-Panzer Division 'Wiking'* were trapped in the pocket. When a relief attempt by *Generalfeldmarschall* von Manstein using the combined forces of XLVII and III *Panzerkorps* failed, the surviving troops in

German Cross in Gold.

the pocket were told they would have to break out on their own. By this point, only 45,000 survivors remained in the pocket of whom around 28,000 succeeded in breaking out though the area appropriately named 'Hell's Gate' near Shanderovka, a tiny gap in the pocket which had by then shrunk to a mere five kilometres in diameter. Nearly 15,000 were killed in the process.

Feldgendarmerie Abteilung 531 was at that point manning the final traffic post at Shanderovka as the final remnants of the desperate German forces pulled out, pursued by the Red Army. As was often the case, the *Feldgendarmerie* manning such posts were the last to leave, once the last retreating German units had passed through the positions they manned.

At Shanderovka, Kandziora became the last man, in the last unit to pull out of the Cherkassy pocket with nothing other than the full might of the Red Army behind him, fulfilling the tradition of 'first in—last out'.

Merit Awards

War Merit Cross

The War Merit Cross was instituted on 18 October 1939 and was intended to reward meritorious conduct which would not normally bring an award of the Iron Cross. It could be awarded with or without swords. Generally those deeds performed by serving soldiers were rewarded by the version with swords though the definition of what would attract the 'with' as opposed to 'without' swords version is not always as clear cut as one might suppose. However, all of the original *Soldbuch/Wehrpass* entries and award documents to *Feldgendarmerie* personnel the author has encountered have been for the 'with' swords version.

The War Merit Cross was awarded for distinguished service or gallantry whilst not necessarily under direct fire from the enemy.

The actions of the *Feldgendarmerie* in successfully directing huge troop movements, protecting supply lines, rounding up and guarding prisoners and many other essential tasks are exactly the type of actions that would qualify for the War Merit Cross and so it is no great surprise that finding an award of the War Merit Cross second class in the *Soldbuch* or *Wehrpass* of a *Feldgendarm* is fairly common, though the first class is relatively scarce.

The award initially consisted of a Maltese style cross in two classes typically measuring 49 mm × 49 mm with on the obverse a central disc bearing the swastika. Swords are crossed through the centre.

The second class is finished in a bronze colour and on the reverse, the central disc contains the date '1939'. It was worn from a ribbon with a black central stripe flanked by narrower stripe sin white and red, effectively reversing the order of colours in the Iron Cross ribbon.

The first class is finished in a matt silver colour with burnished highlights. The reverse is plain and flat with a vertical hinged pin fitting allowing it to be affixed to the left breast of the tunic.

A larger, solid silver Knight's Cross grade was later added to the series on 19 August 1940, but no awards of this higher grade were ever made to members of the *Feldgendarmerie*.

Wound Badge

A badge to recognise those who had been wounded in action was introduced by Kaiser Wilhelm II on 3 March 1918. Not surprisingly, the award was reinstituted in 1939 with the outbreak of the Second Word War, and retained the original design concept of a steel helmet superimposed over crossed swords and surrounded by a wreath of laurel. In the new version the style of helmet was changed to show the more modern M35 type helmet and a large swastika was emblazoned on the side of the helmet. As before, it was to be awarded in three grades:

Black for I-2 wounds

Silver for 3-4 wounds, or for one serious wound.

Gold for 5 or more wounds or for a single wound resulting in a permanent disability such as blindness or loss of a limb.

All grades were in pin back form and worn on the left breast of the tunic. Though *Feldgendarmerie* were not combat troops as such, guiding and escorting large troop movements as they did, they were often first into an area during an advance and last out during a retreat. They were also often in combat against enemy partisans so the opportunities for *Feldgendarmen* to suffer wounds in the performance of their duties were plentiful.

Driving Proficiency Badge—*Kraftfahrbewährungsabzeichen*

Authorised by Adolf Hitler on 23 October 1942 and made retrospective to December 1940, this badge recognised the massive contribution of the transport branch of the *Wehrmacht* and rewarded its drivers for proficiency and merit.

The stamped metal badge consisted of a circular wreath of laurel leaves with a steering wheel in the central field. It was pinned through a circular piece of cloth which was then sewn to the lower left sleeve of the recipients tunic.

Criteria for the award were as follows:

I. Having served in the following areas:

—Yugoslavia, Bulgaria, Romania, Greece.

—Areas north of the old Soviet border (i.e. prior to the Soviet annexation of the Baltic states such as Estonia, Lithuania etc.).

—Finland, Norway and north of the Arctic Circle in Lappland.

—North Africa.

In March 1944 additional qualifying areas were added including:

—Service in Sicily from 1 June 1943.

—Service in Sardinia and Corsica from 1 July 1943.

—Service in southern Italy from 1 August 1943.

—Service in Albania from 9 September 1943.

On 16 May 1944 service on the Eastern Front from February 1944 in the rear areas of Heeresgruppe Nord in Estonia, Latvia and Lithuania was added and finally in September 1944 all rear areas on all fronts were added.

II. Meritorious service in the above areas for the following periods:

Motorcyclists:	90 Days.
Drivers from armed vehicles:	120 Days.
Drivers of miscellaneous vehicles:	150 Days.
Drivers of supply vehicles:	165 Days.
Drivers serving with various commands:	185 Days.

It was awarded in three grades, as follows:

Bronze.

Silver.

Gold.

IM NAMEN DES FÜHRERS
UND OBERSTEN BEFEHLSHABERS
DER WEHRMACHT
VERLEIHE ICH
DEM

Oberfeldwebel Willi Haas
Feldgend.-Tr.296

DAS
KRIEGSVERDIENSTKREUZ
2. KLASSE
MIT SCHWERTERN

Div. Gef.-Stand, DEN 1. Dezember 1942.

(DIENSTSIEGEL)

Generalmajor und Div.-Kdr.
(DIENSTGRAD UND DIENSTSTELLUNG)

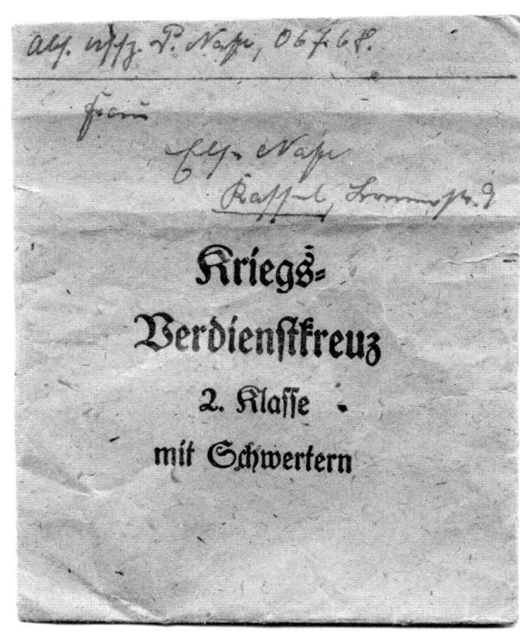

Kriegs-
Verdienstkreuz
2. Klasse
mit Schwertern

Above left: Award Document for the War Merit Cross Second Class to *Oberfeldwebel* Willi Haas of *Feldgendarmerie Trupp* 296.

Above right: An interesting issue packet for the War Merit Cross. The packet was sent home, and is addressed to the wife of the soldier, *Unteroffizier* P. Nase, whose Field Post number is quoted as 06768 (*Feldgendarmerie-Trupp* 116).

An officer and two NCOs of the *Feldgendarmerie* sporting their just awarded War Merit Crosses 2nd Class.

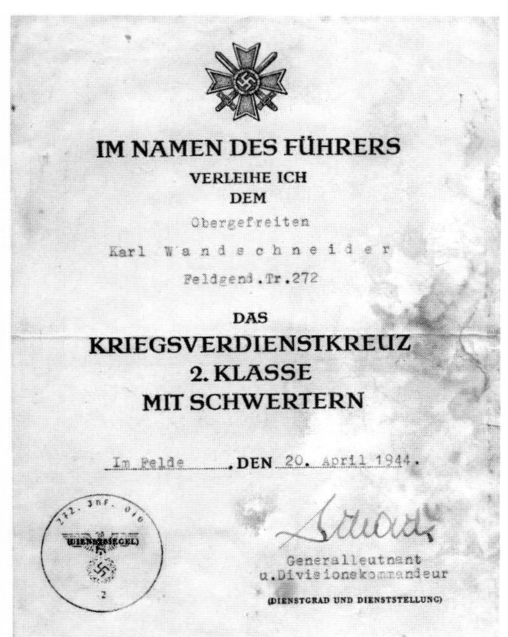

IM NAMEN DES FÜHRERS
VERLEIHE ICH
DEM
Obergefreiten
Karl W a n d s c h n e i d e r
Feldgend.Tr.272
DAS
KRIEGSVERDIENSTKREUZ
2. KLASSE
MIT SCHWERTERN

Im Felde, DEN 20. April 1944.

(DIENSTSIEGEL)

Generalleutnant
u.Divisionskommandeur
(DIENSTGRAD UND DIENSTSTELLUNG)

Award Document for the War Merit Cross Second Class to *Obergefreiter* Karl Wandschneider of *Feldgendarmerie Trupp* 272.

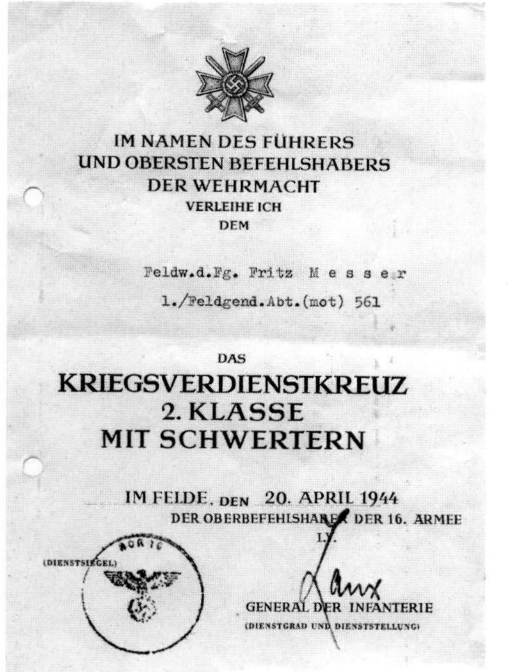

IM NAMEN DES FÜHRERS
UND OBERSTEN BEFEHLSHABERS
DER WEHRMACHT
VERLEIHE ICH
DEM
Feldw.d.Fg. Fritz M e s s e r
1./Feldgend.Abt.(mot) 561
DAS
KRIEGSVERDIENSTKREUZ
2. KLASSE
MIT SCHWERTERN

IM FELDE, DEN 20. APRIL 1944
DER OBERBEFEHLSHABER DER 16. ARMEE
I.V.

(DIENSTSIEGEL)

GENERAL DER INFANTERIE
(DIENSTGRAD UND DIENSTSTELLUNG)

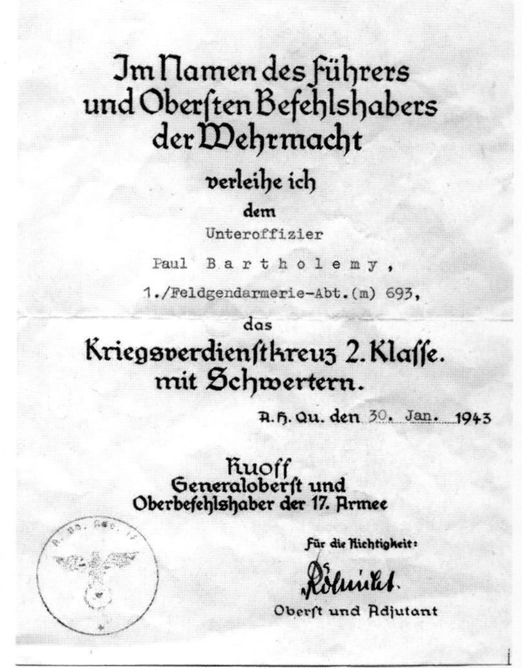

Im Namen des Führers
und Obersten Befehlshabers
der Wehrmacht
verleihe ich
dem
Unteroffizier
Paul B a r t h o l e m y ,
1./Feldgendarmerie-Abt.(m) 693,
das
Kriegsverdienstkreuz 2. Klasse.
mit Schwertern.
A.H.Qu. den 30. Jan. 1943

Ruoff
Generaloberst und
Oberbefehlshaber der 17. Armee

Für die Richtigkeit:

Oberst und Adjutant

Above left: Award Document for the War Merit Cross Second Class to *Feldwebel* Fritz Messer of *Feldgendarmerie Abteilung* 561.

Above right: Award Document for the War Merit Cross Second Class to *Unteroffizier* Paul Bartholomey of *Feldgendarmerie Abteilung* 693.

War Merit Cross Second Class.

Soldbuch of *Unteroffizier* Emil Berger from *Feldgendarmerie-Trupp* 280.

am	für (Zeit)	Erläuterungen	
		Auszeichnungen	

Beurlaubungen über fünf Tage

vom … nach … Grund: Heimaturlaub … den 31. Aug. 1940 … Dienststempel … (Unterschrift des Komp.-, Truppenführers usw.)

Oberzahlmeister

22 23

Awards page from the Berger *Soldbuch* showing the entry for the War Merit Cross Second Class (KVK II Kl. M. Schw).

War Merit Cross First Class.

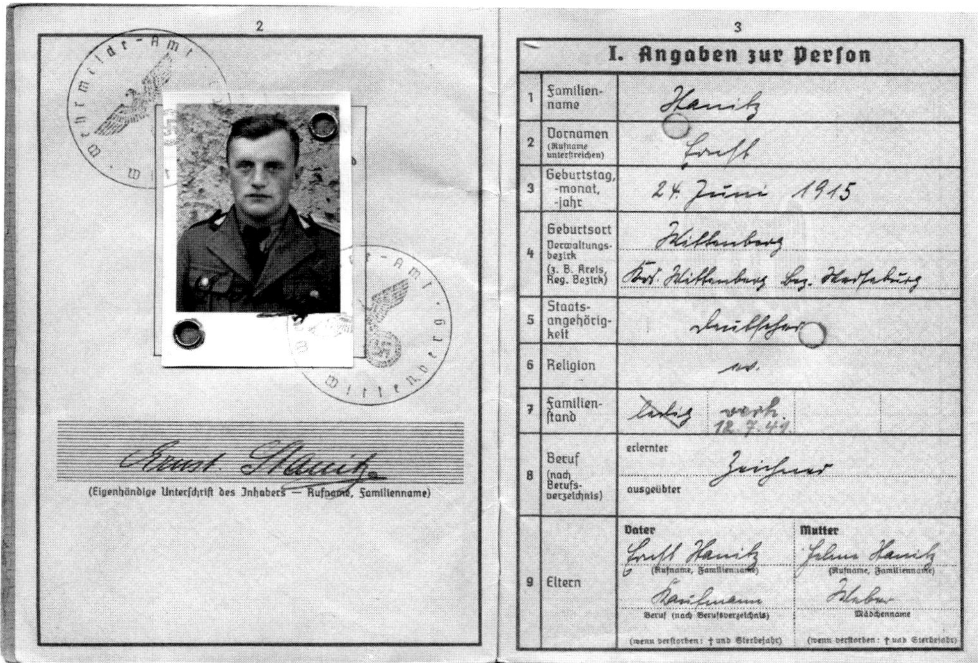

2

Ernst Stanitz

(Eigenhändige Unterschrift des Inhabers — Rufname, Familienname)

3

I. Angaben zur Person

1	Familienname	Stanitz
2	Vornamen (Rufname unterstreichen)	Ernst
3	Geburtstag, -monat, -jahr	24. Juni 1915
4	Geburtsort / Verwaltungsbezirk (z. B. Kreis, Reg. Bezirk)	Wittenberg / Krs. Wittenberg Bez. Merseburg
5	Staatsangehörigkeit	deutsches
6	Religion	ev.
7	Familienstand	ledig / verh. 12.7.41
8	Beruf (nach Berufsverzeichnis)	erlernter: Zeichner / ausgeübter:
9	Eltern	Vater: Ernst Stanitz (Rufname, Familienname) / Kaufmann (Beruf (nach Berufsverzeichnis)) (wenn verstorben: † und Sterbejahr) — Mutter: Selma Stanitz (Rufname, Familienname) / Huber (Mädchenname) (wenn verstorben: † und Sterbejahr)

Wehrpass for *Oberfeldwebel* Ernst Stanitz of *Feldgendarmerie Trupp* b (mot) 183.

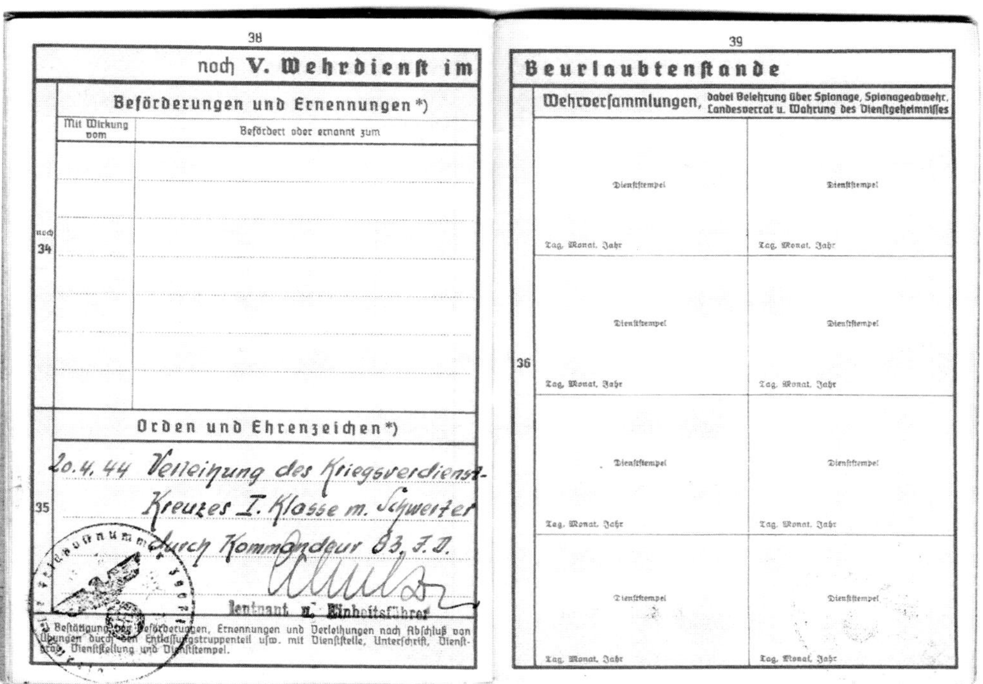

38

noch **V. Wehrdienst im**

Beförderungen und Ernennungen *)

Mit Wirkung vom	Befördert oder ernannt zum

noch 34

Orden und Ehrenzeichen *)

35

20.4.44 Verleihung des Kriegsverdienst-Kreuzes I. Klasse m. Schwertern durch Kommandeur 83. I.D.

Leutnant u. Einheitsführer

*) Bestätigung der Beförderungen, Ernennungen und Verleihungen nach Abschluß von Übungen durch den Entlassungstruppenteil usw. mit Dienststelle, Unterschrift, Dienstgrad, Dienststellung und Dienststempel.

39

Beurlaubtenstande

Wehrversammlungen, dabei Belehrung über Spionage, Spionageabwehr, Landesverrat u. Wahrung des Dienstgeheimnisses

36

Dienststempel / Tag, Monat, Jahr	Dienststempel / Tag, Monat, Jahr
Dienststempel / Tag, Monat, Jahr	Dienststempel / Tag, Monat, Jahr
Dienststempel / Tag, Monat, Jahr	Dienststempel / Tag, Monat, Jahr
Dienststempel / Tag, Monat, Jahr	Dienststempel / Tag, Monat, Jahr

Award entry in the Stanitz *Wehrpass* for the War Merit Cross First Class.

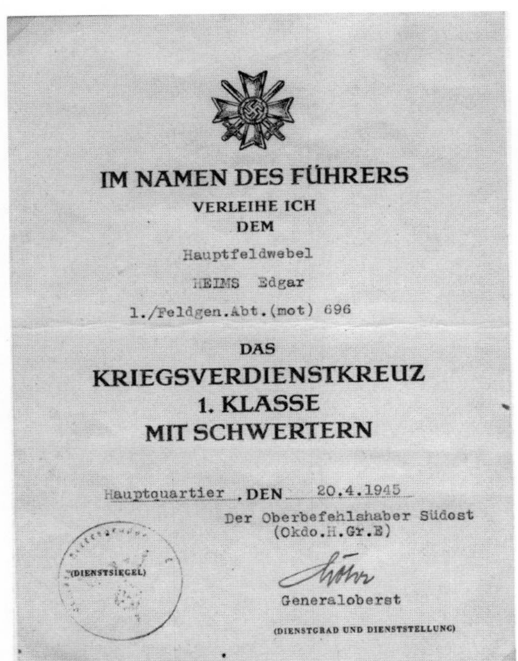

IM NAMEN DES FÜHRERS
VERLEIHE ICH
DEM
Hauptfeldwebel
HEIMS Edgar
1./Feldgen.Abt.(mot) 696
DAS
KRIEGSVERDIENSTKREUZ
1. KLASSE
MIT SCHWERTERN

Hauptquartier , DEN 20.4.1945
Der Oberbefehlshaber Südost
(Okdo.H.Gr.E)
(DIENSTSIEGEL)
Generaloberst
(DIENSTGRAD UND DIENSTSTELLUNG)

Above The Wound Badge, in Black, Silver and Gold grades.

Left: Award Document for the War Merit Cross First Class to a *Feldgendarmerie Hauptfeldwebel.* (*Walter Spiller*)

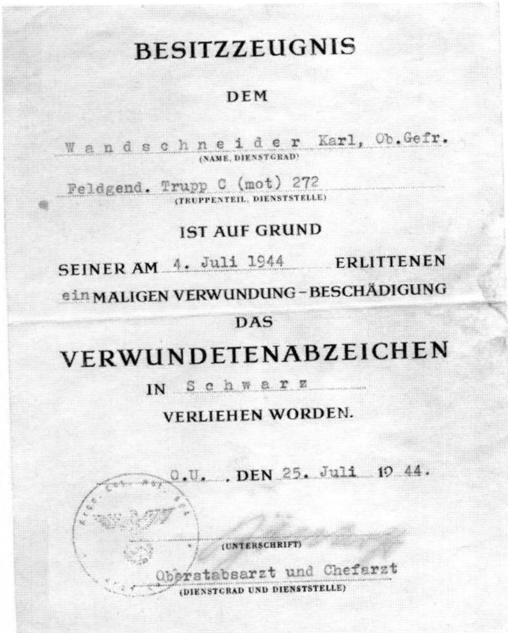

BESITZZEUGNIS
DEM
Wandschneider Karl, Ob.Gefr.
(NAME, DIENSTGRAD)
Feldgend. Trupp C (mot) 272
(TRUPPENTEIL, DIENSTSTELLE)
IST AUF GRUND
SEINER AM 4. Juli 1944 ERLITTENEN
einMALIGEN VERWUNDUNG – BESCHÄDIGUNG
DAS
VERWUNDETENABZEICHEN
IN Schwarz
VERLIEHEN WORDEN.

O.U., DEN 25. Juli 19 44.
(UNTERSCHRIFT)
Oberstabsarzt und Chefarzt
(DIENSTGRAD UND DIENSTSTELLE)

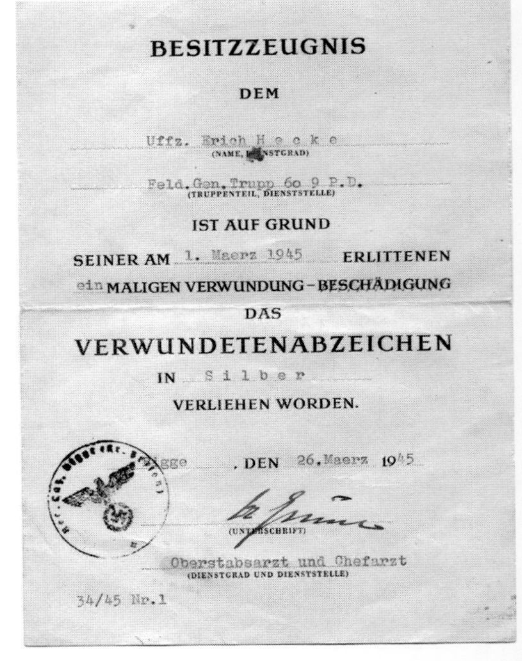

BESITZZEUGNIS
DEM
Uffz. Erich Hecke
(NAME, DIENSTGRAD)
Feld.Gen.Trupp 60 9 P.D.
(TRUPPENTEIL, DIENSTSTELLE)
IST AUF GRUND
SEINER AM 1. Maerz 1945 ERLITTENEN
einMALIGEN VERWUNDUNG – BESCHÄDIGUNG
DAS
VERWUNDETENABZEICHEN
IN Silber
VERLIEHEN WORDEN.

...gge , DEN 26.Maerz 1945
(UNTERSCHRIFT)
Oberstabsarzt und Chefarzt
(DIENSTGRAD UND DIENSTSTELLE)
34/45 Nr.1

Above left: Award Document for the Wound Badge in Black to *Obergefreiter* Karl Wandschneider of *Feldgendarmerie Trupp* c (mot.) 272.

Above right: Award Document for the Wound Badge in Silver to *Unteroffizier* Erich Hecke of *Feldgendarmerie Trupp* 60.

This *Feldgendarmerie* enlisted man wears the ribbon of the East Front Medal in his buttonhole, and the Wound Badge in Black on his breast pocket.

The centre badge on the pocket pleat of this *Oberfeldwebel* is the Wound Badge in Black.

The bronze grade would be awarded on fulfilling the above criteria. To earn the next grade, the fulfilment of the criteria had to be repeated. This for example a motorcyclist would receive the bronze after 90, the silver after 180—and the gold after 270 days. The award could be revoked if the driver was found to have neglected his vehicle, broken the speed limit etc.

Combat Badges

Infantry Assault Badge

Instituted on 20 December 1939 by the C-in-C Army, *Generaloberst* von Brauchitsch, the Infantry Assault Badge was intended to recognise those who had participated in at least three infantry type actions. These included three or more infantry assaults or counter attacks as well as armed reconnaissance actions or hand to hand combat. In all cases only normal infantry type small arms were to have been used.

The badge, some 6.3 cm in height and 4.9 cm wide, consisted of a vertical oval wreath of oakleaves topped by the eagle and swastika. Lying across the wreath was a representation of the standard infantry weapon, the Kar98k *Karabiner*, with fixed bayonet. It featured a matt silvered finish and was to be worn pinned on the left breast of the tunic.

Although not a particularly common find in the personal papers of *Feldgendarmen*, the Infantry Assault Badge was most certainly awarded to *Feldgendarmerie* from time to time as the entry in the *Soldbuch* of Oskar Lösel shown in this volume proves.

General Assault Badge

Introduced on 1 January 1940 by *Generaloberst* von Brauchitsch, the General Assault Badge was intended to recognise those who had taken part in three separate assault actions but who were not eligible for the Infantry Assault Badge. It consisted of an oval wreath of oakleaves encompassing a *Wehrmacht* eagle over a crossed bayonet and stick grenade.

It is uncommon to find an award of the General Assault badge to *Feldgendarmerie* troops but as the actual example of an award document illustrated here proves, it certainly happened.

Anti-Partisan Badge

Instituted on 30 January 1944 by *Reichsführer-SS* Heinrich Himmler, this badge was intended to recognise actions by German military personnel from all branches of the *Wehrmacht* and the police against enemy partisans (whom Himmler had insisted be defined as 'Bandits').

The badge is made from zinc and is oval in form. It shows a sword with a 'sunwheel' style swastika as its crosspiece plunged into a Hydra (the mythical multi-headed beast, representing the Partisans) all within a wreath of oakleaves with a deathshead at its base.

The badge was awarded in three grades which, for ground personnel represented as follows:

Bronze 20 days cumulative combat.

Silver 50 days cumulative combat.

Gold 100 days cumulative combat.

No awards of the Anti-Partisan Badge in gold to *Feldgendarmerie* personnel are known and only a small number in silver though several bronze grade awards were made.

The *Kraftfahrbewährungsabzeichen*, shown here in Bronze.

Feldgendarmerie NCOs from the elite *Grossdeutschland* Division. The NCO at right wears the *Kraftfahrbewährungsabzeichen* on his left sleeve. (*Sebastian Golawski*)

The Infantry Assault Badge.

Note the Infantry Assault Badge worn by the 'Spiess' leaning into the vehicle in this shot.

The General Assault Badge.

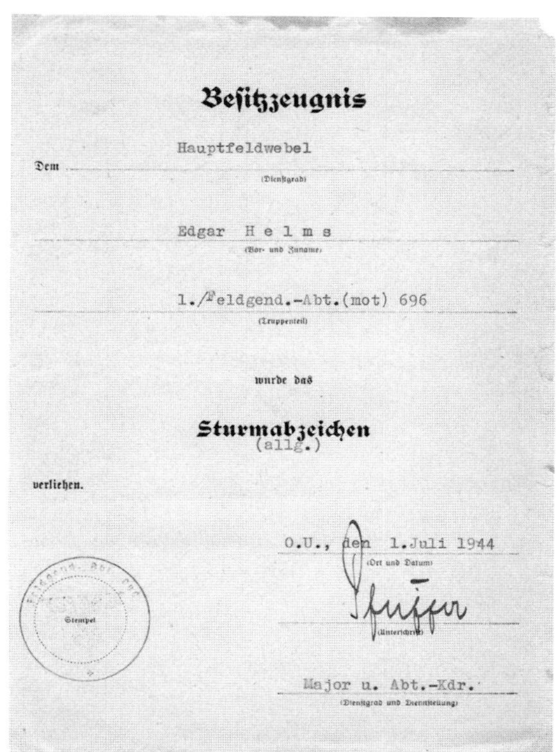

Besitzzeugnis

Dem Hauptfeldwebel
(Dienstgrad)

Edgar H e l m s
(Vor- und Zuname)

1./Feldgend.-Abt.(mot) 696
(Truppenteil)

wurde das

Sturmabzeichen
(allg.)

verliehen.

O.U., den 1.Juli 1944
(Ort und Datum)

(Unterschrift)

Stempel

Major u. Abt.-Kdr.
(Dienstgrad und Dienststellung)

Award Document for the General Assault Badge to a *Feldgendarmerie Hauptfeldwebel*. (*Walter Spiller*)

The Anti-Partisan War Badge.

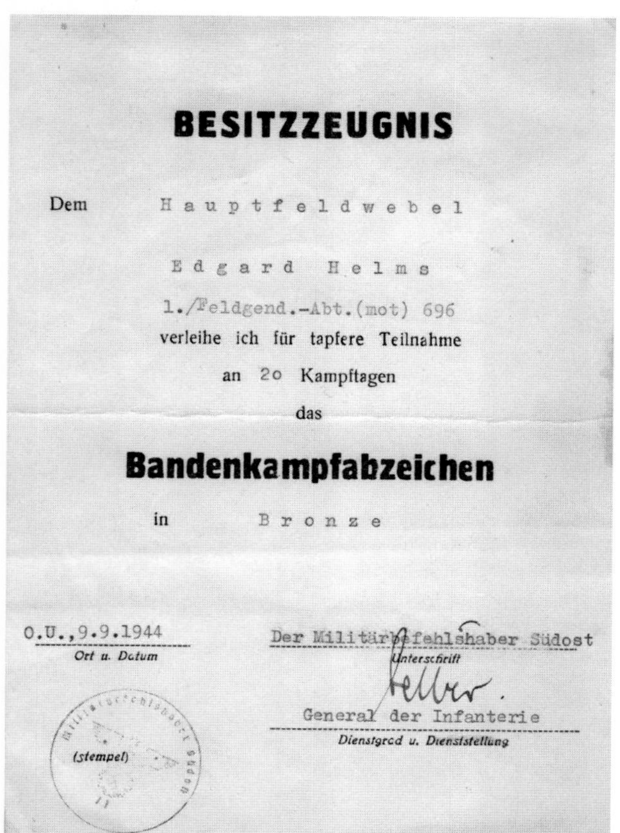

BESITZZEUGNIS

Dem Hauptfeldwebel

Edgard Helms

1./Feldgend.-Abt.(mot) 696

verleihe ich für tapfere Teilnahme

an 20 Kampftagen

das

Bandenkampfabzeichen

in Bronze

O.U.,9.9.1944
Ort u. Datum

Der Militärbefehlshaber Südost
Unterschrift

General der Infanterie
Dienstgrad u. Dienststellung

(Stempel)

An extremely rare example of the award document for the Ant-Partisan Badge, here in bronze, to a *Hauptfeldwebel* of *Feldgendarmerie*. (*Photo courtesy Walter Spiller*)

The *Soldbuch* photo of *Oberfeldwebel* Paul Klementz of *Feldgendarmerie Abteilung* 696.

Auszeichnungen

Datum	Art der Auszeichnung	Verleihungsurkunde	Bestätigung des Komp.- usw. Führers Dienstgrad

22

Awards page from the Klementz *Soldbuch*. The final entry is for the Anti-Partisan Badge in bronze on 20 April 1945.

Luftwaffe Ground Combat Badge

Instituted on 31 March 1942 by Hermann Göring the *Luftwaffe* Ground Combat Badge was intended to reward those *Luftwaffe personnel who had:*

a) taken part in three separate engagements with the enemy on different days.
b) been wounded in action during such an engagement.
c) been awarded a decoration for involvement in an engagement.
d) been killed in action in which case a posthumous award was to be made.

The badge, which measured 56 mm in height and 43 mm in width, consisted of a vertical oval wreath of oakleaves topped by a *Luftwaffe* style eagle and swastika. Within the wreath is shown a darkened thundercloud from which a lightning bolt emerges to strike the ground below.

Feldgendarmerie serving in *Luftwaffe* field units were amongst those who could qualify for this award, as seen in the accompanying example. Prior to the introduction of this badge, *Luftwaffe Feldgendarmen* would have been eligible for the Infantry Assault Badge.

Army Feldgendarmerie Units.

The following list of principal *Feldgendarmerie* units is concentrated on named *Feldgendarmerie* units but it should be noted that as well as specific named units, there were other *Feldgendarmerie* elements within various headquarters which were simply named for that headquarter location, i.e. *Feldgendarmerie der Kreiskommandantur 747, Feldgendarmerie Trupp bei Militär Kommandantur 1016*, etc. and these are not included though some of these were later renamed as specific *Feldgendarmerie* units and are included. The list has been compiled from a number of sources including original documents, Field Post records and personal I.D. papers. There will undoubtedly be some others and the author would be pleased to hear from any readers who can add further information.

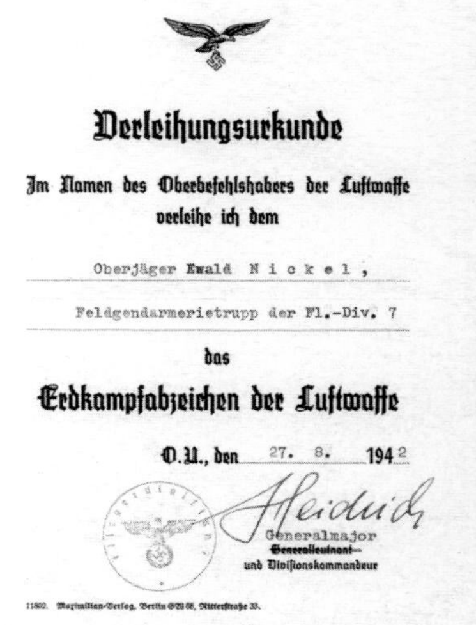

Verleihungsurkunde

Im Namen des Oberbefehlshabers der Luftwaffe
verleihe ich dem

Oberjäger Ewald Nickel,

Feldgendarmerietrupp der Fl.-Div. 7

das

Erdkampfabzeichen der Luftwaffe

O.U., den 27. 8. 1942

Heidrich
Generalmajor
~~Generalleutnant~~
und Divisionskommandeur

11800. Maximilian-Verlag, Berlin SW 68, Ritterstraße 33.

Above left: The Luftwaffe Ground Assault Badge.

Above right: Award Document for the Ground Assault Badge to a Luftwaffe *Feldgendarmerie* Oberjäger.

Unit Christmas Card from the *Feldgendarmerie Trupp* of the *Grossdeutschland* Division in 1944. (*Sebastian Golawski*)

A *Feldgendarmerie* officer poses for a group shot with the NCOs and men of his *Trupp*.

Unit	Parent / Attached Unit where known
Feldgend.-Trupp (mot.) 1	1 Infanterie Div.
Feldgend.-Trupp 2	12 Panzer Div./ 2 Infanterie Div.
Feldgend.-Trupp 3	3 Infanterie Div.
Feldgend.-Trupp a (mot.) 4	4 Infanterie Div. / 14 Panzer Div.
Feldgend.-Trupp 5	5 Jäger Div.
Feldgend.-Trupp a (mot.)	66 Infanterie Div. / Feldkommandantur 520/ 6 Volksgrenadier Div.
Feldgend.-Trupp (mot.) 7	7 Infanterie Div./ Feldkommandantur 682
Feldgend.-Trupp 8	8 Infanterie Div.
Feldgend.-Trupp a (mot.) 9	9 Infanterie Div. / 9 Volksgrenadier Div.
Feldgend.-Trupp (mot.) 10	10 Infanterie Div. / 10 Panzer Div./ 537 Infanterie Div.
Feldgend.-Trupp 11	11 Infanterie Div.
Feldgend.-Trupp 12	12 Infanterie Div.
Feldgend.-Trupp b (mot.) 13	13 Infanterie Div./ 13 Panzer Div.
Feldgend.-Trupp a (mot.) 14	14 Infanterie Div.
Feldgend.-Trupp a (mot.) 15	15 Infanterie Div.
Feldgend.-Trupp 16	16 Infanterie Div./ 16 Panzer Div.
Feldgend.-Trupp (mot.) 17	17 Infanterie Div.
Feldgend.-Trupp (mot.) 18	18 Infanterie Div./ 18 Panzergrenadier Div.
Feldgend.-Trupp a (mot.) 19	19 Infanterie Div. / 19 Panzer Div.
Feldgend.-Trupp b (mot.) 20	20 Infanterie Div. / 20 Panzergrenadier Div.
Feldgend.-Trupp a (mot.) 21	21 Infanterie Div.
Feldgend.-Trupp (mot.) 22	22 Infanterie Div.
Feldgend.-Trupp a (mot.) 23	23 Infanterie Div.
Feldgend.-Trupp a (mot.) 24	24 Infanterie Div.
Feldgend.-Trupp a (mot.) 25	25 Infanterie Div. / 25 Panzergrenadier Div.
Feldgend.-Trupp 26	26 Infanterie Div. / 26 Volksgrenadier Div.
Feldgend.-Trupp a (mot.) 27	27 Infanterie Div. / 17 Panzer Div.
Feldgend.-Trupp 28	Höhererkommando z.b.V.
Feldgend.-Trupp b (mot.) 29	29 Infanterie Div. / 29 Panzergrenadier Div.
Feldgend.-Trupp 30	30 Infanterie Div.
Feldgend.-Trupp a (mot.) 31	31 Infanterie Div. / 31 Volksgrenadier Div./Höhererkommando 31
Feldgend.-Trupp 32	Höhererkommando z.b.V. XXXII Armeekorps
Feldgend.-Trupp 33	33 Infanterie Div./ 15 Panzer Div./15 Panzergrenadier Div.
Feldgend.-Trupp 34	34 Infanterie Div.
Feldgend.-Trupp a (mot.) 35	35 Infanterie Div.
Feldgend.-Trupp a (mot.) 36	36 Infanterie Div./ 36 Grenadier Div./Ortskommandantur 691
Feldgend.-Trupp d 39	Ortskommandantur 691
Feldgend.-Trupp 40	1 Kavallerie Div. / 24 Panzer Div.
Feldgend.-Trupp 44	44 Infanterie Div.
Feldgend.-Trupp 45	45 Infanterie Div./ 45 Grenadier Div.
Feldgend.-Trupp 46	46 Infanterie Div.
Feldgend.-Trupp d 53	Kreiskommandantur 703

Feldgend.-Trupp 54	I Gebirgs Div./ I. Volksgrenadier Div.
Feldgend.-Trupp 55	I Kosaken Div.
Feldgend.-Trupp 57	I leichte Div./ 6 Panzer Div.
Feldgend.-Trupp 58	2 leichte Div./ 7 Panzer Div./ I Panzer Div.
Feldgend.-Trupp 59	3 leichte Div./ 8 Panzer Div.
Feldgend.-Trupp 60	9 Panzer Div.
Feldgend.-Trupp b (mot.) 61	II Panzer Div.
Feldgend.-Trupp c (tmot.) 63	3 Luftwaffen Feldkorps
Feldgend.-Trupp c (tmot.) 64	4 Luftwaffen Feldkorps
Feldgend.-Trupp b (mot.) 66	16 Infanterie Div./ 116 Panzer Div.
Feldgend.-Trupp 67	2 Gebirgs Div.
Feldgend.-Trupp 68	3 Gebirgs Div.
Feldgend.-Trupp 69	3 Kavallerie Brigade / Div.
Feldgend.-Trupp 70	4 Kavallerie Brigade / Div.
Feldgend.-Trupp z.b.V. 71	LXXI Armeekorps/ 230 Infanterie Div.
Feldgend.-Trupp 78	78 Grenadier Div.
Feldgend.-Trupp 81	I Panzer Div.
Feldgend.-Trupp 82	2 Panzer Div.
Feldgend.-Trupp b (mot.) 83	3 Panzer Div.
Feldgend.-Trupp b (mot.) 84	4 Panzer Div.
Feldgend.-Trupp b 85	5 Panzer Div.
Feldgend.-Trupp c (tmot.) 87	25 Panzer Div.
Feldgend.-Trupp b (mot.) 88	18 Panzer Div./Generalkommando XXXV Armeekorps z.b.V./ 18 Artillerie Div.
Feldgend.-Trupp b (mot.) 89	18 Panzer Div./Generalkommando XXXV Armeekorps z.b.V.
Feldgend.-Trupp 90	10 Panzer Div.
Feldgend.-Trupp 91	6 Gebirgs Div.
Feldgend.-Trupp 92	20 Panzer Div.
Feldgend.-Trupp 93	26 Panzer Div.
Feldgend.-Trupp 94	4 Gebirgs Div.
Feldgend.-Trupp 95	5 Gebirgs Div.
Feldgend.-Trupp 97	97 leichte Division/ 97 Jäger Div.
Feldgend.-Trupp 99	7 Gebirgs Div./ 99 Jäger Div.
Feldgend.-Trupp 100	100 leichte Infanterie Div./ 100 Jäger Div.
Feldgend.-Trupp 101	101 leichte Div./ 101 Jäger Div./ (ung.) Div. Kossuth
Feldgend.-Trupp a (mot.) 102	102 Infanterie Div.
Feldgend.-Trupp a (mot.) 104	104 Jäger Div.
Feldgend.-Trupp a (mot.) 106	106 Infanterie Div.
Feldgend.-Trupp 110	110 Infanterie Div.
Feldgend.-Trupp a (mot.) 111	111 Infanterie Div.
Feldgend.-Trupp 112	112 Infanterie Div./ Korps-Abteilung B
Feldgend.-Trupp (mot.) 113	113 Infanterie Div
Feldgend.-Trupp (mot.) 114	114 Jäger Div.
Feldgend.-Trupp 116	?

Feldgend.-Trupp (mot.) 117	*117 Jäger Div.*
Feldgend.-Trupp (mot.) 118	*118 Jäger Div.*
Feldgend.-Trupp 119	*19 Grenadier Div.*
Feldgend.-Trupp 120	*Führer-Begleit-Div.*
Feldgend.-Trupp (mot.) 121	*121 Infanterie Div.*
Feldgend.-Trupp 122	*122 Infanterie Div.*
Feldgend.-Trupp 123	*123 Infanterie Div.*
Feldgend.-Trupp 125	*125 Infanterie Div.*
Feldgend.-Trupp 126	*126 Infanterie Div.*
Feldgend.-Trupp 127	*27 Panzer Div.*
Feldgend.-Trupp 128	*23 Panzer Div.*
Feldgend.-Trupp 129	*129 Infanterie Div.*
Feldgend.-Trupp 131	*131 Infanterie Div.*
Feldgend.-Trupp 132	*132 Infanterie Div.*
Feldgend.-Trupp a (mot.) 133	*Kommandant Festung Kreta*
Feldgend.-Trupp (mot.) 134	*134 Infanterie Div.*
Feldgend.-Trupp (mot.) 137	*137 Infanterie Div.*
Feldgend.-Trupp 138	*38 Infanterie Div.*
Feldgend.-Trupp 139	*39 Infanterie Div.*
Feldgend.-Trupp 140	*79 Infanterie Div.*
Feldgend.-Trupp c (tmot.) 141	*41 Festung Div.*
Feldgend.-Trupp c (tmot.) 142	*42 Jäger Div.*
Feldgend.-Trupp 144	*Panzer Div. Holstein*
Feldgend.-Trupp 147	*47 Volksgrenadier Div.*
Feldgend.-Trupp 148	*148 Infanterie Div.*
Feldgend.-Trupp 149	*49 Infanterie Div.*
Feldgend.-Trupp 150	*50 Infanterie Div.*
Feldgend.-Trupp 152	*52 Infanterie Div./ 1 Ski-Jäger Div.*
Feldgend.-Trupp 155	*Heeresgruppe C*
Feldgend.-Trupp a (mot.) 156	*56 Infanterie Div.*
Feldgend.-Trupp (mot.) 157	*57 Infanterie Div.*
Feldgend.-Trupp a (mot.) 158	*58 Infanterie Div./ 158 Reserve Div.*
Feldgend.-Trupp 159	*59 Infanterie Div.*
Feldgend.-Trupp a (mot.) 160	*60 Infanterie Div.*
Feldgend.-Trupp (mot.) 161	*61 Infanterie Div./ 311 Infanterie Div.*
Feldgend.-Trupp (mot.) 162	*62 Infanterie Div.- Volksgrenadier Div.*
Feldgend.-Trupp 164	*64 Infanterie Div.*
Feldgend.-Trupp a (mot.) 165	*65 Infanterie Div.*
Feldgend.-Trupp 167	*167 Volksgrenadier Div.*
Feldgend.-Trupp a (mot.) 168	*68 Infanterie Div.*
Feldgend.-Trupp (mot.) 169	*69 Infanterie Div.*
Feldgend.-Trupp 170	*70 Infanterie Div.*
Feldgend.-Trupp 171	*71 Infanterie Div.*
Feldgend.-Trupp a (mot.) 172	*72 Infanterie Div.*

Feldgend.-Trupp (mot.) 173	*73 Infanterie Div.*
Feldgend.-Trupp 175	*75 Infanterie Div.*
Feldgend.-Trupp a (mot.) 176	*76 Infanterie Div.*
Feldgend.-Trupp 177	*77 Infanterie Div.*
Feldgend.-Trupp (mot.) 178	*78 Infanterie Div./ 78 Sturm Div.*
Feldgend.-Trupp (mot.) 179	*79 Infanterie Div.*
Feldgend.-Trupp 181	*81 Infanterie Div.*
Feldgend.-Trupp a (mot.) 182	*82 Infanterie Div./Oberfeldkommandantur 672*
Feldgend.-Trupp a (mot.) 183	*83 Infanterie Div./ Feldkommandantur 538/ Oberfeldkommandantur 520*
Feldgend.-Trupp c (tmot.) 184	*84 Infanterie Div.*
Feldgend.-Trupp c (tmot.) 185	*85 Infanterie Div.*
Feldgend.-Trupp (mot.) 186	*86 Infanterie Div.*
Feldgend.-Trupp a (mot.) 187	*87 Infanterie Div.*
Feldgend.-Trupp a 188	*88 Infanterie Div.*
Feldgend.-Trupp c (tmot.) 189	*89 Infanterie Div./ 189 Reserve Div.*
Feldgend.-Trupp 190	*90 Panzergrenadier Div.*
Feldgend.-Trupp c (tmot.) 191	*91 Infanterie Div.*
Feldgend.-Trupp 192	*92 Infanterie Div.*
Feldgend.-Trupp (mot.) 193	*93 Infanterie Div./Oberfeldkommandantur 672*
Feldgend.-Trupp 194	*Divisionstrupp*
Feldgend.-Trupp (mot.) 195	*95 Infanterie Div.*
Feldgend.-Trupp (mot.) 196	*96 Infanterie Div.*
Feldgend.-Trupp (mot.) 198	*98 Infanterie Div.*
Feldgend.-Trupp (mot.) 199	*199 Infanterie Div.*
Feldgend.-Trupp (mot.) 200	*21 Panzer Div.*
Feldgend.-Trupp c (mot.) 203	*203 Infanterie Div.*
Feldgend.-Trupp 205	*205 Infanterie Div./ Feldkommandantur 680*
Feldgend.-Trupp 206	*206 Infanterie Div.*
Feldgend.-Trupp 207	*207 Infanterie Div.*
Feldgend.-Trupp 208	*208 Infanterie Div./ Militärverwaltung Frankreich, Bezirk C / Feldkommandantur 669*
Feldgend.-Trupp 209	*209 Infanterie Div.*
Feldgend.-Trupp 210	*Feldkommandantur 529/Militärverwaltung Frankreich, Bezirk B*
Feldgend.-Trupp 211	*211 Infanterie Div./Militärverwaltung Frankreich, Bezirk B / Feldkommandantur 529*
Feldgend.-Trupp a (mot.) 212	*212 Infanterie Div./ 212 Volksgrenadier Div.*
Feldgend.-Trupp (mot.) 213	*213 Infanterie Div.*
Feldgend.-Trupp (mot.) 214	*214 Infanterie Div.*
Feldgend.-Trupp a (mot.) 215	*215 Infanterie Div./ Militärverwaltung Frankreich, Bezirk C / Feldkommandantur 599*
Feldgend.-Trupp (mot.) 216	*216 Infanterie Div./ Feldkommandantur 588*
Feldgend.-Trupp 217	*217 Infanterie Div.*
Feldgend.-Trupp a (mot.) 218	*218 Infanterie Div.*

Feldgend.-Trupp a (mot.) 219	Korps-Abteilung C / 183 Infanterie Div.
Feldgend.-Trupp c (tmot.) 220	164 Infanterie Div./164 leichte Afrika Div.
Feldgend.-Trupp a (mot.) 221	221 Infanterie Div.
Feldgend.-Trupp c (mot.) 222	181 Infanterie Div.
Feldgend.-Trupp a (mot.) 223	223 Infanterie Div./ Militärverwaltung Frankreich, Bezirk A
Feldgend.-Trupp a (mot.) 225	225 Infanterie Div./ Militärverwaltung Frankreich, Bezirk C/ Feldkommandantur 531
Feldgend.-Trupp 226	226 Infanterie Div.
Feldgend.-Trupp (mot.) 227	227 Infanterie Div.
Feldgend.-Trupp 228	228 Infanterie Div.
Feldgend.-Trupp (tmot.) 229	197 Infanterie Div.
Feldgend.-Trupp (tmot.) 230	169 Infanterie Div./ Generalkommando LXXI Armeekorps
Feldgend.-Trupp a (mot.) 231	231 Infanterie Div.
Feldgend.-Trupp 232	232 Infanterie Div.
Feldgend.-Trupp 233	196 Infanterie Div.
Feldgend.-Trupp c (mot.) 234	163 Infanterie Div.
Feldgend.-Trupp 235	198 Infanterie Div.
Feldgend.-Trupp a (mot.) 236	86 Infanterie Div./ 162 Infanterie Div./XXVII Armeekorps
Feldgend.-Trupp 237	237 Infanterie Div.
Feldgend.-Trupp c (mot.) 238	167 Infanterie Div.
Feldgend.-Trupp 239	239 Infanterie Div.
Feldgend.-Trupp 240	170 Infanterie Div.
Feldgend.-Trupp 241	161 Infanterie Div.
Feldgend.-Trupp c 242	242 Infanterie Div.
Feldgend.-Trupp c 243	243 Infanterie Div.
Feldgend.-Trupp c 244	244 Infanterie Div.
Feldgend.-Trupp d 245	245 Infanterie Div./ Feldkommandantur 245
Feldgend.-Trupp a (mot.) 246	246 Infanterie Div./246 Volksgrenadier Div. /Feldkommandantur 528/ Feldkommandantur 588
Feldgend.-Trupp a (mot.) 248	168 Infanterie Div.
Feldgend.-Trupp a (mot.) 250	250 (span.) Infanterie Div.
Feldgend.-Trupp a (mot.) 251	251 Infanterie Div. /Feldkommandantur 752 / Korps-Abteilung E
Feldgend.-Trupp (mot.) 252	252 Infanterie Div.
Feldgend.-Trupp (mot.) 253	253 Infanterie Div.
Feldgend.-Trupp (mot.) 254	254 Infanterie Div.
Feldgend.-Trupp a (mot.) 255	255 Infanterie Div.
Feldgend.-Trupp a (mot.) 256	256 Infanterie Div./ 256 Volksgrenadier Div./ Korps-Abteilung H
Feldgend.-Trupp a (mot.) 257	257 Infanterie Div./ 257 Volksgrenadier Div. /Volksgrenadier Div. Grossgörschen
Feldgend.-Trupp a (mot.) 258	258 Infanterie Div.
Feldgend.-Trupp 260	260 Infanterie Div.
Feldgend.-Trupp 262	262 Infanterie Div.
Feldgend.-Trupp a (mot.) 263	263 Infanterie Div.
Feldgend.-Trupp c (tmot.) 264	264 Infanterie Div./ Oberbefehlshaber West

Feldgend.-Trupp c (tmot.) 265	265 Infanterie Div.
Feldgend.-Trupp c (tmot.) 266	266 Infanterie Div.
Feldgend.-Trupp 267	267 Infanterie Div.
Feldgend.-Trupp a (mot.) 268	268 Infanterie Div.
Feldgend.-Trupp 269	269 Infanterie Div.
Feldgend.-Trupp c (mot.) 271	113 Infanterie Div,/ 271 Infanterie Div. /576 Volksgrenadier Div.
Feldgend.-Trupp 272	272 Infanterie Div./ 575 Volksgrenadier Div.
Feldgend.-Trupp c (tmot.) 274	274 Infanterie Div.
Feldgend.-Trupp 275	275 Infanterie Div.
Feldgend.-Trupp 276	276 Infanterie Div./ 276 Volksgrenadier Div.
Feldgend.-Trupp 277	277 Infanterie Div./ 574 Volksgrenadier Div.
Feldgend.-Trupp 278	278 Infanterie Div.
Feldgend.-Trupp c (mot.) 280	280 Infanterie Div.
Feldgend.-Trupp c (tmot.) 281	281 Infanterie Div.
Feldgend.-Trupp 282	Generalkommando
Feldgend.-Trupp 286	286 Infanterie Div.
Feldgend.-Trupp 290	290 Infanterie Div.
Feldgend.-Trupp 291	291 Infanterie Div.
Feldgend.-Trupp (tmot.) 292	292 Infanterie Div.
Feldgend.-Trupp 293	293 Infanterie Div.
Feldgend.-Trupp 294	294 Infanterie Div.
Feldgend.-Trupp 295	295 Infanterie Div.
Feldgend.-Trupp 296	296 Infanterie Div.
Feldgend.-Trupp 297	297 Infanterie Div.
Feldgend.-Trupp 298	298 Infanterie Div.
Feldgend.-Trupp 299	299 Infanterie Div.
Feldgend.-Trupp 300	SS-Polizei Div.
Feldgend.-Trupp (tmot.) 302	302 Infanterie Div.
Feldgend.-Trupp 303	303 Infanterie Div.
Feldgend.-Trupp c (mot.) 304	304 Infanterie Div.
Feldgend.-Trupp 305	305 Infanterie Div.
Feldgend.-Trupp 306 c (mot.)	306 Infanterie Div.
Feldgend.-Trupp 307	XXV Armeekorps / 555 Infanterie Div.
Feldgend.-Trupp c (mot.) 308	XXIII Armeekorps
Feldgend.-Trupp a (mot.) 309	5 leichte Div./ Panzer Ersatz Abt. Hamm
Feldgend.-Trupp 310	6 Gebirgs-Div
Feldgend.-Trupp (mot.) 311	XXIV Armeekorps
Feldgend.-Trupp 312	50 Infanterie Div.
Feldgend.-Trupp (mot.) 313	Grenz Abschnitt Kommando 13/Gruppe Schenckendorf/ Höhererkommando z.b.V. XXXV Armeekorps
Feldgend.-Trupp (mot.) 314	Grenz Abschnitt Kommando 14/Höhererkommando 36/Höhererkommando 45
Feldgend.-Trupp a (mot.) 315	72 Infanterie Div.
Feldgend.-Trupp 316	526 Infanterie Div.

Feldgend.-Trupp (mot.) 317	*Grenzkommandantur St. Wendel/Höhererkommando 36/ Korpskommando 12*
Feldgend.-Trupp 319	*319 Infanterie Div.*
Feldgend.-Trupp c (mot.) 320	*320 Infanterie Div./320 Volksgrenadier Div.*
Feldgend.-Trupp c (mot.) 321	*321 Infanterie Div.*
Feldgend.-Trupp 323	*323 Infanterie Div.*
Feldgend.-Trupp 326	*326 Infanterie Div./ 326 Volksgrenadier Div.*
Feldgend.-Trupp c (tmot.) 327	*327 Infanterie Div.*
Feldgend.-Trupp 328	*328 Infanterie Div.*
Feldgend.-Trupp a (mot.) 329	*329 Infanterie Div.*
Feldgend.-Trupp (mot.) 330	*Grenz Abschnitt Kommando 330 /330 Infanterie Div./ Höhererkommando z.b.V. XXXVII Armeekorps*
Feldgend.-Trupp c (tmot.) 331	*331 Infanterie Div.*
Feldgend.-Trupp c (tmot.) 332	*332 Infanterie Div.*
Feldgend.-Trupp a (mot.) 333	*333 Infanterie Div.*
Feldgend.-Trupp 334	*334 Infanterie Div.*
Feldgend.-Trupp c (mot.) 335	*335 Infanterie Div.*
Feldgend.-Trupp 336	*336 Infanterie Div.*
Feldgend.-Trupp c (mot.) 337	*337 Infanterie Div./ 337 Volksgrenadier Div.*
Feldgend.-Trupp c (mot.) 338	*338 Infanterie Div.*
Feldgend.-Trupp 339	*339 Infanterie Div.*
Feldgend.-Trupp 340	*340 Infanterie Div./ 340 Volksgrenadier Div.*
Feldgend.-Trupp (mot.) 341	*311 Infanterie Div.*
Feldgend.-Trupp c (tmot.) 342	*342 Infanterie Div.*
Feldgend.-Trupp c (tmot.) 343	*343 Infanterie Div.*
Feldgend.-Trupp 344	*344 Infanterie Div.*
Feldgend.-Trupp a (mot.) 345	*29 Infanterie Div./ 34 Infanterie Div.*
Feldgend.-Trupp c (tmot.) 346	*346 Infanterie Div.*
Feldgend.-Trupp 347	*347 Infanterie Div.*
Feldgend.-Trupp 348	*348 Infanterie Div.*
Feldgend.-Trupp 349	*349 Infanterie Div./ 349 Volksgrenadier Div.*
Feldgend.-Trupp 352	*352 Infanterie Div./ 352 Volksgrenadier Div.*
Feldgend.-Trupp c (tmot.) 353	*353 Infanterie Div.*
Feldgend.-Trupp c (tmot.) 355	*355 Infanterie Div./ 64 Reserve Korps*
Feldgend.-Trupp c (tmot.) 356	*356 Infanterie Div./ 189 Reserve Div.*
Feldgend.-Trupp 357	*357 Infanterie Div./ 67 Reserve Korps*
Feldgend.-Trupp 359	*359 Infanterie Div.*
Feldgend.-Trupp 360	*XXXXII Armeekorps/ 444 Sicherungs Div.*
Feldgend.-Trupp 361	*361 Infanterie Div./ 361 Volksgrenadier Div.*
Feldgend.-Trupp 362	*362 Infanterie Div.*
Feldgend.-Trupp 363	*363 Infanterie Div.*
Feldgend.-Trupp 365	*365 Infanterie Div.*
Feldgend.-Trupp 367	*367 Infanterie Div.*
Feldgend.-Trupp 369(kroat.)	*369 (kroat.) Infanterie Div.*

Feldgend.-Trupp a (mot.) 370	*370 Infanterie Div.*
Feldgend.-Trupp a (mot.) 371	*371 Infanterie Div.*
Feldgend.-Trupp 372	*?*
Feldgend.-Trupp 373 (kroat.)	*373 (kroat.) Infanterie Div.*
Feldgend.-Trupp 376A	*376 Infanterie Div.*
Feldgend.-Trupp a (mot.) 377	*377 Infanterie Div.*
Feldgend.-Trupp a (mot.) 383	*383 Infanterie Div.*
Feldgend.-Trupp a (mot.) 384	*384 Infanterie Div.*
Feldgend.-Trupp a (mot.) 385	*385 Infanterie Div.*
Feldgend.-Trupp a (mot.) 386	*386 Infanterie Div./ 3 Infanterie Div.*
Feldgend.-Trupp a (mot.) 387	*387 Infanterie Div.*
Feldgend.-Trupp a (mot.) 389	*389 Infanterie Div.*
Feldgend.-Trupp 392 (kroat.)	*392 (kroat.) Infanterie Div.*
Feldgend.-Trupp 393	*393 Infanterie Div.*
Feldgend.-Trupp 395	*395 Infanterie Div.*
Feldgend.-Trupp 399	*399 Infanterie Div.*
Feldgend.-Trupp 401	*I Armeekorps*
Feldgend.-Trupp 402	*II Armeekorps*
Feldgend.-Trupp a (mot.) 403	*III Armeekorps*
Feldgend.-Trupp 404	*IV Armeekorps/ Panzerkorps Feldherrnhalle/ 6 Armee*
Feldgend.-Trupp 405	*V Armeekorps*
Feldgend.-Trupp a (mot.) 406	*VI Armeekorps*
Feldgend.-Trupp 407	*VII Armeekorps/ Generalkommando VII Panzerkorps*
Feldgend.-Trupp 408	*VIII Armeekorps*
Feldgend.-Trupp 409	*IX Armeekorps*
Feldgend.-Trupp a (mot.) 410	*X Armekorps*
Feldgend.-Trupp a (mot.) 411	*Generalkommando XI Armeekorps*
Feldgend.-Trupp 412	*XII Armeekorps*
Feldgend.-Trupp 413	*?*
Feldgend.-Trupp b (mot.) 414	*XIV Armeekorps*
Feldgend.-Trupp b 415	*XV Armeekorps/ Heeresgruppe E/Panzergruppe 3*
Feldgend.-Trupp 416	*416 Infanterie Div.*
Feldgend.-Trupp a (mot.) 417	*XVII Armeekorps*
Feldgend.-Trupp a (mot.) 418	*XVIII Armeekorps/ XXXXIX (Gebirgs) Armeekorps/ XVIII (Gebirgs) Armeekorps*
Feldgend.-Trupp b (mot.) 419	*Gruppe Guderian/ Panzergruppe 2/Generalkommando XIX (Gebirgs) Armeekorps/ Feldgend.-Abt 541*
Feldgend.-Trupp 420	*XX Armeekorps*
Feldgend.-Trupp 421	*I Armeekorps/ XXI Gebirgs-Armeekorps*
Feldgend.-Trupp 422	*XXII Armeekorps/ Panzerarmee Oberkommando I / Heeresgruppe E/XII Gebirgs-Armeekorps*
Feldgend.-Trupp a (mot.) 423	*XXIII Armeekorps*
Feldgend.-Trupp 424	*XXIV Armeekorps*
Feldgend.-Trupp 426	*XXVI Armeekorps/SS-Polizei Div.*

Feldgend.-Trupp a 427	XXVII Armeekorps
Feldgend.-Trupp a (mot.) 428	Generalkommando XXVIII Armeekorps
Feldgend.-Trupp a 429	Generalkommando XXIX Armeekorps
Feldgend.-Trupp c (tmot.) 430	Generalkommando XXX Armeekorps z.b.V.
Feldgend.-Trupp 431	Höhererkommando z.b.V. XXXI Armeekorps
Feldgend.-Trupp 432	Höhererkommando z.b.V. XXXII Armeekorps/ LXXXI Armeekorps
Feldgend.-Trupp (mot.) 433	Korpstrupp
Feldgend.-Trupp (mot.) 435	Höhererkommando z.b.V. XXXV Armeekorps
Feldgend.-Trupp (mot.) 436	Höhererkommando 36
Feldgend.-Trupp (mot.) 437	Höhererkommando z.b.V. XXXVII Armeekorps
Feldgend.-Trupp 438	XXXVIII Armeekorps
Feldgend.-Trupp a (mot.) 439	XXXIX Armeekorps
Feldgend.-Trupp a (mot.) 440	Generalkommando XXXX Armeekorps
Feldgend.-Trupp 441	XXXXI Armeekorps
Feldgend.-Trupp 442	Übergeneralkommando XXI Armeekorps/XXXXII Armeekorps/ 444 Sicherungs Div.
Feldgend.-Trupp 443	XXXXIII Armeekorps
Feldgend.-Trupp (mot.) 444	XXXXIV Armeekorps
Feldgend.-Trupp 446	XXXXVI Armeekorps
Feldgend.-Trupp a (mot.) 447	Generalkommando XXXXVII Panzerkorps
Feldgend.-Trupp 448	XXXXVIII Panzerkorps
Feldgend.-Trupp 449	XVIII (Gebirgs) Armeekorps/ XXXXIX (Gebirgs) Armeekorps
Feldgend.-Trupp 450	L Armeekorps
Feldgend.-Trupp a (mot.) 451	LI Armeekorps
Feldgend.-Trupp 452	LII Armeekorps
Feldgend.-Trupp 453	LIII Armeekorps
Feldgend.-Trupp 455	LV Armeekorps
Feldgend.-Trupp b (mot.) 456	Generalkommando LVI Armeekorps
Feldgend.-Trupp 457	LVII Armeekorps/ Armeeoberkommando II/ Armeeoberkommando 7 / LVII Panzerkorps
Feldgend.-Trupp b (mot.) 458	Generalkommando LVIII Panzerkorps
Feldgend.-Trupp 459	LIX Armeekorps/ Höhererkommando 59
Feldgend.-Trupp 460	LXXXIV Armekorps
Feldgend.-Trupp c (tmot.) 462	Korück 525
Feldgend.-Trupp (mot.) 463	Übergeneralkommando XXI Armeekorps/181 Infanterie Div./Gebirgskorps Norwegen
Feldgend.-Trupp a (mot.) 464	Generalkommando LXIV Armeekorps
Feldgend.-Trupp d 465	Generalkommando LXV Armeekorps z.b.V.
Feldgend.-Trupp d (tmot.) 466	66 Reserve Korps
Feldgend.-Trupp 467	LXVII Armeekorps
Feldgend.-Trupp z.b.V. 468	Generalkommando LXVIII Armeekorps z.b.V.
Feldgend.-Trupp c (tmot.) 472	Generalkommando LXXII Armeekorps
Feldgend.-Trupp b (mot.) 473	XVI Armeekorps
Feldgend.-Trupp a (mot.) 474	Generalkommando LXXIV Armeekorps

Feldgend.-Trupp a (mot.) 475	*Generalkommando LXXV Armeekorps*
Feldgend.-Trupp a (mot.) 476	*Oberbefehlshaber Süd*
Feldgend.-Trupp 477	*LXX Armeekorps*
Feldgend.-Trupp 478	*Generalkommando I Kavalleriekorps*
Feldgend.-Trupp a (mot.) 485	*Generalkommando LXXXV Armeekorps*
Feldgend.-Trupp 486	*?*
Feldgend.-Trupp 487	*137 Infanterie Div./ Heeresgruppe C/Generalkommando LXXXVII Armeekorps*
Feldgend.-Trupp c (tmot.) 491	*Generalkommando LXXXXI Armeekorps*
Feldgend.-Trupp 495	*?*
Feldgend.-Trupp 497	*Heerestrupp*
Feldgend.-Trupp (mot.) 498	*Generalkommando Deutsches Afrikakorps/Oberbefehlshaber Süd*
Feldgend.-Trupp b (mot.) 500	*Panzerkorps Grossdeutschland*
Feldgend.-Trupp 503	*Heerestrupp*
Feldgend.-Trupp 505	*Militärverwaltung Frankreich, Bezirk Bordeaux*
Feldgend.-Trupp d 507	*Oberfeldkommandantur Warschau*
Feldgend.-Trupp d 508	*Oberfeldkommandantur Lemberg/ Deutsche Befehlshaber Westungarn*
Feldgend.-Trupp 509	*Militär Befehlshaber Frankreich, Militärverwaltung Bezirk C*
Feldgend.-Trupp a (mot.) 510	*Militärverwaltung Frankreich, Bezirk B*
Feldgend.-Trupp 511	*Ortskommandantur 511/ 311 Infanterie Div./Feldkommandantur 581/ Feldkommandantur 748/ Chef der Militärverwaltung, Bezirk B*
Feldgend.-Trupp 512	*Platzkommandantur I Bologna/Platzkommandantur II Modena*
Feldgend.-Trupp 513	*Heerestrupp*
Feldgend.-Trupp 515	*Militär Befehlshaber Frankreich, Militärverwaltung Bezirk A*
Feldgend.-Trupp a (mot.) 516	*Militärverwaltung Frankreich, Bezirk C*
Feldgend.-Trupp a (mot.) 517	*Feldkommandantur 517*
Feldgend.-Trupp 518	*Militärverwaltung Frankreich, Bezirk B*
Feldgend.-Trupp 520	*Heerestrupp*
Feldgend.-Trupp a (mot.) 524	*Militärverwaltung Bezirk Bordeaux/Militärverwaltung Bezirk B Südwest Frankreich*
Feldgend.-Trupp d 526	*Militärkommandantur 1006 Ferrera/ 526 Reserve Div.*
Feldgend.-Trupp 527	*Militärverwaltung Bezirk A*
Feldgend.-Trupp 528	*Militärverwaltung Bezirk B*
Feldgend.-Trupp 532	*Heerestrupp*
Feldgend.-Trupp 535	*Heerestrupp*
Feldgend.-Trupp 536	*Heerestrupp*
Feldgend.-Trupp 537	*Heerestrupp*
Feldgend.-Trupp 539	*Militärverwaltung Frankreich, Bezirk Bordeaux*
Feldgend.-Trupp 540	*Militärverwaltung Frankreich, Bezirk Bordeaux*
Feldgend.-Trupp 542	*Militär-Befehlshaber Frankreich*
Feldgend.-Trupp 543	*Militär-Befehlshaber Frankreich/78 Grenadier Div./ Kreiskommandantur 533*

Feldgend.-Trupp 544	Militär-Befehlshaber Frankreich, Militär-Verwaltung Bezirk A
Feldgend.-Trupp 545	?
Feldgend.-Trupp 546	Heerestrupp
Feldgend.-Trupp 547	Chef der Militärverwaltung Bezirk B
Feldgend.-Trupp 549	?
Feldgend.-Trupp a (mot.) 550	Militär-Befehlshaber Frankreich, Militärverwaltung Bezirk C
Feldgend.-Trupp 552	Militär-Befehlshaber Frankreich, Militärverwaltung Bezirk C
Feldgend.-Trupp 553	Militärverwaltung Bezirk C
Feldgend.-Trupp 554	554 Infanterie Div./ Platzkommandantur Asti
Feldgend.-Trupp 555	XXV Armeekorps
Feldgend.-Trupp a (mot.) 556	556 Infanterie Div.
Feldgend.-Trupp 557	Heerestrupp
Feldgend.-Trupp 558	Militär-Befehlshaber Frankreich, Militärverwaltung Bezirk C
Feldgend.-Trupp 559	559 V olksgrenadier Div./ Deutsche Wehrmacht in Italien
Feldgend.-Trupp 560	Militär-Befehlshaber Frankreich, Militärverwaltung Bezirk C
Feldgend.-Trupp 562	Militär-Befehlshaber Frankreich, Militärverwaltung Bezirk C
Feldgend.-Trupp 563	Militär-Befehlshaber Frankreich, Militärverwaltung Bezirk C
Feldgend.-Trupp 564	Militärverwaltung Bezirk Bordeaux/Kommandant Heeres Gebeit Süd Frankreich/Kommandant Gross-Paris/325 Sicherungs Div.
Feldgend.-Trupp 565	565 Volksgrenadier Div./ Deutsche Wehrmacht in Italien
Feldgend.-Trupp 566	Militärverwaltung Bezirk C
Feldgend.-Trupp 567	Militär-Befehlshaber Frankreich, Militärverwaltung Bezirk A
Feldgend.-Trupp 568	568 Volksgrenadier Div.
Feldgend.-Trupp 569	569 Volksgrenadier Div.
Feldgend.-Trupp 571	Gruppe 21/ Befehlshaber Oslo Südwest/199 Infanterie Div.
Feldgend.-Trupp 577	Militär-Befehlshaber Frankreich, Militärverwaltung Bezirk A
Feldgend.-Trupp c (tmot.) 579	Militär-Befehlshaber Frankreich, Militärverwaltung Bezirk A/ Befehlshaber Nordwest Frankreich
Feldgend.-Trupp 581	581 Volksgrenadier Div.
Feldgend.-Trupp 582	Chef der Militärverwaltung Bezirk B
Feldgend.-Trupp 583	Militärverwaltung Bezirk A, Nordwest Frankreich
Feldgend.-Trupp 584	Ortskommandantur 584/Militär-Befehlshaber Westpreussen Danzig/ Generalkommando IX Armeekorps/ Kommandantur der Befehlshaber Saarpfalz /Generalkommando XXIII Armekorps/Chef der Militärverwaltung Bezirk Paris/ Festungkommandantur Thorn
Feldgend.-Trupp 585	Feldkommandantur 589
Feldgend.-Trupp 586	Militärverwaltung Frankreich, Bezirk B
Feldgend.-Trupp 588	Feldkommandantur 588
Feldgend.-Trupp 589	Feldkommandantur 589/ Militär-Befehlshaber Frankreich, Militärverwaltung Bezirk A/Feldkommandantur 894
Feldgend.-Trupp a (mot.) 590	Militär-Befehlshaber Frankreich, Militärverwaltung Bezirk C
Feldgend.-Trupp 591	Feldkommandantur 591

Feldgend.-Trupp 592	*Feldkommandantur 750*
Feldgend.-Trupp 594	*Militärverwaltung Frankreich, Bezirk C*
Feldgend.-Trupp 596	*Militärverwaltung Frankreich, Bezirk C*
Feldgend.-Trupp d 597	*Militärverwaltung Frankreich, Bezirk B*
Feldgend.-Trupp c (tmot.) 600	*281 Sicherungs Div.*
Feldgend.-Trupp a (mot.) 602	*Kraftwagentransport Regt. 602/Feldkommandantur 602*
Feldgend.-Trupp c (tmot.) 603	*Behelshaber der deutschen Truppe Dänemark*
Feldgend.-Trupp 604	*Feldkommandantur 602*
Feldgend.-Trupp a (mot.) 605	*Kraftwagentransport Regt. 605*
Feldgend.-Trupp c (tmot.) 606	*Feldkommandantur Lillehammer*
Feldgend.-Trupp 607	*Militärverwaltung Frankreich, Bezirk B*
Feldgend.-Trupp 608	*Militärbefehlshaber Frankreich, Bezirk Chef C/ Feldkommandantur 531*
Feldgend.-Trupp 609	*Militärverwaltung Frankreich, Bezirk B*
Feldgend.-Trupp d 610	*Militärbefehlshaber Serbien*
Feldgend.-Trupp 611	*Heerestrupp*
Feldgend.-Trupp 612	*Kreiskommandantur 612/ LXVI Armeekorps/ 612 Infanterie Division/Armeeoberkommando 7/Feldkommandantur 684*
Feldgend.-Trupp 613 (trop.)	*Feldkommandantur 615*
Feldgend.-Trupp 615	*Militärverwaltung Bezirk Bordeaux*
Feldgend.-Trupp a (mot.) 616	*Feldkommandantur 677/Feldkommandantur 665*
Feldgend.-Trupp c (tmot.) 617	*LXXXVIII Armeekorps*
Feldgend.-Trupp c (tmot.) 618	*Generalkommando V Armeekorps*
Feldgend.-Trupp 620	*Militärverwaltung Frankreich, Bezirk C*
Feldgend.-Trupp 621	*Feldkommandantur 560*
Feldgend.-Trupp 622	*Militärverwaltung Frankreich, Bezirk C*
Feldgend.-Trupp c (mot.) 623	*Militärbefehlshaber Frankreich*
Feldgend.-Trupp 624	*Militärverwaltung Bezirk C*
Feldgend.-Trupp 627	*Militärverwaltung Frankreich, Bezirk C*
Feldgend.-Trupp 628	*?*
Feldgend.-Trupp 629	*Militärverwaltung Frankreich, Bezirk C*
Feldgend.-Trupp c (tmot.) 630	*Generalkommando LXXI Armeekorps*
Feldgend.-Trupp 631	*?*
Feldgend.-Trupp 634	*Chef der Militärverwaltung Frankreich, Bezirk C*
Feldgend.-Trupp 635	*Militärverwaltung Frankreich, Bezirk B*
Feldgend.-Trupp 641	*Feldkommandantur 589*
Feldgend.-Trupp 643	*Standortoffizier Olbia/ Standortoffizier Belluno*
Feldgend.-Trupp 645	*Chef der Militärverwaltung Frankreich, Bezirk A*
Feldgend.-Trupp a (mot.) 646	*1 Fallschirm Div.*
Feldgend.-Trupp a (mot.) 647	*2 Fallschirm Div.*
Feldgend.-Trupp a (mot.) 648	*3 Fallschirm Div.*
Feldgend.-Trupp 649	*Militärbefehlshaber Frankreich*
Feldgend.-Trupp 650	*4 Fallschirm Div.*
Feldgend.-Trupp 651	*Militärverwaltung Frankreich, Bezirk Bordeaux*

Feldgend.-Trupp 652	Kommando Sardinien/ Oberbefehlshaber Südwest
Feldgend.-Trupp d 653	Oberbefehlshaber Südwest
Feldgend.-Trupp 654	5 Fallschirm Div.
Feldgend.-Trupp 655	Militärverwaltung Bezirk Bordeaux
Feldgend.-Trupp 656	Chef der Militärverwaltung Frankreich, Bezirk C
Feldgend.-Trupp c (tmot.) 657	Militärverwaltung Frankreich, Bezirk Bordeaux
Feldgend.-Trupp 658	Chef der Militärverwaltung Frankreich, Bezirk C
Feldgend.-Trupp 659	Militärverwaltung Frankreich, Bezirk Bordeaux
Feldgend.-Trupp 660	Chef der Militärverwaltung Frankreich, Bezirk C
Feldgend.-Trupp 661	Chef der Militärverwaltung Frankreich, Bezirk C
Feldgend.-Trupp d 662	Oberbefehlshaber Südost
Feldgend.-Trupp d 663	Oberbefehlshaber Südost
Feldgend.-Trupp 665	Militärverwaltung Frankreich, Bezirk B
Feldgend.-Trupp d 666	Oberbefehlshaber Südost
Feldgend.-Trupp 667	Militärvbefehlshaber Frankreich
Feldgend.-Trupp d 670	Oberbefehlshaber Südost
Feldgend.-Trupp d 671	Oberbefehlshaber Südost
Feldgend.-Trupp d 672	Oberbefehlshaber Südost
Feldgend.-Trupp 673	Feldkommandantur 673/Armeeoberkommando Norwegen
Feldgend.-Trupp d 674	Oberbefehlshaber Südost
Feldgend.-Trupp a (mot.) 675	Oberbefehlshaber West/ II Fallschirmjägerkorps
Feldgend.-Trupp 676	I Fallschirmjägerkorps
Feldgend.-Trupp a (mot.) 677	Militärverwaltung Frankreich Bezirk B
Feldgend.-Trupp 678	Feldkommandantur 678
Feldgend.-Trupp 680	Feldkommandantur 680
Feldgend.-Trupp 684	Militärbefehlshaber Frankreich Bezirk A
Feldgend.-Trupp b (mot.) 685	Befehlshaber Nordwest Frankreich
Feldgend.-Trupp b (mot.) 687	Befehlshaber Südwest Frankreich
Feldgend.-Trupp b 688	Befehlshaber Nordost Frankreich
Feldgend.-Trupp b (mot.) 689	Kommandant Heeres Gebeit Süd Frankreich
Feldgend.-Trupp b (mot.) 690	Kommandant Heeres Gebiet Süd Frankreich
Feldgend.-Trupp d 691	Befehlshaber Nordwest Frankreich
Feldgend.-Trupp d 692	Befehlshaber Südwest Frankreich
Feldgend.-Trupp d 693	Militärbefehlshaber Frankreich
Feldgend.-Trupp d 694	Kommandant Heeres Gebiet Süd Frankreich
Feldgend.-Trupp d 695	Kommandant Heeres Gebiet Süd Frankreich
Feldgend.-Trupp d (mot.) 699	Militärbefehlshaber Frankreich
Feldgend.-Trupp 702	702 Infanterie Div.
Feldgend.-Trupp 704	704 Infanterie Div.
Feldgend.-Trupp 706	Militärverwaltung Frankreich Bezirk C
Feldgend.-Trupp 708	708 Infanterie Div./ 708 Volksgrenadier Div.
Feldgend.-Trupp 709	709 Infanterie Div./ 709 Volksgrenadier Div.
Feldgend.-Trupp 710	710 Infanterie Div.
Feldgend.-Trupp 711	Kreiskommandantur 622/Kreiskommandantur 711/ 711 Infanterie Div.

The armband worn by those acting as temporary *Feldgendarmen*, machine woven version.

Armband worn by Military Police acting as traffic controllers, printed version.

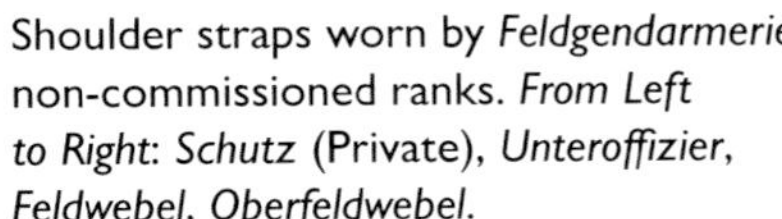

Shoulder straps worn by *Feldgendarmerie* non-commissioned ranks. *From Left to Right: Schutz* (Private), *Unteroffizier, Feldwebel, Oberfeldwebel.*

Feldgendarmerie shoulder straps. *From Left to Right: Fahnenjunkeroberfeldwebel* (senior Officer candidate), *Feldwebel* of the *Grossdeutschland* Division, *Unteroffizier* for tropical uniform.

Feldgendarmerie junior officers shoulder straps. *From Left to Right*: *Leutnant, Oberleutnant, Hauptmann.*

Senior officer's shoulder straps. *From Left to Right*: Major, *Oberstleutnant, Oberst.*

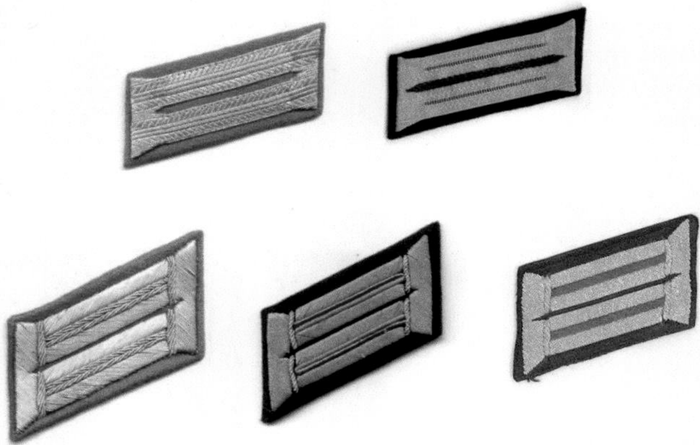

Feldgendarmerie collar tabs. *From Left to Right from top*: Lower ranks parade tunic, lower ranks field blouse, officer parade tunic, officer field blouse, late pattern woven officers.

Feldgendarmerie sleeve eagle for lower ranks (*left*) and officers (*right*).

Standard pattern *Feldgendarmerie* sleeve eagle (*left*) and variant with three wing segments (*right*).

Aluminium thread hand embroidered variants of the *Feldgendarmerie* cufftitle.

The three known woven variants of original wartime *Feldgendarmerie* cufftitles. All are similar though minor detail differences may be seen on close examination.

The reverse faces of the machine woven bands show very different manufacturing techniques.

The *Feldgendarmerie* gorget as worn by *Feldgendarm*en of the *Heer*, *Waffen-SS* and many *Luftwaffe* units. The buttons, eagle and lettering are luminous. This example, by the Assmann firm has a dark grey finish.

A further example of the *Feldgendarmerie* gorget, by the Maedicke firm of Berlin has the more typical silvered finish.

Reverse of the *Feldgendarmerie* gorget. The central prong was slotted into the tunic buttonhole to prevent it from swinging around when the wearer moved.

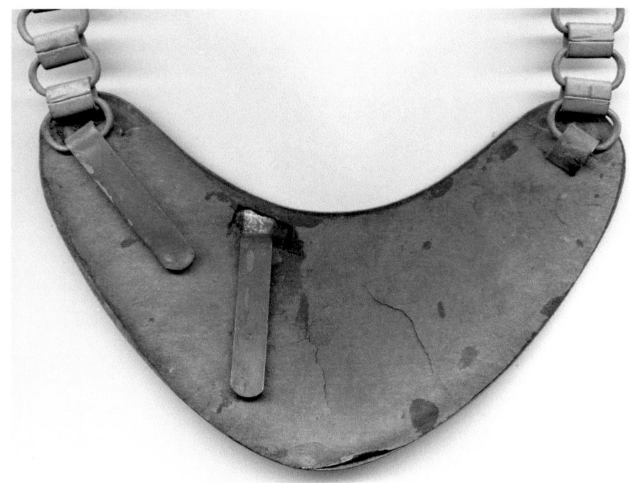

Above left: The exceptionally rare variant of the gorget worn by *Feldgendarmerie* in the *Grossdeutschland* Division. One of only a handful known to still exist.

Above right: Feldgendarmerie officer's orange piped visor cap by the well-known firm of Clemens Wagner.

Right: Visor cap for enlisted and NCO ranks of the *Feldgendarmerie* distinguished by the use of a leather chinstrap rather than aluminium thread cords.

Officer's tunic for a *Leutnant* of *Feldgendarmerie*.

Left: NCO field blouse for an *Oberfeldwebel* of *Feldgendarmerie*.

Below: Gorget worn by members of patrol groups from the local military headquarters or *Kommandantur*. (*Firma Helmut Weitze, Photo by Christoph Schultz*)

Armband worn by members of the *Bahnhofswache* prior to the introduction of the gorget.

Bahnhofswache gorget. The Roman numeral is the *Wehrkreis* or Military District number. (*Firma Helmut Weitze, Photo by Christoph Schultz*)

Gorget worn by members of the *Zugwache*. The numerals in the centre represent the *Abteilung* number.

Gültigkeitsdauer

bis 31. Dez. 44.

bis

bis

bis

bis

bis

Kdr. d. Heeresstreifendienstes
für Reiseverkehr Südrußland O. U., den 12. April 1944

Ausweis Nr. 173

Schtz. Müller Edmund gehört zur

Zugwachabteilung 507

[Verf.: OKH (Ch H Rüst und BdE) AHA/Ia (II) Nr. 21172/41]

Er hat die Berechtigung, gegebenenfalls die Verpflichtung, allen Angehörigen der Wehrmacht und des Wehrmachtgefolges — mit Ausnahme von Generalen und im Generalsrang stehenden Wehrmachtbeamten — in bezug auf seinen Aufgabenkreis Befehle zu erteilen.

Gegenüber Offizieren und Wehrmachtbeamten im Offizierrang haben nur Offiziere Befehlsgewalt und Prüfungsrecht.

Alle Truppenteile und Dienststellen sowie jeder Wehrmachtangehörige sind verpflichtet, die Transportführer und Zugwachen auf Anforderung mit allen erforderlichen Mitteln zu unterstützen.

Kdr. d. Heeresstreifendienstes für Reiseverkehr Südrußland

(Unterschrift)

Oberstlt. u. Kommandeur

Zugwache Ausweis for a member of *Zugwachabteilung* 507 serving on the Eastern Front.

Dem Inhaber dieses Ausweises obliegt die Kontrolle aller Wehrmachtreisenden - einschl. Angehörigen des Wehrmachtgefolges - in den Zügen. Er hat in Ausübung seines Dienstes die Eigenschaft einer militärischen Wache im Sinne des § 111, Abs. 2 MStGB.

Er ist berechtigt, in und außer Dienst Pistole zu tragen.

Soweit dienstliche Notwendigkeit vorliegt, ist er bei Flakbeschuß und Luftalarm von luftschutzmäßigem Verhalten und vom Aufsuchen von Luftschutzräumen befreit.

Auszug aus MStGB.

§ 111 (H. Dv. 275)

Wer eine militärische Wache im Dienste oder in Beziehung auf eine Diensthandlung mit der Begehung eines Verbrechens oder Vergehens bedroht oder wer sich ihr gegenüber einer Beleidigung, eines Ungehorsams, einer Widersetzung oder einer Tätlichkeit schuldig macht, wird ebenso bestraft, als wenn er die Handlung gegen einen Vorgesetzten begangen hätte.

The *Zugwache Ausweis* details the authority of the bearer and includes an extract from the German Military Penal Code.

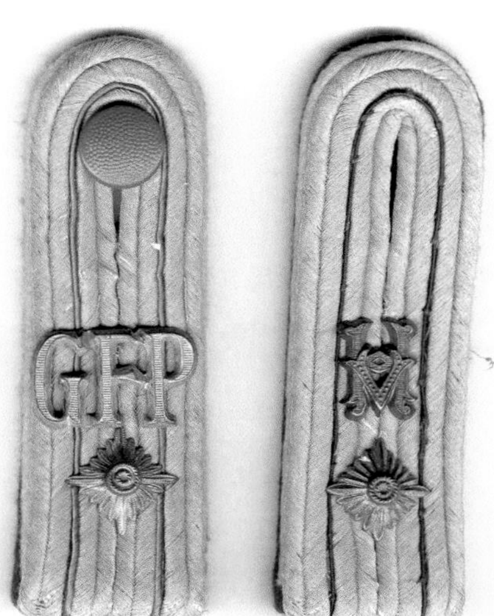

Above left: Rare tropical issue field cap with *Feldgendarmerie* orange-red *soutache* over the national cockade. *(David Bunch)*

Above right: At left is a shoulder strap for a *Feldpolizeiinspektor* of the *Geheimefeldpolizei*. At right is a strap for an army Justice Official with the rank of *Heeresjustizinspektor*. Both feature the same light blue underlay but note that the GFP strap also has a thin blue cord between the braid, as opposed to a dark green cord for the Justice official.

The collar patch for junior GFP Officers also featured light blue centres to the collar *'Litzen'* and piping around the rear, top and bottom edges, but not to the front. (*Courtesy Lundström Collection*)

Left: from left to right: Shoulder strap for *Stabsfeldwebel* of *Feldgendarmerie* attached to the GFP, shoulder strap for *Feldpolizeidirektor* of GFP and collar tab for senior ranks in the GFP. *Feldpolizeidirektor* strap. (*Courtesy Peter Whamond/Collectors Guild*)

Below: The cufftitle authorised and manufactured for the GFP, but probably never worn.

Extremely rare original tunic for a *Feldpolizeiobersekretär* of the *Geheime Feldpolizei.* (*Brecht Schotte*)

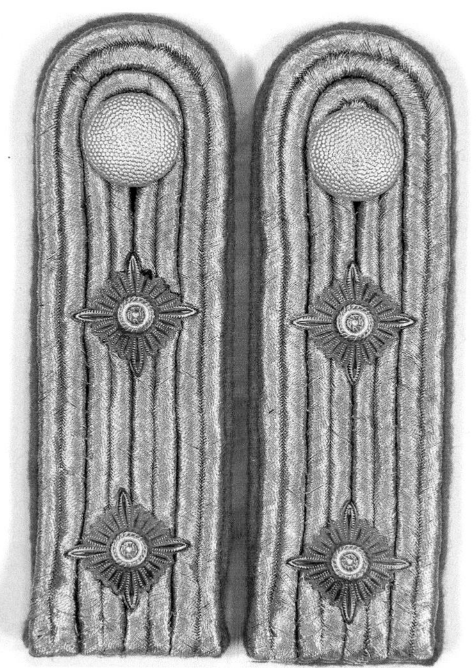

Above left: Collar patch and shoulder strap for *Feldpolizeidirektor* of *Luftwaffe* GFP.

Above right: Shoulder straps for an *Unterfeldwebel* of *Luftwaffe Feldgendarmerie*, post June 1943.

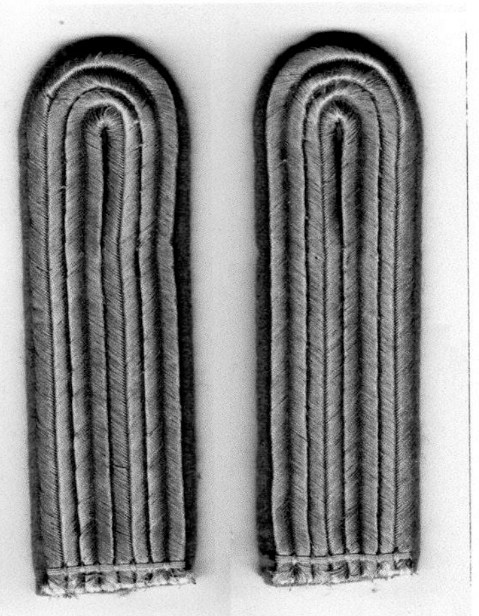

Above left: Shoulder straps for a *Luftwaffe Hauptmann* of *Feldgendarmer*iue, post June 1943.

Above right: Luftwaffe Feldgendarmerie gorget. (*George Petersen*)

Above left: Shoulder straps as worn by a *Luftwaffe Leutnant* of *Feldgendarmerie*, pre-June 1943 with light blue underlay.

Above right: Collar patch and shoulder strap for a *Feldpolizeikomissar* of *Luftwaffe* GFP.

An original gorget of the *Feldjägerkorps*. (*Bill Shea*)

One of the two known designs of armband worn by the Feldjäger.

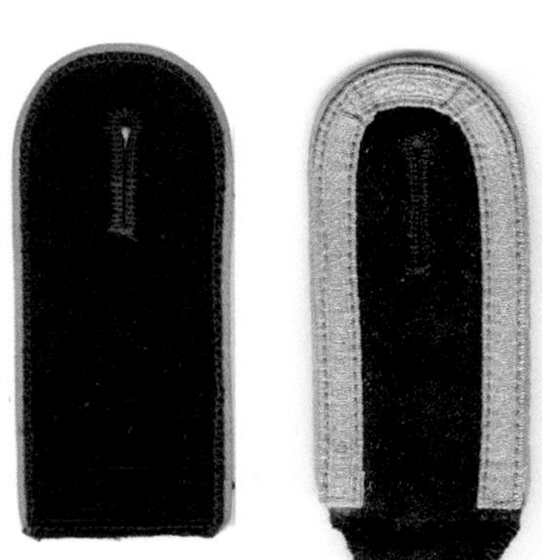

Above: Machine woven cufftitle worn by the *SS-Feldgendarmerie* from 1942–1944.

Left: Shoulder straps for a *Schutze and Unterscharführer* of *SS-Feldgendarmerie. Schutze* strap. (*Courtesy Peter Whamond/ Collectors Guild*)

Tunic of an *SS-Feldgendarmerie Sturmmann* of the 3rd *SS-Panzer Division Totenkopf*. (*Courtesy of Willi Schumacher*)

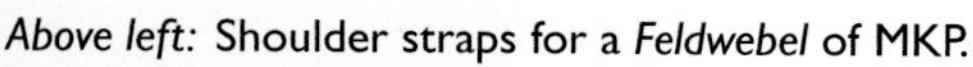

Above left: Shoulder straps for a *Feldwebel* of MKP.

Above right: Wasserschutzpolizei pattern shoulder straps for a *Revier-Oberwachtmeister*.

Nr. 61

Ausweis als Militär-Polizei-Unteroffizier

Inhaber ist der ....

....

Er versieht den Dienst als Militär-Polizei-Unteroffizier im Standort Swinemünde und ist berechtigt, in Ausübung dieses Dienstes Waffen zu tragen.

Alle Unteroffiziere und Mannschaften (ausschließlich der ihnen auf Grund eines besonderen Vorgesetztenverhältnisses vorgesetzten Unteroffiziere) der Wehrmacht haben seinen dienstlichen Anordnungen und Anforderungen nachzukommen.

Inhaber ist berechtigt, auch im Dienst Zivilkleidung zu tragen.

Swinemünde, den 17. Nov. 1938

Kommandantur der Befestigungen der pommerschen Küste

Konteradmiral

Sichtvermerk der Polizei-Verwaltung Swinemünde.

Die Beamten der Stadt- und Kriminalpolizei werden angewiesen, dem M.-P.-U. in Ausübung seines Dienstes Schutz und Beistand zu gewähren.

Swinemünde,

den 22. 11. 1938

Der Bürgermeister als Ortspolizeibehörde

Im Auftrage:

A pre-war *Ausweis* for a naval NCO serving as a military policeman.

Marineküstenpolizei cufftitle.

Gorget of the *Marineküstenpolizei*

Police pattern sleeve eagles in embroidered and machine woven form as worn by the MKP.

Naval pattern visor cap with WSP insignia as worn by MKP NCOs during the transitional period before the use of full *Kriegsmarine* insignia.

Feldgend.-Trupp d (mot.) 712	*712 Infanterie Div.*
Feldgend.-Trupp c 715	*715 Infanterie Div.,*
Feldgend.-Trupp 716	*716 Infanterie Div.*
Feldgend.-Trupp c (mot.) 718	*Kommandant Festung Kreta/Ortskommandantur 718/Kreiskommandantur Agaeis*
Feldgend.-Trupp 719	*719 Infanterie Div.*
Feldgend.-Trupp 721	*Militärbefehlshaber Frankreich Militärverwaltung Bezirk C/ Kreiskommandantur 622*
Feldgend.-Trupp 722	*Militärbefehlshaber Frankreich Militärverwaltung Bezirk A*
Feldgend.-Trupp 723	*Militärbefehlshaber Frankreich Militärverwaltung Bezirk A*
Feldgend.-Trupp 724	*Feldkommandantur 724*
Feldgend.-Trupp 726	*Militärverwaltung Frankreich, Bezirk C*
Feldgend.-Trupp 727	*Militärverwaltung Frankreich, Bezirk C*
Feldgend.-Trupp 728	*Militärverwaltung Frankreich, Bezirk C*
Feldgend.-Trupp 729	*Militärverwaltung Frankreich, Bezirk B*
Feldgend.-Trupp 730	*Militärverwaltung Frankreich, Bezirk Bordeaux*
Feldgend.-Trupp 731	*Militärbefehlshaber Frankreich-Militärverwaltung Frankreich, Bezirk A*
Feldgend.-Trupp 732	*Militärverwaltung Frankreich, Bezirk Bordeaux/ Korück 588 Bordeaux*
Feldgend.-Trupp 733	*Feldkommandantur 752*
Feldgend.-Trupp 734	*Militärverwaltung Frankreich, Bezirk Bordeaux/ Panzer Armeeoberkommando 5*
Feldgend.-Trupp 735	*Militärverwaltung Frankreich, Bezirk B*
Feldgend.-Trupp 736	*Militärverwaltung Frankreich, Bezirk Bordeaux*
Feldgend.-Trupp 737	*Militärverwaltung Frankreich, Bezirk C*
Feldgend.-Trupp d 738	*Ortskommandantur 738/Kreiskommandantur 738/ Kreiskommandantur 895*
Feldgend.-Trupp d 739	*Militärverwaltung Frankreich, Bezirk Bordeaux*
Feldgend.-Trupp 740	*Ortskommandantur 740/Feldkommandantur 752*
Feldgend.-Trupp 741	*Militärbefehlshaber Frankreich, Militärverwaltung Bezirk A*
Feldgend.-Trupp 742	*Militärbefehlshaber Frankreich, Militärverwaltung Bezirk A*
Feldgend.-Trupp d (mot.) 743	*Kreiskommandantur 743/Kreiskommandantur 773*
Feldgend.-Trupp 744	*Militärbefehlshaber Frankreich, Bezirk C*
Feldgend.-Trupp 745	*Militärbefehlshaber Frankreich, Militärverwaltung Bezirk A*
Feldgend.-Trupp 747	*Militärbefehlshaber Frankreich*
Feldgend.-Trupp 748	*Militärverwaltung Frankreich Bezirk B*
Feldgend.-Trupp 750	*Chef der Militärverwaltung Bezirk B*
Feldgend.-Trupp a (mot.) 751	*Feldkommandantur 751/Militärbefehlshaber Frankreich, Militärverwaltung Bezirk A*
Feldgend.-Trupp 752	*Feldkommandantur 752/ Befehlshaber Südwest Frankreich*
Feldgend.-Trupp c (tmot.) 753	*Feldkommandantur 753/Feldkommandantur 517*
Feldgend.-Trupp a (mot.) 754	*Befehlshaber Nordwest Frankreich*
Feldgend.-Trupp a (mot.) 756	*Militärbefehlshaber Frankreich, Militärverwaltung Bezirk B*

Feldgend.-Trupp a (mot.) 757	Feldkommandantur 757
Feldgend.-Trupp 758	Feldkommandantur 758
Feldgend.-Trupp 759	Kreiskommandantur 759
Feldgend.-Trupp 760	Militärverwaltung Frankreich, Bezirk C
Feldgend.-Trupp 764	Militärverwaltung Frankreich, Bezirk Bordeaux
Feldgend.-Trupp 765	Kreiskommandantur 734/Kreiskommandantur 798
Feldgend.-Trupp 766	Wehrkreis XIII
Feldgend.-Trupp 766	Wehrkreis XIII
Feldgend.-Trupp 767	Militärverwaltung Frankreich Bezirk C
Feldgend.-Trupp 768	Militärverwaltung Frankreich Bezirk B
Feldgend.-Trupp d 769	Militärverwaltung Frankreich Bezirk C
Feldgend.-Trupp 770	Wehrkreis XIII
Feldgend.-Trupp 773	?
Feldgend.-Trupp 774	Feldkommandantur 774
Feldgend.-Trupp 778	Sturmbrigade RFSS
Feldgend.-Trupp d 776	Militärbefehlshaber Frankreich, Militärverwaltung Bezirk A
Feldgend.-Trupp 777	Militärverwaltung Frankreich Bezirk Bordeaux
Feldgend.-Trupp 779	Militärverwaltung Frankreich Bezirk Bordeaux
Feldgend.-Trupp 780	Kreiskommandantur 780/Kreiskommandantur 747
Feldgend.-Trupp 785	?
Feldgend.-Trupp 788	Wehrkreis XIII
Feldgend.-Trupp 789	Militärbefehlshaber Frankreich, Militärverwaltung Bezirk A
Feldgend.-Trupp 792	Kreiskommandantur 792
Feldgend.-Trupp 793	Militärverwaltung Frankreich, Bezirk B
Feldgend.-Trupp 794	Chef der Militärverwaltung Frankreich, Bezirk B
Feldgend.-Trupp 795	Militärverwaltung Frankreich Bezirk C/Kreiskommandantur 706
Feldgend.-Trupp d 796 La Rochelle	Militärverwaltung Frankreich Bezirk B/Kommandantur 505
Feldgend.-Trupp 797 Kreiskommandantur 645	Militärbefehlshaber Frankreich Militärverwaltung Bezirk A/
Feldgend.-Trupp 798	Wehrkreis XIII
Feldgend.-Trupp 800	Chef der Militärverwaltung Frankreich Bezirk A
Feldgend.-Trupp d 801	Ortskommandantur 699/Feldkommandantur 678
Feldgend.-Trupp d 802	Ortskommandantur 701/Feldkommandantur 589
Feldgend.-Trupp d 803	Ortskommandantur 940/Feldkommandantur 589
Feldgend.-Trupp d 804	Oberfeldkommandantur 589/ Ortskommandantur 687/ Militärbefehlshaber Frankreich Verwaltung Bezirk A
Feldgend.-Trupp d 805	Ortskommandantur 639
Feldgend.-Trupp a 806	Feldkommandantur 581/Ortskommandantur 642/Feldkommandantur 670
Feldgend.-Trupp a (mot.) 807	Oberfeldkommandantur 589
Feldgend.-Trupp 808	Ortskommandantur 691/Oberfeldkommandantur 589
Feldgend.-Trupp 809	Wehrkreis IX/ Ortskommandantur 715/ Oberfeldkommandantur 670

Feldgend.-Trupp a (mot.) 810	*Oberfeldkommandantur 672*
Feldgend.-Trupp c (mot.) 811	*Oberfeldkommandantur 672/Generalkommando XI Armeekorps*
Feldgend.-Trupp d 812	*Ortskommandantur 636/Oberfeldkommandantur 589*
Feldgend.-Trupp a (mot.) 813	*Oberfeldkommandantur 670*
Feldgend.-Trupp a 814	*Ortskommandantur 703/Oberfeldkommandantur 670/*
Kreiskommandantur 703	
Feldgend.-Trupp a (mot.) 815	*Oberfeldkommandantur 670*
Feldgend.-Trupp a 816	*Ortskommandantur 914/Oberfeldkommandantur 670*
Feldgend.-Trupp d 817	*Ortskommandantur 689/Oberfeldkommandantur 672*
Feldgend.-Trupp a 818	*Ortskommandantur 692/Oberfeldkommandantur 670*
Feldgend.-Trupp d 819	*Ortskommandantur 693*
Feldgend.-Trupp a (mot.) 820	*Feldkommandantur 681/Oberfeldkommandantur 672*
Feldgend.-Trupp 821	*Generalkommando XI Armeekorps/Feldkommandantur 520*
Feldgend.-Trupp a 822	*Ortskommandantur 707/Oberfeldkommandantur 670*
Feldgend.-Trupp a (mot.) 823	*Oberfeldkommandantur 670*
Feldgend.-Trupp a 824	*Ortskommandantur 714/Oberfeldkommandantur 670*
Feldgend.-Trupp d 825	*Ortskommandantur 771*
Feldgend.-Trupp d 826	*Ortskommandantur 913*
Feldgend.-Trupp d 827	*Ortskommandantur 643*
Feldgend.-Trupp d 828	*Ortskommandantur 772*
Feldgend.-Trupp d 829	*Ortskommandantur 694/Oberfeldkommandantur 672*
Feldgend.-Trupp 830	*Wehrkreis Böhmen-Mähren/Ortskommandantur 702/ Oberfeldkommandantur 672*
Feldgend.-Trupp 831	*Generalkommando XI Armeekorps/Oberfeldkommandantur 672*
Feldgend.-Trupp d 832	*Ortskommandantur 635*
Feldgend.-Trupp c (tmot.) 833	*Oberfeldkommandantur 670*
Feldgend.-Trupp d 834	*Ortskommandantur 713*
Feldgend.-Trupp 835	*?*
Feldgend.-Trupp c (mot.) 836	*Oberfeldkommandantur 672/Generalkommando XI Armeekorps*
Feldgend.-Trupp a (mot.) 837	*Oberfeldkommandantur 589*
Feldgend.-Trupp 838	*Oberfeldkommandantur 520*
Feldgend.-Trupp d 839	*Ortskommandantur 614/Oberfeldkommandantur 520*
Feldgend.-Trupp 840	*Ortskommandantur 630/Oberfeldkommandantur 570*
Feldgend.-Trupp d 841	*Ortskommandantur 510/Oberfeldkommandantur 570*
Feldgend.-Trupp a (mot.) 842	*Oberfeldkommandantur 570*
Feldgend.-Trupp 843	*Wehrkreis VI/Oberfeldkommandantur 520*
Feldgend.-Trupp d 844	*Ortskommandantur 688/Oberfeldkommandantur 520*
Feldgend.-Trupp d 845	*Ortskommandantur 613/Oberfeldkommandantur 520*
Feldgend.-Trupp d 846	*Wehrkreis VI/ Ortskommandantur 705/ Oberfeldkommandantur 520/ Ortskommandantur 636/ Oberfeldkommandantur 690*
Feldgend.-Trupp d 847	*Oberfeldkommandantur 570/Ortskommandantur 690*
Feldgend.-Trupp 848	*Oberfeldkommandantur 570/Ortskommandantur 654*
Feldgend.-Trupp 849	*Ortskommandantur 708/Oberfeldkommandantur 570*
Feldgend.-Trupp d 850	*Ortskommandantur 632/Oberfeldkommandantur 570*

Feldgend.-Trupp d 851	*Generalkommando XI Armeekorps/Ortskommandantur 616/*
Oberfeldkommandantur 520	
Feldgend.-Trupp d 852	*Ortskommandantur 652/Generalkommando XI Armeekorps*
Feldgend.-Trupp 853	*Oberfeldkommandantur 570*
Feldgend.-Trupp a (mot.) 854	*Oberfeldkommandantur 570*
Feldgend.-Trupp d 855	*Ortskommandantur 663/Oberfeldkommandantur 570*
Feldgend.-Trupp 856	*Wehrkreis VI/ Ortskommandantur 942/*
Oberfeldkommandantur 520	
Feldgend.-Trupp c (tmot.) 857	*Militärbefehlshaber Serbien*
Feldgend.-Trupp c (tmot.) 858	*Oberbefehlshaber Südost*
Feldgend.-Trupp c (tmot.) 859	*Militärbefehlshaber Serbien*
Feldgend.-Trupp 860	*Militärverwaltung Frankreich Bezirk Bordeaux*
Feldgend.-Trupp c (tmot.) 861	*Militärbefehlshaber Serbien*
Feldgend.-Trupp d 864	*Kreiskommandantur 832*
Feldgend.-Trupp d 865	*Militärbefehlshaber Serbien*
Feldgend.-Trupp 866	*Militärverwaltung Frankreich, Bezirk A*
Feldgend.-Trupp d 867	*Militärbefehlshaber Serbien*
Feldgend.-Trupp c (tmot.) 868	*Militärbefehlshaber Serbien*
Feldgend.-Trupp d 869	*Militärbefehlshaber Serbien*
Feldgend.-Trupp d 870	*Militärbefehlshaber Serbien*
Feldgend.-Trupp d 871	*Militärbefehlshaber Serbien*
Feldgend.-Trupp 872	*Feldkommandantur 872/Feldkommandantur 748*
Feldgend.-Trupp c (mot.) 873	*Feldkommandantur 674*
Feldgend.-Trupp c (mot.) 874	*Feldkommandantur 724*
Feldgend.-Trupp d 875	*Militärbefehlshaber Serbien*
Feldgend.-Trupp 876	*Militärbefehlshaber Frankreich-Militärverwaltung Bezirk A*
Feldgend.-Trupp 877	*Militärverwaltung Frankreich, Bezirk B*
Feldgend.-Trupp d 881	*Wehrmacht Befehlshaber Dänemark*
Feldgend.-Trupp 882	*Militärbefehlshaber Frankreich Militärverwaltung Bezirk A*
Feldgend.-Trupp 884	*Militärbefehlshaber Frankreich Militärverwaltung Bezirk A*
Feldgend.-Trupp 885	*Wehrkreis XIII*
Feldgend.-Trupp 887	*Kreiskommandantur 887*
Feldgend.-Trupp 888	*Militärbefehlshaber Frankreich Bezirk Chef C/ Kreiskommandantur 563*
Feldgend.-Trupp 889	*Militärbefehlshaber Frankreich Militärverwaltung Bezirk C*
Feldgend.-Trupp 890	*Kreiskommandantur 890/ Militärverwaltung Frankreich Bezirk C*
Feldgend.-Trupp 891	*Militärbefehlshaber Frankreich Militärverwaltung Bezirk C*
Feldgend.-Trupp 892	*Militärverwaltung Frankreich Bezirk C –Dijon*
Feldgend.-Trupp 893	*Militärverwaltung Frankreich Bezirk C*
Feldgend.-Trupp 894	*?*
Feldgend.-Trupp d 895	*Feldkommandantur 758*
Feldgend.-Trupp 896	*Kreiskommandantur 896 Paris/Militärbefehlshaber Frankreich*
Feldgend.-Trupp b (mot.) 897	*Oberfeldkommandantur Warschau*
Feldgend.-Trupp 898	*?*

Feldgend.-Trupp b (mot.) 899	Oberfeldkommandantur Krakau/Oberfeldkommandantur 226
Feldgend.-Trupp 900	Heerestrupp
Feldgend.-Trupp 901	Militärverwaltung Frankreich Bezirk C/Feldkommandantur 591
Feldgend.-Trupp a (mot.) 902	Militärbefehlshaber Frankreich Militärverwaltung Bezirk A/ Feldkommandantur 758/160 Reserve Div.
Feldgend.-Trupp a (mot.) 903	Militärbefehlshaber Frankreich
Feldgend.-Trupp a (mot.) 904	Kommandant Festung Kreta
Feldgend.-Trupp 905	?
Feldgend.-Trupp 907	?
Feldgend.-Trupp 908	Militärverwaltung Frankreich, Bezirk C
Feldgend.-Trupp c (tmot.) 909	Oberbefehlshaber Südwest
Feldgend.-Trupp 910	Oberbefehlshaber Südwest
Feldgend.-Trupp d (tmot.) 911	Oberbefehlshaber Südwest
Feldgend.-Trupp 912	Oberbefehlshaber Südwest
Feldgend.-Trupp a (mot.) 913	Militärbefehlshaber Frankreich
Feldgend.-Trupp c (tmot.) 914	Oberfeldkommandantur Warschau
Feldgend.-Trupp c (tmot.) 916	Wehrkreis Generalgouvernement
Feldgend.-Trupp c (tmot.) 917	Oberfeldkommandantur 379
Feldgend.-Trupp 919	Wehrmacht Befehlshaber Südost
Feldgend.-Trupp 920	Wehrmacht Befehlshaber Südost
Feldgend.-Trupp 921	Wehrmacht Befehlshaber Südost/Befehlshaber Nordost Frankreich
Feldgend.-Trupp 922	Wehrmacht Befehlshaber Südost
Feldgend.-Trupp c (tmot.) 923	Militärbefehlshaber Frankreich
Feldgend.-Trupp d 924	Feldgendarmerie Ausbildungs- Abteilung II
Feldgend.-Trupp 925	Militärverwaltung Frankreich, Bezirk C
Feldgend.-Trupp 926	?
Feldgend.-Trupp a (mot.) 929	Feldkommandantur 564
Feldgend.-Trupp (mot.) 930	Generalkommando LXXI Armeekorps
Feldgend.-Trupp 931	?
Feldgend.-Trupp c (tmot.) 932	Kommandant Heeres Gebiet Süd- Frankreich
Feldgend.-Trupp c (tmot.) 933	Militärbefehlshaber Frankreich
Feldgend.-Trupp d (tmot.) 934	Wehrkreis Generalgouvernement
Feldgend.-Trupp d (tmot.) 935	Wehrkreis Generalgouvernement
Feldgend.-Trupp d (tmot.) 936	Wehrkreis Generalgouvernement
Feldgend.-Trupp d (tmot.) 937	Wehrkreis Generalgouvernement
Feldgend.-Trupp d (tmot.) 938	Wehrkreis Generalgouvernement
Feldgend.-Trupp d (tmot.) 939	Wehrkreis Generalgouvernement
Feldgend.-Trupp d (tmot.) 940	Wehrkreis Generalgouvernement
Feldgend.-Trupp d (mot.) 941	Kommandant Festung Kreta/Kreiskommandantur Agaeis
Feldgend.-Trupp d (tmot.) 942	Wehrkreis Generalgouvernement
Feldgend.-Trupp d (tmot.) 943	Wehrkreis Generalgouvernement
Feldgend.-Trupp d (tmot.) 944	Wehrkreis Generalgouvernement
Feldgend.-Trupp d (tmot.) 945	Wehrkreis Generalgouvernement

Feldgend.-Trupp d (tmot.) 946	Wehrkreis Generalgouvernement
Feldgend.-Trupp d (tmot.) 947	Wehrkreis Generalgouvernement
Feldgend.-Trupp d (tmot.) 948	Wehrkreis Generalgouvernement
Feldgend.-Trupp d (tmot.) 949	Wehrkreis Generalgouvernement
Feldgend.-Trupp d (tmot.) 950	Wehrkreis Generalgouvernement
Feldgend.-Trupp d (tmot.) 951	Wehrkreis Generalgouvernement
Feldgend.-Trupp d (tmot.) 952	Wehrkreis Generalgouvernement
Feldgend.-Trupp 953	Wehrkreis Generalgouvernement
Feldgend.-Trupp 954	Wehrkreis Generalgouvernement
Feldgend.-Trupp 955	Wehrkreis Generalgouvernement
Feldgend.-Trupp 956	Wehrkreis Generalgouvernement
Feldgend.-Trupp 957	Wehrkreis Generalgouvernement
Feldgend.-Trupp d 958	Kommandant Heeres Gebeit Süd- Frankreich
Feldgend.-Trupp d 960	Ortskommandantur 891/Feldkommandantur 197
Feldgend.-Trupp d 961	Kommandant Heeres Gebeit Süd- Frankreich
Feldgend.-Trupp d 962	Kommandant Heeres Gebeit Süd- Frankreich
Feldgend.-Trupp d 963	Kommandant Heeres Gebeit Süd- Frankreich
Feldgend.-Trupp d 964	Kommandant Heeres Gebeit Süd- Frankreich
Feldgend.-Trupp d 965	Kommandant Heeres Gebeit Süd- Frankreich
Feldgend.-Trupp d 966	Kommandant Heeres Gebeit Süd-Frankreich
Feldgend.-Trupp d 967	Kommandant Heeres Gebeit Süd- Frankreich
Feldgend.-Trupp d 968	Kommandant Heeres Gebeit Süd- Frankreich
Feldgend.-Trupp d 969	Kommandant Heeres Gebeit Süd- Frankreich
Feldgend.-Trupp d 970	Kommandant Heeres Gebeit Süd- Frankreich
Feldgend.-Trupp d 971	Kommandant Heeres Gebeit Süd- Frankreich
Feldgend.-Trupp d 972	Kommandant Heeres Gebeit Süd- Frankreich
Feldgend.-Trupp d 973	Kommandant Heeres Gebeit Süd- Frankreich
Feldgend.-Trupp d 974	Kommandant Heeres Gebeit Süd- Frankreich
Feldgend.-Trupp d 975	Kommandant Heeres Gebeit Süd- Frankreich
Feldgend.-Trupp d 976	Kommandant Heeres Gebeit Süd- Frankreich
Feldgend.-Trupp d 977	Kommandant Heeres Gebeit Süd- Frankreich
Feldgend.-Trupp d 978	Kommandant Heeres Gebeit Süd- Frankreich
Feldgend.-Trupp d 979	Kommandant Heeres Gebeit Süd- Frankreich
Feldgend.-Trupp d 980	Kommandant Heeres Gebeit Süd- Frankreich
Feldgend.-Trupp a (mot.) 981	Kraftwagentransport Regt. Stab 981
Feldgend.-Trupp a (mot.) 982	Kraftwagentransport Regt. Stab 982
Feldgend.-Trupp c (tmot.) 983	Kommandant Heeres Gebeit Süd- Frankreich
Feldgend.-Trupp a (mot.) 984	Kraftwagentransport Regt. Stab z.b.V. 984
Feldgend.-Trupp c (mot.) 985	Kommandant Festung Kreta
Feldgend.-Trupp d 986	Kommandant Heeres Gebeit Süd- Frankreich
Feldgend.-Trupp 987	999 leichte Afrika Div./ Kommandant Heeres Gebeit Süd-Frankreich
Feldgend.-Trupp a 988	Kommandant Heeres Gebeit Süd-Frankreich
Feldgend.-Trupp 989	Sturm Div. Rhodos

Feldgend.-Trupp d 991	*Kommandant Heeres Gebeit Süd- Frankreich*
Feldgend.-Trupp d 992	*Kommandant Heeres Gebeit Süd- Frankreich*
Feldgend.-Trupp d 993	*Kommandant Heeres Gebeit Süd- Frankreich*
Feldgend.-Trupp d 994	*Kommandant Heeres Gebeit Süd- Frankreich*
Feldgend.-Trupp d 995	*Kommandant Heeres Gebeit Süd- Frankreich*
Feldgend.-Trupp 998	*Militärverwaltung Frankreich Bezirk C/Wehrmacht Ortskommandantur Gross Kopenhagen*
Feldgend.-Trupp (mot.) 999	*Sturmdiv. Rhodos*
Feldgend.-Trupp (tmot.) 1016	*Wehrkreis Generalgouvernement*
Feldgend.-Trupp 1017	*Heerestrupp*
Feldgend.-Trupp (tmot.) 1018	*Festung Ymuiden*
Feldgend.-Trupp (tmot.) 1019	*Festung Hök von Holland*
Feldgend.-Trupp (tmot.) 1020	*Festung Duenkirchen*
Feldgend.-Trupp (tmot.) 1021	*Festung Boulogne*
Feldgend.-Trupp (tmot.) 1022	*Festung Le Havre*
Feldgend.-Trupp (tmot.) 1023	*Festung Cherbourg*
Feldgend.-Trupp (tmot.) 1024	*Festung St. Malo*
Feldgend.-Trupp (tmot.) 1025	*Festung Brest*
Feldgend.-Trupp (tmot.) 1026	*Festung Lorient*
Feldgend.-Trupp (tmot.) 1027	*Festung St. Nazaire*
Feldgend.-Trupp (tmot.) 1033	*Festung Girondemündung Nord*
Feldgend.-Trupp (tmot.) 1034	*Festung Girondemündung Süd*
Feldgend.-Trupp 1035	*?*
Feldgend.-Trupp 1036	*Panzer Div. Holste*
Feldgend.-Trupp d (mot.) 1043	*Heeresgruppe Süd*
Feldgend.-Trupp d (tmot.) 1044	*Heeresgruppe Süd*
Feldgend.-Trupp d (tmot.) 1045	*Heeresgruppe Mitte*
Feldgend.-Trupp 1046	*148 Reserve Div./ Oberkommando Heeresgruppe A*
Feldgend.-Trupp d (tmot.) 1047	*Oberkommando Heeresgruppe A*
Feldgend.-Trupp d (tmot.) 1048	*156 Reserve Div.*
Feldgend.-Trupp 10498	*Gebirgs Div./Kommandant Böhmen-Mähren*
Feldgend.-Trupp 1056	*156 Reserve Div.*
Feldgend.-Trupp 1057	*?*
Feldgend.-Trupp 1058	*?*
Feldgend.-Trupp 1059	*159 Infanterie Div.*
Feldgend.-Trupp 1062	*Wehrkreis XXI*
Feldgend.-Trupp 1063	*Wehrkreis XXI*
Feldgend.-Trupp 1064	*188 Gebirgs Div./ Wehrkreis XXI*
Feldgend.-Trupp 1071	*189 Infanterie Div.*
Feldgend.-Trupp 1088	*191 Reserve Div.*
Feldgend.-Trupp 1089	*189 Infanterie Div.*
Feldgend.-Trupp 1091	*191 reserve Div.*
Feldgend.-Trupp d 1109	*Wehrkreis XXI*
Feldgend.-Trupp d 1110	*Wehrkreis XXI*

Feldgend.-Trupp d 1122	Feldkommandantur 605
Feldgend.-Trupp d 1123	Feldkommandantur 725
Feldgend.-Trupp d 1124	Feldkommandantur 817
Feldgend.-Trupp d 1125	Feldkommandantur 1030
Feldgend.-Trupp d 1126	Feldkommandantur 1034
Feldgend.-Trupp d 1127	Feldkommandantur 1039
Feldgend.-Trupp d 1128	Feldkommandantur 1040
Feldgend.-Trupp 1129	Feldkommandantur 1042
Feldgend.-Trupp 114	1176 Infanterie Div./ Oberfeldkommandantur Lublin
Feldgend.-Trupp 1142	Deutsche Wehrmacht in Italien
Feldgend.-Trupp d (tmot.) 1144	Wehrmacht Kommandantur Rotterdam
Feldgend.-Trupp d (tmot.) 1145	Feldkommandantur 243
Feldgend.-Trupp d (tmot.) 1146	Feldkommandantur 245
Feldgend.-Trupp d (tmot.) 1147	Wehrmacht Kommandantur Amsterdam
Feldgend.-Trupp d (tmot.) 1148	Wehrmacht Kommandantur Minsk
Feldgend.-Trupp d (tmot.) 1149	Wehrmacht Kommandantur Riga
Feldgend.-Trupp 1151	Kommando Böhmen-Mähren
Feldgend.-Trupp d (tmot.) 1152	Oberbefehlshaber Südost
Feldgend.-Trupp 1176	541 Volksgrenadier Div.
Feldgend.-Trupp 1180	542 Volksgrenadier Div.
Feldgend.-Trupp 1316	16 Infanterie Div.
Feldgend.-Trupp c (mot.) 1340	Wehrkreis XXI
Feldgend.-Trupp c (tmot.) 1416	Generalkommando XVI Armeekorps
Feldgend.-Trupp c (tmot,) 1463	Generalkommando LXIII Armeekorps
Feldgend.-Trupp 1541	543 Grenadier Div.
Feldgend.-Trupp 1542	542 Grenadier Div.
Feldgend.-Trupp 1543	543 Grenadier Div.
Feldgend.-Trupp 1544	544 Grenadier Div.
Feldgend.-Trupp 1545	545 Grenadier Div.
Feldgend.-Trupp 1546	546 Grenadier Div.
Feldgend.-Trupp c 1547	547 Grenadier Div.
Feldgend.-Trupp c 1548	548 Grenadier Div.
Feldgend.-Trupp c 1549	549 Grenadier Div.
Feldgend.-Trupp c 1550	550 Grenadier Div.
Feldgend.-Trupp c 1551	551 Grenadier Div.
Feldgend.-Trupp c 1552	552 Grenadier Div.
Feldgend.-Trupp c c (tmot.) 1553	553 Grenadier Div.
Feldgend.-Trupp c 1558	558 Grenadier Div.
Feldgend.-Trupp c 1559	559 Grenadier Div.
Feldgend.-Trupp 1560	?
Feldgend.-Trupp c 1561	561 Grenadier Div.
Feldgend.-Trupp c 1562	562 Grenadier Div.
Feldgend.-Trupp 1563	Grenadier Lehr Div.
Feldgend.-Trupp 1564	564 Volksgrenadier Div.

Feldgend.-Trupp 1565	565 Volksgrenadier Div.
Feldgend.-Trupp 1566	566 Volksgrenadier Div.
Feldgend.-Trupp 1567	567 Volksgrenadier Div.
Feldgend.-Trupp 1568	568 Volksgrenadier Div.
Feldgend.-Trupp 1569	569 Volksgrenadier Div.
Feldgend.-Trupp 1570	570 Volksgrenadier Div.
Feldgend.-Trupp 1571	571 Volksgrenadier Div.
Feldgend.-Trupp 1572	572 Volksgrenadier Div.
Feldgend.-Trupp 1573	573 Volksgrenadier Div.
Feldgend.-Trupp 1574	574 Volksgrenadier Div.
Feldgend.-Trupp 1575	575 Volksgrenadier Div.
Feldgend.-Trupp 1576	576 Volksgrenadier Div.
Feldgend.-Trupp 1577	577 Volksgrenadier Div.
Feldgend.-Trupp 1578	578 Volksgrenadier Div.
Feldgend.-Trupp 1579	579 Volksgrenadier Div.
Feldgend.-Trupp 1580	580 Volksgrenadier Div.
Feldgend.-Trupp 1581	581 Volksgrenadier Div.
Feldgend.-Trupp 1582	582 Volksgrenadier Div.
Feldgend.-Trupp 1600	600 (russ.) Infanterie Div.
Feldgend.-Trupp 1606	606 Infanterie Div. z.b.V.
Feldgend.-Trupp 1609	18 Volksgrenadier Div.
Feldgend.-Trupp 1650	650 (russ.) Infanterie Div.
Feldgend.-Trupp 1818	18 Volksgrenadier Div.
Feldgend.-Trupp a (mot.) z.b.V. 1901	Wehrkreis Böhmen-Mähren
Feldgend.-Trupp a (mot.) z.b.V. 1902	Wehrkreis Böhmen-Mähren
Feldgend.-Trupp a (mot.) z.b.V. 1903	Wehrkreis Böhmen-Mähren
Feldgend.-Trupp a (mot.) z.b.V. 2901	Wehrkreis Böhmen-Mähren
Feldgend.-Trupp a (mot.) z.b.V. 2902	Wehrkreis Böhmen-Mähren
Feldgend.-Trupp a (mot.) z.b.V. 2903	Wehrkreis Böhmen-Mähren
Feldgend.-Trupp a (mot.) z.b.V. 3901	Wehrkreis Böhmen-Mähren
Feldgend.-Trupp a (mot.) z.b.V. 3902	Wehrkreis Böhmen-Mähren
Feldgend.-Trupp a (mot.) z.b.V. 3903	Wehrkreis Böhmen-Mähren
Feldgend.-Trupp Feldherrnhalle	Panzergrenadier Div. Feldherrnhalle
Feldgend.-Trupp Führer-Grenadier-Brigade	Führer-Grenadier-Brigade

Feldgend.-Trupp Panzer Div. Jüterbog	Panzer Div. Jüterbog
Feldgend.-Trupp Panzer Div. Schlesien	Panzer Div. Schlesien
Feldgend.-Trupp Brandenburg	Panzergrenadier Div. Brandenburg
Feldgend.-Trupp Div. Ulrich v. Hutten	Div. Ulrich v. Hutten
Feldgend.-Trupp Panzer Div. Muncheberg	Panzer Div. Muncheberg
Feldgend.-Trupp 10 Panzer Div.	10 Panzer Div.
Feldgend.-Trupp Grossdeutschland	Panzergrenadier Div. Grossdeustchland
Feldgend.-Trupp 500 Grossdeustchland	Generalkommando Panzerkorps Grossdeutschland
Feldgend.-Trupp Kfz. Transport Regt. 602	Kfz. Transport Regt. 602
Feldgend.-Trupp Kfz. Transport Regt. 605	Kfz. Transport Regt. 605
Feldgend.-Trupp Sonderverband 287	Sonderverband 287
Feldgend.-Trupp Sardinien	?
Feldgend.-Trupp Stabsoffizier Dänemark	S tabsoffizier Dänemark
Feldgend.-Trupp Festung Kreta	?
Feldgend.-Trupp z.b.V. AOK Norwegen	AOK Norwegen
Feldgend.-Trupp Oderkorps	?
Feldgend.-Trupp Ostpreussen 1	?
Feldgend.-Trupp Ostpreussen 2	?
Feldgend.-Trupp z.b.V	?
Feldgend.-Trupp Landwehr 161	?
Feldgend.-Trupp Höheres Kommando LIX	Höheres Kommando LIX
Feldgend.-Trupp Venedig	?
Feldgend.-Trupp Div. Generalgouvernement	?
Feldgend.-Trupp 2/238	?
Feldgend.-Trupp 90 leichte Div.	90 leichte Div.
Feldgend.-Trupp Panzer-Lehr Div.	Panzer-Lehr Div.
Feldgendarmerie Abteilung 501	Korück 501/ Militärverwaltung Frankreich/ Korück 560/ Befehlshaber Südgriechenland/ Armeeoberkommando 12/ Heeresgruppe E

Feldgendarmerie Abteilung 521	*Korück 520/ Panzerarmeeoberkommando 4/ Heeresgruppe Nordukraine*
Feldgendarmerie Abteilung 531	*Korück 530/ 9 Armee*
Feldgendarmerie Abteilung 541	*Korück 540/ 6 Armee/ Heeresgruppe C/ 14 Armee*
Feldgendarmerie Abteilung 551	*Korück 550/ 7 Armee/ Panzerarmeeoberkommando 3/ 4 Panzerarmee*
Feldgendarmerie Abteilung 561	*Korück 560/ 16 Armee*
Feldgendarmerie Abteilung 571	*Korück 570/ 6 Armee*
Feldgendarmerie Abteilung 581	*Korück 580/ 4 Armee/ 2 Armee*
Feldgendarmerie Abteilung 591	*Korück 590/ 1 Armee/ 2 Panzerarmee*
Feldgendarmerie Abteilung 613	*Panzerarmee Afrika*
Feldgendarmerie Abteilung 682	*1 Panzerarmee/ Heeresgruppe Süd/ Heeresgruppe A*
Feldgendarmerie Abteilung 683	*Korück 540/ 10 Armee/12 Armee/11 Armee /Korück 553/ 8 Armee/ Korück 558*
Feldgendarmerie Abteilung 685	*Heeresgruppe Süd/ 2 Armee/17 Armee/ 1 Panzerarmee/ 4 Armee*
Feldgendarmerie Abteilung 689	*Armeeoberkommando 18*
Feldgendarmerie Abteilung 690	*Befehlshaber Rückw. Heeresgebeit Mitte/ Befehlshaber Weissruthenien/7 Armee*
Feldgendarmerie Abteilung 691	*Befehlshaber Rückw. Heeresgebeit Nord/ Befehlshaber Ostungarn/17 Armee*
Feldgendarmerie Abteilung 692	*Befehlshaber Rückw. Heeresgebeit Süd/ 10 Armee*
Feldgendarmerie Abteilung 693	*17 Armee/Panzerarmeeoberkommando 5/15 Armee*
Feldgendarmerie Abteilung 694	*3 Panzerarmee/ 17 Armee/Heeresgruppe Südukraine/Heeresgruppe Süd*
Feldgendarmerie Abteilung 695	*4 Armee/ 3 Panzerarmee/Feldgendarmerie Abteilung 696 4 Armee/ 2 Armee/ Heeresgruppe E*
Feldgendarmerie Abteilung 697	*4 Panzerarmee/ Feldkommandantur Heeresgruppe Nord*
Feldgendarmerie Abteilung 698	*Rückw. Heeresgebeit derHeeresgruppe A*
Feldgendarmerie-Ersatz-Abteilung 1	*Feldgendarmerie Ersatz Regiment*
Feldgendarmerie-Ersatz-Abteilung 2	*Feldgendarmerie Ersatz Regiment*
Feldgendarmerie-Ersatz-Abteilung 3	*Feldgendarmerie Ersatz Regiment*
Feldgendarmerie Kompanie B1	
Feldgendarmerie Kompanie B2	
Feldgendarmerie Kompanie B3	
Feldgendarmerie Kompanie B4	
Feldgendarmerie Kompanie B5	
Feldgendarmerie Kompanie B7	
Feldgendarmerie Kompanie G1	
Feldgendarmerie Kompanie G2	
Feldgendarmerie Kompanie G3	

Feldgendarmerie Kompanie G5	
Feldgendarmerie Kompanie G6	
Feldgendarmerie Kompanie G7	
Feldgendarmerie Kompanie G8	
Feldgendarmerie Kompanie G9	
Feldgendarmerie Kompanie G10	
Feldgendarmerie Kompanie 19	*XXIII Armeekorps*
Feldgendarmerie Kompanie 61	*II Panzer Division*
Feldgendarmerie Kompanie 64	*404 Infanterie Division*
Feldgendarmerie Kompanie 66	*?*
Feldgendarmerie Kompanie (mot.) 220	*164 Infanterie Division (Festungs Division Kreta)*
Feldgendarmerie Kompanie (mot.) 236	*162 (turk.) Infanterie Division*
Feldgendarmerie Kompanie 602	*Korück 566 Afrika*
Feldgendarmerie Kompanie 613	*Panzerarmee Afrika/Heerestrupp (Trop.)*
Feldgendarmerie Kompanie 614 (Tunis)	*?*
Feldgendarmerie Kompanie 684	*413 Infanterie Division*
Feldgendarmerie Kompanie (mot.) 757	*Wehrkreis XX*
Feldgendarmerie Kompanie 904	*Festung Division Kreta*
Feldgendarmerie Kompanie 914	*Oberfeldkommandantur Warschau*
Feldgendarmerie Kompanie Grossdeutschland	*Panzergrenadier Div. Grossdeutschland*
Feldgendarmerie Kompanie Aufrichtungstab 16	*?*
Feldgendarmerie Einsatz-Kompanie z.b.V. B.d.O. Italien	*B.d.O. Italien*
Feldgendarmerie-Gruppe Neapel	*Deutsche Standortoffizier Neapel*
Feldgendarmerie-Gruppe 466	*66 Reserve Korps*
Feldgendarmerie-Gruppe 577	*Kommandant, Heeres Gebiet Süd- Frankreich*
Feldgendarmerie-Gruppe 642 Livorno	*Standortoffizier Livorno*
Feldgendarmerie-Gruppe 644 Reggio	*Standortoffizier Reggio*
Feldgendarmerie-Gruppe 659	*Kommandant, Heeres Gebiet Süd- Frankreich*
Feldgendarmerie-Gruppe 711	*Kommandant, Heeres Gebiet Süd- Frankreich*
Feldgendarmerie-Gruppe 730	*Kommandant, Heeres Gebiet Süd- Frankreich*
Feldgendarmerie-Gruppe 732	*Kommandant, Heeres Gebiet Süd- Frankreich*
Feldgendarmerie-Gruppe 734	*Kommandant, Heeres Gebiet Süd-Frankreich*
Feldgendarmerie-Gruppe 739	*Kommandant, Heeres Gebiet Süd-Frankreich*
Feldgendarmerie-Gruppe 747	*Kommandant, Heeres Gebiet Süd- Frankreich*
Feldgendarmerie-Gruppe 761	*Kommandant, Heeres Gebiet Süd-Frankreich*

Feldgendarmerie-Gruppe 792	*Kommandant, Heeres Gebiet Süd-Frankreich*
Feldgendarmerie-Gruppe 798	*Kommandant, Heeres Gebiet Süd-Frankreich*
Feldgendarmerie-Gruppe 800	*Kommandant, Heeres Gebiet Süd-Frankreich*
Feldgendarmerie-Gruppe 802	*Kommandant, Heeres Gebiet Süd-Frankreich*
Feldgendarmerie-Gruppe 806	*Kommandant, Heeres Gebiet Süd- Frankreich*
Feldgendarmerie-Gruppe d 964	*Kommandant, Heeres Gebiet Süd- Frankreich*
Feldgendarmerie-Gruppe d 967	*Kommandant, Heeres Gebiet Süd- Frankreich*
Feldgendarmerie-Gruppe 983	*Kommandant, Heeres Gebiet Süd-Frankreich*
Feldgendarmerie-Gruppe d 986	*Kommandant, Heeres Gebiet Süd-Frankreich*
Feldgendarmerie-Gruppe 987	*Kommandant, Heeres Gebiet Süd-Frankreich*
Feldgendarmerie-Gruppe 988	*Kommandant, Heeres Gebiet Süd-Frankreich*
Feldgendarmerie-Gruppe 989	*Kommandant, Heeres Gebiet Süd-Frankreich*
Feldgendarmerie-Gruppe 990	*Kommandant, Heeres Gebiet Süd-Frankreich/416 Infanterie Div.*
Feldgendarmerie-Gruppe 992	*Kommandant, Heeres Gebiet Süd-Frankreich*
Feldgendarmerie-Gruppe 993	*Kommandant, Heeres Gebiet Süd-Frankreich*
Feldgendarmerie-Gruppe 994	*Kommandant, Heeres Gebiet Süd-Frankreich*
Feldgendarmerie-Gruppe 995	*Kommandant, Heeres Gebiet Süd-Frankreich*
Feldgendarmerie-Gruppe 996	*Kommandant, Heeres Gebiet Süd-Frankreich/416 Infanterie Div.*
Feldgendarmerie-Gruppe 997	*Kommandant, Heeres Gebiet Süd-Frankreich/416 Infanterie Div.*
Feldgendarmerie-Gruppe 998	*Militärbefehlshaber in Frankreich, Militärverwaltung Bezirk C*
Feldgendarmerie-Gruppe 1009	*Oberkommando Heeresgruppe B*
Feldgendarmerie-Gruppe 1010	*Oberkommando Heeresgruppe B*
Feldgendarmerie-Gruppe 1011	*Oberkommando Heeresgruppe B*
Feldgendarmerie-Gruppe 1012	*Oberkommando Heeresgruppe B*
Feldgend Staffel 1-2, Wehrmacht Wirtschafts Erfassungs	*Kommando 9*
Feldgendarmerie-Kompanie beim Rhein-Kommandant I	*Rhein-Kommandant I*
Feldgendarmerie Kommando Grob der Feldjager Regt 3	*Feldjäger Regtment 3*
Feldgendarmerie Feld-Ersatz-Komp 183	*?*
1. Kompanie Feldgendarmerie-Bataillon Hauptquartier Ob.d.L.,	*H.Q. Ob.d.L.*
2. Kompanie Feldgendarmerie-Bataillon Hauptquartier Ob.d.L.,	*H.Q. Ob.d.L.*
3. Kompanie Feldgendarmerie-Bataillon Hauptquartier Ob.d.L.	*H.Q. Ob.d.L.*
Feldgendarmerie Ersatz Regiment	*Litzmannstadt/ Prague*

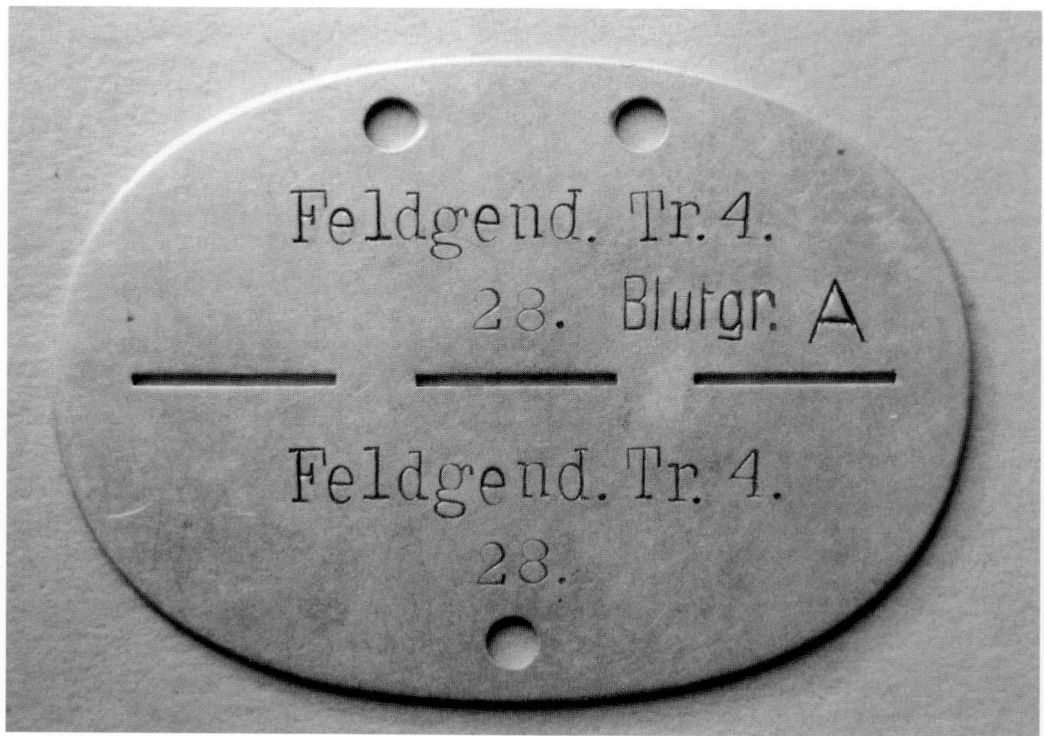

Feldgendarmerie ID Disc. The disc records the name of the unit, the individual's roster number within the unit and the individual's blood group.

Feldgendarmerie from I Gebirgs Division at a unit formal dinner.

Off duty *Feldgendarmen* relax with a few bottles of wine. Just visible in the centre background a gorget can be seen hanging from a peg.

Feldgendarmen pose outside their duty room, occupied Russia May 1942.

Personnel from *Feldgendarmerie Trupp* 468. Note that only a minority wear the *Feldgendarmerie* cufftitle.

Feldgendarmen survey the devastation caused by German bombardment at Dnjepropetrovsk.

The *Feldgendarm* in this shot wears a summer uniform in light weight field grey drill material.

A *Feldgendarm* patrolling the streets of a bombed out district. Prevention of looting was an occasional duty for the military police. (*Josef Charita*)

In walking out dress and camera in hand, an off-duty *Feldgendarm* enjoys a stroll somewhere in occupied Europe.

Feldgendarmerie often provided security for senior officers. Note the NCO in the background at this meeting of *Generaloberst* Ewald von Kleist and *SS-Gruppenführer* 'Sepp' Dietrich. (*Clyde R. Davis*)

Feldgendarmerie with uniformed and plain clothes members of the French *Gendarmerie* after the fall of France in 1940.

Feldgendarmerie pose with some local peasants in occupied Russia.

A rather stern looking *Feldgendarmerie* NCO with captured French colonial troops, France 1940.

Feldgendarmerie guarding a minor river crossing. Note the map case worn by the NCO.

Two *Feldgendarmerie Unteroffiziere*. The fact that only one wears the steel helmet suggests that they are not in a combat zone.

Feldgendarmerie Gefreiter in greatcoat with the duty gorget. (Sebastian Golawski)

Note, from the figure on the right, that wearing of the bayonet was normal, off duty, even when the rifle itself was not carried.

Off duty *Feldgendarmerie* NCOs with motorcyclist wearing the duty gorget.

A *Feldgendarmerie Unteroffizier* bids farewell to his family on his return to his unit after a period of leave.

Taken by a *Feldgendarm*, this photo shows the huge POW holding area at Uman in the Ukraine.

On this shot of *Feldgendarm*en from *Sonderverband* 287, the Infantry Assault Badge can just be seen on the pocket of the soldier at extreme left.

France 1940 and *Feldgendarmerie* NCOs pose with a captured British Mk IV Cruiser tank.

Above: A *Feldgendarmerie* ID disc. This rare example is to a member of the Cossack (Ost) *Kompanie* of *Feldgendarmerie Abteilung* 581.

Right: Although on duty, as signified by the gorget, this enlisted rank appears unarmed, suggesting he is based on the home front.

Feldgendarm guarding Soviet POWs. Given that he is unarmed, there is obviously no expectation that they would abscond.

*Feldgendarm*en taking a rest. Presumably on the home front or rear area as the dog accompanying them appears to be a pet.

Knocked out enemy vehicles were a popular spot to pose for photos. Here a *Feldgendarm* sits on a knocked out Soviet KV I.

An extremely rare metal vehicle pennant for the *Feldgendarmerie Trupp* of the elite *Grossdeutschland* Division. (*Sebastian Golawski*)

Traffic Control Batallions—*Verkehrsregelungsbataillonen*

The movement of huge field armies during the early weeks of the Second World War had shown that the existing military police formations were inadequate to ensure efficient movement of so many troops. This resulted in the formation of ten new battalions of transport control troops. Each fully motorised battalion consisted of a staff element plus two companies of 150 NCOs and men.

Ultimately, the growth of the *Feldgendarmerie* meant that these separate units were no longer required and during the course of 1942 they were gradually disbanded, as their tasks were completely taken over by the *Feldgendarmerie*. Most were distributed to various *Feldgendarmerie* units and in some cases entire new *Feldgendarmerie* units were formed by direct transfers from VKB units.

The only special insignia worn by these troops was an armband worn on the left sleeve. It was normally in an orange colour though variations exist in a pinkish shade, with the text '*Verkehrs-Aufsicht*' in Latin script.

Order of Battle—*Verkehrsregelungs-Bataillonen*

Verkehrsregulierungs Staffel VI. This short lived unit is believed to have been formed in October 1940 and was disbanded in February 1941.

Verkehrsregelungs-Bataillon 751. Formed 28 October 1939 *Wehrkreis V*, disbanded 1942. Served in France and Russia with *16 Armee*.

Verkehrsregelungs-Bataillon 752 Formed 30 October 1939 *Wehrkreis VI*, disbanded 1942. Served in France and Russia with *9 Armee*.

Verkehrsregelungs-Bataillon 753 Formed 30 October 1939 *Wehrkreis VI*, disbanded 1942. Served in France with *4 Armee* and Russia with *18 Armee*.

Verkehrsregelungs-Bataillon 754 Formed 28 October 1939 *Wehrkreis IX*, disbanded 1942. Served in France and Russia with *4 Armee*.

Verkehrsregelungs-Bataillon 755 Formed 26 October 1939 *Wehrkreis IX* ,disbanded 1942. Served in France with *Gruppe von Kleist* and Russia with *2 Panzerarmee*. Elements were used to constitute *Feldgendarmerie Kompanie 755*.

Verkehrsregelungs-Bataillon 756 Formed 26 October 1939 *Wehrkreis IX* , disbanded 1942. Served in France and Russia with *11 Armee*. Elements were used to constitute *Feldgendarmerie Kompanie 756*.

Verkehrsregelungs-Bataillon 757 Formed 26 October 1939 *Wehrkreis IX*, disbanded 1942. Served in France with *12 Armee* and in Russia with *2 Armee*. Elements were used to constitute *I./. Feldgendarmerie Abteilung 698* and the remainder were transferred to *Feldgendarmerie Abteilung 581*.

Verkehrsregelungs-Bataillon 758 Formed 30 October 1939 *Wehrkreis X*, disbanded 1942. Served

France and Russia with *2 Armee*.

Verkehrsregelungs-Bataillon 759 Formed 30 October 1939 *Wehrkreis X*, disbanded 1942. Served France and in Russia with *6 Armee*. Elements were used to constitute *3./ Feldgendarmerie Abteilung 698* and the remainder were transferred to *Feldgendarmerie Abteilung 571*.

Verkehrsregelungs-Bataillon 760 Formed 30 October 1939 *Wehrkreis XIII* , disbanded 1942. Served France with *2 Armee* and in Russia with *17 Armee*. Elements were used to constitute 2./ *Feldgendarmerie* Abteilung 698 whilst the remainder were reformed as *Feldgendarmerie* Kompanie 760.

Above left: Traffic points duty in occupied Russia. The fact that there appears to be no traffic present suggests a staged shot!

Above right: Feldgendarm with camouflage painted Horch heavy field car. (*Josef Charita*)

A *Feldgendarm* directing traffic over a bridge in Russia.

Controlling and directing military traffic was one of the most important of all the *Feldgendarmerie*'s tasks.

(ii) Feldgendarmerie der Luftwaffe

During the early part of the war, the *Luftwaffe* had no need for its own military police branch, the few small field units of the Regiment *General Göring* would in any case not, under normal circumstances, have been entitled to a *Feldgendarmerie-Trupp*.

By 1942 however, Göring's overwhelming ambitions had seen not only the expansion of his personal regiment to divisional status, but the creation of the first of the *Luftwaffe* field divisions. Eventually, 22 such divisions would be created.

Initially, the *Feldgendarmerie* sections of these *Luftwaffe* field units were considered as part of the divisional transport and supply (*Nachschub*) element. This situation remained until *Luftwaffen Verordnungsblatt 43, Nr. 1115* of 3 June 43 decreed that the *Feldgendarmerie* was to be considered a separate branch in its own right.

Each major field unit of the *Luftwaffe* was allocated a *Feldgendarmerie-Trupp* and the *Trupp* was the standard *Feldgendarmerie* unit strength throughout the *Luftwaffe*. There were no *Feldgendarmerie-Abteilungen* within the Order of Battle of the *Luftwaffe*. The exception to the use of *Trupp* sized units was a battalion comprising an HQ element and three companies of *Feldgendarmerie* which was located with Göring's personal headquarter, the *Feldgendarmerie-Bataillon Hauptquartier Oberbefehlshaber der Luftwaffe*.

It should be noted that the *Feldgendarmerie* of the *Luftwaffe* existed solely to support its field units (with the exception of Göring's headquarters battalion). The *Luftwaffe* did not maintain the widespread network of units fielded by the army through the various *Wehrkreis* on the home front, or with *Orts-* and *Feldkommandantura*. Any tasks required by these areas were carried out by *Feldgendarmerie* units of the *Heer*.

Uniforms and Insignia

Feldgendarmerie personnel within the *Luftwaffe* wore absolutely standard *Luftwaffe* uniforms and equipment, only the use of the following special insignia indicating their status as military policemen.

The principal form of dress which appears, from photographic evidence to have been worn by *Luftwaffe Feldgendarmerie* were the *Fliegerbluse*, tropical tunic in hot climates, camouflaged smock worn over the *Fliegerbluse* by *Fallschirmjäger* units and four pocket M43 style tunic worn by the *Hermann Göring* Division.

This shot is one of several unexplained images that emerged recently showing Police troops wearing a *Luftwaffe* gorget. It is however a standard bearers gorget not a *Feldgendarmerie* gorget, though it seems certain they are carrying out some sort of provost function.

Above left: Luftwaffe NCO once again clearly wearing the army pattern gorget.

Above right: A *Feldgendarm* from the elite Hermann Göring Division. (*Ludwig Dinger*)

Two soldiers appear in front of a *Luftwaffe* Field Court Martial. (*Herbert Kail*)

Note the sign on this Opel Blitz truck '*Feldgericht der Lw*' (Luftwaffe Field Court Martial). (*Herbert Kail*)

Even at the front, the military policeman was plagued with paperwork. Shown here is *Unteroffizier* Herbert Kail from *Feldgendarmerie*trupp 'HG'. (*Herbert Kail*)

Feldgendarmerie from the Hermann Göring Division on the Eastern Front. (*Herbert Kail*)

Luftwaffe Feldgendarmen on Sicily. (*Herbert Kail*)

Hermann Göring Division *Feldgendarm* with the Divisional band in the background. Most of the members of the '*Musikzug*' were absorbed into the *Feldgendarmerie*trupp. (Herbert Kail)

Shoulder straps

Initially, as stated above, until June 1943 the *Feldgendarmerie* were considered as part of the divisional transport and supply element as as such wore the pale blue *Waffenfarbe* of this branch as piping to the grey blue NCO and enlisted shoulder straps and as underlay to officer's shoulder straps.

After June 1943, *Luftwaffe* military policemen would wear the same orange-red *Waffenfarbe* as members of the *Heer* and *SS-Feldgendarmerie*. The only exception to this was the *Feldgendarmerie* elements of the *Fallschirmjäger* divisions who are said to have worn the basic golden-yellow *Waffenfarbe* applicable to *Fallschirmjäger* personnel. There is however, some evidence that this may not have been the case and that *Fallschirmjäger Feldgendarmerie* may have worn the same *Waffenfarbe* colours as members of the field divisions and *Hermann Göring Division*.

Collar tabs

The standard collar tabs colour for the field divisions was the so-called 'rifle green' with white as the base colour for the *Hermann Göring Division*.

From inception until 1943, enlisted and NCO personnel of the field divisions wore *Waffenfarbe* piping in the branch colour around the edges of the collar tabs, matching that worn on the shoulder straps. This piping is believed to have been removed in April 1943 (at the same time as piping was ordered removed from tabs for the *Hermann Göring Division*) after which only the *Waffenfarbe* on the shoulder straps indicated the wearer's branch.

Finally, in early 1944, collar tabs became virtually defunct and enlisted men and NCOs either wore no collar adornment, or pinned the small metal rank wings from the collar tabs directly to the tunic collar. This of course applies to field tunics. The four pocket *Luftwaffe 'Rock'* would have retained the use of collar tabs.

Thus the appearance of the *Feldgendarm* in a *Luftwaffe* field division would be along the following lines:

Enlisted Men/NCOs

1942–43: Green collar tabs with light blue piping. Light blue piping to shoulder straps.
1943–44: Green collar tabs without piping. Orange piping to shoulder straps.
1944–45: No collar tabs. Orange piping to shoulder straps.

Officers

1942–43: Green collar tabs. Light blue underlay to shoulder straps.
1943–44: Green collar tabs. Orange underlay to shoulder straps.
1944–45: No collar tabs. Orange underlay to shoulder straps.

The *Hermann Göring* division followed a similar timetable. Initially enlisted men's/ NCOs collar tabs were worn with piping in *Waffenfarbe* colours, then had the piping removed and this was followed by cessation in the use of collar tabs on field uniforms. The appearance of a *Feldgendarm* in the *Hermann Göring* division would be along the following lines:

Enlisted Men/NCOs

1942–43: White collar tabs with light blue piping. Light blue piping to shoulder straps.
1943–44: White collar tabs without piping. Orange piping to shoulder straps.
1944–45: No Collar tabs. Orange piping to shoulder straps.

Officers
1942–43: White collar tabs. Light blue underlay to shoulder straps.
1943–44: White collar tabs. Orange underlay to shoulder straps.
1944–45: No collar tabs. Orange underlay to shoulder straps.

As previously mentioned, it has been reported that *Feldgendarmen* serving in *Fallschirmjäger* divisions wore the normal golden yellow *Waffenfarbe* of the *Fallschirmjäger*. However, photographic evidence shows *Feldgendarmen* wearing collar tabs that do not appear to be the light shade that yellow would appear as even in monotone photographs. The difficulty in establishing colours in a black and white image with any degree of certainty means that this question must, for now, remain somewhat of a mystery.

Cuffbands

Members of the *Luftwaffe Feldgendarmerie* wore the same standard machine woven rayon cuffband as their counterparts in the Heer as has been established in several original photographs. As with their *Heer* comrades, this would have ceased to be worn when the cuffband was ordered removed in 1944.

Arm Eagle

The use of the police style arm eagle by *Feldgendarmen* of the *Luftwaffe* seems to have been extremely rare. However, at least one wartime photo exists which shows the police arm eagle worn on the sleeve of the *Fliegerbluse*. Given the paucity of evidence of its wear it seems unlikely that a special version would have been made on *Luftwaffe* field blue cloth backing and the example seen on the photograph in question is most likely a standard army issue type on field grey.

Gorget

Once again we are faced with photographic evidence that the *Luftwaffe* made widespread use of the regular army pattern gorget. Certainly, as far as the *Fallschirmjäger* divisions are concerned, photographs show the army gorget in wear. The author is not aware of any photographs emerging which show the use of the special *Luftwaffe* pattern gorget by these units. What is clear however, is that the *Luftwaffe* pattern gorget was worn widely within the *Hermann Göring Division* and may also have been used by the *Luftwaffe* field divisions.

The *Luftwaffe* gorget is identical in design and construction to its *Heer* counterpart with the sole exception that the regular national emblem is replaced by a *Luftwaffe* style eagle and swastika. Original surviving examples of the *Luftwaffe* gorget are extremely rare, no doubt influenced by the fact that most of the units which used it fought predominantly on the Eastern Front.

Headgear

Visor caps for *Luftwaffe* officers from *Leutnant* to *Oberst* were piped in woven aluminium cord for all ranks regardless of branch so no special examples specific to the *Feldgendarmerie* existed.

Visor caps for enlisted men and NCOs did however carry crown and cap band piping in the appropriate *Waffenfarbe* colour. It appears that it was to say the least unusual to find NCOs within the field divisions wearing visor caps, the overseas cap or M43 field cap being the standard for of headdress. However, visor caps would be the normal form of dress with the four pocket tunic and as field division tunics in this pattern exist, it is likely that visor caps would have been worn with them. Theoretically at least, visor caps for those serving in the *Feldgendarmerie* of the field divisions would have been piped in light blue until the introduction of orange-red *Waffenfarbe* in June 1943. As the group photograph of *Luftwaffe Feldgendarmen* accompanying this text shows, visor caps were certainly worn by some *Feldgendarmen* though at this stage it is not possible to ascertain the colour of piping used on these caps, whether the rifle green of the field divisions, or the light blue or orange of the *Feldgendarmerie* branch. It is assumed that any visor caps worn by enlisted and NCO ranks of the *Hermann Göring Division* would have utilised that units unique white *Waffenfarbe*.

Unteroffizier Herbert Kail of the Hermann Göring Division can clearly be seen to be wearing the army pattern *Feldgendarmerie* cufftitle. (*Herbert Kail*)

Fine study of *Feldgendarmerie Unteroffizier* Ewald Nickel with his wife. Note the *Feldgendarmerie* cufftitle, and the *Luftwaffe* Ground Combat Badge.

Unteroffizier from the *Feldgendarmerie* of a *Luftwaffe Feld* Division. Though difficult to discern, he also wears the *Feldgendarmerie* sleeve eagle, rarely seen on *Luftwaffe* uniforms.

Horses were often used by *Feldgendarmerie* on the eastern front. This NCO is wearing the *Luftwaffe* pattern gorget. (*Herbert Kail*)

A group of *Luftwaffe Feldgendarmen* wearing the army pattern gorget. Note the MP40 carried by the junior NCO in the centre.

Luftwaffe Feldgendarmerie Units

Field Divisions

Initially, *Luftwaffe Feldgendarmerie* units were designated by name, e.g *Feldgendarmerie-Trupp der I Luftwaffen Feld Division*. This was subsequently changed some time around March 1943 so that all of the *Luftwaffe* field division units were allocated a four digit number in the 1100 range, thus the above became *Feldgendarmerie-Trupp 1101*. These units may (though by no means always) have the suffix *'der Luftwaffe'* added, so the first field division military police troop may be variously encountered as:

Feldgendarmerie-Trupp der I Luftwaffen Feld Division.
Feldgendarmerie-Trupp der Luftwaffe 1101.
Feldgendarmerie-Trupp 1101.

For the sake of simplicity, only the numerical designation is used in the following list. The last digit or pair of digits therefore indicating the feld division number. i.e. 1116 = *16 Luftwaffen Feld Division*.

Feldgendarmerie-Trupp 1101	*1 Luftwaffen Feld Division*
Feldgendarmerie-Trupp 1102	*2 Luftwaffen Feld Division*
Feldgendarmerie-Trupp 1103	*3 Luftwaffen Feld Division*
Feldgendarmerie-Trupp 1104	*4 Luftwaffen Feld Division*
Feldgendarmerie-Trupp 1105	*5 Luftwaffen Feld Division*
Feldgendarmerie-Trupp 1106	*6 Luftwaffen Feld Division*
Feldgendarmerie-Trupp 1107	*7 Luftwaffen Feld Division*
Feldgendarmerie-Trupp 1108	*8 Luftwaffen Feld Division*
Feldgendarmerie-Trupp 1109	*9 Luftwaffen Feld Division*
Feldgendarmerie-Trupp 1110	*10 Luftwaffen Feld Division*
Feldgendarmerie-Trupp 1111	*11 Luftwaffen Feld Division*
Feldgendarmerie-Trupp 1112	*12 Luftwaffen Feld Division*
Feldgendarmerie-Trupp 1113	*13 Luftwaffen Feld Division*
Feldgendarmerie-Trupp 1114	*14 Luftwaffen Feld Division*
Feldgendarmerie-Trupp 1115	*15 Luftwaffen Feld Division*
Feldgendarmerie-Trupp 1116	*16 Luftwaffen Feld Division*
Feldgendarmerie-Trupp 1117	*17 Luftwaffen Feld Division*
Feldgendarmerie-Trupp 1118	*18 Luftwaffen Feld Division*
Feldgendarmerie-Trupp 1119	*19 Luftwaffen Feld Division*
Feldgendarmerie-Trupp 1120	*20 Luftwaffen Feld Division*
Feldgendarmerie-Trupp 1121	*21 Luftwaffen Feld Division*
Feldgendarmerie-Trupp 1122	*22 Luftwaffen Feld Division*

Note:

The *Luftwaffe* field divisions were not a military success. So poor was their general level of achievement (though admittedly with some exceptions) that in November 1943, all those which had not already been destroyed were removed from *Luftwaffe* control and absorbed into the *Heer*. They retained their number but were then re-titled as, for example *16 Feld-Division (L)*

For some reason, a study of the German field post system does not reveal a field post number allocated for *Feldgendarmerie-Trupp 1107*. Given the very short life of this unit before it was virtually destroyed on the Eastern Front, it is possible that it was never allocated its own number and may have been administered by and dealt with under the same number as the divisional *Nachschub* element.

Fallschirmjäger Feldgendarmerie Units

Unlike the Field Divisions, the *Fallschirmjäger Feldgendarmerie* units were usually numbered in the same three digit system as their Heer counterparts.

Feldgendarmerie-Trupp a (mot.) 646	*1 Fallschirmjäger Div.*
Feldgendarmerie-Trupp a (mot.) 647	*2 Fallschirmjäger Div.*
Feldgendarmerie-Trupp a (mot.) 648	*3 Fallschirmjäger Div.*
Feldgendarmerie-Trupp a (mot.) 650	*4 Fallschirmjäger Div.*
Feldgendarmerie-Trupp a (mot.) 654	*5 Fallschirmjäger Div.*
Feldgendarmerie-Trupp 6 Fj. Div.	*6 Fallschirmjäger Div.*

Hermann Göring Division Feldgendarmerie Units

At approximately the same time that the *Feldgendarmerie* elements of the field units changed from a named to a numbered format, the *Feldgendarmerie* of the *Hermann Göring Division* did the same, becoming *Feldgendarmerie-Trupp 1000.*

Feldgend.-Trupp Panzer Div. Hermann Göring	Mar 43 to Sep 43.
Feldgend.-Trupp 1000	Sep 43 to Apr 44.
Feldgend.-Trupp Fallschirm Panzer Div. Hermann Göring	Nov 44 to May 45.
Feldgend.-Trupp Fallschirm Panzer Div. Hermann Göring 2	Nov 44 to May 45.

Corps Units

As with the *Heer*, the *Luftwaffe* fielded *Feldgendarmerie* units at corps level as part of the administrative machinery to support the control of the divisions for which the corps was responsible. In a similar manner to the field divisions, these began with named designations before changing to numbers.

Unit	**Period**	**Parent**
Feldgend.-Trupp III Luftwaffen Feldkorps	Jan 40 to Mar 43	*III Luftwaffen Feldkorps*
Feldgend.-Trupp c (tmot.) 63	Sep 43 to Apr 44	*III Luftwaffen Feldkorps*
Feldgend.-Trupp IV Luftwaffen Feldkorps	Jan 40 to Mar 43	*IV Luftwaffen Feldkorps*
Feldgend.-Trupp c (tmot.) 64	Sep 43 to Apr 44	*IV Luftwaffen Feldkorps*
Feldgend.-Trupp V Luftwaffen Feldkorps	Jan 40 to Sep 43	*V Luftwaffen Feldkorps*
Feldgend.-Trupp XIII Luftwaffen Fliegerkorps	Jan 40 to Mar 43	*XIII Fliegerkorps*
Feldgend.-Trupp b (mot.) 675	From May 44	*I Fallschirmkorps*
Feldgend.-Trupp b (mot.) 676	From Jan 44	*II Fallschirmkorps*

Soldbuch
zugleich Personalausweis
Nr.
für
den Wachtmeister
(Dienstgrad)
ab
ab
ab Lt. d. Feldgend.
(Vor- und Zuname)
Erkennungsmarke
Blutgruppe
Gasmaskengröße
Wehrnummer
1

Soldbuch of *Leutnant* der *Feldgendarmerie* Alfons Liehr. The photo shows him as a *Stabsfeldwebel* before his commissioning. He previously served with the *Feldgendarmerie* of II *Luftwaffen Feld* Division before command of these *Luftwaffe* units was taken over by the Army, hence his photograph in army uniform.

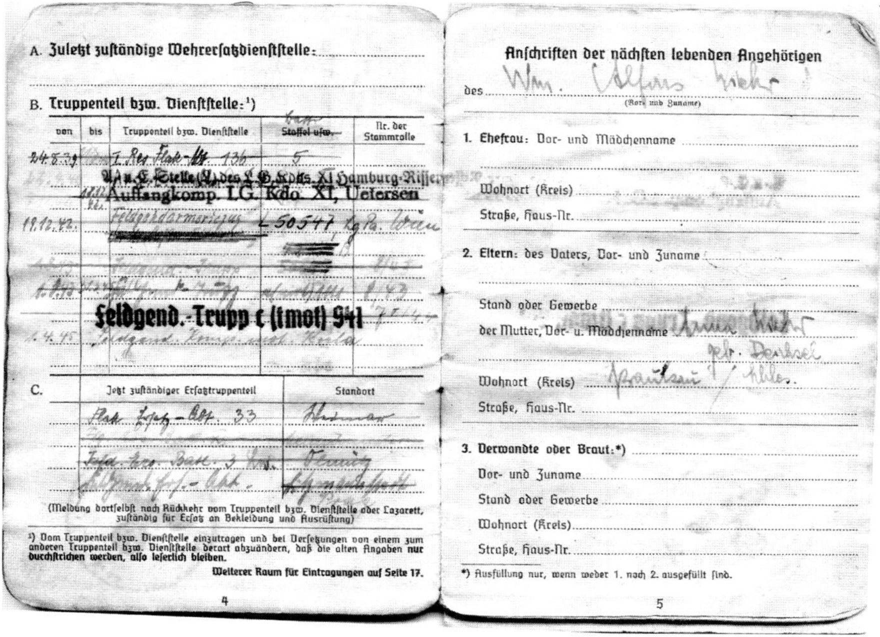

A. Zuletzt zuständige Wehrersatzdienststelle:

B. Truppenteil bzw. Dienststelle:¹)

von	bis	Truppenteil bzw. Dienststelle	Staffel usw.	Nr. der Stammrolle
		A. u. E. Stelle (L) des L.G. Kdos. XI Hamburg-Rissen		
		Auffangkomp. LG. Kdo. XI, Uetersen		
		Feldgend.-Trupp c (mot) 941		

C.

Jetzt zuständiger Ersatztruppenteil	Standort

(Meldung dortselbst nach Rückkehr vom Truppenteil bzw. Dienststelle oder Lazarett, zuständig für Ersatz an Bekleidung und Ausrüstung)

¹) Vom Truppenteil bzw. Dienststelle einzutragen und bei Versetzungen von einem zum anderen Truppenteil bzw. Dienststelle derart abzuändern, daß die alten Angaben nur durchstrichen werden, also leserlich bleiben.

Weiterer Raum für Eintragungen auf Seite 17.

4

Anschriften der nächsten lebenden Angehörigen

des
(Vor- und Zuname)

1. Ehefrau: Vor- und Mädchenname
Wohnort (Kreis)
Straße, Haus-Nr.

2. Eltern: des Vaters, Vor- und Zuname
Stand oder Gewerbe
der Mutter, Vor- u. Mädchenname
Wohnort (Kreis)
Straße, Haus-Nr.

3. Verwandte oder Braut:*)
Vor- und Zuname
Stand oder Gewerbe
Wohnort (Kreis)
Straße, Haus-Nr.

*) Ausfüllung nur, wenn weder 1. noch 2. ausgefüllt sind.

5

The Liehr *Soldbuch* with the marked entry showing *Feldgendarmerietrupp* a (mot) IIII, the *Feldgendarmerie* unit of II *Luftwaffen Feld* Division.

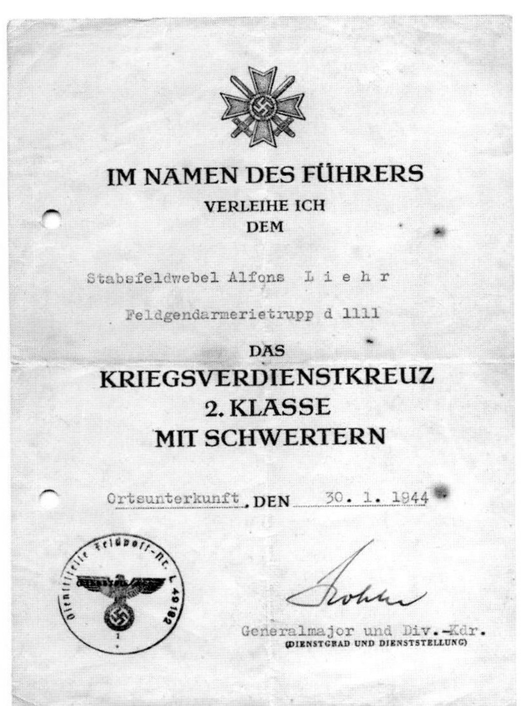

IM NAMEN DES FÜHRERS
VERLEIHE ICH
DEM

Stabsfeldwebel Alfons Liehr

Feldgendarmerietrupp d 1111

DAS
KRIEGSVERDIENSTKREUZ
2. KLASSE
MIT SCHWERTERN

Ortsunterkunft, DEN 30. 1. 1944

Generalmajor und Div.-Kdr.
(DIENSTGRAD UND DIENSTSTELLUNG)

Award document for the War Merit Cross to Alfred Liehr of II *Luftwaffen Feld* Division.

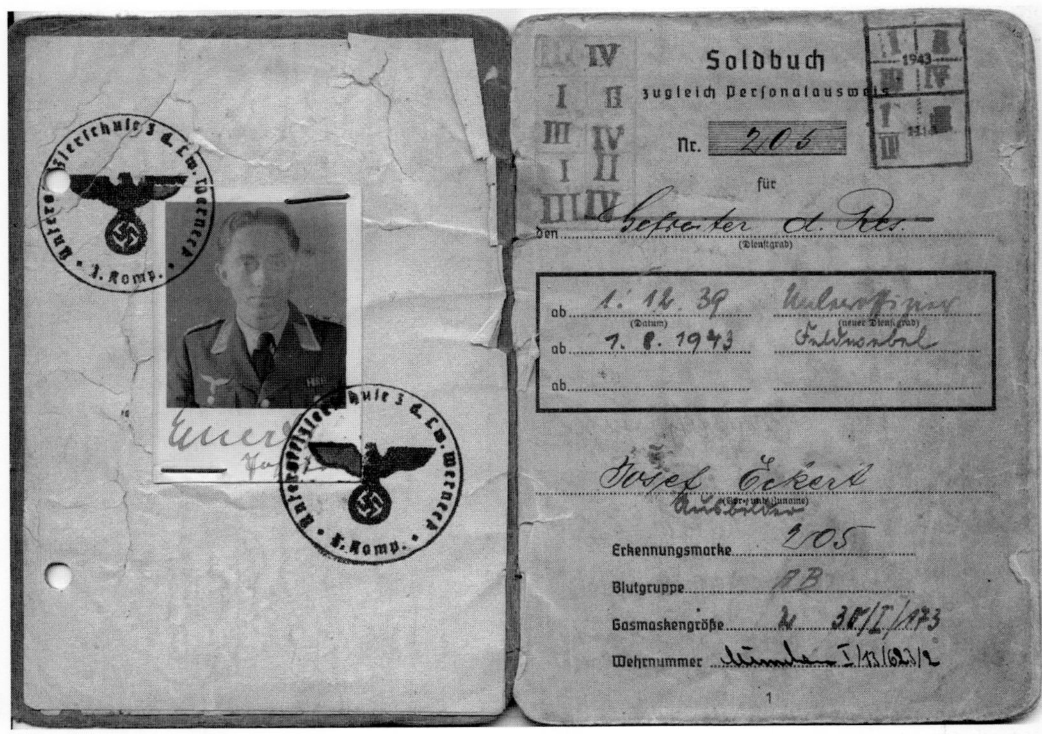

Soldbuch
zugleich Personalausweis
Nr. 205
für
den Gefreiter d. Res.
(Dienstgrad)
ab 1. 12. 39
(Datum) (neuer Dienstgrad)
ab 1. 8. 1943
ab
Josef Eckert
(Vor- und Zuname)
Erkennungsmarke 205
Blutgruppe AB
Gasmaskengröße
Wehrnummer
1

Soldbuch of *Feldwebel* Josef Eckert who served in the *Luftwaffe Feldgendarmerie*.

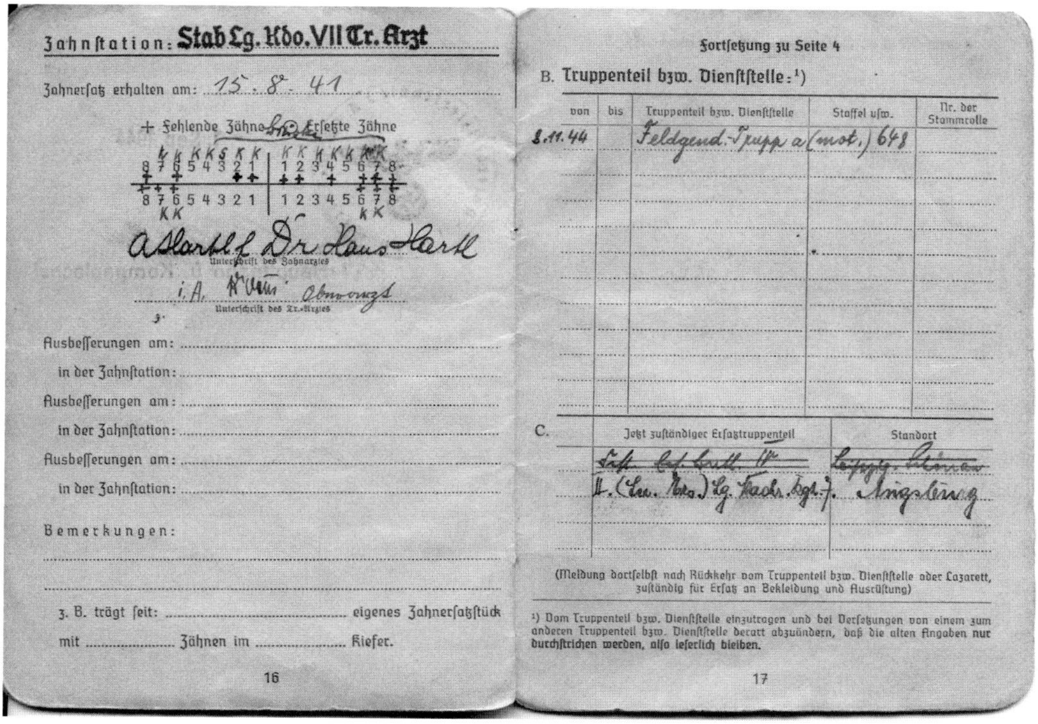

Zahnstation: Stab Lg. Kdo. VII Tr. Arzt

Zahnersatz erhalten am: 15. 8. 41

+ Fehlende Zähne Ersetzte Zähne

8 7 6 5 4 3 2 1 | 1 2 3 4 5 6 7 8

8 7 6 5 4 3 2 1 | 1 2 3 4 5 6 7 8

Unterschrift des Zahnarztes

i. A. Obmmzt

Unterschrift des Tr.-Arztes

Ausbesserungen am:

in der Zahnstation:

Ausbesserungen am:

in der Zahnstation:

Ausbesserungen am:

in der Zahnstation:

Bemerkungen:

z. B. trägt seit: .... eigenes Zahnersatzstück

mit .... Zähnen im .... Kiefer.

16

Fortsetzung zu Seite 4

B. Truppenteil bzw. Dienststelle:[1])

von	bis	Truppenteil bzw. Dienststelle	Staffel usw.	Nr. der Stammrolle
8.11.44		Feldgend.-Trupp a (mot.) 648		

C.

Jetzt zuständiger Ersatztruppenteil	Standort
~~Ers. Abt. Batl.~~	~~Leipzig~~
II. (Erg. Abs.) Lg. Nachr. Rgt. 7.	Augsburg

(Meldung dortselbst nach Rückkehr vom Truppenteil bzw. Dienststelle oder Lazarett, zuständig für Ersatz an Bekleidung und Ausrüstung)

[1]) Vom Truppenteil bzw. Dienststelle einzutragen und bei Versetzungen von einem zum anderen Truppenteil bzw. Dienststelle derart abzuändern, daß die alten Angaben nur durchstrichen werden, also leserlich bleiben.

17

Entry in the Eckert *Soldbuch* showing his attachment to *Feldgendarmerie Trupp* a (mot) 648, the military police element of 3 Fallschirm Division.

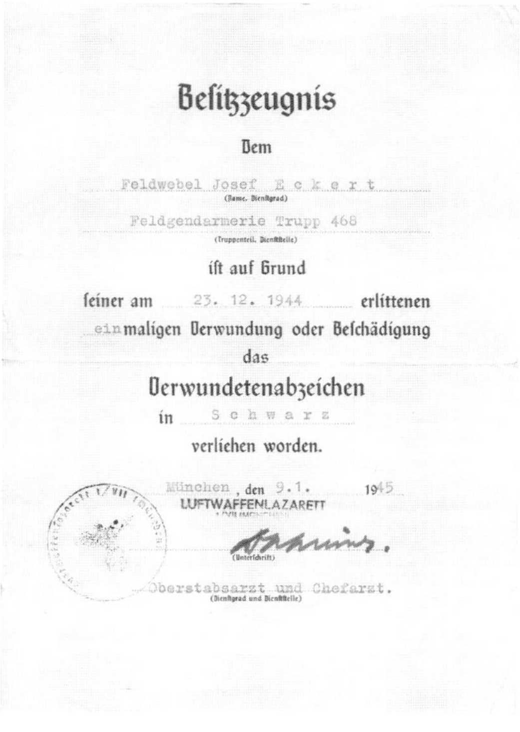

Besitzzeugnis

Dem

Feldwebel Josef E c k e r t

(Name, Dienstgrad)

Feldgendarmerie Trupp 468

(Truppenteil, Dienststelle)

ist auf Grund

seiner am 23. 12. 1944 erlittenen

einmaligen Verwundung oder Beschädigung

das

Verwundetenabzeichen

in S c h w a r z

verliehen worden.

München, den 9.1. 1945

LUFTWAFFENLAZARETT

(Unterschrift)

Oberstabsarzt und Chefarzt.

(Dienstgrad und Dienststelle)

Award Document for Eckert's Wound Badge, earned for wounds received during the Ardennes Offensive.

Headquarter Units

As previously mentioned only one large *Feldgendarmerie* unit was created for the *Luftwaffe*, and was attached to Görings personal headquarters.

Stab Feldgend.-Bataillon Hauptquartier Oberbefehlshaber der Luftwaffe.
I Komp./ Feldgend.-Bataillon Hauptquartier Oberbefehlshaber der Luftwaffe.
2 Komp./ Feldgend.-Bataillon Hauptquartier Oberbefehlshaber der Luftwaffe.
3 Komp./ Feldgend.-Bataillon Hauptquartier Oberbefehlshaber der Luftwaffe.

Fallschirmjäger Feldgendarmerie, instantly recognisable by the distinctive paratroop helmets being worn. (*Josef Charita*)

(iii) Feldgendarmerie der Waffen-SS

Prior to the outbreak of war, the still very small *SS-Verfügungstruppe* had no particular need for its own *Feldgendarmerie* branch. Even though it participated in large scale troop movements such as the occupation of the Sudetenland, the *Anschluss* with Austria etc., any required provost support was provided by the same *Motorisierte Gendarmerie* troops assigned to the army for the same purpose.

By the outbreak of war however, the *SS-Verfügungsdivision* and *SS-Totenkopf Division* each fielded a *Feldgendarmerie-Trupp*. As the now renamed Waffen-SS grew, so each new division would be assigned its own *Feldgendarmerie-Trupp*, and in the case of some of the larger and more powerful units, its own *Feldgendarmerie-Kompanie*.

Not every *Waffen-SS* division which existed on paper however, ever reached full strength status in reality and in the case of some of these units, no trace can be found of any intended *Feldgendarmerie-Trupp* actually being created.

Although as a general rule, only field units of divisional size or greater would be allocated its own *Feldgendarmerie-Trupp*, in a small number of cases brigade sized units in the *Waffen-SS* were also allocated their own *Feldgendarmerie*. Corps and headquarters establishments were also known to have had *Feldgendarmerie* elements attached.

As with the *Feldgendarmerie* of the *Luftwaffe*, those of the *Waffen-SS* existed to provide provost support to *Waffen-SS* divisions in the field. Within the borders of the *Reich* all military police functions were carried out by the *Feldgendarmerie* of the *Heer*. Members of the *Waffen-SS* for example committing disciplinary infringements whilst on leave in Germany would be dealt with by military policemen of the army attached to the local *Kommandantur*.

SS-Unterscharführer Erwin Bartmann was a member of the elite LAH (*Leibstandarte SS Adolf Hitler*), the unit which began life as the personal bodyguard of the *Führer*. Based in the capital of the *Reich*, the LAH was extremely 'high profile' and mounted guard at the *Reichskanzlei*.

Despite his NCO rank and membership of this influential unit, on committing some minor *faux pas* when travelling through Berlin, Bartmann was 'collared' by the military police and reported to his unit. The army *Feldgendarmerie* had no qualms about disciplining a member of the powerful SS. Interestingly, the same veteran could not recall ever having seen an *SS-Feldgendarm*. This is perhaps not all that surprising. At the front, troops are more likely to encounter *Feldgendarmen* directing traffic at crossroads or manning checkpoints when they would often be wearing the protective motorcycle coat. With no distinctive SS insignia visible, it might easily be assumed such troops were from the army *Feldgendarmerie*. Like their army counterparts, the *Waffen-SS* units seem to have drawn their *Feldgendarmerie* personnel from the civilian police. Or at least the initial cadre staff of experienced officers and NCOs, with men drawn from its own ranks gradually being trained to fulfil the provost role.

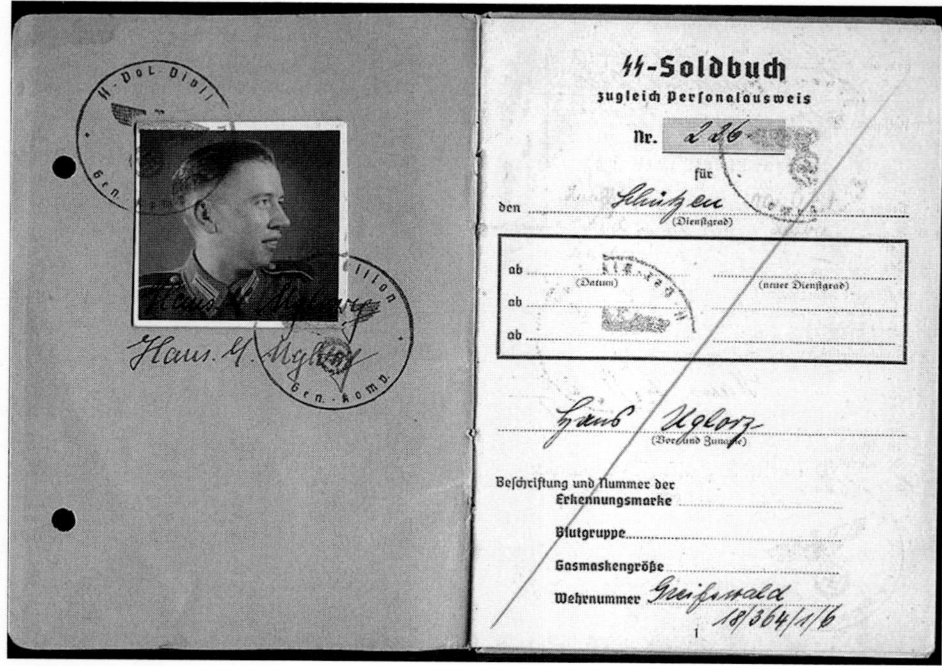

SS-Soldbuch
zugleich Personalausweis
Nr. 226
für
den Schützen (Dienstgrad)
ab (Datum) (neuer Dienstgrad)
ab
ab
Hans Uglorz (Vor- und Zuname)
Beschriftung und Nummer der Erkennungsmarke
Blutgruppe
Gasmaskengröße
Wehrnummer Greifswald 18/364/1/6
1

Soldbuch to *Schützen* Hans Uglorz who served with the *SS-Feldgendarmerie* in the *SS-Polizei* Division. (*Henner Lindlar*)

A. Zuletzt zuständige Wehrersatzdienststelle:

B. Zum Feldheer abgesandt von:[1])

	Ersatztruppenteil	Kompanie	Nr. der Truppenstammrolle
a	Pol.-Ausb. Batl. (E) Spandau		
b	1. Komp.		
c			

C.

	Feldtruppenteil[2])	Kompanie	Nr. der Kriegsstammrolle
a	E./Pol.Rgt.3		
b	d.SS-Pol.-Div.		
c	Feldgend.-Kp.		

D.

Jetzt zuständiger Ersatztruppenteil[2])	Standort

und Ausrüstungsstücke

Anschriften der nächsten lebenden Angehörigen

des Hans Uglorz (Vor- und Zuname)

1. Ehefrau: Vor- und Mädchenname
(ggf. Vermerk „ledig")
Wohnort (Kreis)
Straße, Haus-Nr.

2. Eltern: des Vaters, Vor- und Zuname
Stand oder Gewerbe
der Mutter, Vor- u. Mädchenname
Wohnort (Kreis)
Straße, Haus-Nr. 31

3. Verwandte oder Braut:[1])
Vor- und Zuname
Stand oder Gewerbe
Wohnort (Kreis)
Straße, Haus-Nr.

[1]) Ausfüllung nur, wenn weder 1. noch 2. ausgefüllt sind.

5

Note the entry in Section C of the Uglorz *Soldbuch* for service with the *Feldgendarmerie-Leutnant* of the *Polizei* Division. (*Henner Lindlar*)

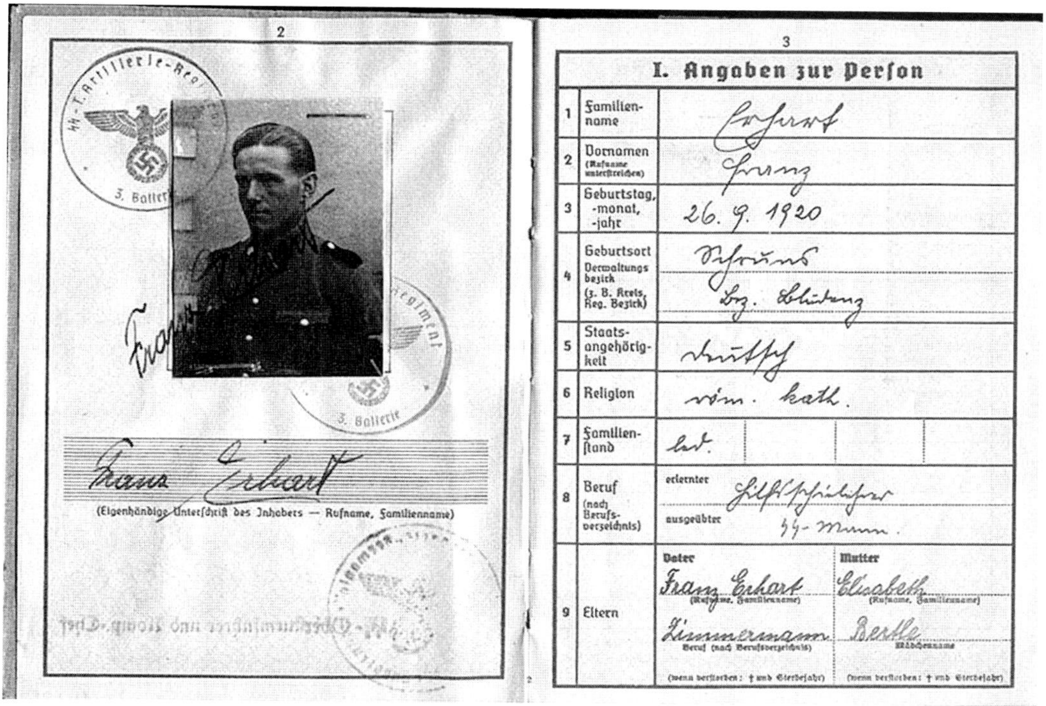

2

SS-T.-Artillerie-Regiment 3. Batterie

Franz Erhart

(Eigenhändige Unterschrift des Inhabers — Rufname, Familienname)

SS-Unterscharführer und Komp.-Chef

3

I. Angaben zur Person

1	Familienname	Erhart
2	Vornamen (Rufname unterstreichen)	Franz
3	Geburtstag, -monat, -jahr	26. 9. 1920
4	Geburtsort Verwaltungsbezirk (z. B. Kreis, Reg. Bezirk)	Schruns Bz. Bludenz
5	Staatsangehörigkeit	deutsch
6	Religion	röm. kath.
7	Familienstand	led.
8	Beruf (nach Berufsverzeichnis)	erlernter: Hilfsschlosser ausgeübter: SS-Mann
9	Eltern	Vater: Franz Erhart (Rufname, Familienname); Zimmermann Beruf (nach Berufsverzeichnis) Mutter: Elisabeth (Rufname, Familienname); Bertle Mädchenname (wenn verstorben: † und Sterbejahr)

Werpass of *Unterscharführer* Franz Erhart who served with the *SS-Feldgendarmerie* of the *Totenkopf Division*. (*Henner Lindlar*)

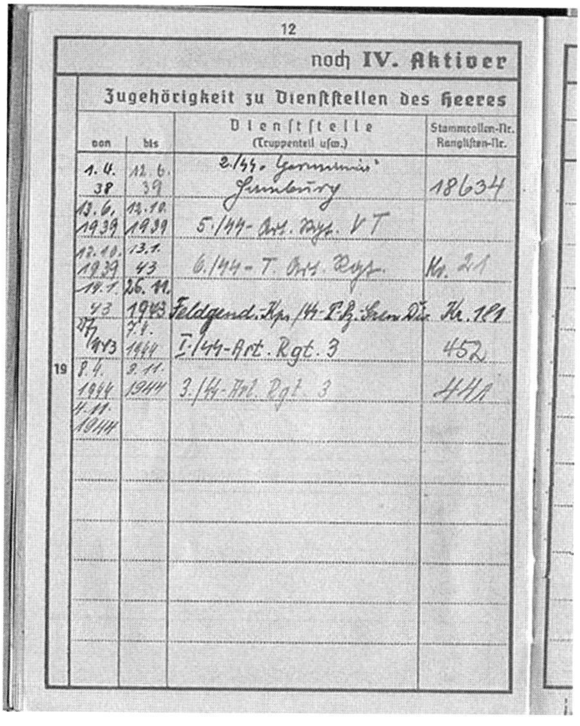

12

noch IV. Aktiver

Zugehörigkeit zu Dienststellen des Heeres

	von	bis	Dienststelle (Truppenteil usw.)	Stammrollen-Nr. Ranglisten-Nr.
	1.4.38	12.6.39	2/SS. Germania Hamburg	18634
	13.6.1939	12.10.1939	5./SS-Art. Rgt. VT	
	13.10.1939	13.1.43	6./SS-T. Art. Rgt.	Kr. 21
	14.1.43	26.11.1943	Feldgend.-Kp./SS-T-Pz.Gren.Div.	Kr. 191
	27/11/43	7.4.1944	I./SS-Art. Rgt. 3	452
19	8.4.1944	3.11.1944	3./SS-Art. Rgt. 3	441
	4.11.1944			

The fourth entry from the Erhart *Wehrpass* shown here reads 'Feldgend. Kp/ SS-T-Pz. Gren.Div.' or '*Feldgendarmerie Leutnant*/ *SS*-Totenkopf Panzer Grenadier Division'. (*Henner Lindlar*)

Medals are awarded to members of the *Feldgendarmerie* from the *SS-Totenkopf* Division. The army pattern cufftitle is worn. (*Gary Wood*)

An *SS-Feldgendarm* on duty at a traffic post for SS vehicles. (*Henner Lindlar*)

Uniforms and Insignia

SS-Feldgendarmen wore exactly the same range of uniforms and equipment as their regular comrades, only certain special insignia identifying their particular role and authority.

Shoulder Straps

Feldgendarmen of the *Waffen-SS* wore the same orange-red *Waffenfarbe* as their army counterparts. It was featured as piping to the edge of enlisted mens and NCOs straps and as intermediate underlay between the braid and black wool base material of officers straps. As of course no *Waffenfarbe* was featured on regulation *SS* collar tabs, the shoulder strap was the principal bearer of the distinctive *Waffenfarbe* colour.

Headgear

The standard *Waffenfarbe* colour for piping on *Waffen-SS* visor caps was white for all branches of the service. For short period however, between May and November 1940, piping in branch colours was permitted. Photographs exist of *SS-Feldgendarmen* where it is quite clear that the piping to the crown and cap band of the visor cap is certainly not white, and can therefore be assumed to be in orange-red.

Notwithstanding the fact that branch-piped *SS* visor caps for the *Feldgendarmerie* must have existed, such caps have been so expertly faked in recent times that it is almost impossible to find an example over which agreement on originality can be established between experienced collectors.

Waffenfarbe colour in the form of and inverted rayon chevron of Russia Braid or soutache enclosing the *Totenkopf* was also worn on the field cap and once again, photos of SS-*Feldgendarmen* wearing field caps with what can only be an orange-red *Waffenfarbe* soutache exist.

Arm Eagles

Typically, throughout the war, the standard arm eagle worn by *SS-Feldgendarmen* was the basic machine woven or machine embroidered *SS* sleeve eagle. Less common though it certainly occurred and can be proven through original period photos, the best known of which show *Feldgendarmerie* personnel from the *Handschar Division*, was the use of the *Feldgendarmerie* police style arm eagle embroidered in orange thread on a field grey base. In fact this police style eagle was prescribed for *SS-Feldgendarmerie* units in 1942 though it would appear that most continued to wear the regular *SS* arm eagle. In any case, the use of this police style arm eagle was abolished altogether (also for the *Heer*) in October 1944. There do exist photos which show the use of a police style arm eagle worn below the *SS* eagle. Even from black and white photos, it appears that in these cases, the eagle being worn is that of the *Schutzpolizei*, embroidered in green, not orange thread.

In 1943, the *SS* introduced a diamond shaped sleeve badge (*Ärmelraute*) as a 'tradition' badge to indicate the wearers former status as a member of the police, and it is believed that the police eagles seen worn below the *SS* arm eagle on such photographs are *Schutzpolizei* eagles used for the same purpose and are not *Feldgendarmerie* eagles. In any case, no regulation has been discovered allowing the use of two arm eagles on *Waffen-SS* uniform (as opposed to one eagle and a 'tradition' badge).

Mealtime for the *Feldgendarm*en of the *SS-Totenkopf* Division. Note that they wear the runic collar patch, not the normal deaths-head patch of the *Totenkopf* Division. (*Gary Wood*)

Two *SS-Rottenführer* from the *SS-Feldgendarmerie* of the elite *Leibstandarte* escorting British prisoners. Although somewhat blurred, the photo shows both the Divisional 'Adolf Hitler' cufftitle and the '*SS-Feldgendarmerie*' cufftitle are being worn. (*Josef Charita*)

Cuffbands

On the outbreak of war, members of the *SS-Feldgendarmerie* were issued with the same machine woven grey on brown rayon cuffband as used by the *Heer* and *Luftwaffe*. In August 1942 however, a specific *SS* version of the cuffband was introduced. It was 3.2 cm wide, woven in silver grey rayon on black with the text *SS-Feldgendarmerie* in Latin script letters. This band was worn until November 1944 when the *Feldgendarmerie* of the *Waffen-SS*, like their *Wehrmacht* counterparts, ceased to wear a cuffband.

Gorget

The gorget worn by the *SS-Feldgendarmerie* the standard Heer pattern.

In the recent publication 'Ringkragen und Brustschilder im Dritten Reich', authors Wim Saris and Andrew Mollo show a interesting variant of the *Fedgendarmerie* gorget which is similar in concept to the special version created for the *Grossdeutschland* Division. In this case however, the additional thin sheet metal plate added across the top of the gorget features a so-called *Sonnenrad* or "Sunwheel" type circular swastika. This was the emblem used by *5 SS-Panzer Division 'Wiking'*, so although so far no photographs have emerged showing this gorget being worn by members of *SS-Feldgendarmerietrupp 5*, it seems likely that this gorget was indeed, like its GD counterpart, a unit modified variant for the military police of this elite unit.

Waffen-SS Feldgendarmerie Units

Initially, the *Waffen-SS* tended to title their *Feldgendarmerie* units with the name of the parent unit, but eventually settled on a numerical system where the number of the *Feldgendarmerie-Trupp* followed that of the parent division, thus *SS-Feldgendarmerie-Trupp 12* was part of *12 SS-Panzer Division "Hitlerjugend"*.

Divisional Units	**Parent**
SS-Feldgend.-Komp 1	*1 SS-Panzer Div."LSSAH"*
SS-Feldgend.-Komp 2	*2 SS-Panzer Div." Das Reich"*
SS-Feldgend.-Komp 3	*3 SS-Panzer Div. "Totenkopf"*
SS-Feldgend.-Komp 4	*4 SS-Polizei-Division*
SS-Feldgend.-Komp 5	*5 SS-Panzer Div.,,"Wiking"*
SS-Feldgend.-Komp 6	*6 SS-Gebirgs-Div. "Nord"*
SS-Feldgend.-Trupp 7	*7 SS-Gebirgs-Div."Prinz Eugen"*
SS-Feldgend.-Trupp 8	*8 SS-Kavallerie-Div. "Florian Geyer"*
SS-Feldgend.-Trupp 9	*9 SS-Panzer Div. "Hohenstaufen"*
SS-Feldgend.-Komp 10	*10 SS-Panzer Div. "Frundsberg"*
SS-Feldgend.-Komp 11	*11 SS-Panzergrenadier Div. "Nordland"*
SS-Feldgend.-Komp 12	*12 SS-Panzer Div. "Hitlerjugend"*
SS-Feldgend.-Trupp 13	*13 Waffen-Gebirgs-Div. der SS "Handschar"*
SS-Feldgend.-Trupp 14	*14 Waffen-Grenadier-Div. der SS*
SS-Feldgend.-Trupp 15	*15 Waffen-Grenadier-Div. der SS*
SS-Feldgend.-Komp 16	*16 SS-Panzergrenadier Div. "Reichsführer-SS"*
SS-Feldgend.-Komp 17	*17 SS-Panzergrenadier Div. "Gotz v. Berlichingen"*
SS-Feldgend.-Komp 18	*18 SS-Freiwilligen Panzergrenadier Div. "Horst Wessel"*
SS-Feldgend.-Trupp 19	*19 Waffen-Grenadier-Div. der SS*

SS-Feldgend.-Trupp 20	*20 Waffen-Grenadier-Div. der SS*
SS-Feldgend.-Trupp 21	*21 Waffen-Gebirgs-Div. der SS "Skanderbeg"*
SS-Feldgend.-Trupp 26	*26 Waffen-Grenadier-Div. der SS*
SS-Feldgend.-Trupp 27	*27 Freiwilligen-Grenadier-Div. der SS "Langemarck"*
SS-Feldgend.-Trupp 31	*31 Freiwilligen-Grenadier-Div. der SS*
SS-Feldgend.-Trupp 37	*37 SS-Freiwilligen Kavallerie Div.*

Corps Units	**Parent**
SS-Feldgendarmerie-Kompanie SS-Panzerkorps LAH	*I SS-Panzerkorps*
SS-Feldgendarmerie-Kompanie I SS-Panzerkorps	*I SS-Panzerkorps*
SS-Feldgendarmerie-Kompanie 101	*I SS-Panzerkorps*
SS-Feldgendarmerie-Kompanie II SS-Panzerkorps	*II SS-Panzerkorps*
SS-Feldgendarmerie-Kompanie 102	*II SS-Panzerkorps*
SS-Feldgendarmerie-Kompanie III (germ.) SS-Panzerkorps	*III SS-Panzerkorps*
SS-Feldgendarmerie-Kompanie 103	*III SS-Panzerkorps*
SS-Feldgendarmerie-Kompanie IV SS-Panzerkorps	*IV SS-Panzerkorps*
SS-Feldgendarmerie-Kompanie 104	*IV SS-Panzerkorps*
SS-Feldgendarmerie-Kompanie 105	*V SS-Panzerkorps*
SS-Feldgendarmerie-Kompanie 106	*VI SS-Panzerkorps*
SS-Feldgendarmerie-Kompanie 107	*VII SS-Korps*
SS-Feldgendarmerie-Kompanie 109	*IX SS-Korps*
SS-Feldgendarmerie-Kompanie 509	*IX SS-Korps*
SS-Feldgendarmerie-Kompanie 111	*XI SS-Korps*
SS-Feldgendarmerie-Kompanie 112	*XII SS-Korps*
SS-Feldgendarmerie-Kompanie 113	*XIII SS-Korps*
SS-Feldgendarmerie-Kompanie XVIII SS-Korps	*XVIII SS-Korps*

Brigade Units	**Parent**
Feldgendarmerie-Trupp SS-Brigade 1	*I SS-Brigade*
Feldgendarmerie-Trupp SS-Infanterie Brigade 1	*I SS-Infanterie Brigade*
SS-Feldgendarmerie-Trupp 51	*I SS-Infanterie Brigade*
Feldgendarmerie-Trupp SS-Brigade 2 RFSS	*SS-Brigade RFSS*
Feldgendarmerie-Trupp SS-Infanterie Brigade 2	*2 SS-Infanterie Brigade*
SS-Feldgendarmerie-Trupp 52	*2 SS-Infanterie Brigade*
SS-Feldgendarmerie-Trupp 54	*SS-Brigade Nederland*
Feldgendarmerie-Trupp SS-Kavallerie Brigade	*SS-Kavallerie Brigade*
SS-Feldgendarmerie-Trupp franz. SS-Brigade	*französische SS-Brigade*

Miscellaneous

Feldgendarmerie-Trupp Generalkommando Waffen-(Gebirgs) Armeekorps SS

I. Feldgendarmerie-Trupp Kommandostab rückwärtige Dienst Reichsführer-SS

I. Feldgendarmerie-Trupp Reichsführer-SS

Feldgendarmerie-Trupp Reichsführer-SS

SS-Feldgendarmerie-Kompanie Reichsführer-SS

Above left: A fine portrait study of an *SS-Hauptscharführer* wearing the machine woven '*SS-Feldgendarmerie*' cufftitle. Note also the Infantry Assault Badge being worn.

Above right: A fine portrait shot of a *Oberschutze of SS-Feldgendarmerie.* (*Henner Lindlar*)

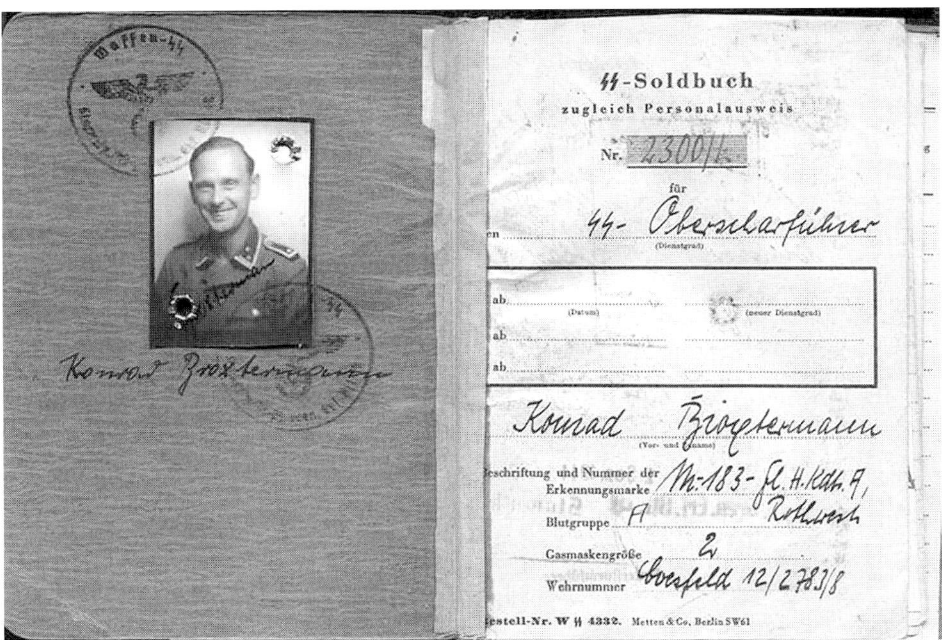

Waffen-SS

Konrad Broxtermann

SS-Soldbuch

zugleich Personalausweis

Nr. 2300/...

für

...n SS-Oberscharführer
(Dienstgrad)

ab .... (Datum) .... (neuer Dienstgrad)

ab

ab

Konrad Broxtermann
(Vor- und Zuname)

...eschriftung und Nummer der Erkennungsmarke

Blutgruppe A

Gasmaskengröße 2

Wehrnummer

...estell-Nr. W SS 4332. Metten & Co. Berlin SW61

Soldbuch of Oberscharführer Konrad Broxtermann who served with the *SS-Feldgendarmerie* attached to the famed 'Wiking' Division. (*Henner Lindlar*)

A. Zuletzt zuständige Wehrersatzdienststelle
SS-Erg. Stelle VI Wart
B. Zum Feldheer abgesandt von[1])

	Ersatztruppenteil	Kompanie	Nr. der Truppenstammrolle
a	Gren.Ers.Btl. 18	Stammkp.	U 444/L
b			
c			

C.	Feldtruppenteil[2])	Kompanie	Nr. der Kriegsstammrolle
a	~~SS-F.A.B.5~~	~~1~~	~~1030~~
b	5.SS Pz.-Div. „Wiking" Feldgend.-Komp.		171
c			

D.	Jetzt zuständiger Ersatztruppenteil[1])	Standort
	~~SS-Pz.Gren.Ers.Btl.18~~	~~Breslau~~
	~~SS-Gren.Ausb.u.Ers.Btl. 5~~	~~Ellwangen~~
	SS-Feldgend.A.u.E.Kp.	Weimar/Bu

(Meldung dortselbst nach Rückkehr vom Feldheer oder Lazarett, zuständig für Ersatz an Bekleidung und Ausrüstung.)

[1]) Vom Ersatztruppenteil einzutragen, von dem der Soldbuchinhaber zum Feldheer abgesandt wird.
[2]) Vom Feldtruppenteil einzutragen und bei Versetzungen von einem zum anderen Feldtruppenteil derart abzuändern, daß die alten Angaben nur durchstrichen werden, also leserlich bleiben.

Weiterer Raum für Eintragungen auf Seite 25

4

Anschriften der nächsten lebenden Angehörigen

Konrad Broxtermann (Vor- und Zuname)
Ehefrau: Vor- und Mädchenname Liesel geb. Bölle (gegebenenfalls Vermerk „ledig")
Wohnort (Kreis) Thringshausen b/Kassel
Straße, Haus-Nr. Ackerhagener Str. 75

Eltern: des Vaters Vor- und Zuname
Stand oder Gewerbe
der Mutter Vor- und Mädchenname
Wohnort (Kreis)
Straße, Haus-Nr.

Verwandte oder Braut:*)
Vor- und Zuname
Stand oder Gewerbe
Wohnort (Kreis)
Straße, Haus-Nr.

*) Ausfüllung nur, wenn weder 1 noch 2 ausgefüllt sind.

5

The Broxtermann *Soldbuch*. Note the entry in Section C ' 5 SS. P-Div '*Wiking*' *Feldgend.-Komp.*' (*Henner Lindlar*)

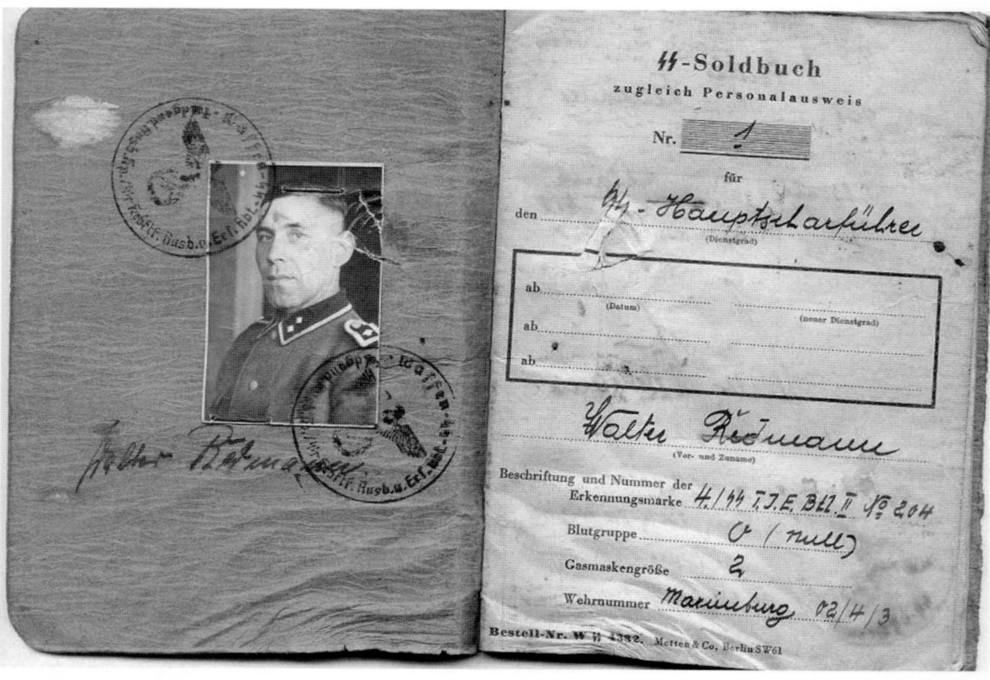

SS-Soldbuch
zugleich Personalausweis
Nr. 1
für
den SS-Hauptscharführer (Dienstgrad)
ab (Datum) (neuer Dienstgrad)
ab
ab
Walter Redmann (Vor- und Zuname)
Beschriftung und Nummer der Erkennungsmarke 4/SS T.J.E.Btl.II No 204
Blutgruppe 0 (null)
Gasmaskengröße 2
Wehrnummer Marienburg 02/4/3
Bestell-Nr. W SS 4382. Metten & Co., Berlin SW 61

Soldbuch to *Hauptscharführer* of *SS-Feldgendarmerie* Walter Redmann.

A. Zuletzt zuständige Wehrersatzdienststelle
WMA Marienburg
B. Zum Feldheer abgesandt von[1])

	Ersatztruppenteil	Kompanie	Nr. der Truppenstammrolle
a	SS-Feldgend. A. u. E. Komp. Weimar-Buchenwald		
b			
c			

C.

	Feldtruppenteil[2])	Kompanie	Nr. der Kriegsstammrolle
a	SS Pz. Div. Wiking	Feldg.-Trupp	47
b	SS-Pz. Div. Frundsberg	Feldgend. Kp.	159
c			

D.

	Jetzt zuständiger Ersatztruppenteil[3])	Standort
a)	Feldg.-Ausb. u. Ers.-Komp.	Weimar-Buchenwald

(Meldung dortselbst nach Rückkehr vom Feldheer oder Lazarett, zuständig für Ersatz an Bekleidung und Ausrüstung.)

[1]) Vom Ersatztruppenteil einzutragen, von dem der Soldbuchinhaber zum Feldheer abgesandt wird.
[2]) Vom Feldtruppenteil einzutragen und bei Versetzungen von einem zum anderen Feldtruppenteil derart abzuändern, daß die alten Angaben nur durchstrichen werden, also leserlich bleiben.
Weiterer Raum für Eintragungen auf Seite 25.

4

Anschriften der nächsten lebenden Angehörigen
des Walter Redmann
(Vor- und Zuname)

1. Ehefrau: Vor- und Mädchenname Erna Hoffmann
(gegebenenfalls Vermerk „ledig")
Wohnort (Kreis) Marienburg / Westpr.
Straße, Haus-Nr. Ordensweg 2

2. Eltern: des Vaters Vor- und Zuname
Stand oder Gewerbe
der Mutter Vor- und Mädchenname
Wohnort (Kreis)
Straße, Haus-Nr.

3. Verwandte oder Braut:*)
Vor- und Zuname
Stand oder Gewerbe
Wohnort (Kreis)
Straße, Haus-Nr.

*) Ausfüllung nur, wenn weder 1 noch 2 ausgefüllt sind.

5

Entries from the Redmann *Soldbuch* showing service with the *SS-Feldgendarmerie* units of two elite Panzer Divisions, '*Wiking*' and '*Frundsberg*'.

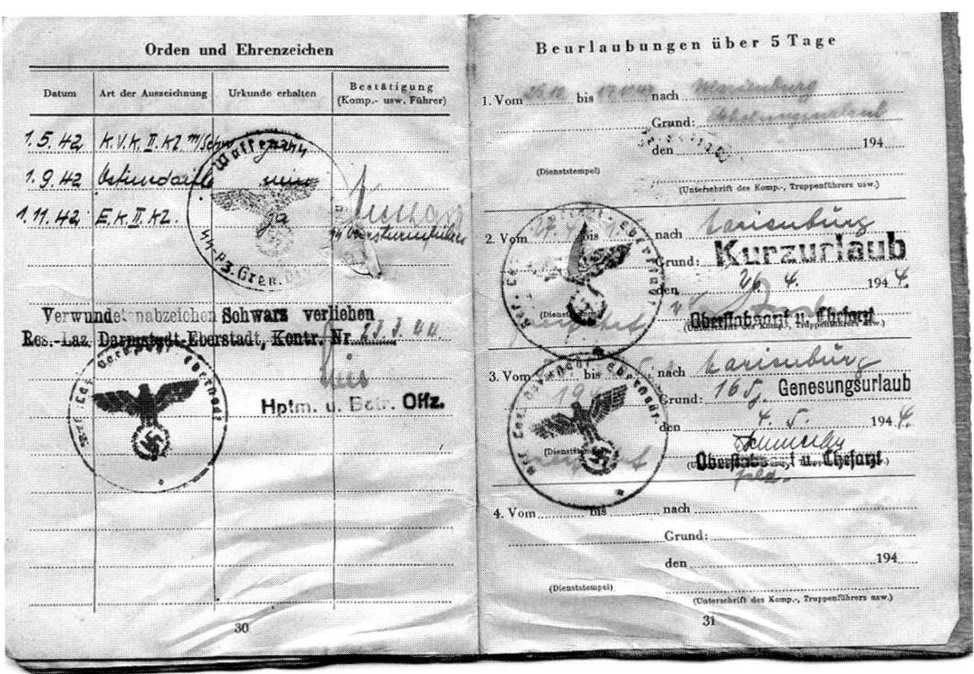

Orden und Ehrenzeichen

Datum	Art der Auszeichnung	Urkunde erhalten	Bestätigung (Komp.- usw. Führer)
1.5.42	K.V.K. II. Kl. m/Schw.		
1.9.42	Ostmedaille		
1.11.42	E.K. II. Kl.		

Verwundetenabzeichen Schwarz verliehen
Res.-Laz. Darmstadt-Eberstadt, Kontr. Nr.
Hptm. u. Betr. Offz.

30

Beurlaubungen über 5 Tage

1. Vom ... bis ... nach ...
Grund: ...
den ... 194...
(Dienststempel)
(Unterschrift des Komp.-, Truppenführers usw.)

2. Vom ... bis ... nach Marienburg
Grund: Kurzurlaub
den 26. 4. 1944
Oberstabsarzt u. Chefarzt

3. Vom ... bis ... nach Marienburg
Grund: 16 T. Genesungsurlaub
den 4. 5. 1944
Oberstabsarzt u. Chefarzt

4. Vom ... bis ... nach ...
Grund: ...
den ... 194...
(Dienststempel)
(Unterschrift des Komp.-, Truppenführers usw.)

31

Award entries from the Redmann *Soldbuch* showing the War Merit Cross 2nd Class , East Front Medal, Iron Cross 2nd Class and Wound Badge in Black.

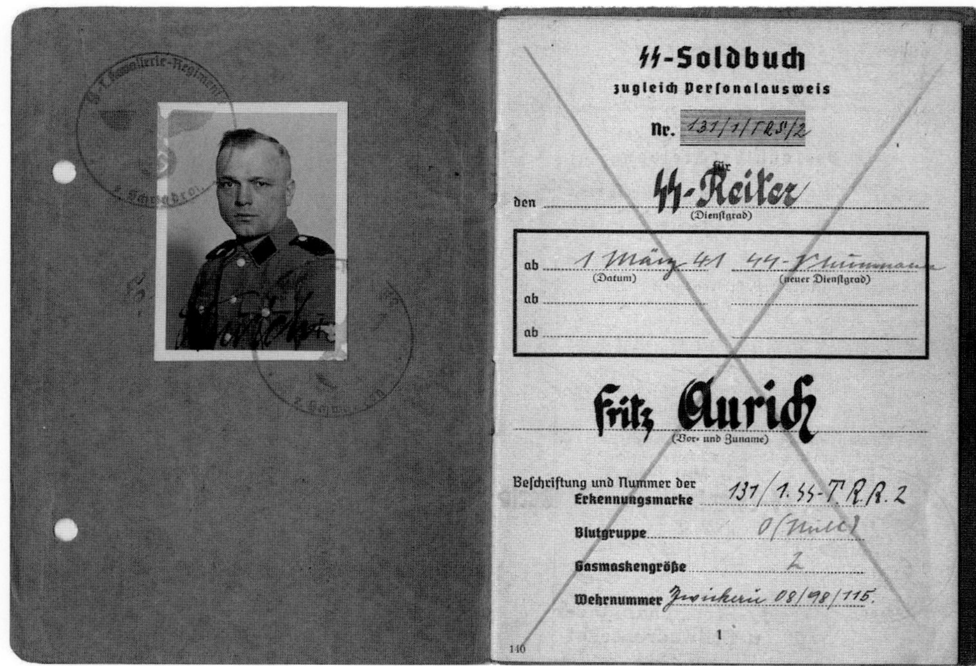

SS-Soldbuch
zugleich Personalausweis
Nr. 137/1/TRR/2
für
den SS-Reiter
(Dienstgrad)
ab 1 März 41 SS-Sturmmann
(Datum) (neuer Dienstgrad)
ab
ab
Fritz Aurich
(Vor- und Zuname)
Beschriftung und Nummer der Erkennungsmarke 137/1.SS-T.R.R.2
Blutgruppe 0 (Mittel)
Gasmaskengröße 2
Wehrnummer Zwickau 08/98/115.
1

Soldbuch to *SS-Sturmmann* of *Feldgendarmerie* Fritz Aurich. (*Henner Lindlar*)

A. Zuletzt zuständige Wehrersatzdienststelle:
SS-Ergzt. IV Elbe

B. Zum Feldheer abgesandt von:[1]

	Ersatztruppenteil	Kompanie	Nr. der Truppen-stammrolle
a			
b			
c			

C.

	Feldtruppenteil[2]	Kompanie	Nr. der Kriegs-stammrolle
a	~~1/2 SS-T.R.R.~~		~~131~~
b	~~1/1 SS-T.Kav.Rgt.~~	~~1~~	~~41~~
c	SS Kavallerie-Brigade Feldgend. Trupp		-36-

D.

Jetzt zuständiger Ersatztruppenteil[2]	Standort
~~1/2 SS-T.R.R.~~	~~Goerlitz~~
~~1/1 SS-T.Kav.Rgt.~~	~~Lublin~~
~~SS-Führungshauptamt~~	~~Berlin~~
1.SS Kraft. Ers. Abt.	Berlin Lichterfelde

(Meldung dortselbst nach Rückkehr vom Feldheer oder Lazarett, zuständig für Ersatz an Bekleidung und Ausrüstung)

[1]) Vom Ersatztruppenteil einzutragen, von dem der Soldbuchinhaber zum Feldheer abgesandt wird.

[2]) Vom Feldtruppenteil einzutragen und bei Versetzungen von einem zum anderen Feldtruppenteil derart abzuändern, daß die alten Angaben nur durchstrichen werden, also leserlich bleiben.

Weiterer Raum für Eintragungen auf Seite 17.

4

Anschriften der nächsten lebenden Angehörigen

des Fritz Aurich,
(Vor- und Zuname)

1. Ehefrau: Vor- und Mädchenname Elisabeth Dillmann
(ggf. Vermerk „ledig")
Wohnort (Kreis) Zwickau, Stadt.
Straße, Haus-Nr. Crossener Str. 92.

2. Eltern: des Vaters, Vor- und Zuname
Stand oder Gewerbe
der Mutter, Vor- u. Mädchenname
Wohnort (Kreis)
Straße, Haus-Nr.

3. Verwandte oder Braut:*)
Vor- und Zuname
Stand oder Gewerbe
Wohnort (Kreis)
Straße, Haus-Nr.

*) Ausfüllung nur, wenn weder 1. noch 2. ausgefüllt sind.

5

The Aurich *Soldbuch* showing the unit entry for his service with the *Feldgendarmerietrupp* of the *SS Kavallerie-Brigade*. (*Henner Lindlar*)

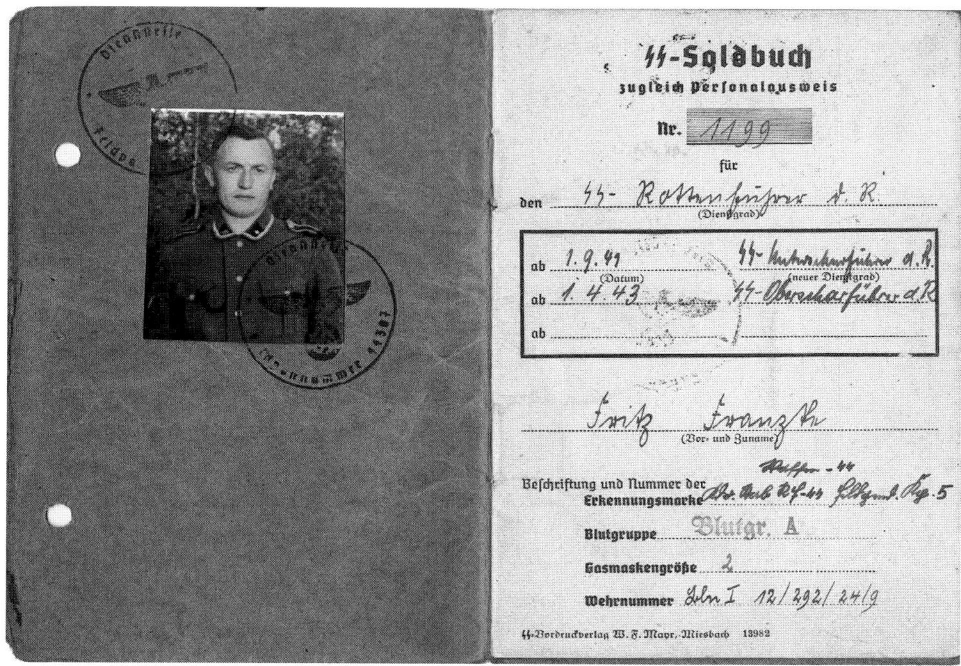

SS-Soldbuch
zugleich Personalausweis
Nr. 1199
für
den SS-Rottenführer d.R.
(Dienstgrad)
ab 1.9.41 (Datum) SS-Unterscharführer d.R. (neuer Dienstgrad)
ab 1.4.43 SS-Oberscharführer d.R.
ab
Fritz Franzke
(Vor- und Zuname)
Beschriftung und Nummer der Erkennungsmarke
Blutgruppe Blutgr. A
Gasmaskengröße 2
Wehrnummer Berlin I 12/292/24/9
SS-Vordruckverlag W. F. Mayr, Miesbach 13982

Extremely rare *Soldbuch* to *Oberscharführer* Fritz Franzke who served with the *SS-Feldgendarmerie* attached to the personal staff of *Reichsführer-SS* Heinrich Himmler. (*Henner Lindlar*)

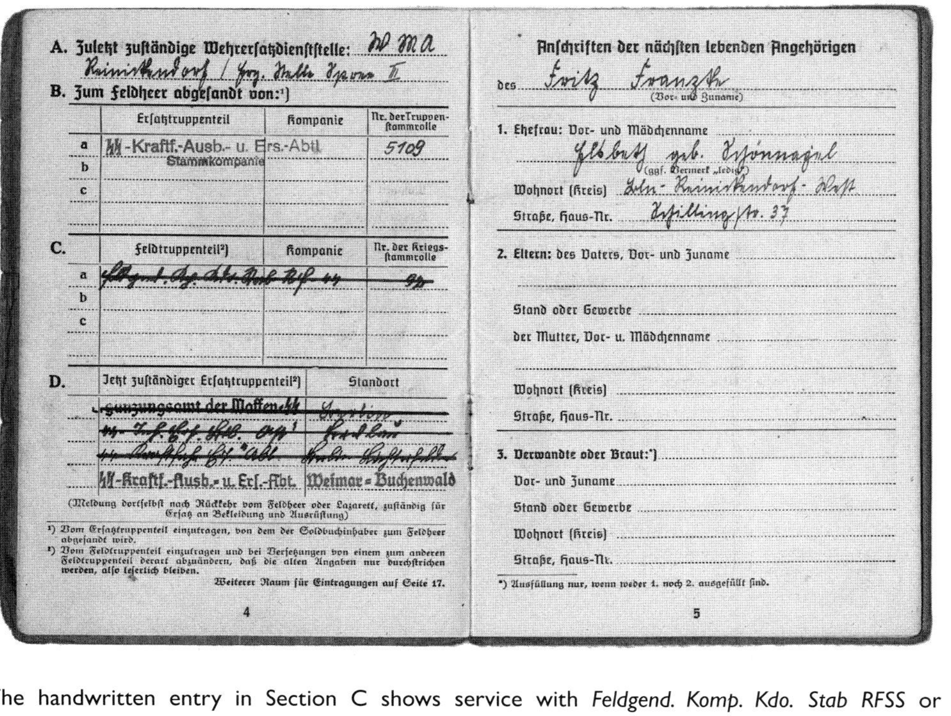

A. Zuletzt zuständige Wehrersatzdienststelle: W.M.A. Reinickendorf
B. Zum Feldheer abgesandt von:[1])

	Ersatztruppenteil	Kompanie	Nr. der Truppen-stammrolle
a	SS-Kraftf.-Ausb.- u. Ers.-Abt.	Stammkompanie	5109
b			
c			

C.

	Feldtruppenteil[2])	Kompanie	Nr. der Kriegs-stammrolle
a	[struck through]		
b			
c			

D.

Jetzt zuständiger Ersatztruppenteil[2])	Standort
Ergänzungsamt der Waffen-SS [struck through]	[struck through]
[struck through]	[struck through]
[struck through]	[struck through]
SS-Kraftf.-Ausb.- u. Erf.-Abt.	Weimar-Buchenwald

(Meldung dortselbst nach Rückkehr vom Feldheer oder Lazarett, zuständig für Ersatz an Bekleidung und Ausrüstung)

[1]) Vom Ersatztruppenteil einzutragen, von dem der Soldbuchinhaber zum Feldheer abgesandt wird.

[2]) Vom Feldtruppenteil einzutragen und bei Versetzungen von einem zum anderen Feldtruppenteil derart abzuändern, daß die alten Angaben nur durchstrichen werden, also leserlich bleiben.

Weiterer Raum für Eintragungen auf Seite 17.

4

Anschriften der nächsten lebenden Angehörigen
des Fritz Franzke
(Vor- und Zuname)

1. Ehefrau: Vor- und Mädchenname
Elisabeth geb. Schönnagel
(ggf. Vermerk „ledig")
Wohnort (Kreis) Berlin-Reinickendorf-West
Straße, Haus-Nr. Schillingstr. 37

2. Eltern: des Vaters, Vor- und Zuname
Stand oder Gewerbe
der Mutter, Vor- u. Mädchenname
Wohnort (Kreis)
Straße, Haus-Nr.

3. Verwandte oder Braut:*)
Vor- und Zuname
Stand oder Gewerbe
Wohnort (Kreis)
Straße, Haus-Nr.

*) Ausfüllung nur, wenn weder 1. noch 2. ausgefüllt sind.

5

The handwritten entry in Section C shows service with *Feldgend. Komp. Kdo. Stab RFSS* or *Feldgendarmerie Leutnant Kommandostab RFSS*. (*Henner Lindlar*)

Marineküstenpolizei

Having decided that a police branch was required for the Navy, the high command of the *Kriegsmarine* took the logical step of following their army counterparts by drafting in experienced police personnel from the civil sector to create this new force. Where the army had turned to the *Gendarmerie* to provide the initial cadres around which the *Feldgendarmerie des Heeres* was formed, the *Kriegsmarine* turned to the civil waterways police, the *Wasserschutzpolizei* or WSP.

Unlike the *Feldgendarmerie* however which was formed shortly before the outbreak of war as Germany began to mobilize, the *Marineküstenpolizei* or MKP was not formed until 1940. With *Unternehmung Weserübung*, and the occupation of Denmark and Norway the Germans found themselves with a vastly increased amount of coastline to secure.

A decree issued by the *Chef der Ordnungspolizei* dated 20 April 1940 (O-KdO g2 (O 7) Nr 23—40g) authorised the transfer of police personnel to the newly formed MKP. A letter issued on 10 May 1940 listed a number of police personnel from various WSP units throughout Germany who were ordered to assemble at the railway station in Wilhelmshaven on 13 May 1940 for duty with the MKP. At the same time two harbour patrol motor boats previously used by the police, were transferred to the naval authorities and were to report to the port of Emden with their crews on the same day.

The MKP at this time recruited exclusively from serving WSP officials and reservists who from this time on were no longer considered police personnel but came under the control of the *Kriegsmarine*, more specifically the *2. Admiral der Nordsee* or *2. Admiral der Ostsee*. (The *2. Admiral* or 2nd Admiral was the Flag Officer responsible for administration rather than operations.)

Within the *Reich*, the authority of the MKP extended over the inshore coastal areas and ports and in occupied countries also to inland rivers and lakes. Its areas of responsibility included the security of rivers and river mouths, protection of fisheries, controlling order and discipline of personnel onboard ships whilst in port and also of naval land units in coastal areas.

Duties included the arrest of miscreants and their delivery to either the military justice system if a court martial was appropriate, or to a responsible civilian court in other cases, the monitoring and observing of coastal areas, prevention of the escape of wanted persons by sea from occupied areas and general assistance to the military authorities. It can be seen that whilst some of their duties might seem similar to 'Shore Patrol' personnel in the USN or Royal Navy, the range of duties they carried out was far wider than what might be considered their allied equivalents. The MKP were effectively a naval version of the military police though with their own very specific tasks.

Members of the *Wasserschutzpolizei* in their '*Hafenboot*'. In April 1940 an initial tranche of 71 WSP personnel, together with their *Hafenboote*, were transferred to the *Marineküstenpolizei*. (*Josef Charita*)

An NCO of the *Wasserschutzpolizei*. On transfer to the MKP, personnel initially retained their full WSP uniform.

Above: A senior NCO of the MKP shown here wearing his original WSP uniform.

Left: The same NCO, now in regulation *Kriegsmarine* uniform though note, without sleeve eagle. His colleagues still wear their original WSP uniforms.

The same NCO once again. This time the emblem of the MKP, an unfouled anchor, can be seen on his shoulder strap.

In photographs such as this it can be impossible to be sure whether the individual is a member of the WSP or MKP.

An order of the day number 192 dated 9 September 1941 set out some of the details regarding the new formation:

Provisional Regulations for the Marineküstenpolizei
Arrangement, Assumption, Employment

1. The *Oberkommando der Kriegsmarine* can request members of the *Wasserschutzpolizei* (active and reservist) from the *Reichsführer SS und Chef der Deutschen Polizei* for tasks in the occupied areas in wartime as members of the *Marineküstenpolizei*. The number of the WSP officials available is restricted

2. The *Marineküstenpolizei* (MKP) is to consist of officers and NCOs who are specially trained for the execution of water protection police type tasks of every kind.

3. As a rule the MKP will not be used in closed units, their members will be distributed in the local harbour monitoring posts in the numbers as required. Exceptionally, if the employment of a closed MKP unit is required, it will be ordered by the responsible command office of the *Kriegsmarine* (Naval Commander or Admiral Commanding the Coast),

Service Conditions
7. Officers and NCOs of the MKP are soldiers on an equal footing as the appropriate ranks of the *Kriegsmarine*. They are subject to military laws and regulations.

8. Members of the MKP carry the standard military rank designations with the suffix '*der MKP*' (e.g. *Feldwebel der MKP, Leutnant der MKP*)

Rank designations of the MKP

Polizei	***MKP***
Rottwachtmeister	*Maat*
Wachtmeister	*Obermaat*
Oberwachtmeister	*Feldwebel*
Revieroberwachtmeister	*Oberfeldwebel*
Hauptwachtmeister (less than 12 years service)	*Oberfeldwebel*
Hauptwachtmeister (more than 12 years service)	*Stabsoberfeldwebel*
Meister	*Sonderführer (Lt. der MKP)*
Revierleutnant	*Sonderführer(Oblt der MKP)*
Revieroberleutnant	,,

Officer ranks of the *Polizei* (insofar as military ranks are concerned) on call up as naval officers or appointment thereto and/or as *Sonderführer* in officer ranks are not fixed.

The ranks of naval officers of equal standing will have the suffix 'der MKP'.

Members of the MKP who hold a higher rank as reservists in another branch of the armed forces than he would hold after his rank was adjusted after transfer, is to be accorded that higher rank.

9. Ranks of *Meister*, *Revierleutnant* and *Revieroberleutnant* are to be appointed as *Sonderführer* in the *Kriegsmarine* only if their use in an officer position is definitely required. In other cases they are to be transferred back to a home service post.

The same arrangement is valid for *Polizei* reservists in respect of the allocation of ranks of *Maat* and *Obermaat*.

10. Service conditions of the *Ordnungspolizei* taken over by the MKP correspond to the service conditions of members of the reserves who are called up for military service.

11. On discharge from the MKP, former officials and reservists from the *Ordnungspolizei* will return to their home service post. No special rights arise from affiliation to the MKP.

Uniforms and Insignia

In the same way in which police uniforms were worn during a transitional phase by members of the civilian police transferred into the army to serve in the *Feldgendarmerie*, so WSP uniforms were initially worn by those transferred into the navy to serve in the MKP.

For several months after the formation of the MKP, personnel transferred from the WSP continued to wear their WSP rank insignia (as confirmed in OTB 41, Nr 52 XVI of 12 March 1941). An exception to this was if the police member held a reserve rank in the navy, in which case he would wear *Kriegsmarine* uniform with the insignia of the appropriate naval *Sonderführer* (Specialist) rank. The same order however indicated that although the WSP uniform would be worn, it should have the naval version of the national emblem sewn on to the right breast in the same manner as for naval uniforms.

Not long afterwards, on 24 July 1941, the order previously referred to (OTB 41, Nr 192) prescribed the use of standard issue naval garments as follows:

Armament, Clothing, Equipment

For the MKP, the normal naval clothing regulations are to be followed in principle, with the following deviations:

a) All members of the MKP wear on the left upper arm of the blue jacket and the greatcoat the national emblem of the water protection police (without district designation) and on the left lower arm of the blue jacket (for officers between sleeve strips and career badges of the naval officers and/or officers of the naval artillery) and the greatcoat a light blue band with the inscription '*Marineküstenpolizei*' in yellow embroidery in accordance with the special sample.

b) On duty, NCOs of the MKP carry on the right breast, a pin-on MKP insignia in white metal with the lettering '*Marineküstenpolizei*' in luminous letters as on the special sample.

Paragraph 33 of the same order confirmed the issue of personal kit to MKP personnel, thus:

> The MKP in service with the *Kriegsmarine* is equipped with pistol, belt with bayonet, bread bag, canteen, drinking cup, and mess kit and, further, with any weapons and equipment necessary for the execution of their tasks, as well as with the M.K.P. Insignia.
>
> Furthermore the M.K.P. member receives the same *Soldbuch* and identity discs as the regular soldiers of the *Kriegsmarine*.

The special MKP insignia worn on the standard naval uniform can thus be summarised as follows.

Cuffband

The narrow MKP cuffband is made from cornflower blue cloth 2.2 cm in width, with yellow-gold Russia braid edging. In the centre was machine- embroidered the legend *Marine-Küstenpolizei* in Gothic script in the same golden-yellow colour as the edging. Examples may also be encountered with edging and lettering in gold coloured wire and these are presumed to be for officer or senior NCO ranks.

Sleeve Eagle

The WSP pattern sleeve eagle was worn. This was either in machine embroidered or machine-woven form and had the police pattern national emblem in golden yellow colour on a navy blue backing. Officer grade examples would be hand embroidered in gold coloured wire.

Gorget

The special 'Insignia' referred to in the OTB of 24 July 1941 was in fact a gorget plate. This was similar in shape to the *Feldgendarmerie* example but smaller at just 13 cm wide, and was unique in that it featured a hinged horizontal pin fitting on the reverse rather than being suspended from a neck chain.

The plate was stamped from thin sheet metal with a raised edge with the legend *Marine-Küsten/ Polizei* in two lines, and had a silver painted finish. At each side and just above the lettering are positioned two naval style buttons with the traditional fouled anchor motif. The buttons and lettering were painted with a pale yellow luminous paint. The reverse face of the plate was covered in field grey coloured wool. The MKP gorget was unusual in that there were two prescribed methods of wear. On the jacket, it was worn on the right breast, just below the naval breast eagle, with the pin through thread loops sewn onto the jacket (in a similar manner to loops sewn on to uniforms to hold badges and awards).

Perhaps it is because of this position, directly below the national emblem on the jacket, that the gorget lacks the national emblem found on the *Feldgendarmerie* gorget as this would have seemed superfluous. When worn on the greatcoat however, which of course did not feature a national emblem on the right breast, two short 9 cm lengths of chain were attached to the gorget by means of passing the gorget pin through links in the chain. The other ends of the chain had small hooks attached which then served to attach the assembly to small loops sewn under the greatcoat collar.

When the assembly was worn, it had the appearance of a conventional gorget, worn centred on the chest by a neck chain. The MKP gorget is one of the rarer types and not too often encountered on the collector market. Even rarer however, are photos of the gorget being worn.

Although the officer here is in WSP uniform, the fact he is accompanied by an armed *Kriegsmarine* sailor suggests he may be acting as an MKP officer. (*Josef Charita*)

As this photo was reputed taken in Norway the officer in the centre is almost certainly acting as MKP as the WSP did not operate outside of the Reich.

It is to be expected that with such a small branch as the MKP, good photos of its personnel would be relatively scarce. It is interesting that photos have been found with the gorget in wear and with the cuffband in wear, but so far the author has not encountered a photo showing both in wear at the same time!

As stated in the original regulations for the creation of the MKP, these were as a rule not formed up as self-contained unit as were their *Feldgendarmerie* counterparts. Instead, a small handful of MKP personnel would be allocated to the office of the local Harbour Commander (*Hafenkommandant*).

This being the case, the normal means of identifying the branch of service of a member of a military police type unit by examining the entries in the *Soldbuch* showing their unit allocation cannot be used in this case as these entries would simply show the individual allocated to the local harbour or installation commander.

Virtually the only way therefore of identifying such documents to these troops is by the addition of the suffix 'der MKP' to the individuals rank as shown in the book.

Above left: There is no question in this case that the individual in the centre is MKP. In full *Kriegsmarine* uniform with the addition of the *Polizei* sleeve eagle and '*Marineküstenpolizei*' cufftitle. (*Josef Charita*)

Above right: An interesting transitional uniform is shown here. The jacket is WSP with the sleeve rings of an NCO, but with the addition of a *Kriegsmarine* breast eagle and the use of a regulation *Kriegsmarine* NCO visor cap.

Right: Unfouled anchor badge worn on the left sleeve by Junior NCO ranks serving with the MKP.

Below: An extremely rare photograph, one of only a handful known to exist, showing the MKP gorget in wear, in the regulation position under the breast eagle.

Soldbuch
zugleich Personalausweis
Nr. 180
Obermaat der MKP 77
(Dienstgrad) (Wehrsoldgruppe)

befördert:	zum:	
ab .... (Datum)	/ .... (neuer Dienstgrad)	/ .... (Wehrsoldgruppe)
ab	/	/ ....
ab	/	/ ....
ab	/	/ ....
ab	/	/ ....

Heinz Eberhard (Vor- und Zuname)
Beschriftung und Nummer der Erkennungsmarke N 75456 S.
Blutgruppe B
Gasmaskengröße 3
Marine-Stammrollen-Nr. L.M.St.A. 07514 S
Stamm-Marineteil Mar. Stamm Reg. Beverloo
1

Soldbuch of *Marineküstenpolizei Oberbootsmann* Heinz Eberhard. Only the use of the suffix „der MKP" to the ranks indicates he is from the naval police. (*Ian Jewison*)

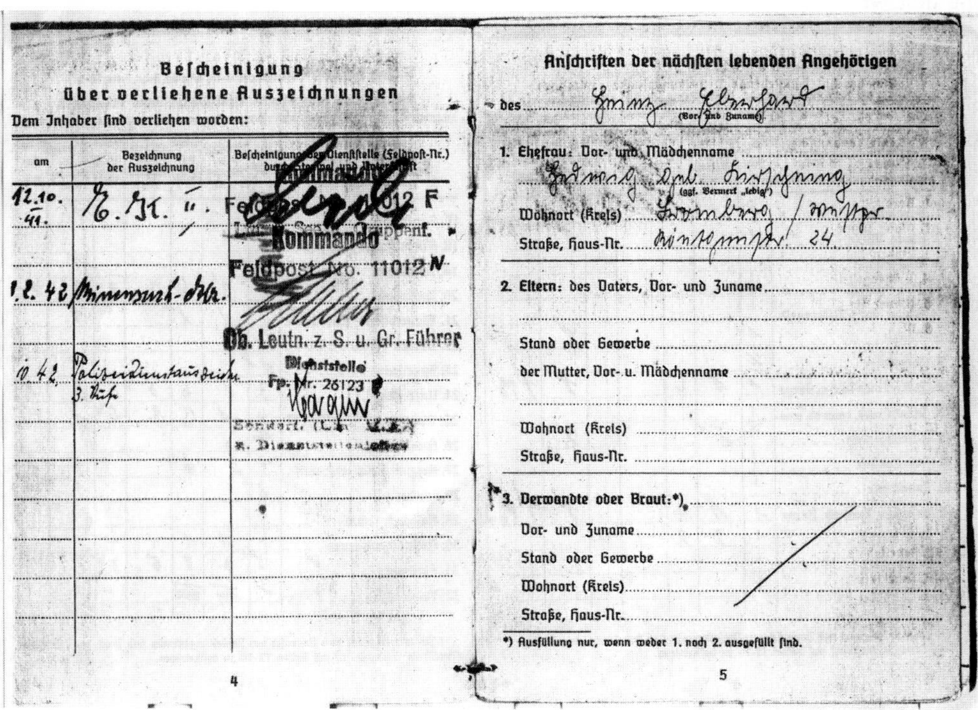

Bescheinigung
über verliehene Auszeichnungen
Dem Inhaber sind verliehen worden:

am	Bezeichnung der Auszeichnung	Bescheinigung der Dienststelle (Feldpost-Nr.) durch Stempel und Unterschrift
12.10.41.	E.K. II.	Feldpost-Nr. 11012 F Kommando
1.2.42	Minensuch-Abz.	Feldpost No. 11012 N Ob. Leutn. z. S. u. Gr. Führer
10.42	Polizeidienstauszeichn. 3. Stufe	Dienststelle Fp. Nr. 26123

4

Anschriften der nächsten lebenden Angehörigen
des Heinz Eberhard (Vor- und Zuname)

1. Ehefrau: Vor- und Mädchenname .... (ggf. Vermerk „ledig")
Wohnort (Kreis) ....
Straße, Haus-Nr. 24

2. Eltern: des Vaters, Vor- und Zuname ....
Stand oder Gewerbe ....
der Mutter, Vor- u. Mädchenname ....
Wohnort (Kreis) ....
Straße, Haus-Nr. ....

3. Verwandte oder Braut:*) ....
Vor- und Zuname ....
Stand oder Gewerbe ....
Wohnort (Kreis) ....
Straße, Haus-Nr. ....

*) Ausfüllung nur, wenn weder 1. noch 2. ausgefüllt sind.

5

The awards page from the Eberhard *Soldbuch* showing the issue of a Police Long Service Medal, another clue to his police origins. (*Ian Jewison*)

Feldjägerkorps

During the second half of the war, as Germany's military fortunes waned, morale and motivation of the German front line troops began to decline. Indiscipline and desertion rates increased to worrying proportions. In addition it rapidly became clear that huge levels of manpower and equipment was being effectively wasted in the occupied areas, especially in countries like France where occupation troops often lived in what seemed like luxurious circumstances compared to their comrades on the Eastern Front.

One of the major factors leading to the creation of the *Feldjägerkorps* was a visit to occupied France by *Generaloberst* Jodl to inspect the preparations for the anticipated allied invasion. Jodl was shocked at the relative luxury in which senior command elements had housed themselves, clean luxury hotels or châteaux with carpeted floors, comfortably furnished and richly decorated. One unit which he reportedly went to visit were all absent on a hunt!

In addition, as front line units were decimated in fighting on the eastern front, there resulted a large number of non-combatant elements which existed to supply these combat units, but had no units left to support. Clearly the situation of bloated rear area formations living in relative safety and luxury, consuming vast amounts of food, fuel and manpower whilst the front line combat units suffered could not be allowed to continue.

In December 1943, a *Führer* decree was issued creating the *Feldjägerkommandos.*

> The *Feldjägerkommandos* and battalions are *Wehrmacht* troops and are directly subordinate to the OKW. The have the task of checking and combing out units of the army, navy air-force and *Waffen-SS.* These tasks will be carried out in close connection with the territorial commanders. The commanders of the *Feldjägerkommandos* are responsible solely to the Chief of the OKW. Enforcement measures, task forces, patrol services should be made available to the *Feldjägerkommandos.*

So we can see that not only were the *Feldjägerkommandos* given supreme authority to carry out their tasks in relation to *Wehrmacht* forces, but *Waffen-SS* also, and that they had the power to call on whatever support they needed from the local commanders.

The following definitions of the tasks of the *Feldjäger* were published by the OKH (*Oberkommando des Heeres*—High Command of the Army) in September 1944 (O.K.H. (Ch H Rüst u. BdE), 15 September 44—7378/44—Stab/.Ia2.) and also in a special supplement to army orders bulletin (*Heeresmitteilungsblatt*) as H.M. 1944, Issue Nr 24.

1. *Feldjäger* have the task, as ordered by the *Führer* and under direct command of the Chief of the *Oberkomando der Wehrmacht* in the rear areas, to maintain temporary and complete authority, military discipline and order in all situations, if necessary by ruthless measures up to the immediate use of firearms.

2. *Feldjäger* are special, proven front soldiers, whose activities have the sole aim of supporting the front line. They ensure the area behind the front is kept secure. They expect therefore and with good reason the greatest appreciation for their difficult task, primarily from frontline soldiers of all ranks.

3. *Feldjäger* have received from the *Führer*, in order to accomplish their assigned tasks, particularly wide ranging power and authority over members of all parts of the armed forces, the *Waffen-SS* and organisations used in the support of the armed forces (OT, NSKK etc.)

4. *Feldjäger* co-operate closely with all Order services in the area in which they are employed (*Wehrmachtstreifendienst, Feldgendarmerie, Kommandanturen, Polizei,* Guards, Patrols and Sentries of all kinds). They carry out their tasks as required by the prevailing situation at the front. Criticisms of, or resistance to, *Feldjäger* orders are unjustified and are also considered as proof of the lack of correct military attitude and insight due to indiscipline.

5. *Feldjäger* eliminate all possibility of mismanagement in the area between fighting front and homeland front, which disparage the great sacrifices of every good German and the combatants of the armed forces.

6. *Feldjäger* ensure the delivery of redundant and surplus personnel and material from rear agencies and units and the supply of personnel and material fit for the front, to the fighting troops.

7. *Feldjäger* fight behind the front against disobedience, desertion, self-interest, neglect and sloppy work of any type. They are strictly monitored in the performance of their duties by their superiors, with any misdemeanours particularly severely punished and discharged from the *Feldjägerkorps*.

8. *Feldjäger* on duty are recognizable by gorgets, red armbands and a special *Ausweis*.

Their service is difficult, self sacrificing and highly responsible.

All are required to help and to facilitate, by disciplined behaviour, the difficult task of the *Feldjäger*, because the military discipline of the German soldier is the guarantee of victory. In this regard the *Feldjäger* is a strict and fair helper.

Special Insignia

Feldjäger were recruited from experienced personnel from the *Wehrmacht* and *Waffen-SS*, though the *Luftwaffe* element was minimal. *Heer* and *Waffen-SS* members were expected to be combat veterans though *Luftwaffe* personnel generally came from redundant aircrew and ground crew so the combat experience would not be appropriate.

Former *Feldjäger, SS-Unterscharführer* Gottfried Schwittalla remembers:

> It is correct that the members of the OKW *Feldjäger* should have been experienced front line Officers and NCOs as patrol leaders and members.
>
> This requirement was mostly not met by the *Luftwaffe* as the *Luftwaffe* element consisted mainly of ground crew personnel, while from the army, as a minimum, decorated front line soldiers were required.
>
> In my unit, the company commander, *SS-Hauptsturmführer* Brehm and I, and one sergeant from the army, *Feldwebel* Kastl, held the Iron Cross Ist Class.
>
> In December 1943 while I was acting as an instructor at the *SS-Pionier-Ersatz und Ausbildungs Bataillon* in Dresden after seeing combat action and being wounded on the Eastern Front, I had to report to the adjutant, *SS-Hauptsturmführer* Tarneden. He told me that the battalion commander, *SS-Sturmbannführer* Tietz, had decided that I would be transferred to the newly formed OKW *Feldjäger* detachment near Vienna. My qualification for the position was front line experience and possession of the Iron Cross Ist Class.
>
> The transfer to the *Feldjäger* followed in February 1944 and we were accommodated in the barracks of a replacement battalion for the *Panzertruppe* in Spratzern. I was assigned the 3rd[d] Company. My company commander was *SS-Hauptsturmführer* Brehm and my platoon leader was from the *Luftwaffe*, *Hauptmann* Isermann

With personnel drawn from so many varied units, there was no dedicated *Waffenfarbe* colour worn by the *Feldjäger*, the *Waffenfarbe* of the soldier's original unit being worn as was the wearers original uniform so that within a single *Feldjäger* patrol uniforms of the *Heer, Waffen-SS* and *Luftwaffe* might all be seen at the same time. Three special forms of identification were used:

Armband

Two versions of the *Feldjäger* armband are known. The most commonly encountered on wartime photos is the red armband with white lettering *OKW/Feldjäger.* A further variant exists however, with the printed legend *Oberkommando der Wehrmacht/Feldjäger* in black. Both variants were normally worn on the lower left sleeve.

Ausweis

Feldjäger were issued with a special *Ausweis* printed on red card, which set out the level of their authority from the OKW.

An army officer serving with the *Feldjägerkorps*. Apart from the armband, no special insignia is worn. (*Otto Spronk Photo Files*)

Feldjäger armbands were also made in printed form in black on red. Originals are of great rarity and the example illustrated is an accurate post-war replica.

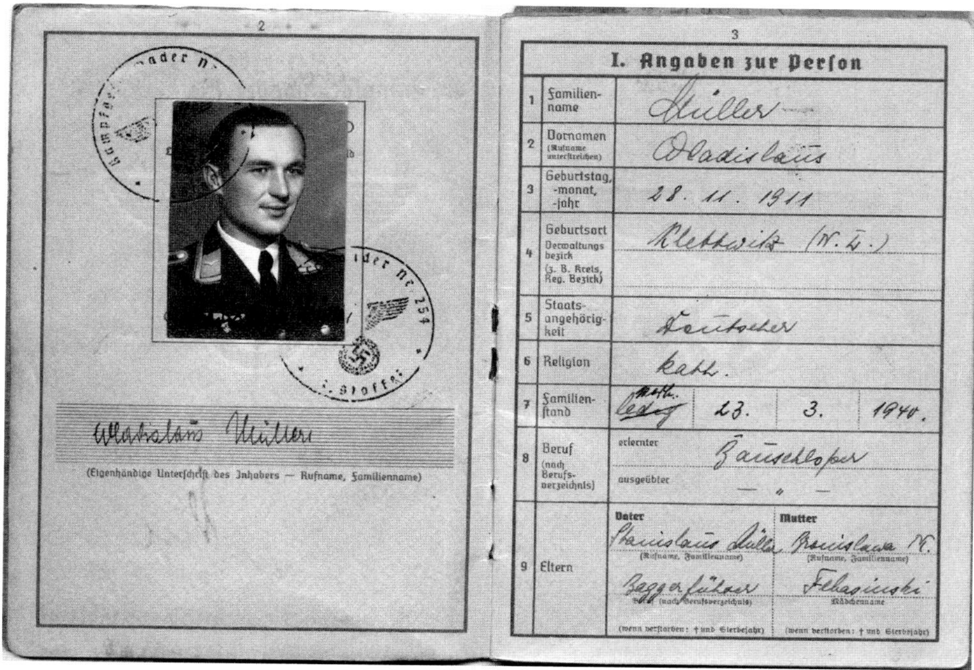

2

Wladislaus Müller

(Eigenhändige Unterschrift des Inhabers — Rufname, Familienname)

3

I. Angaben zur Person

1	Familienname	Müller
2	Vornamen (Rufname unterstreichen)	Wladislaus
3	Geburtstag, -monat, -jahr	28. 11. 1911
4	Geburtsort, Verwaltungsbezirk (z. B. Kreis, Reg. Bezirk)	Klettwitz (N. L.)
5	Staatsangehörigkeit	Deutscher
6	Religion	kath.
7	Familienstand	ledig / verh. 23. 3. 1940.
8	Beruf (nach Berufsverzeichnis)	erlernter: Bauschlosser; ausgeübter: — " —
9	Eltern	Vater: Stanislaus Müller (Rufname, Familienname); Baggerführer (nach Berufsverzeichnis); (wenn verstorben: † und Sterbejahr) — Mutter: Stanislawa M. (Rufname, Familienname); Felsasinski (Mädchenname); (wenn verstorben: † und Sterbejahr)

Wehrpass to Wladislaus Müller, a *Luftwaffe Stabsfeldwebel* who served with the *Feldjäger.*

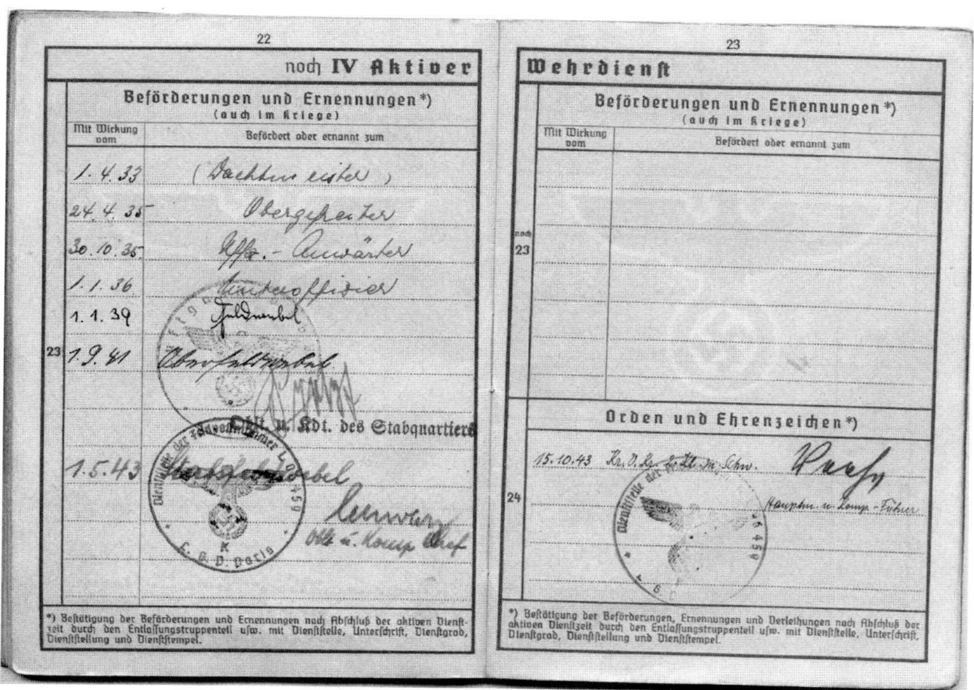

22

noch **IV Aktiver**

Beförderungen und Ernennungen*) (auch im Kriege)

Mit Wirkung vom	Befördert oder ernannt zum
1.4.33	(Dachdecker)
24.4.35	Obergefreiter
30.10.35	Uffz.-Anwärter
1.1.36	Unteroffizier
1.1.39	Feldwebel
1.9.41	Oberfeldwebel
	Oblt. u. Kdt. des Stabquartiers
1.5.43	Stabsfeldwebel
	Oblt. u. Komp. Chef

*) Bestätigung der Beförderungen und Ernennungen nach Abschluß der aktiven Dienstzeit durch den Entlassungstruppenteil usw. mit Dienststelle, Unterschrift, Dienstgrad, Dienststellung und Dienststempel.

23

Wehrdienst

Beförderungen und Ernennungen*) (auch im Kriege)

Mit Wirkung vom	Befördert oder ernannt zum

Orden und Ehrenzeichen*)

15.10.43 Kr.V.K. 2. Kl. m. Schw.

Hauptm. u. Komp.-Führer

*) Bestätigung der Beförderungen, Ernennungen und Verleihungen nach Abschluß der aktiven Dienstzeit durch den Entlassungstruppenteil usw. mit Dienststelle, Unterschrift, Dienstgrad, Dienststellung und Dienststempel.

The Müller *Wehrpass* . During 1940/41 Müller served with *Kampfgeschwader Boelcke* but apart from his Combined Pilot-Observer badge, the only award shown is the humble War Merit Cross 2nd Class.

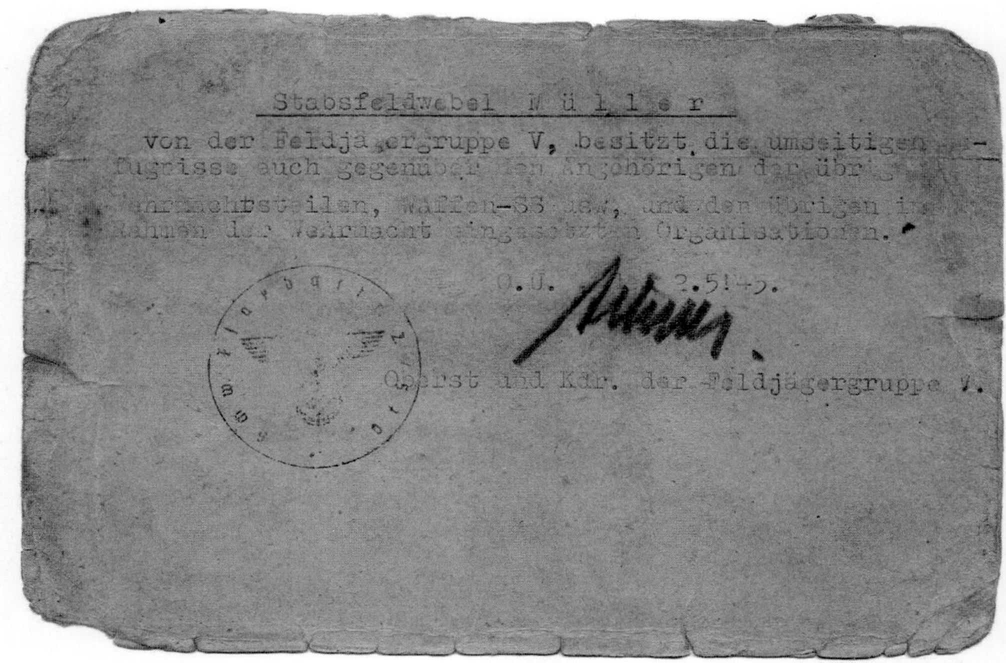

Stabsfeldwebel M ü l l e r

von der Feldjägergruppe V, besitzt die umseitigen [illegible]fugnisse auch gegenüber den Angehörigen der übrigen [illegible]ehrmachtsteilen, Waffen-SS usw, und den übrigen im Rahmen der Wehrmacht eingesetzten Organisationen.

O.U. [illegible] 2.5.45.

Oberst und Kdr. der Feldjägergruppe V.

The Müller *Wehrpass* shows no indication that he served with the *Feldjäger*. However with the *Wehrpass* is an *Ausweis* issued by the commander of *Feldjägergruppe* V confirming his position and that his authority extended over all branches of the *Wehrmacht* as well as the *Waffen-SS*.

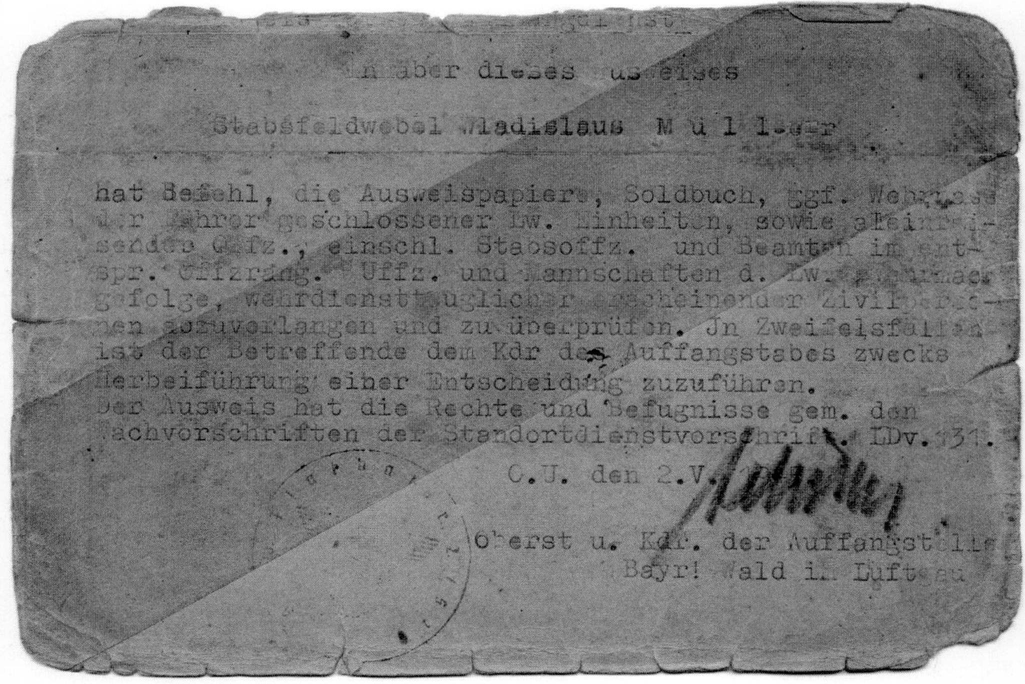

[illegible]nhaber dieses [illegible]usweises

Stabsfeldwebel Wladislaus M ü l l e r

hat Befehl, die Ausweispapiere, Soldbuch, Wehrpass der Führer geschlossener Lw. Einheiten, sowie [illegible] sendes [illegible]ffz., einschl. Stabsoffz. und Beamten im entspr. Offzrang. Uffz. und Mannschaften d. Lw. [illegible]gefolge, wehrdiensttauglicher erscheinender Zivilpersonen [illegible]verlangen und zu überprüfen. Jn Zweifelsfällen ist der Betreffende dem Kdr des Auffangstabes zwecks Herbeiführung einer Entscheidung zuzuführen.
Der Ausweis hat die Rechte und Befugnisse gem. den Wachvorschriften der Standortdienstvorschrift [illegible] LDv. 131.

O.U. den 2.V.[illegible]

Oberst u. Kdr. der Auffangstelle
Bayr! Wald in Luftgau

Reverse of the Müller *Ausweis*, further setting out his duties and authority.

A *Feldjäger* wearing the variant armband with white lettering on red. The scroll on the gorget is impossible to read and may be the regular *Feldgendarmerie* type. (*Otto Spronk Photo Files*)

Gorget

A special gorget was produced, identical to the *Feldgendarmerie* gorget, but with the scroll bearing the legend *Feldjägerkorps*. The gorget was certainly manufactured and original examples have survived, but whether it saw any widespread use is debatable. Once again, Gottfried Schwitalla remembers:

> Our uniforms were without additional characteristics, thus without the gorget. They told us that we would be issued gorgets with the designation '*Feldjäger*', however we never received them. When on patrol service we wore only a red armband on the left arm with the inscription '*OKW Feldjäger*'.

In terms of insignia, it was also intended that ultimately, a special shoulder strap emblem consisting of the Latin letters Fj, for *Feldjäger*, would be introduced and that white would be adopted for the *Waffenfarbe* of these formations. It does not appear however that adoption of this distinctive insignia was ever achieved before the end of the war. In terms of equipment, the *Feldjägerkorps* was fairly lightly equipped, though at *Feldjägerkommando* level, each had Fieseler Storch communications aircraft available.

As the *Feldjäger* operated mostly as small independent four man patrols (one officer and three NCOs or two NCOs and a driver), no heavy vehicles were required and the typical equipment for each patrol was a requisitioned civilian vehicle.

From Gottfried Schwitalla:

> I was patrol member of an officer-led patrol. As our vehicle we had a Citroen passenger vehicle. The driver was a private first class of the *Luftwaffe*.

Armament normally comprised a pistol for the officer, and Mauser Kar98k carbines for the NCOs and junior ranks such as the driver. As with the *Feldgendarmerie*, only a small number of machine-pistols were issued to *Feldjäger*.

Organisation

The basic organisation of the *Feldjägerkorps* was simple. A command element or *Feldjägerkommando*, with control over a single *Feldjägerabteilung** (later increased to a *Feldjägerregiment*). The *Feldjägerabteilung* was divided into 5 *Kompanien*, the later, larger *Feldjägerregiment* was divided into 5 *Feldjägerabteilungen* each of which consisted of 3 *Kompanien*.
Each *Kompanie* would typically field 4 patrols or *Streifen*.

**Abteilung* simply means a military detachment or unit. The word is often used in connection with a battalion sized unit and in the case of the *Feldjägerkorps Abteilung* and *Bataillon* can be considered as synonymous.

Equipment Levels

Feldjägerkommando (mot.)

Command element

9 officers, 1 admin official*, 5 NCOs, 21 enlisted men.

- 10 × pistols.
- 24 × carbines.
- 2 × machine pistols.
- 1 × heavy field car.
- 4 × medium field cars.
- 2 × light field cars (4 seat).
- 1 × 2 ton truck.
- 1 × 15 seat bus.

*Admin officials were civilians with specialist skills (such as paymasters, legal officers etc.) put into uniform 'for the duration' with officer status and with their own specific career paths separate to the regular army. In addition to the above a *Flugbereitschaft* or flight section consisting of three spotter/communication aircraft (Fieseler Storch) was available to each *Feldjägerkommando.*

Feldjägerregiment (mot.)

Command Group

5 officers, 2 admin officials, 9 NCOs and 17 enlisted men.

- 10 × pistols.
- 22 × carbines.
- 1 × machine pistol.
- 1 × light machine gun.
- 1 × medium field car.
- 3 × light field cars (4 seat).
- 1 × 2 ton truck.
- 1 × 15 seat bus.

Motor Transport Section

1 admin official, 2 NCOs, 8 enlisted men.
1 × pistol.
10 × carbines.
3 × light field cars.
1 × 3 ton truck.

Feldjägerabteilung

Command Group

4 officers and 5 enlisted ranks (despatch riders, drivers).
4 × pistols.
5 × carbines.
1 × motorcycle.
1 × motorcycle with sidecar.
3 × light field cars.

Patrol (*Streifen*) Group

A number of 4 man *Streifen* were grouped into a *Kompanie* as required. The total strength of a *Kompanie* could vary as circumstances required.

3 officers, 9 NCOs and 6 enlisted men.
6 × pistols.
6 × carbines.
6 × machine pistols.
6 × light field cars.

Special Purpose Patrol Group

2 officers, 8 NCOs and 15 enlisted men.
5 × pistols.
15 × carbines.
5 × machine pistols.
5 × medium field cars.
2 × motorcycles.

Supply element

7 NCOs and 17 enlisted men.
3 × pistols.
21 × carbines.
6 × 3 ton trucks (2 for field kitchens, 1 for packs, 1 for fuel, 1 for supplies and 1 for personnel).

Repair troop

2 NCOs and 2 enlisted men.
1 × pistol.
3 × carbines.
1 × light field car.
1 × 2 ton truck.

Soldbuch
zugleich Personalausweis

Nr. 733

für

Kraftfahrer
(Dienstgrad)

ab 1.1.1942 Oberkraftfahrer
(Datum) (neuer Dienstgrad)
ab 1.1.1943 Gefreiter
ab 1.12.1943 Obergefreiter

Gustav Rösener
(Vor- und Zuname)

Beschriftung und Nummer der Erkennungsmarke 1./Kf. Ers. Abt. 20 733

Blutgruppe 0

Gasmaskengröße 2

Wehrnummer Hagen 11/7/6/15

1

Soldbuch for *Obergefreiter* Gustav Rösener who served with *Feldjäger* Regiment I.

A. Zuletzt zuständige Wehrersatzdienststelle: W. B. A. Schwelm

B. Zum Feldheer abgesandt von:[1])

	Ersatztruppenteil	Kompanie	Nr. der Truppenstammrolle
a	1. Komp. Kraftf. Ers. Abt. 20		VI/138
b			
c			

C.

	Feldtruppenteil[2])	Kompanie	Nr. der Kriegsstammrolle
a			468
b	4/Kraftf.Abt.901		468
c	Feldjäger-Rgt (mot) I	IV	Kr. 213/44

D.

Jetzt zuständiger Ersatztruppenteil[2])	Standort
~~Kraftf. Ers. Abt. 20~~	~~Gera~~
Kf. Ers. Abt. 3.	Rathenow

(Meldung dortselbst nach Rückkehr vom Feldheer oder Lazarett, zuständig für Ersatz an Bekleidung und Ausrüstung)

[1]) Vom Ersatztruppenteil einzutragen, von dem der Soldbuchinhaber zum Feldheer abgesandt wird.
[2]) Vom Feldtruppenteil einzutragen und bei Versetzungen von einem zum anderen Feldtruppenteil derart abzuändern, daß die alten Angaben nur durchstrichen werden, also leserlich bleiben.

Weiterer Raum für Eintragungen auf Seite 17.

4

Anschriften der nächsten lebenden Angehörigen

des Gustav Rösener
(Vor- und Zuname)

1. Ehefrau: Vor- und Mädchenname Else Rösener
(21) (ggf. Vermerk „ledig")
Wohnort (Kreis) Altenvoerde
Straße, Haus-Nr. Nr. 15

2. Eltern: des Vaters, Vor- und Zuname

Stand oder Gewerbe

der Mutter, Vor- u. Mädchenname

Wohnort (Kreis)

Straße, Haus-Nr.

3. Verwandte oder Braut:*)

Vor- und Zuname

Stand oder Gewerbe

Wohnort (Kreis)

Straße, Haus-Nr.

*) Ausfüllung nur, wenn weder 1. noch 2. ausgefüllt sind.

5

Section C of the Rösener *Soldbuch* shows his service with *Feldjäger*-Rgt (mot.) I

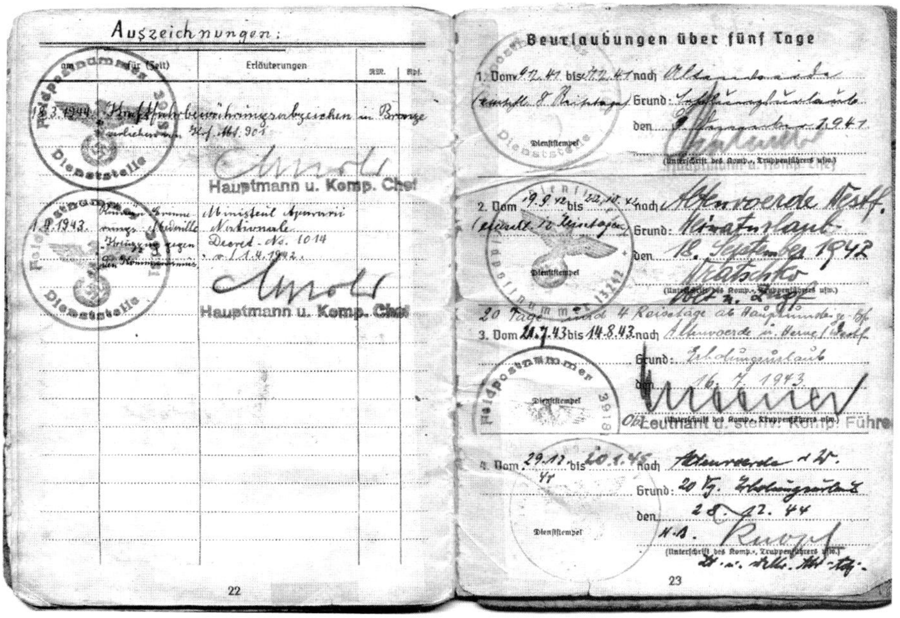

Auszeichnungen:

(Zeit)	Erläuterungen	RM.	Rpf.
8.3.1944	Kraftfahrbewährungsabzeichen in Bronze ... Kf. Abt. 901		
	Hauptmann u. Komp. Chef		
1.8.1943	Ministerul Apararii Nationale Decret No. 1014 ...		
	Hauptmann u. Komp. Chef		

22

Beurlaubungen über fünf Tage

1. Vom 9.12.41 bis 17.12.41 nach ... Grund: ... den ... 1941 (Unterschrift des Komp.-, Truppenführers usw.)

2. Vom 9.9.42 bis 22.10.42 nach Altenvoerde Westf. Grund: Heimatsurlaub den 18. September 1942 (Unterschrift des Komp.-, Truppenführers usw.)

20 Tage und 4 Reisetage ...

3. Vom 21.7.43 bis 14.8.43 nach Altenvoerde i. Westf. Grund: Erholungsurlaub den 16. 7. 1943 Oblt. Leutnant u. stellv. Komp. Führer

4. Vom 29.12.44 bis 20.1.45 nach Altenvoerde ... Grund: 20 Tg. Erholungsurlaub den 28.12.44 (Unterschrift des Komp.-, Truppenführers usw.)

23

The awards page from the Rösener *Soldbuch* gives the lie to the theory that all *Feldjäger* were decorated combat veterans with at least an Iron Cross. Rösener held just the *Kraftfahrbewährungsabzeichen* and the Romanian Medal for the 'Crusade against Communism'.

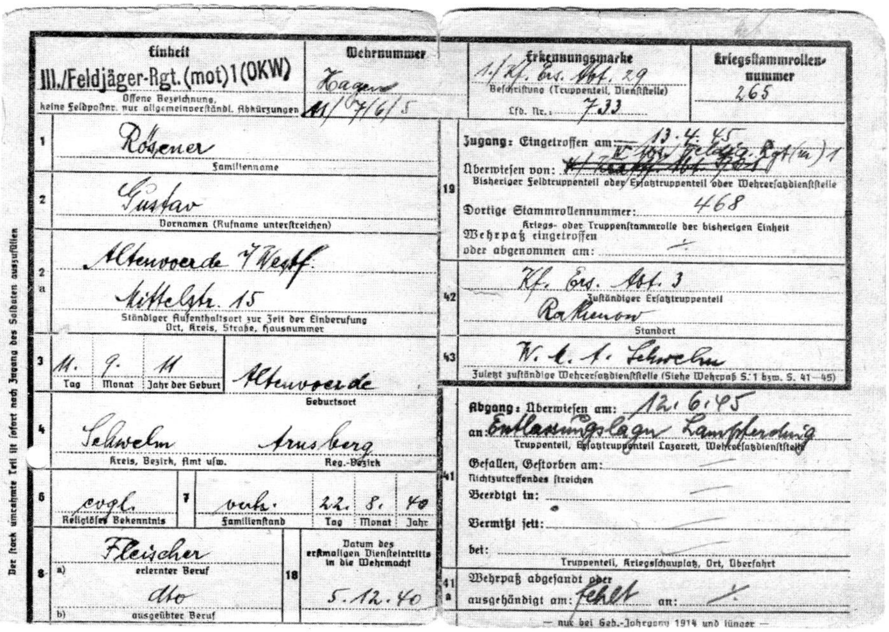

Einheit: III./Feldjäger-Rgt. (mot) 1 (OKW)
Offene Bezeichnung, keine Feldpostnr. nur allgemeinverständl. Abkürzungen

Wehrnummer: Hagen 11/7/6/5

Erkennungsmarke: 1./Kf. Ers. Abt. 29 — Lfd. Nr.: 733

Kriegsstammrollennummer: 265

1. Rösener — Familienname
2. Gustav — Vornamen (Rufname unterstreichen)
2a. Altenvoerde i. Westf. Mittelstr. 15 — Ständiger Aufenthaltsort zur Zeit der Einberufung Ort, Kreis, Straße, Hausnummer
3. 11. 9. 11 — Tag, Monat, Jahr der Geburt — Altenvoerde — Geburtsort
4. Schwelm, Arnsberg — Kreis, Bezirk, Amt usw. — Reg.-Bezirk
5. evgl. — Religiöses Bekenntnis; 7. verh. — Familienstand; 22. 8. 40 — Tag, Monat, Jahr
8. a) Fleischer — erlernter Beruf; b) dto — ausgeübter Beruf
18. Datum des erstmaligen Diensteintritts in die Wehrmacht: 5.12.40

19. Zugang: Eingetroffen am: 13.4.45 ... Überwiesen von: ... Bisheriger Feldtruppenteil oder Ersatztruppenteil oder Wehrersatzdienststelle. Dortige Stammrollennummer: 468. Kriegs- oder Truppenstammrolle der bisherigen Einheit. Wehrpaß eingetroffen oder abgenommen am: —

42. Kf. Ers. Abt. 3 — Zuständiger Ersatztruppenteil — Rathenow — Standort

43. W. B. K. Schwelm — Zuletzt zuständige Wehrersatzdienststelle (Siehe Wehrpaß S. 1 bzw. S. 41—45)

41. Abgang: Überwiesen am: 12.6.45 an: Entlassungslager Landsberg ... Truppenteil, Ersatztruppenteil, Lazarett, Wehrersatzdienststelle. Gefallen, Gestorben am: — Nichtzutreffendes streichen. Beerdigt in: — Vermißt seit: — bei: — Truppenteil, Kriegsschauplatz, Ort, Überfahrt

41a. Wehrpaß abgesandt oder ausgehändigt am: fehlt an: —
— nur bei Geb.-Jahrgang 1914 und jünger —

Der stark umrahmte Teil ist sofort nach Zugang des Soldaten auszufüllen

False entries for rare units in an original *Soldbuch* are not unknown but Rösener's service in the *Feldjägerkorps* is confirmed by his personal data sheet from the unit.

The Feldjägerkorps

Feldjäger-Kommando I

Formed 25 December 1943 by the high command of *Wehrkreis I.*

Commander:

General der.Flieger Ernst Müller (December 1943–May 1945).

Feldjäger Bataillon I

Formed 25 December 1943. Based in Stablack in *Wehrkreis I* with five fully motorised *Kompanien.*

Feldjäger Regiment I

Created on 25 April 1944 with the enlargement of the original five companies into battalions (*Abteilungen*). The same *Feldpost* numbers were retained by the companies which had now been elevated to battalion status. Each new *Abteilung* fielded three *Kompanie* sized units. These did not appear to have been issued with individual *Feldpost* numbers.

Feldjäger-Kommando II

Formed 25 December 1943 by the high command of *Wehrkreis VIII.*

Commanders:

General der Panzertruppe Kempf (Dec 1943–17 May 1944).
General der Infanterie Karl von Oven (17 May 1944–5 Feb 1945).
General der Artillerie Willi Moser (5 Feb 1945–8 May 1945).

Feldjäger Bataillon II

Formed 25 December 1943 from a mixture of *Heer, Luftwaffe* and *Waffen-SS* personnel organised into five fully motorised *Kompanien.* It operated exclusively on the Eastern Front. All elements appear to have initially used the same *Feldpost* number.

Feldjäger Regiment II

Created on 25 April 1944 with the enlargement of the original five companies into battalions. Again, each of the new *Abteilungen* contained three *Kompanie* sized sub-units.

Feldjäger-Kommando III

Formed 25 December1943 by the high command of *Wehrkreis XVII.*

Commanders:

General d. Infanterie Scheele (Dec 1943–Aug 1944).
General d. Infanterie Grase (Aug 1944–12 Mar 1945).
General d. Flieger Speidel (12 Mar 1945–23 Jun 1945).

Feldjäger Bataillon III

Formed 23 December 1943 with five fully motorised *Kompanien*. All appear to have used the same *Feldpost* number.

Feldjäger Regiment III
Created on 25 April 1944 with the enlargement of the original five companies into battalions.

Feldjäger Regiment 3 is interesting in that on its strength appears to have been a platoon specifically designated for carrying out sentences passed by the court martial element of the *Kommando*. On the list of field post numbers for the period from November 1944, FP Nr 42693 is listed as covering not only the *Regiment* but also a *Strafvollstreckungszug*. (punishment platoon).

Also part of the Order of Battle of the *Feldjägerkorps* was a training and replacement unit, *Feldgendarmerie Ersatz Regiment* I which appears to have been formed in November 1944 to train and prepare personnel for service in their new role.

Only one sub-unit is known, *I (Grenadier Bataillon) Feldgendarmerie Ersatz Regiment I* (FP Nr 04833) created at the same time.

Geheime Feldpolizei

The GFP was brought into being on 21 July 1939 following the signing of a new document, *Heeres Dienstvorschrift (geheim)150*, by *Generaloberst* Wilhelm Keitel.

The members of this new force were classed as *Wehrmachtbeamte* and not as professional career soldiers, though regular members of the armed forces could also be temporarily attached to the GFP as required, where they brought a specific skill that was required for the execution of a specific task, whether that skill might be technical, in languages or whatever. As well as suitable personnel from other branches, soldiers from the *Feldgendarmerie* were also occasionally attached to the GFP.

Organisational Structure

Each *Armeeoberkommando* had an attached GFP *Gruppe*, commanded by an official with the rank of *Feldpolizeidirektor*.

GFP Gruppen were also attached to district commands (*Abschnittskommandos*) of the *Grenzschutz* to help protect the security of the borders of the *Reich*.

Tasks

(i) To investigate all threats to the state, especially espionage and treasonous activities and to combat sabotage and hostile propaganda.

(ii) To collect and evaluate evidence and the results of investigations undertaken.

(iii) To supervise the implementation counter-measures for the protection of operational areas and provide support and advice to the military Staffs.

Performance of such tasks could include general measures for the personal protection of the senior personnel of the *Armee* staff where this was not otherwise provided; providing support to special courts in cases of espionage; assisting the police authorities in searching premises, especially in areas recently occupied and investigation and prevention of the use and abuse of German uniforms by enemy intelligence services.

In areas just occupied, GFP would become involved in securing all written material and telegrams in various institutions, post offices, railway stations and also securing any mail still in post boxes. Any of such documents might well contain useful intelligence material.

GFP could also be involved in searching recently abandoned military establishments, accommodation barracks etc and the seizure of any documents found in these places for delivery to military intelligence.

Searches would also be made for other means of communication which might potentially be used for espionage or sabotage operations by the enemy, such as courier pigeons, hidden radios transmitters, morse transmitters, printing presses etc.

In operational areas police investigations into matters within their remit were carried out by the GFP, and in such cases they were entitled to require any other military units including the *Feldgendarmerie*, to provide assistance.

GFP would also be involved in watching for the release of parachutes from aircraft which might contain material for saboteurs and for the release of enemy propaganda leaflets. They would also occasionally monitor establishments such as restaurants and cafes for suspicious persons. They could also monitor churches and other places where the public gathered, listening for subversive or provocative utterings.

Within the *Reich*, investigations were to be carried out in co-operation with the local civil police authorities. In this case GFP personnel had equal powers to the civilian police authorities. The GFP might also become involved in operations against smuggling, both of contraband and of people.

Although, generally, when operating outside the *Reich*, GFP officials would be in uniform and when operating within the *Reich* they would be in civilian clothing, in fact they were authorised to wear whatever civil or military clothing was deemed appropriate for them to carry out their investigations, indicating that they could in fact wear the uniform of other branches of the *Wehrmacht* if this was authorised, for them to operate 'under cover'.

A suspect, with *Feldgendarmerie* escort is interrogated by two GFP officials. On the original print, the distinctive GFP style *Waffenfarbe* surround around the officer's collar tabs is visible. (*Josef Charita*)

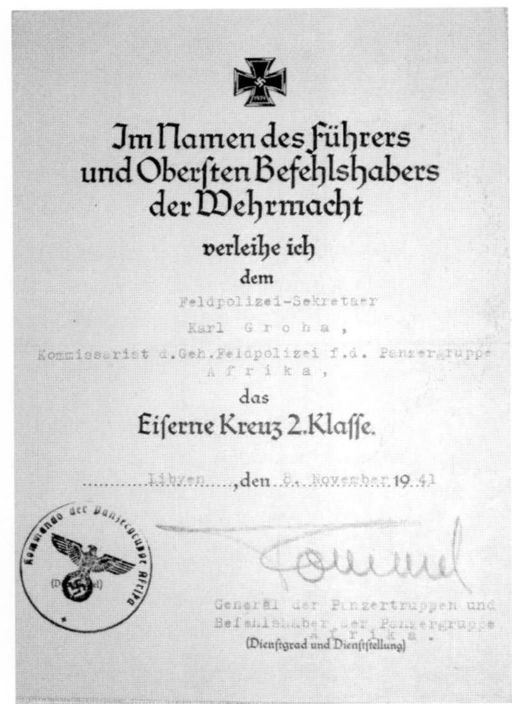

Im Namen des Führers
und Obersten Befehlshabers
der Wehrmacht
verleihe ich
dem
Feldpolizei-Sekretaer
Karl G r o h a ,
Kommissariat d.Geh.Feldpolizei f.d. Panzergruppe
A f r i k a ,
das
Eiserne Kreuz 2.Klasse.

Libyen, den 8. November 1941

General der Panzertruppen und
Befehlshaber der Panzergruppe
A f r i k a .
(Dienstgrad und Dienststellung)

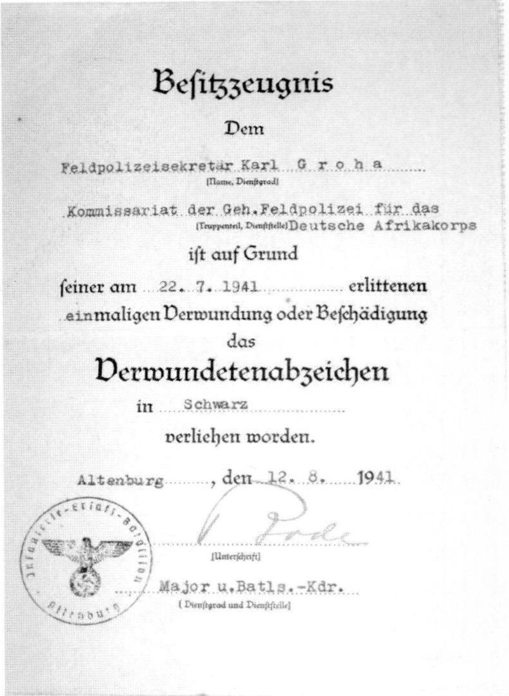

Besitzzeugnis

Dem

Feldpolizeisekretär Karl G r o h a
(Name, Dienstgrad)

Kommissariat der Geh.Feldpolizei für das
(Truppenteil, Dienststelle) Deutsche Afrikakorps

ist auf Grund
seiner am 22. 7. 1941 erlittenen
einmaligen Verwundung oder Beschädigung
das
Verwundetenabzeichen
in Schwarz
verliehen worden.

Altenburg, den 12. 8. 1941

(Unterschrift)
Major u.Batls.-Kdr.
(Dienstgrad und Dienststelle)

Above left: A very rare Award Document for the Iron Cross Second Class to a GFP officer, *Feldpolizeisekretär* Karl Groha, serving in North Africa, and signed by Rommel. (*David Bunch*)

Above right: Award Document for the Wound Badge in Black to Groha, also issued for wounds received during his service in North Africa. (*David Bunch*)

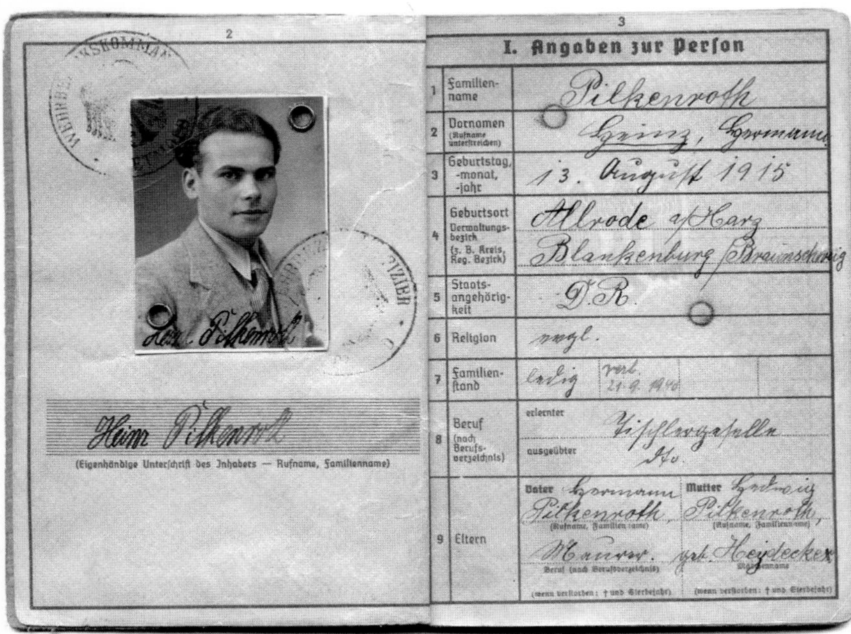

2

Heinz Pilkenroth
(Eigenhändige Unterschrift des Inhabers — Rufname, Familienname)

3

I. Angaben zur Person

1	Familien-name	Pilkenroth
2	Vornamen (Rufname unterstreichen)	Heinz, Hermann
3	Geburtstag, -monat, -jahr	13. August 1915
4	Geburtsort, Verwaltungs-bezirk (z. B. Kreis, Reg. Bezirk)	Allrode a/Harz Blankenburg / Braunschweig
5	Staats-angehörig-keit	D.R.
6	Religion	evgl.
7	Familien-stand	ledig / verh. 21.9.1940
8	Beruf (nach Berufs-verzeichnis)	erlernter: Tischlergeselle; ausgeübter: do.
9	Eltern	Vater: Hermann Pilkenroth (Rufname, Familienname), Maurer (Beruf (nach Berufsverzeichnis)) (wenn verstorben: † und Sterbejahr); Mutter: Hedwig Pilkenroth (Rufname, Familienname), geb. Heydecker (Mädchenname) (wenn verstorben: † und Sterbejahr)

Wehrpass of Heinz Pilkenroth an army soldier who served on temporary attachment to the GFP.

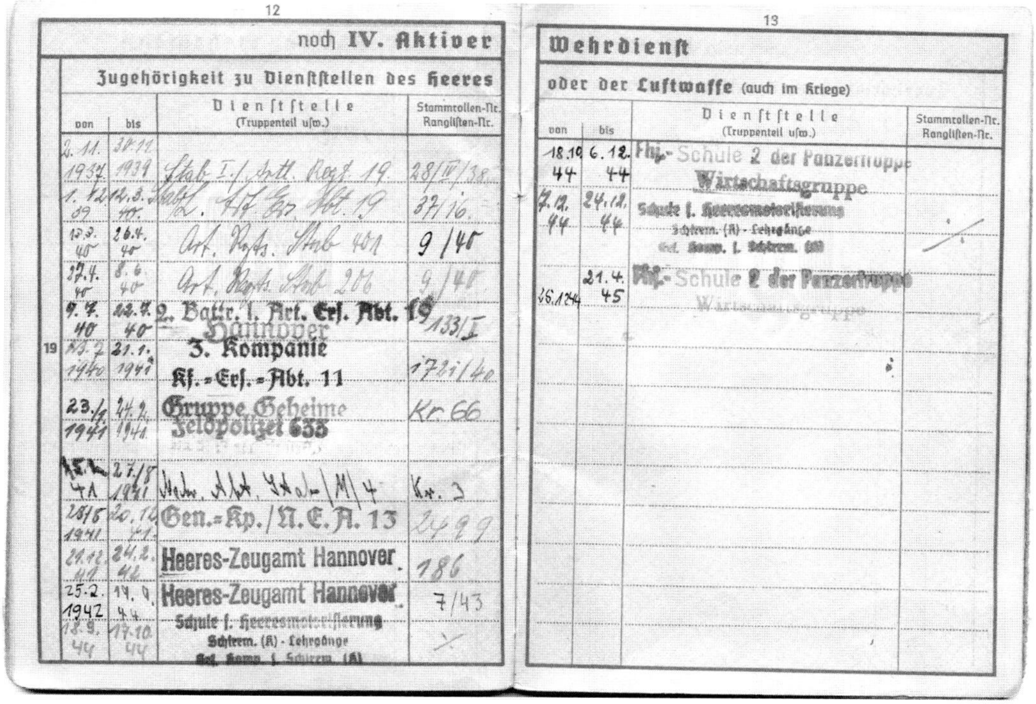

Note the entry in the Pilkenroth *Wehrpass* showing a brief attachment to *Gruppe* GFP 633. Such brief assignments, followed by a release to normal duties was Common at NCO level.

Uniforms and Insignia

GFP personnel wore the uniform appropriate to the *Heeresbeamte*, whose *Waffenfarbe* was dark green but with light-blue *Nebenfarbe* or secondary colour as their branch identifier and with a white metal Latin script 'GFP' emblem on the shoulder strap. A cuffband bearing the legend *Geheime Feldpolizei* was also produced but so far no evidence has emerged of this cuffband actually being worn. It is normally made from black rayon with the lettering woven in aluminium thread though hand embroidered versions also exist.

A visor cap also exists which has been attributed to the GFP. In normal Army style, it has a brown rather than dark green band to the cap, with blue-grey *Waffenfarbe* piping. Once again, no photographic evidence of its wear has yet emerged. Indeed although this type of cap may be contemporary, there is no firm evidence whatsoever to link it to the GFP, and it is most likely that the standard *Heeresbeamte* visor cap with dark green band and dark green piping was most often worn. Other troops temporarily attached to the GFP wore the uniform of their original branch but also used the metal GFP shoulder strap emblem.

Every member of the GFP, in common with all other military personnel, carried a *Soldbuch* and an *Erkennungsmarke* as a form of identification. In terms of their police status however, they also carried a special *Ausweis*, printed on green paper, and with their photograph in both uniform and civil clothing. This *Ausweis* carried details of their police powers including confirmation that they were entitled to require other military and civil powers to render assistance when required.

A metal '*Dienstmarke*' or warrant disc was also carried. Unlike those carried by their civilian equivalents, the GFP disc was circular. On the obverse was shown the *Wehrmacht* style eagle with wings outspread whilst the reverse had the legend '*Oberkommando des Heeres*' around the top edge and '*Geheime /Feldpolizei*' in the centre, over the serial number of the disc.

Amongst the entitlements brought by the possession of the *Ausweis* and *Dienstmarke* were the right to pass through military checkpoints, to enter military buildings, to use all military means of communication, to use any armed forces vehicles, to request accommodation and food assuming of course that these were necessary to the performance of his duties, and to free use of all public transport.

Devisenschutzkommando

One of the more unusual, and certainly less well known, of the GFPs functions were the duties it carried out for the *Devisenschutzkommando* or 'Currency Protection Command'.

This organisation was formed in the wake of the Westfeldzug, as German forces began their occupation of Denmark, Norway, France and the Low Countries.

Under German occupation, the citizens of these countries were prohibited from owning foreign currency and stocks (including German) and the *Devisenschutzkommando* assisted by the GFP, had the task of tracking down a seizing such assets in order that they be used to support the German economy.

Responsibility for such activities was passed to the *Reichsfinanzverwaltung* in 1941.

The following elements of the GFP were employed on these duties:

GFP Gruppe z.b.V. Devisenschutz Kommando Frankreich
GFP Gruppe (Devisenschutz) Kommando Frankreich
GFP Gruppe (Devisenschutz) Aussenstelle Nordfrankreich
GFP Gruppe (Devisenschutz) Kdo. Frankreich Aussenstelle Nancy
GFP Gruppe (Devisenschutz) Aussenstelle Nancy
GFP Gruppe (Devisenschutz) Aussenstelle Ghent
GFP Gruppe (Devisenschutz) Aussenstelle Antwerpen
GFP Gruppe (Devisenschutz) Kommando Belgien

GFP Units

Gruppe Geheime Feldpolizei 1

Formed on 26 August 1939 in *Wehrkreis II* (Rostock). Employed initially in Poland, then in occupied France, Germany, Russia and finally in Italy.

Gruppe Geheime Feldpolizei 2

Formed on 26 August 1939 in *Wehrkreis II* (Stralsund). Employed primarily in occupied France and the Netherlands. Ultimately absorbed into the *Sicherheitsdienst*.

Gruppe Geheime Feldpolizei 3

Formed on 25 August 1939 in *Wehrkreis VIII* (Leobschütz). Employed primarily in occupied France and the Netherlands.

Gruppe Geheime Feldpolizei 7

Formed on 23 August 1939 in *Wehrkreis V* (Donaueschingen). Employed in occupied France. Ended the war in the Lorient fortress. May have been absorbed into the *Sicherheitsdienst*.

Gruppe Geheime Feldpolizei 8

Formed on 26 August 1939 in *Wehrkreis VI* (Soest). Employed in France, Belgium Germany and Denmark.

Gruppe Geheime Feldpolizei 9

Formed on 26 August 1939 in *Wehrkreis VI* (Aachen). Employed in the Netherlands and ultimately in Croatia.

Gruppe Geheime Feldpolizei 11

Formed in August 1939. Employed in Germany and France. Absorbed into the *Sicherheitsdienst* in 1942.

Gruppe Geheime Feldpolizei 13

Formed on 26 September 1939 in *Wehrkreis VIII* (Glogau). Employed in Poland and in the West, ultimately in Silesia.

Gruppe Geheime Feldpolizei 14

Formed on 26 August 1939 in Breslau. Employed in Poland and France. Absorbed into the *Sicherheitsdienst* in 1942.

Gruppe Geheime Feldpolizei 20

Formed on 26 August 1939 in *Wehrkreis XVIII* (Salzburg). Employed in Austria.

Gruppe Geheime Feldpolizei 30

Formed on 26 August 1939 in *Wehrkreis XVII* (Vienna). Employed in Poland, and in France. Absorbed into the *Sicherheitsdienst* in 1942.

Gruppe Geheime Feldpolizei 131

Formed on 26 August 1939 in East Prussia. Employed in France and the Netherlands.

Gruppe Geheime Feldpolizei 161

Formed on 26 August 1939 in East Prussia. Employed in France.

Gruppe Geheime Feldpolizei 171

Formed on 26 August 1939 in East Prussia. Employed in Denmark and ultimately in Romania.

Gruppe Geheime Feldpolizei 312

Formed on 26 August 1939 in Küstrin. Employed initially in France and ultimately in Hungary.

Gruppe Geheime Feldpolizei 501

Formed on 16 August 1939 in *Wehrkreis I* (Königsberg). Employed in Poland, France, Northern Russia and Latvia.

Photograph from the *Soldbuch* of a GFP officer with the rank of *Feldpolizeiinspektor*. The distinctive piping around the collar tab can be clearly seen. (*Ian Jewison*)

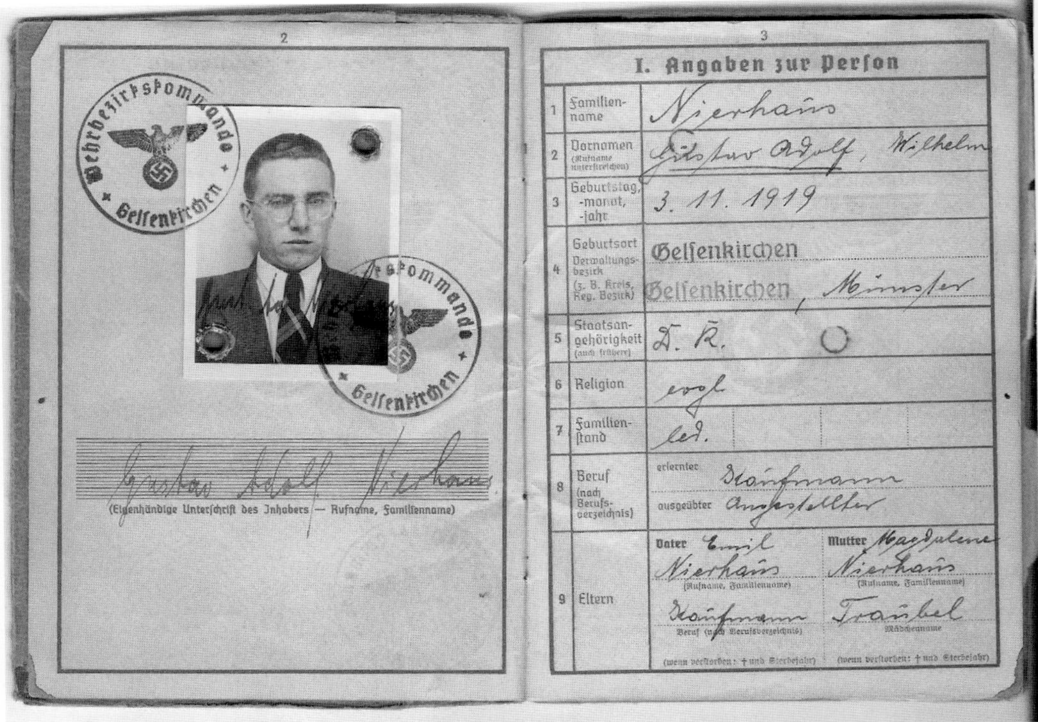

2

Wehrbezirkskommando Gelsenkirchen

Gustav Adolf Nierhaus

(Eigenhändige Unterschrift des Inhabers — Rufname, Familienname)

3

I. Angaben zur Person

1	Familienname	Nierhaus
2	Vornamen (Rufname unterstreichen)	Gustav Adolf, Wilhelm
3	Geburtstag, -monat, -jahr	3. 11. 1919
4	Geburtsort Verwaltungsbezirk (z. B. Kreis, Reg. Bezirk)	Gelsenkirchen Gelsenkirchen, Münster
5	Staatsangehörigkeit (auch frühere)	D. R.
6	Religion	evgl.
7	Familienstand	led.
8	Beruf (nach Berufsverzeichnis)	erlernter Kaufmann ausgeübter Angestellter
9	Eltern	Vater Emil Nierhaus (Rufname, Familienname) Kaufmann Beruf (nach Berufsverzeichnis) (wenn verstorben: † und Sterbejahr) Mutter Magdalene Nierhaus (Rufname, Familienname) Traubel Mädchenname (wenn verstorben: † und Sterbejahr)

Wehrpass for *Unteroffizier* Gustav Nierhaus who served with GFP *Gruppen* 7 and 560. (*Kevin Huckfield*)

12

noch IV. Aktiver

Zugehörigkeit zu Dienststellen des Heeres

von	bis	Dienststelle (Truppenteil usw.)	Stammrollen-Nr. Ranglisten-Nr.
24.8. 1939	8.4. 1942	Grp. geh. Feldpol. 560	Nr. 10
9.4. 42	8.5. 42	2./Inf.-Ers.-Batl. Altenburg	278/42
11.5. 42	11.11. 42	Geh. Feldpolizei Gr. 7	103
12.11. 42	30.11. 42	[illegible] Feldpolizeidirektor beim [illegible]befehlshaber in Frankreich	
7.12. 42	3.2. 43	Genes. Kp./Ers. Batl. 600	923/43
4.2. 43	24.3. 43	Heeres Entlassungsstelle 1 des Wehrkreises VI	4061

13

Wehrdienst

oder der Luftwaffe (auch im Kriege)

von	bis	Dienststelle (Truppenteil usw.)	Stammrollen-Nr. Ranglisten-Nr.

Above: Nierhaus was already serving with the GFP when war broke out and spent the majority of his military career with this organisation. (*Kevin Huckfield*)

Right: Award Document for the Eastern Front Medal to Gustav Nierhaus. (*Kevin Huckfield*)

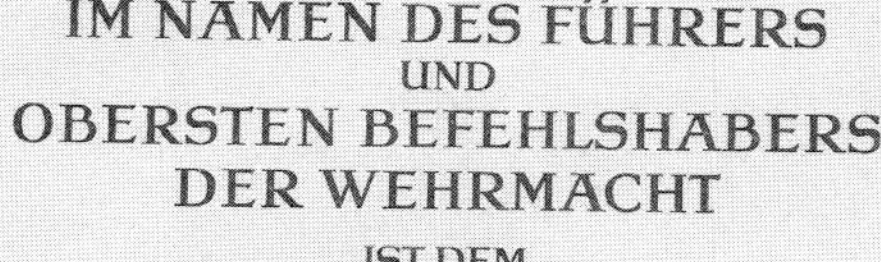

IM NAMEN DES FÜHRERS
UND
OBERSTEN BEFEHLSHABERS
DER WEHRMACHT
IST DEM

Unteroffizier Gustav N i e r h a u s ,
Gruppe Geheime Feldpolizei 560,

AM 1. September 1942

DIE MEDAILLE
WINTERSCHLACHT IM OSTEN
1941/42
(OSTMEDAILLE)
VERLIEHEN WORDEN.

FÜR DIE RICHTIGKEIT:

Generalmajor
und
Chef des Generalstabes AOK 19

Gruppe Geheime Feldpolizei 510

Formed on 26 August 1939 in *Wehrkreis XVII* (Vienna). Employed in Poland , the West, the Balkans.

Gruppe Geheime Feldpolizei 520

Formed on 15 August 1939 in *Wehrkreis VII* (Vienna). Employed in Poland, the West, Russia and Latvia.

Gruppe Geheime Feldpolizei 530

Formed on 2 August 1939 in *Wehrkreis III* (Berlin). Employed in Poland, Belgium and France.

Gruppe Geheime Feldpolizei 540

Formed on 2 August 1939 in *Wehrkreis IV* (Dresden). Employed in Poland and in France.

Gruppe Geheime Feldpolizei 550

Formed on 26 August 1939 in *Wehrkreis V* (Stuttgart). Employed in France and absorbed into the *Sicherheitsdienst* in 1942.

Gruppe Geheime Feldpolizei 560

Formed on 24 August 1939 in *Wehrkreis VI* (Münster). Employed in France, Southern Russia and Germany.

Gruppe Geheime Feldpolizei 570

Formed on 26 August 39 in *Wehrkreis XI* (Nürnberg). Employed in Poland, France, Central Russia and ultimately in East Prussia.

Gruppe Geheime Feldpolizei 580

Formed on 15 August 1939 in *Wehrkreis IV* (Dresden). Employed in Poland, France, Belgium and Central Russia.

Gruppe Geheime Feldpolizei 581

Formed on 25 August 1939 in *Wehrkreis IX* (Kassel). Employed on the Western Front.

Gruppe Geheime Feldpolizei 590

Formed on 25 August 1939 in *Wehrkreis IX* (Kassel). Employed in France.

Gruppe Geheime Feldpolizei 603

Formed on 26 August 1939 in *Wehrkreis III* (Berlin). Employed in Poland, France and the Netherlands. Absorbed into the Sicherheitsdienst in November 1942.

Gruppe Geheime Feldpolizei 610

Formed on 26 August 1939 in *Wehrkreis X* (Hamburg). Employed in France, Southern Russia and Italy.

Gruppe Geheime Feldpolizei 611

Formed on 26 August 1939 in *Wehrkreis XI* (Hannover). Employed in the West and in the Balkans, ultimately in Croatia.

Gruppe Geheime Feldpolizei 612
Formed on 26 August 1939 in *Wehrkreis XII* (Wiesbaden). Employed in the West, Balkans, Central Russia and West Prussia.

Gruppe Geheime Feldpolizei 621
Formed on 28 February 1940 in *Wehrkreis I* (Königsberg). Employed in France and Belgium, the Balkans and ultimately in Croatia.

Gruppe Geheime Feldpolizei 625
Formed on 15 February 1940 in *Wehrkreis V* (Stuttgart). Employed in France.

Gruppe Geheime Feldpolizei 626
Formed in early 1940 in *Wehrkreis VI* (Münster). Employed in France, Russia and Slovakia.

Gruppe Geheime Feldpolizei 627
Formed on 24 February 1940 in *Wehrkreis VII* (Munich). Employed in France and absorbed into the *Sicherheitsdienst* in November 1942.

Gruppe Geheime Feldpolizei 629
Formed February 1940 in *Wehrkreis XII* (Wiesbaden). Employed in Norway.

Gruppe Geheime Feldpolizei 631
Formed on 21 August 1939 in *Wehrkreis III* (Berlin). Employed on security duties at OKH headquarters.

Gruppe Geheime Feldpolizei 632
Formed on 17 February 1940 in *Wehrkreis XII* (Wiesbanden). Employed in France and absorbed into the *Sicherheitsdienst* in November 1942.

Gruppe Geheime Feldpolizei 633
Formed on 26 February 1940 in Wehrkreis XI (Hannover). Employed in France and absorbed into the *Sicherheitsdienst* in November 1942.

Gruppe Geheime Feldpolizei 637
Formed on 15 February 1940 in *Wehrkreis IV* (Dresden). Employed in Belgium and Italy.

Gruppe Geheime Feldpolizei 639
Formed on 10 September 1940 im *Wehrkreis V* (Stuttgart). Employed with *Panzergruppe 2/2 Panzerarmee*.

Gruppe Geheime Feldpolizei 640
Formed on 19 September 1940 in *Wehrkreis XX* (Danzig). Employed in the Balkans and Croatia.

Gruppe Geheime Feldpolizei 644
Formed on 10 September 1940 in *Wehrkreis IV* (Dresden).
Employed In France.

Gruppe Geheime Feldpolizei 647
Formed on 10 September 1940 in *Wehrkreis VII* (Munich). Employed in France, Southern Russia and Slovakia.

Gruppe Geheime Feldpolizei 648
Formed on 10 September 1940 im *Wehrkreis VIII* (Breslau). Employed in Belgium, France and ultimately in Bohemia.

Gruppe Geheime Feldpolizei 649
Formed on 9 September 1940 in *Wehrkreis IX* (Kassel). Employed in France and absorbed into the *Sicherheitsdienst* in November 1942.

Gruppe Geheime Feldpolizei 701
Formed on 26 April 1941 in *Wehrkreis IV* (Dresden). Employed in France and absorbed into the *Sicherheitsdienst* in November 1942

Gruppe Geheime Feldpolizei 702
Formed on 26 April 1941 in *Wehrkreis IV* (Dresden). Employed with *285 Sicherungs Division* in Russia and ultimately with *Heeresgruppe Süd* in Vienna.

Gruppe Geheime Feldpolizei 703
Formed on 26 April 1941 in *Wehrkreis IV* (Dresden). Employed in Russia with *Pz.Gruppe 3*

Gruppe Geheime Feldpolizei 704
Formed on 26 April 1941 in *Wehrkreis IV* (Dresden). Employed with *Pz.Gruppe 4*

Gruppe Geheime Feldpolizei 705
Formed on 26 April 1941 in *Wehrkreis IV*(Dresden). Employed with *281. Sicherungs Division* in Russia

Gruppe Geheime Feldpolizei 706
Formed on 26 April 1941 in *Wehrkreis IV* (Dresden). Employed with *403 Sicherungs Division* in Central Russia, later in Southern Russia and ultimately in Silesia.

Gruppe Geheime Feldpolizei 707
Formed on 26 April 1941 in *Wehrkreis IV* (Dresden). Employed in Central Russia and from early 1945 on the Western Front.

Gruppe Geheime Feldpolizei 708
Formed on 26 April 1941 in *Wehrkreis IV*. (Dresden). Employed in Southern Russia and ultimately in Hungary and Austria.

Gruppe Geheime Feldpolizei 709
Formed on 26 April 1941 in *Wehrkreis IV* (Dresden). Employed in central Russia.
Gruppe Geheime Feldpolizei 710

Formed on 26 April 1941 in *Wehrkreis IV* (Dresden). Employed in Central Russia and from early 1945 on the Western Front.

Gruppe Geheime Feldpolizei 711
Formed on 26 April 1941 im *Wehrkreis IV* (Dresden). Employed in Southern Russia and absorbed into the Sicherheitsdienst in April 1944.

Gruppe Geheime Feldpolizei 712
Formed on 26 April 1941 in *Wehrkreis IV* (Dresden). Employed in Belgium and France and absorbed into the *Sicherheitsdienst* in April 1944.

Gruppe Geheime Feldpolizei 713
Formed on 21 Mayl 1941 in *Wehrkreis IV* (Dresden). Employed in Northern Russia and ultimately in West Prussia.

Gruppe Geheime Feldpolizei 714
Formed on 21 May 1941 in *Wehrkreis IV* (Dresden). Employed in Northern Russia and ultimately in West Prussia.

Gruppe Geheime Feldpolizei 715
Formed on 21 May 1941 in *Wehrkreis IV* (Dresden. Employed in Northern Russia and absorbed into the *Sicherheitsdienst* in mid 1944.

Gruppe Geheime Feldpolizei 716
Formed on 21 May 1941 in *Wehrkreis IV* (Dresden). Employed in Central Russia, with the V-Weapon programme in the West and ultimately in the Netherlands.

Gruppe Geheime Feldpolizei 717
Formed on 21 May 1941 in *Wehrkreis IV* (Dresden). Employed in Central Russia and from 1945 on the Western Front.

Gruppe Geheime Feldpolizei 718
Formed on 21 May 1941 in *Wehrkreis IV* (Dresden). Employed in Central Russia and absorbed into the *Sicherheitsdienst* in early 1944.

Gruppe Geheime Feldpolizei 719
Formed on 21 May 1941 in *Wehrkreis IV* (Dresden). Employed in Southern Russia and from 1945 in Silesia.

Gruppe Geheime Feldpolizei 720
Formed on 21 May 1941 in *Wehrkreis IV* (Dresden). Employed in Southern Russia and from 1945 in Vienna.

Gruppe Geheime Feldpolizei 721

Formed on 21 May 1941 in *Wehrkreis IV* (Dresden). Employed in Southern Russia, ultimately in Hungary.

Gruppe Geheime Feldpolizei 722
Formed on 21 May 1941 in *Wehrkreis IV* (Dresden). Employed in Northern Russia and absorbed into the *Sicherheitsdienst* in September 1944.

Gruppe Geheime Feldpolizei 723
Formed on 21 May 1941 in *Wehrkreis IV* (Dresden).; Herbst 1944 (?). Employed in Central Russia and believed disbanded in Autumn 1944.

Gruppe Geheime Feldpolizei 724
Formed on 21 May 1941 in *Wehrkreis IV* (Dresden). Employed in Central Russia and absorbed into the *Sicherheitsdienst* in the Autumn of 1944.

Gruppe Geheime Feldpolizei 725
Formed on 21 May 1941 in *Wehrkreis IV* (Dresden). Employed in Southern Russia and from 1945 in Central Russia.

Gruppe Geheime Feldpolizei 726
Formed on 21 May 1941 in *Wehrkreis IV* (Dresden). Employed in Southern Russia.

Gruppe Geheime Feldpolizei 727
Formed on 21 June 1941 in *Wehrkreis IV* (Dresden). Employed in Northern Russia and from 1945 in Latvia.

Gruppe Geheime Feldpolizei 728
Formed on 21 June 1941 in *Wehrkreis IV* (Dresden). Employed in Northern Russia and Estonia.

Gruppe Geheime Feldpolizei 729
Formed on 21 June 1941 in *Wehrkreis IV* (Dresden). Employed in Central Russia, Central Russia and East Prussia.

Gruppe Geheime Feldpolizei 730
Formed on 21 June 1941 in *Wehrkreis IV* (Dresden). Employed in Southern Russia and absorbed into the *Sicherheitsdienst* in mid 1944.

Gruppe Geheime Feldpolizei 731
Formed on 21 June 1941 im *Wehrkreis IV* (Dresden). Employed in France and absorbed into the *Sicherheitsdienst* in November 1942.

Gruppe Geheime Feldpolizei 732
Formed on 21 June 1941 in *Wehrkreis IV* (Dresden). Employed in France and absorbed into the *Sicherheitsdienst* in November 1942.

Gruppe Geheime Feldpolizei 733

Formed on 21 June 1941 in *Wehrkreis IV* (Dresden). Employed in France and absorbed into the *Sicherheitsdienst* in November 1942.

Gruppe Geheime Feldpolizei 734
Formed on 21 June 1941 in *Wehrkreis IV* (Dresden). Employed in France and absorbed into the *Sicherheitsdienst* in November 1942.

Gruppe Geheime Feldpolizei 735
Formed on 21 June 1941 in *Wehrkreis IV* (Dresden). Employed in France, Lappland and Norway.

Gruppe Geheime Feldpolizei 736
Formed on 21 June 1941 in *Wehrkreis IV* (Dresden). Employed in France and absorbed into the *Sicherheitsdienst* in November 1942.

Gruppe Geheime Feldpolizei 737
Formed on 21 June 1941 in *Wehrkreis IV* (Dresden).

Gruppe Geheime Feldpolizei 738
Formed on 21 June 1941 in *Wehrkreis IV* (Dresden). Employed in Belgium and France and disbanded in Autumn 1944.

Gruppe Geheime Feldpolizei 739
Formed on 21 June 1941 in *Wehrkreis IV* (Dresden). Employed in Belgium, France and Southern Russia and absorbed into the *Sicherheitsdienst* in September 1944.

Gruppe Geheime Feldpolizei 740
Formed on 21 June 1941 in *Wehrkreis IV* (Dresden). Employed in Belgium, France and Southern Russia and absorbed into the *Sicherheitsdienst* in September 1944

Gruppe Geheime Feldpolizei 741
Formed on 15.10. 1941 in North Africa to serve the *Afrikakorps*. Employed in North Africa and Italy.

Gruppe Geheime Feldpolizei 742
Formed in the Winter of 1942/43 in *Wehrkreis XXI* (Posen) for service with the Luftwaffe.

Gruppe Geheime Feldpolizei 743
Formed in 1943 in *Wehrkreis XXI* (Posen). Employed on the Western Front.

Gruppe Geheime Feldpolizei 744
Formed in the Winter of 1943/44 im *Wehrkreis XXI* (Posen) for employment by the *Luftwaffe*.

Gruppe Geheime Feldpolizei 745
Formed in the Winter of 1943/44 in *Wehrkreis XXI* (Posen). Employed in Southern Russia.
Gruppe Geheime Feldpolizei 751

Formed on 2 August 1943 in *Wehrkreis XXI* (Posen). Employed in Italy.

Gruppe Geheime Feldpolizei z.b.V.

Formed in early September 1939 from members of the *Reichssicherheitsdienst-Gruppe z.b.V. (Führersicherheit)* who had previously been tasked with Hitler's personal security. It gradually took responsibility for the security of other leading figures both political and military, the latter incuding *Reichsmarschall* Göring and *Grossadmiral* Dönitz.

Equipment Levels

GFP Gruppe

2 officers, 14 admin officials, 6 NCOs and 51 enlisted ranks.

66 × pistols.
55 × carbines.

Motor Section

4 NCOs and 27 enlisted men.

13 × pistols.
30 × carbines.
25 × light field cars.
1 × 15 seat Bus.
1 × 3 ton truck.
3 × motorcycles.
2 × motorcycles with sidecars.

It is interesting to note that the weapons allocation suggests that the non-officer ranks were issued a pistol as well as a carbine.

During the second half of the war, the *Luftwaffe* formed its own GFP branch. Like their army equivalents, they wore the uniform of the *Beamter* or official, rather than a career soldier. All insignia were that of the normal *Luftwaffenbeamter*, with the exception of the shoulder straps which bore the GFP letters in gilt, in conjunction with a wine-red *Nebenfarbe* between the aluminium braid and the green base of the strap.

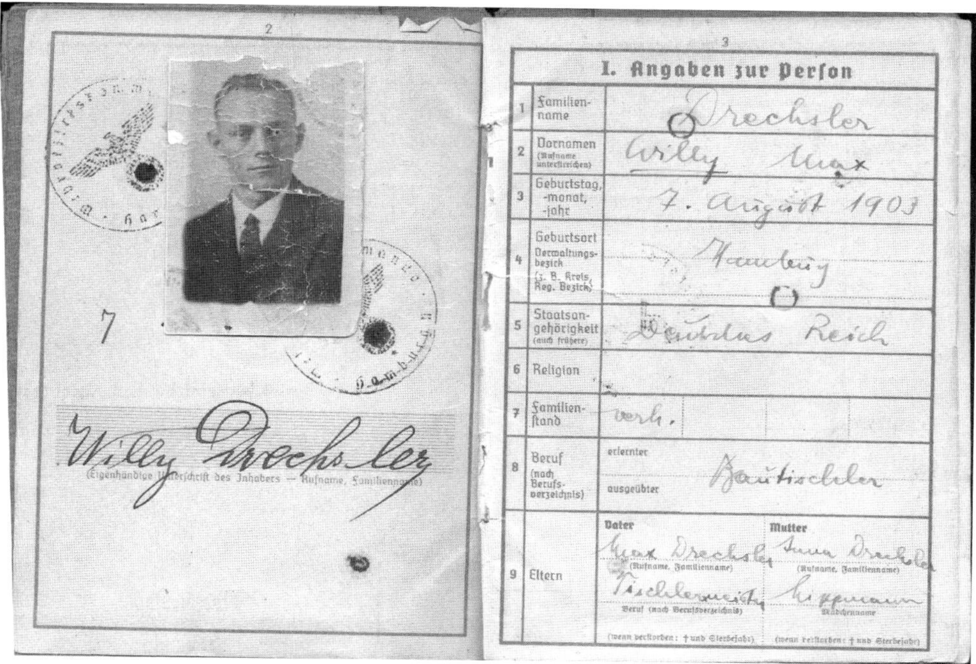

2

7

Willy Drechsler
(Eigenhändige Unterschrift des Inhabers — Rufname, Familienname)

3

I. Angaben zur Person

1	Familienname	Drechsler
2	Vornamen (Rufname unterstreichen)	Willy Max
3	Geburtstag, -monat, -jahr	7. August 1903
4	Geburtsort Verwaltungsbezirk (z. B. Kreis, Reg. Bezirk)	Hamburg
5	Staatsangehörigkeit (auch frühere)	Deutsches Reich
6	Religion	
7	Familienstand	verh.
8	Beruf (nach Berufsverzeichnis) erlernter / ausgeübter	Bautischler
9	Eltern	Vater: Max Drechsler (Rufname, Familienname), Tischlermeister (Beruf (nach Berufsverzeichnis)); Mutter: Anna Drechsler (Rufname, Familienname), Lippmann (Mädchenname)

(wenn verstorben: † und Sterbejahr) (wenn verstorben: † und Sterbejahr)

Wehrpass of GFP official Willy Dreschler. Note that the identity photo though it does show Dreschler, is not the original photo from the *Wehrpass*.

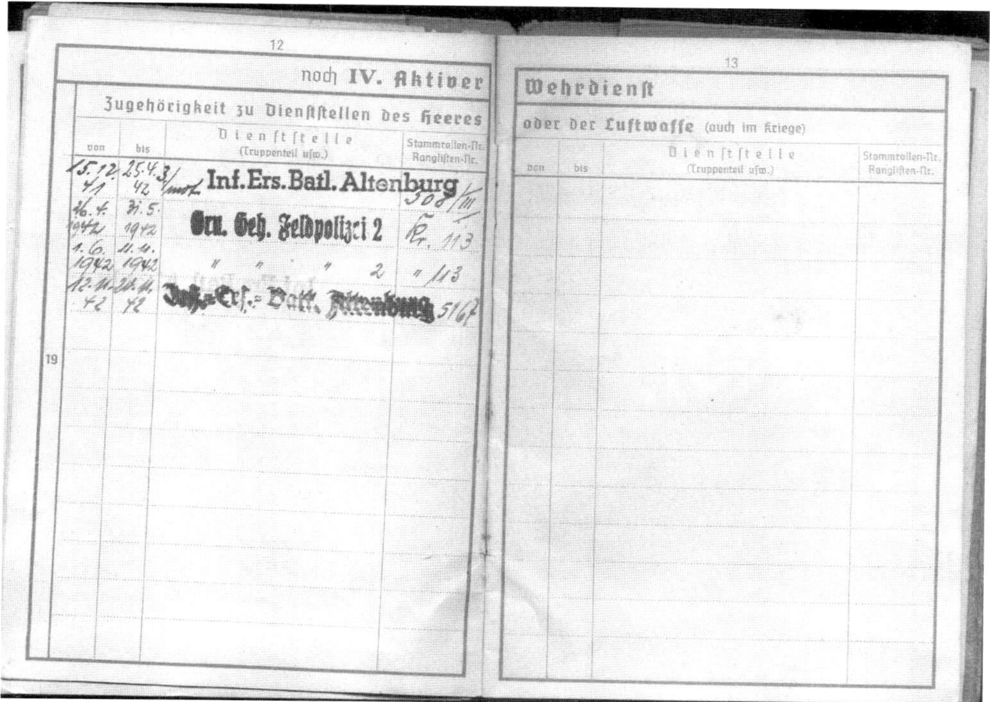

12 13

noch IV. Aktiver Wehrdienst

Zugehörigkeit zu Dienststellen des Heeres oder der Luftwaffe (auch im Kriege)

von	bis	Dienststelle (Truppenteil usw.)	Stammrollen-Nr. Ranglisten-Nr.
15.12.41	25.4.42	3/mot. Inf.Ers.Batl. Altenburg	308/III
16.4.1942	31.5.1942	Gru. Geh. Feldpolizei 2	Gr. 113
1.6.1942	11.11.1942	" " " 2	" /113
12.11.42	24.11.42	Inf.-Ers.-Batl. Altenburg	5167

19

Ehbauer's *Soldbuch* shows he served within *Wehrkreis* XIII, the military district centred on Nuremberg.

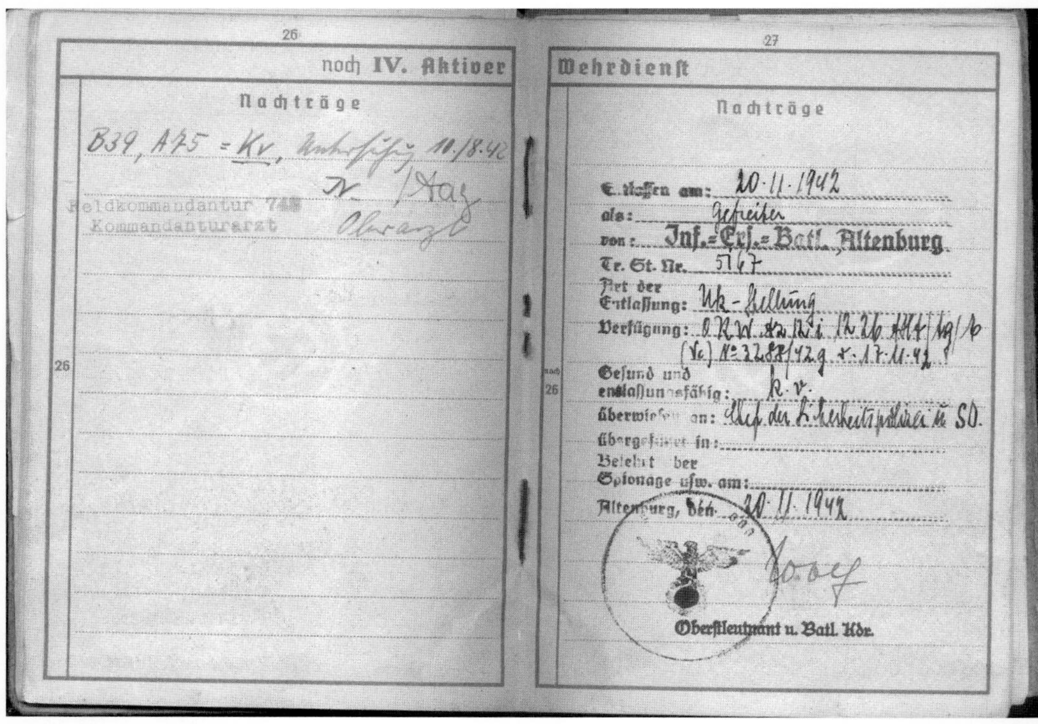

26

noch IV. Aktiver

Nachträge

B39, A75 = Kv, Untersuchung 10/18.42

Dr. [illegible]

Feldkommandantur 7[illegible]
Kommandanturarzt
Oberarzt

27

Wehrdienst

Nachträge

Entlassen am: 20.11.1942

als: Gefreiter

von: Inf.-Ers.-Batl. Altenburg

Tr. St. Nr. 5747

Art der Entlassung: Uk-Stellung

Verfügung: OKW [illegible]

Gesund und entlassungsfähig: k.v.

überwiesen an: Chef der Sicherheitspolizei u. SD.

übergeführt in:

Belehrt der Spionage usw. am:

Altenburg, den 20.11.1942

Oberstleutnant u. Batl. Kdr.

Deschler's origins are clear from the entry shown here which indicates that when released from his military duties he is returned to the '*Chef der Sicherheitspolizei* u. SD' (Chief of the Security Police and Security Service). Amt IV (Department IV) of the *Sicherheitspolizei* was the Gestapo.

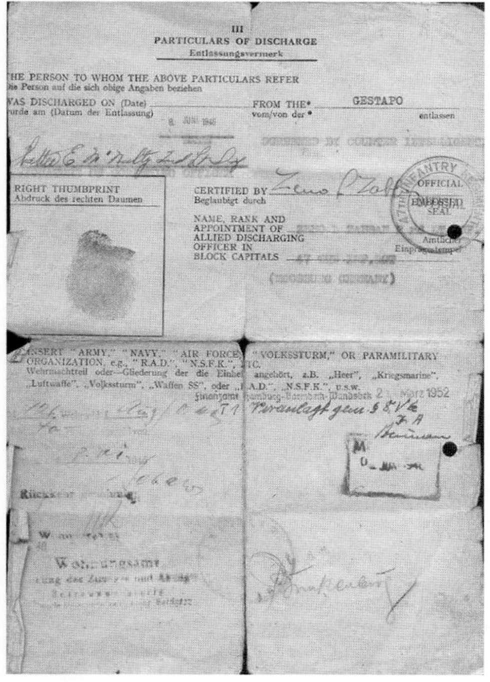

III
PARTICULARS OF DISCHARGE
Entlassungsvermerk

THE PERSON TO WHOM THE ABOVE PARTICULARS REFER
Die Person auf die sich obige Angaben beziehen
WAS DISCHARGED ON (Date) 8. JUNI 1946 FROM THE* GESTAPO
wurde am (Datum der Entlassung) vom/von der* entlassen

RIGHT THUMBPRINT
Abdruck des rechten Daumen

CERTIFIED BY
Beglaubigt durch

NAME, RANK AND APPOINTMENT OF ALLIED DISCHARGING OFFICER IN BLOCK CAPITALS

OFFICIAL EMBOSSED SEAL
Amtlicher Einprägestempel

*INSERT "ARMY," "NAVY," "AIR FORCE," "VOLKSSTURM," OR PARAMILITARY ORGANIZATION, e.g., "R.A.D.", "N.S.F.K.", ETC.
Wehrmachtteil oder—Gliederung der die Einheit angehört, z.B. „Heer", „Kriegsmarine", „Luftwaffe", „Volkssturm", „Waffen SS", oder „R.A.D.", „N.S.F.K.", u.s.w.

Finanzamt Hamburg-Barmbek-Wandsbek 2[illegible] März 1952

Deschler's discharge from captivity as a POW confirms he is being discharged from the 'Gestapo'.

Supporting Provost Branches

The Streifendienst

The chaotic military situation which existed in the late part of the Second World War and the need for robust disciplinary elements such as the *Feldjäger* is well known. More surprising perhaps is the fact that even at the very start of the war, the German military, perceived as being highly organised and disciplined, was facing severe problems with the behaviour of its troops.

With the general mobilisation prior to war, vast numbers of men were called up who had had prior military service in the First World War, and were by 1939 in the older age groups, men of over 40 years of age, many of whom were family men, and who had no wish to be in uniform again. These troops of course were not used as front line combatants, that being the lot of the younger, fitter generation. Used as second or third line elements, these men were often ill-disciplined and had a less than positive attitude. During the so-called 'Phoney-War' or Sitzkrieg, some were alleged to have fraternised with the French.

It was not only these older, less reliable troops who caused problems however, even some of the younger troops, including officers, were causing problems including theft, disobedience and drunkenness. Things were serious enough for the *Oberbefehlshaber des Heeres*, *Generaloberst* von Brauchitsch, to compare their behaviour to that of the *Landsknecht* (the often undisciplined German mercenaries of the sixteenth century)

For many of the highest ranking officers in the German military, memories of the breakdown in discipline which preceded the collapse of the German armies in 1918 were still fresh and led to the creation of the *Streifendienst* in a move intended to reinforce discipline and good behaviour, especially in places where bad behaviour could adversely effect the reputation of the *Wehrmacht*, i.e. where the public could witness any such behaviour.

On 18 November 1939, the formation of the *Heeresstreifendienst* was announced in *Heeresmitteilungsblatt* 41, Nr 526.

The central command for these units lay with the so-called *Generäle zbV IV*, based at the *Oberkommando der Wehrmacht* in Berlin. Under the control of this department were included the commanders of the patrol services in the homeland military districts (*Heimat Wehrkreise*) whose responsibilities included railway station guard units (*Bahnhofswache*), train guard units (*Zugwache*) as well as patrol services in garrison areas.

Outside of Germany, i.e. in the operational areas and occupied countries, officers rather awkwardly entitled 'commanders for monitoring leave', were established in early 1942. Under their control were patrol groups (initially of the *Heer* but later for the whole of the *Wehrmacht*), *Wehrmacht* patrol commanders in the senior levels of the armies in the field as well as temporary patrol units organized at a local level for the armies in the field.

Gruppe Heeresstreifendienst A.H.Qu., 4.7.40.
A. O. K. 16

Ausweis.

Der Jnhaber dieses Ausweises ist der
Unteroffz. Nabinger,
Angehöriger der Feldwebelstreife 4 des Heeres-
streifendienstes im Bereich des A.O.K.16.

Oberstlt. u. Kommandeur.

A very early and very simple typewritten *Ausweis* to *Unteroffizier* Friedrich Nabinger identifying him as a member of the *Streifendienst.*

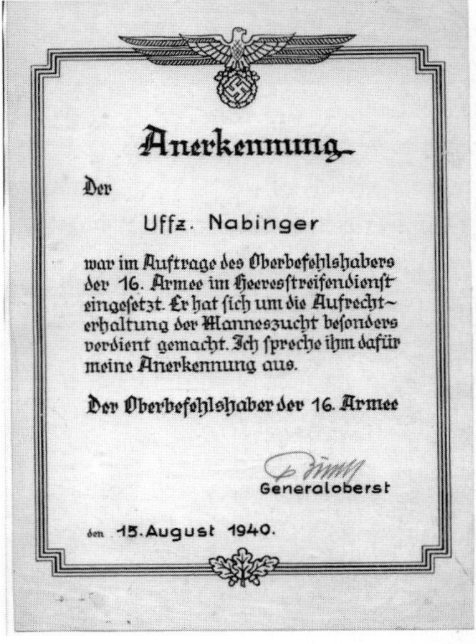

Anerkennung

Der

Uffz. Nabinger

war im Auftrage des Oberbefehlshabers der 16. Armee im Heeresstreifendienst eingesetzt. Er hat sich um die Aufrechterhaltung der Manneszucht besonders verdient gemacht. Ich spreche ihm dafür meine Anerkennung aus.

Der Oberbefehlshaber der 16. Armee

Generaloberst

den 15. August 1940.

Above left: The *Streifendienst* was unusual in not using a gorget or armband as a symbol of authority but rather an aiguilette a simplified version of that worn by adjutants. (*Ian Jewison*)

Above right: A commendation certificate to Nabinger from *Generaloberst* (later *Generalfeldmarschall*) Busch in respect of his service with the *Streifendienst.*

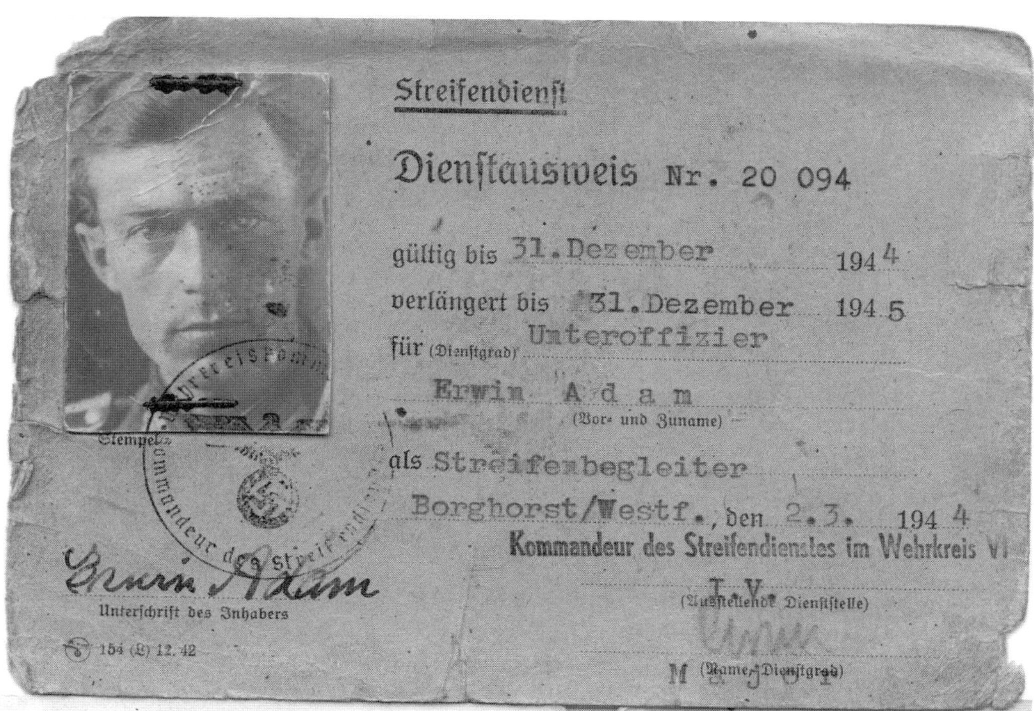

Streifendienst

Dienstausweis Nr. 20 094

gültig bis 31. Dezember 1944

verlängert bis 31. Dezember 1945

für (Dienstgrad) Unteroffizier

Erwin Adam

(Vor- und Zuname)

als Streifenbegleiter

Borghorst/Westf., den 2.3. 1944

Kommandeur des Streifendienstes im Wehrkreis VI

I.V.

(Ausstellende Dienststelle)

(Name, Dienstgrad)

Stempel

Unterschrift des Inhabers

154 (L) 12. 42

Streifendienst *Ausweis* to *Unteroffizier* Erwin Adam. The *Ausweis* was issued in *Wehrkreis* VI (Dresden). (*Ian Jewison*)

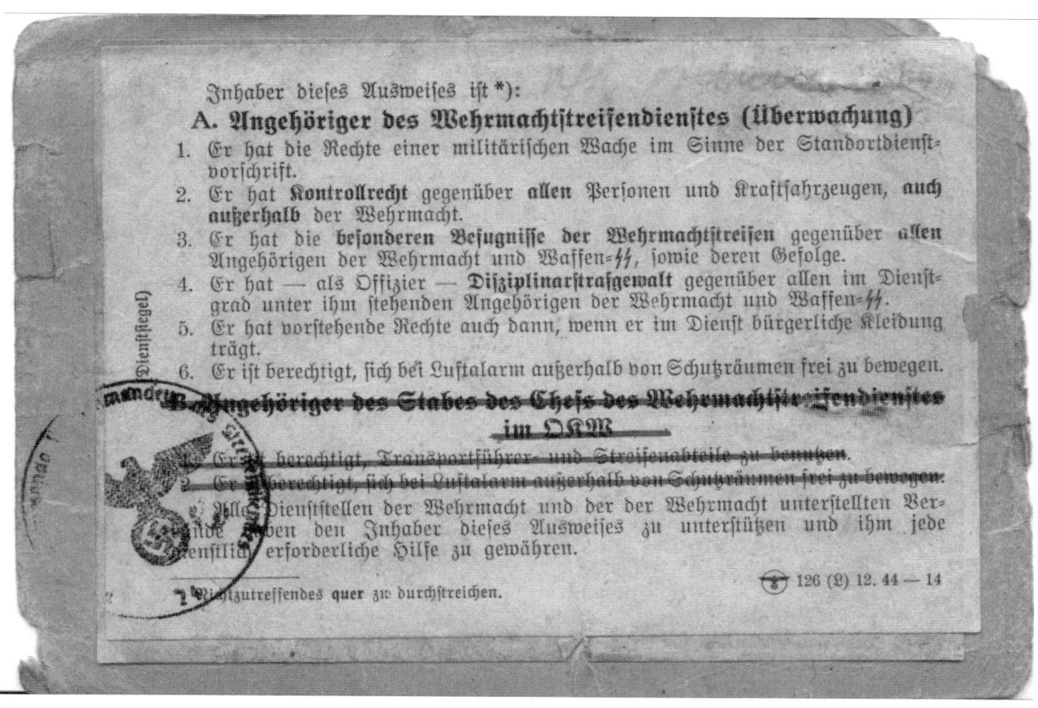

Inhaber dieses Ausweises ist *):

A. Angehöriger des Wehrmachtstreifendienstes (Überwachung)

1. Er hat die Rechte einer militärischen Wache im Sinne der Standortdienstvorschrift.
2. Er hat **Kontrollrecht** gegenüber **allen** Personen und Kraftfahrzeugen, **auch außerhalb** der Wehrmacht.
3. Er hat die **besonderen Befugnisse der Wehrmachtstreifen** gegenüber **allen** Angehörigen der Wehrmacht und Waffen-SS, sowie deren Gefolge.
4. Er hat — als Offizier — **Disziplinarstrafgewalt** gegenüber allen im Dienstgrad unter ihm stehenden Angehörigen der Wehrmacht und Waffen-SS.
5. Er hat vorstehende Rechte auch dann, wenn er im Dienst bürgerliche Kleidung trägt.
6. Er ist berechtigt, sich bei Luftalarm außerhalb von Schutzräumen frei zu bewegen.

~~B. Angehöriger des Stabes des Chefs des Wehrmachtstreifendienstes im OKW~~

1. ~~Er ist berechtigt, Transportführer- und Streifenabteile zu benutzen.~~
2. ~~Er ist berechtigt, sich bei Luftalarm außerhalb von Schutzräumen frei zu bewegen.~~
3. Alle Dienststellen der Wehrmacht und der der Wehrmacht unterstellten Verbände haben den Inhaber dieses Ausweises zu unterstützen und ihm jede dienstlich erforderliche Hilfe zu gewähren.

(Dienstsiegel)

*) Nichtzutreffendes **quer** zu durchstreichen.

126 (L) 12. 44 — 14

The reverse of the *Streifendienst Ausweis* sets out the responsibilities and authority of the bearer. (*Ian Jewison*)

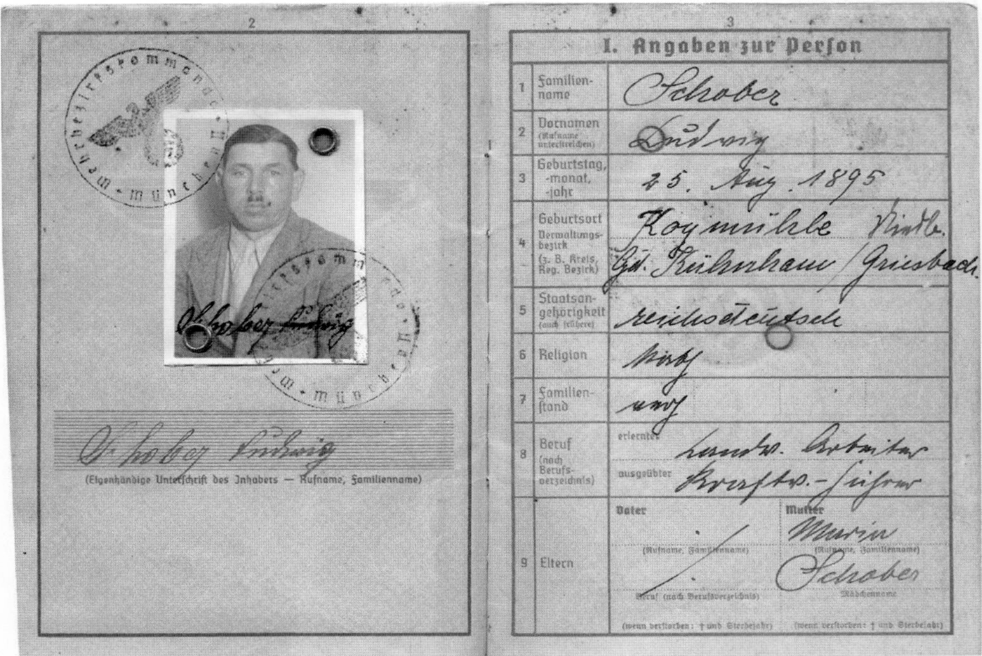

2

(Eigenhändige Unterschrift des Inhabers — Rufname, Familienname)

Schober Ludwig

3

	I. Angaben zur Person	
1	Familienname	Schober
2	Vornamen (Rufname unterstreichen)	Ludwig
3	Geburtstag, -monat, -jahr	25. Aug. 1895
4	Geburtsort, Verwaltungsbezirk (z. B. Kreis, Reg. Bezirk)	Koymühle [illegible], Gd. Kühnham / Griesbach
5	Staatsangehörigkeit (auch frühere)	reichsdeutsch
6	Religion	kath
7	Familienstand	verh
8	Beruf (nach Berufsverzeichnis)	erlernter: Landw. Arbeiter; ausgeübter: Kraftw.-Führer
9	Eltern	Vater: — (Rufname, Familienname); Beruf (nach Berufsverzeichnis) (wenn verstorben: † und Sterbejahr) — Mutter: Maria (Rufname, Familienname) Schober (Mädchenname) (wenn verstorben: † und Sterbejahr)

Wehrpass to *Unteroffizier* Ludwig Schober who served with the *Heeresstreifendienst*.

12 | 13

noch IV. Aktiver Wehrdienst

Zugehörigkeit zu Dienststellen des Heeres oder der Luftwaffe (auch im Kriege)

	von	bis	Dienststelle (Truppenteil usw.)	Stammrollen-Nr. Ranglisten-Nr.
	21.3.15	4.2.19	Kraftf. Ers. Abtlg. 1.	
	29.8.39	20.11.39	Betr. St. Kol. 572	—
	27.11.39	24.3.42	2./Kraftf. Ers. Abt. 7 München	IV/113
	25.3.42	5.6.42	Gruppe Heeres-Streifendienst beim Deutschen Wehrmachts-Attaché in Rom	87
19	6.6.42	19.7.42	2. Gen. Kp. I. E. B. 61	399/42
	20.7.42	31.7.42	2. Kompanie Inf. Ers. Btl. 61	1189/42
	[illegible] 42	9.10.1942	Heeres Verpfleg. Magazin Berditschew	40
	10.10.42	5.12.42	Ldsch. Ers. Batl. 7./Gen.-Komp.	1863

As we can see, *Streifendienst* not only operated in Germany and the occupied territories, but anywhere German troops were present, including friendly states. Schober served in the *Streifendienst* attached to the German Military Attaché in Rome.

Wehrkreis level commands

Command	**Location**
Kdr. des Streifendienstes im Wehrkreis I:	*Königsberg.*
Kdr. des Streifendienstes im Wehrkreis II	*Stettin.*
Kdr. des Streifendienstes im Wehrkreis III	*Berlin.*
Kdr. des Streifendienstes im Wehrkreis IV:	*Dresden.*
Kdr. d. Streifendienstes im Wehrkreis V:	*Stuttgart*
Kdr. d. Streifendienstes im Wehrkreis VI	*Münster*
Kdr. des Streifendienstes im Wehrkreis VII	*München.*
Kdr. des Streifendienstes im Wehrkreis VIII	*Breslau.*
Kdr. des Streifendienstes im Wehrkreis IX	*Kassel.*
Kdr. des Streifendienstes im Wehrkreis X	*Hamburg*
Kdr. des Streifendienstes im Wehrkreis XI	*Hannover.*
Kdr. des Streifendienstes im Wehrkreis XII:	*Wiesbaden*
Kdr. des Streifendienstes im Wehrkreis XIII	*Nürnberg*
Kdr. der Streifendienste im Wehrkreis XVII	*Wien*
Kdr. der Streifendienste im Wehrkreis XVIII	*Salzburg*
Kdr. des Streifendienstes im Wehrkreis XX	*Danzig*
Kdr. des Streifendienstes im Wehrkreis XXI	*Posen*

Kdr des Streifendienstes im Generalgouvernement
(Formed on 15 August 1941 in Wehrkreis VIII and from 17 September 1943 renamed as ‚*Kdr. des Streifendienstes im Wehrkreis Generalgouvernement*' Disbanded 17 August1944.)

Field Units of the Army and Wehrmacht

All units which were initially formed as *Heeres-Streifendienst* were redesignated as *Wehrmacht-Streifendienst* in 1944.

Gruppe Heeresstreifendienst z. b. V. 1:

Formed on 9 December 1941 in *Wehrkreis VIII*, from 29 December 1941 as *Gruppe Heeres-Streifendienst beim AOK Norwegen*. Reformed 17 February 1942 in *Wehrkreis XI* 1944/45 with *Oberbefehlshaber West*, lastly located at Freiburg/Breisgau.

Gruppe Heeresstreifendienst z. b. V. 2:

Formed 17 December 1941 in *Wehrkreis XI*, 1944 attached to *Heeresgruppe A*,
1945 attached to *Heeresgruppe Mitte*.

Gruppe Heeresstreifendienst z. b. V. 3:

Formed 1 September1942 im *Wehrkreis III*; 1944/45 in Italy with *Oberbefehlshaber Südwest*.

Gruppe Heeresstreifendienst z. b. V. 4:

Formed 3 September 1942 in *Wehrkreis IV*; 1944/45 in Italy.

Soldbuch
zugleich Personalausweis
Nr. 24
für
den [illegible] (Dienstgrad)

ab 1. 9. 1940 (Datum) [illegible] (neuer Dienstgrad)
ab 1. 1. 1943 Stabsfeldwebel
ab

Franz Ehbauer (Vor- und Zuname)

Beschriftung und Nummer der Erkennungsmarke 24
Blutgruppe 0
Gasmaskengröße 2
Wehrnummer [illegible]

1

Soldbuch to *Stabsfeldwebel* Franz Ehbauer who served in the *Streifendienst* on the home front.

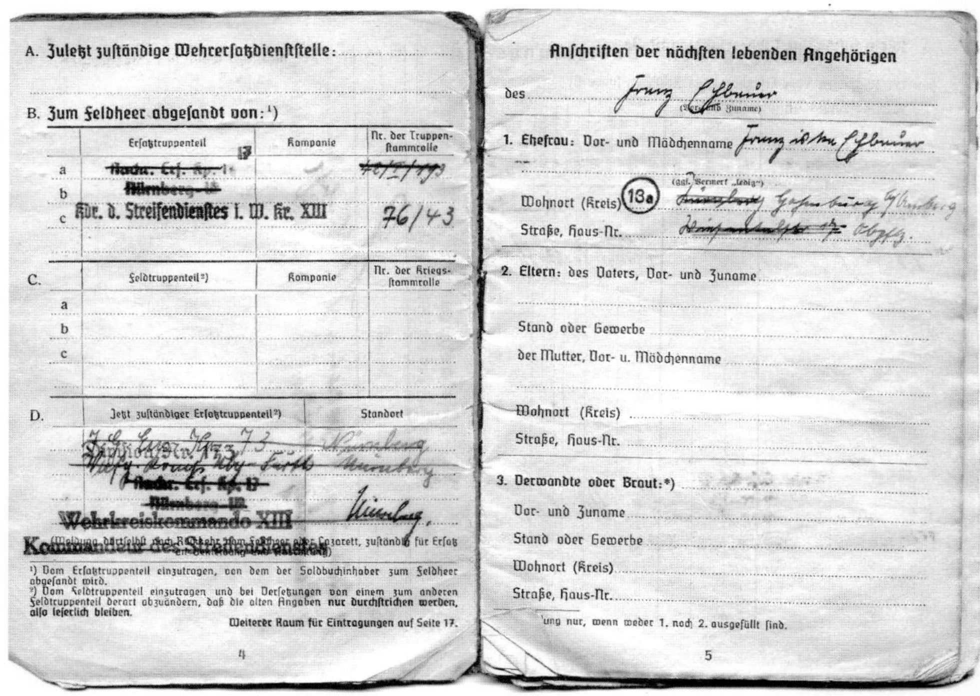

A. Zuletzt zuständige Wehrersatzdienststelle:

B. Zum Feldheer abgesandt von:[1])

	Ersatztruppenteil	Kompanie	Nr. der Truppenstammrolle
a	~~Nachr. Ers. Kp. 17~~		~~[illegible]~~
b	~~Allenberg 13~~		
c	Kdr. d. Streifendienstes i. W. Kr. XIII		76/43

C.	Feldtruppenteil[2])	Kompanie	Nr. der Kriegsstammrolle
a			
b			
c			

D.	Jetzt zuständiger Ersatztruppenteil[2])	Standort
	~~Nachr. Ers. Kp. 17~~	
	~~Allenberg 13~~	
	~~Wehrkreiskommando XIII~~	Nürnberg
	Kommandeur des Streifendienstes	

(Meldung dortselbst nach Rückkehr vom Feldheer oder Lazarett, zuständig für Ersatz ...)

[1]) Vom Ersatztruppenteil einzutragen, von dem der Soldbuchinhaber zum Feldheer abgesandt wird.
[2]) Vom Feldtruppenteil einzutragen und bei Versetzungen von einem zum anderen Feldtruppenteil derart abzuändern, daß die alten Angaben **nur durchstrichen werden, also leserlich bleiben.**

Weiterer Raum für Eintragungen auf Seite 17.

4

Anschriften der nächsten lebenden Angehörigen

des Franz Ehbauer (Vor- und Zuname)

1. Ehefrau: Vor- und Mädchenname [illegible]
(ggf. Vermerk „ledig")
Wohnort (Kreis) 13a [illegible]
Straße, Haus-Nr. [illegible]

2. Eltern: des Vaters, Vor- und Zuname
Stand oder Gewerbe
der Mutter, Vor- u. Mädchenname
Wohnort (Kreis)
Straße, Haus-Nr.

3. Verwandte oder Braut:*)
Vor- und Zuname
Stand oder Gewerbe
Wohnort (Kreis)
Straße, Haus-Nr.

*) ... nur, wenn weder 1. noch 2. ausgefüllt sind.

5

Entries from the Drechsler *Wehrpass* showing his service with *Gruppe* GFP 2.

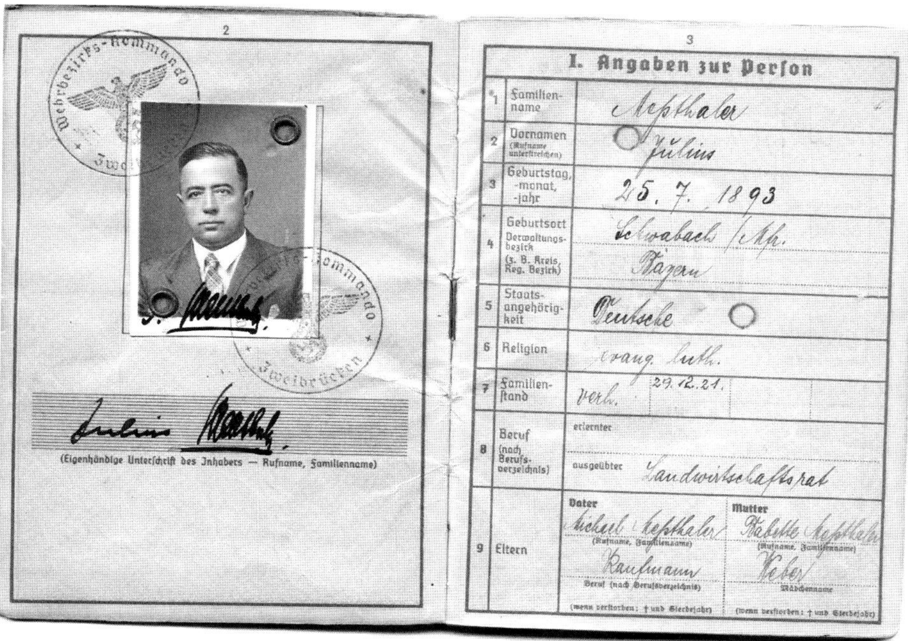

2

(Eigenhändige Unterschrift des Inhabers — Rufname, Familienname)

3

I. Angaben zur Person

1	Familienname	Meßthaler
2	Vornamen (Rufname unterstreichen)	Julius
3	Geburtstag, -monat, -jahr	25. 7. 1893
4	Geburtsort, Verwaltungsbezirk (z. B. Kreis, Reg. Bezirk)	Schwabach / Mfr. Bayern
5	Staatsangehörigkeit	Deutsche
6	Religion	evang. luth.
7	Familienstand	verh. 29.12.21.
8	Beruf (nach Berufsverzeichnis)	erlernter: — ausgeübter: Landwirtschaftsrat
9	Eltern	Vater: Michael Meßthaler (Rufname, Familienname), Kaufmann (Beruf (nach Berufsverzeichnis)) (wenn verstorben: † und Sterbejahr) — Mutter: Babette Meßthaler (Rufname, Familienname), Weber (Mädchenname) (wenn verstorben: † und Sterbejahr)

Wehrpass to Major Julius Messthaler, commander of *Wehrmachstreifengruppe* z.b.V. 24 a combat infantry veteran before serving with the *Streifendienst.*

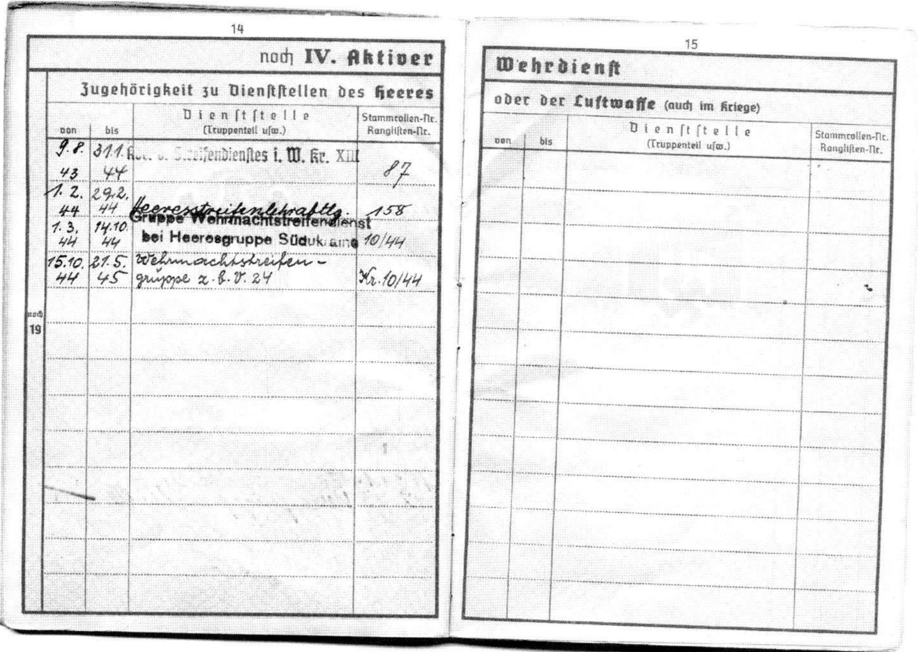

14

noch IV. Aktiver

Zugehörigkeit zu Dienststellen des Heeres

von	bis	Dienststelle (Truppenteil usw.)	Stammrollen-Nr. Ranglisten-Nr.
9.8.43	31.1.44	Kdr. d. Streifendienstes i. W. Kr. XIII	87
1.2.44	29.2.44	Heeresstreifenbefehlsh.	158
1.3.44	14.10.44	Gruppe Wehrmachtstreifendienst bei Heeresgruppe Südukraine	10/44
15.10.44	21.5.45	Wehrmachtstreifengruppe z.b.V. 24	Nr. 10/44

noch 19

15

Wehrdienst

oder der Luftwaffe (auch im Kriege)

von	bis	Dienststelle (Truppenteil usw.)	Stammrollen-Nr. Ranglisten-Nr.

Messthaler's *Wehrpass* shows that he served with the *Streifendienst* on the home front as well as in Russia.

Gruppe Heeresstreifendienst z.b.V. 5:
Formed 5 September 1942 in *Wehrkreis XI*; 1944 *Heeresgruppe A*, 1945 *Heeresgruppe Mitte (17. Armee)* in Oberschlesien.

Gruppe Heeresstreifendienst z. b.V. 6:
Formed April 1943 in *Wehrkreis III*; 1944/45 in Italy.

Gruppe Heeresstreifendienst z. b.V. 7:
Formed April 1943 in *Wehrkreis III* (Berlin-Spandau); in 1944 with *Heeresgruppe A /Mitte* in Silesia.

Gruppe Heeresstreifendienst 8:
Formed March 1943 in *Wehrkreis I*; 1944 with *Oberbefehlshaber West*, 1945 on the Oder with *Heeresgruppe Weichsel*.

Gruppe Heeresstreifendienst 9:
Formed March 1943 in *Wehrkreis XIII*; 1944 with *Heeresgruppe A*,
1945 with *Heeresgruppe Mitte*.

Gruppe Heeresstreifendienst z. b.V. 10:
Formed March 1943 in *Wehrkreis IV*; 1945 on the western front with *Heeresgruppe G*, Oberrhein, Saarpfalz.

Gruppe Heeresstreifendienst z. b.V. 11:
Formed March 1943 in *Wehrkreis VI*; 1944 with *Heeresgruppe A* in southern Poland. 1945 with *Heeresgruppe Mitte* in Silesia.

Gruppe Heeresstreifendienst z. b.V. 12:
Formed February 1943 in *Wehrkreis III* (Berlin-Spandau); 1944 with *4. Armee* in East Prussia.

Gruppe Heeresstreifendienst z. b.V. 13:
Formed September 1943 in *Wehrkreis VIII*; in 1944/45 with *Oberbefehlshaber Südost*, finally in Cilli/ Steiermark.

Gruppe Heeresstreifendienst z. b.V. 14:
Formed September 1943 in *Wehrkreis XIII* (Bayreuth); November 1943 with *Militär Befehlshaber Nordostfrankreich*, 1944 with *Oberbefehlshaber West*,
1945 in Idar-Oberstein.

Gruppe Heeresstreifendienst 15:
Formed Aug. 1943 in *Wehrkreis XI*; 1944 with *Heeresgruppe E* in Serbia, 1945 in Croatia.

Wehrmachtsstreifengruppe z.b.V. 16:
Formed March 1944 by renaming *'Gruppe Wehrmachtsstreifendienst bei Heeresgruppe Süd'*; employed with *Heeresgruppe A* in southern Poland, 1945 in Prague.

Gruppe Wehrmachtsstreifendienst z.b.V. 17:
Formed August 1944 in *Wehrkreis III*; employed in the west with *Heeresgruppe G*, In 1945 at St. Wendel/Saar (l.Armee).

Gruppe Wehrmachtsstreifendienst z.b.V. 18:
Formed Aug. 1944 im *Wehrkreis IV*; employed firstly in the west, by the end of 1944 with *Heeresgruppe A* in southern Poland, 1945 in Bautzen.

Gruppe Wehrmachtsstreifendienst z.b.V. 19:
Formed August 1944 in *Wehrkreis XI*; Hannover. Employed initially in *Wehrkreis XII*, Wiesbaden, then with *Heeresgruppe A* in southern Poland, and ultimately with *Heeresgruppe Mitte* in Silesia.

Wehrmachtstreifengruppe z. b.V. 20:
Formed Aug. 1944 from *Kommandeur Heeres-Streifendienst beim Befehlshaber Rückwärtigen Heeresgebiet Mitte*; action with *3. PzArmee*, in East Prussia.
In 1945 with *2. Armee* on the Vistula front.

Wehrmachtstreifengruppe z. b.V. 21:
Formed April 1944 in *Wehrkreis III* (Belzig); action in Hungary.

Wehrmachtstreifengruppe 22:
Formed September 1944 in Slovakia.

Wehrmachtstreifengruppe 23:
Formed October 1944 from *Wehrmacht-Streifengruppe 2 bei Heeresgruppe Nord* and ultimately served in Kurland.

Wehrmachtstreifengruppe 24:
Formed in October 1944 from *Wehrmacht-Streifengruppe Heeresgruppe Süd* and ultimately serbed in Slovakia.

Wehrmachtstreifengruppe 25:
Formed Winter 1944/45; ultimately active in East Prussia.

Wehrmachtstreifengruppe z.b.V. 26:
Formed summer 1944 in Hungary from the *Kommandeur der Heeresstreifendienstes Ungarn* and disbanded at the end of 1944.

Wehrmachtstreifengruppe 27:
Formed November 1944 from *Gruppe Heeresstreifendienst beim deutschen Wehrmachtattaché Rom*, Employed in Italy.

Wehrmachtstreifengruppe 28:
No information available.

Wehrmachtstreifengruppe z. b. V. 29:
Formed October 1944 from the renamed *Gruppe Wehrmachtstreifendienst beim WB Dänemark.*

Wehrmachtstreifengruppe 30:
Formed January 1945 active in Bohemia-Moravia.

Wehrmachtstreifengruppe 31:
Formed January 1945 and active with *Panzer Armeeoberkommando 6* in Hungary.

Wehrmacht-Streifengruppe 32:
Formed January 1945 and active around Prenzlau with *Heeresgruppe Weichsel.*

Wehrmacht-Streifengruppe 33:
Formed January 1945. No other details known.

Wehrmacht-Streifengruppe 34:
Formed January 1945. No other details known.

Wehrmacht-Streifengruppe 35:
Formed January 1945 and served with *Heeresgruppe B.*

Wehrmacht-Streifengruppe 36:
Formed January 1945 and based in Berlin-Hirschgraben.

Wehrmacht-Streifengruppe 37:
Formed February 1945 active around Falkensee.

Wehrmacht-Streifengruppe 38:
Formed February 1945 active in Potsdam.

Wehrmacht-Streifengruppe 39:
Formed February 1945 and active with *Heeresgruppe Süd.*

Wehrmacht-Streifengruppe 40:
Formed February 1945 and based in Danzig.

Wehrmacht-Streifengruppe 41:
Formed April 1945. No other details known.

Wehrmacht-Streifengruppe 42:
Formed April 1945. No other details known.

Wehrmacht-Streifengruppe 43:
Formed April 1945. No other details known.

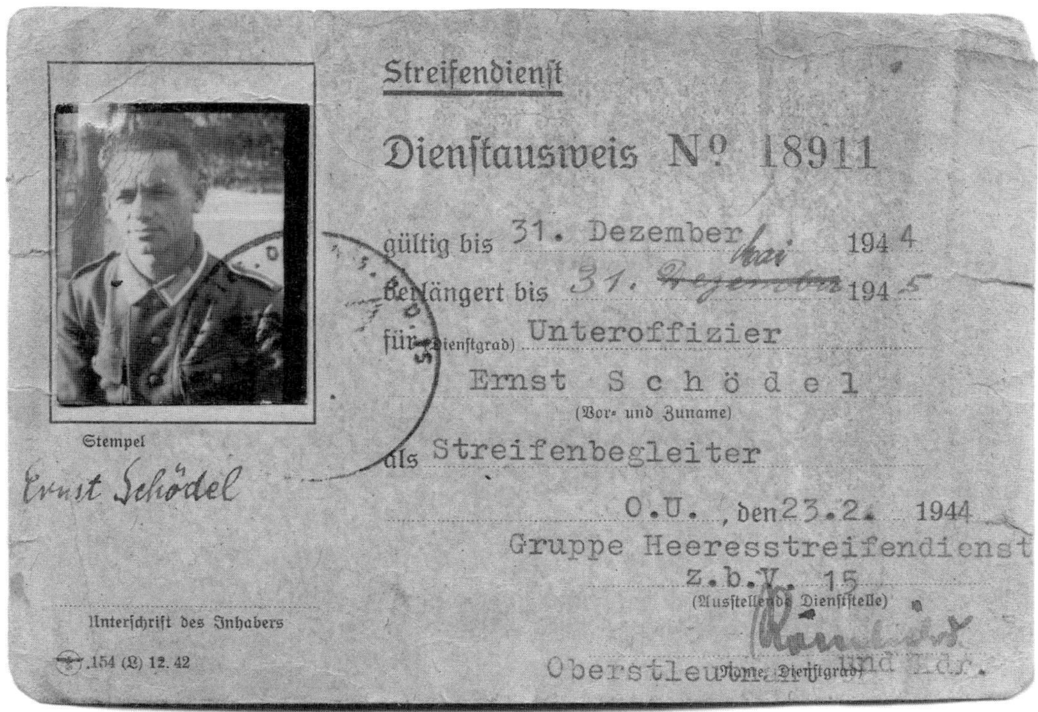

Streifendienst

Dienstausweis Nº 18911

gültig bis 31. Dezember / Mai 1944

verlängert bis 31. ~~Dezember~~ 1945

für (Dienstgrad) Unteroffizier

Ernst Schödel

(Vor- und Zuname)

als Streifenbegleiter

O.U., den 23.2. 1944

Gruppe Heeresstreifendienst

z.b.V. 15

(Ausstellende Dienststelle)

Oberstleutnant und Kdr.

(Name, Dienstgrad)

Stempel

Ernst Schödel

Unterschrift des Inhabers

.154 (L) 12.42

Ausweis of *Unteroffizier* Ernst Schödel as a member of *Gruppe Heeresstreifendienst* z.b.V. 15

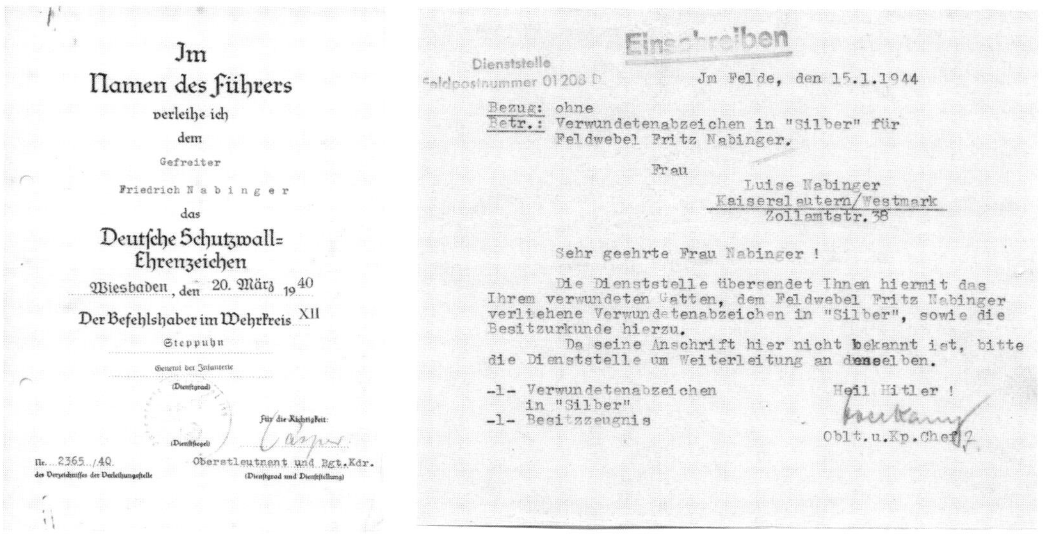

Im Namen des Führers

verleihe ich

dem

Gefreiter

Friedrich N a b i n g e r

das

Deutsche Schutzwall-Ehrenzeichen

Wiesbaden, den 20. März 1940

Der Befehlshaber im Wehrkreis XII

Steppuhn

General der Infanterie

(Dienstgrad)

Für die Richtigkeit:

(Dienstsiegel)

Oberstleutnant und Rgt.Kdr.

(Dienstgrad und Dienststellung)

Nr. 2365./40.

des Verzeichnisses der Verleihungsstelle

Einschreiben

Dienststelle

Feldpostnummer 01 208 D

Jm Felde, den 15.1.1944

Bezug: ohne

Betr.: Verwundetenabzeichen in "Silber" für Feldwebel Fritz Nabinger.

Frau

Luise Nabinger

Kaiserslautern/Westmark

Zollamtstr. 38

Sehr geehrte Frau Nabinger !

Die Dienststelle übersendet Ihnen hiermit das Ihrem verwundeten Gatten, dem Feldwebel Fritz Nabinger verliehene Verwundetenabzeichen in "Silber", sowie die Besitzurkunde hierzu.

Da seine Anschrift hier nicht bekannt ist, bitte die Dienststelle um Weiterleitung an denselben.

-1- Verwundetenabzeichen in "Silber"

-1- Besitzzeugnis

Heil Hitler !

Oblt.u.Kp.Chef/7

Above left: Award document for the West Wall Medal awarded to Nabinger for his service on the defensive fortifications on Germany's border with France prior to May 1940, whilst serving with the *Streifendienst.*

Above right: Nabinger would later serve as a combat infantryman. This covering letter was to accompany the Wound Badge in Silver and its award document being sent to his wife by his then unit, *Infanterie* Regiment 118.

Equipment Levels

Gruppe Heeresstreifendenst

HQ

1 officer, 1 NCO and 3 enlisted ranks.

- 2 × pistols.
- 3 × carbines.
- 1 × machine pistol.
- 1 × automobile.

Officer Patrols

1 officer, 1 NCO and 1 enlisted rank.

- 1 × pistol.
- 1 × carbine.
- 1 × machine pistol.
- 1 × automobile.

NCO Patrols

2 NCOs and 1 enlisted rank.

- 1 × pistol.
- 1 × carbine.
- 1 × machine pistol.
- 1 × automobile.

Gruppe Heeresstreifendenst a—Occupied Territories

HQ

2 officers, 3 NCOs and 6 enlisted ranks.

- 7 × pistols.
- 4 × carbines.
- 2 × machine pistols.
- 1 × heavy field car.

Officer Patrols

9 officers, 9 NCOs and 9 enlisted ranks.

- 18 × pistols.
- 9 × carbines.
- 9 × machine pistols.
- 6 × medium field cars.
- 3 × light field cars.

NCO Patrols

6 NCOs and 3 enlisted ranks.

- 6 × pistols.
- 3 × carbines.

3 × machine pistols.
1 × medium field car.
1 × heavy field car.

Gruppe Heeresstreifendenst b—Occupied Territories

HQ

2 officers, 3 NCOs and 6 enlisted ranks.
9 × pistols.
6 × carbines.
2 × machine pistols.
1 × heavy field car.

Officer Patrols

12 officers, 12 NCOs and 12 enlisted ranks.
24 × pistols.
12 × carbines.
12 × machine pistols.
8 × medium field cars.
4 × light field cars.

NCO Patrols

12 NCOs and 6 enlisted ranks.
12 × pistols.
6 × carbines.

Wehrmacht - Streifendienst
Dienstausweis № 32201
gültig bis 31. Dezember 1945
verlängert bis .... 194...
für (Dienstgrad) Oberfeldwebel
Paul Stegmann
(Vor- und Zuname)
als Wehrmachtstreifenführer
Dienstsiegel
Hbg.-Wandsbk., den 21.4. 1945
Kommandeur der Wehrmachtordnungstr. Hbg
In Vertretung des Kommandeurs
(Ausstellende Dienststelle)
Unterschrift des Inhabers
(Name, Dienstgrad) Major
203 (2) 1. 45 — 3

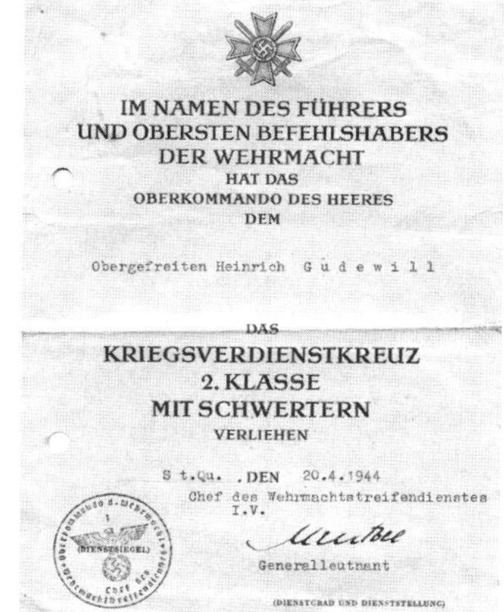

IM NAMEN DES FÜHRERS
UND OBERSTEN BEFEHLSHABERS
DER WEHRMACHT
HAT DAS
OBERKOMMANDO DES HEERES
DEM
Obergefreiten Heinrich Güdewill
DAS
KRIEGSVERDIENSTKREUZ
2. KLASSE
MIT SCHWERTERN
VERLIEHEN
St.Qu., DEN 20.4.1944
Chef des Wehrmachtstreifendienstes
I.V.
Generalleutnant
(DIENSTGRAD UND DIENSTSTELLUNG)

A *Above left:* 1945 *Ausweis* to *Oberfeldwebel* Paul Stegmann. Notice that a prefix 'Wehrmacht' has been added to the heading after all *Heerestreifendienst* elements were renamed as *Wehrmachtstreifendienst.*

Above right: Award Document for the War Merit Cross to *Obergefreiten* Heinrich Gudewill for service in the *Streifendienst.*

6 × machine pistols.
4 × medium field cars.
2 × heavy field cars.

Gruppe Heeresstreifendenst c—Occupied Territories

HQ

2 officers, 3 NCOs and 6 enlisted ranks.
7 × pistols.
4 × carbines.
2 × machine pistols.
1 × heavy field car.

Officer Patrols

3 officers, 4 NCOs and 16 enlisted ranks.
42 × pistols.
21 × carbines.
21 × machine pistols.
16 × medium field cars.
5 × heavy field cars.

NCO Patrols

30 NCOs and 15 enlisted ranks.
30 × pistols.
15 × carbines.
15 × machine pistols.
10 × light field cars.
5 × medium field cars.

Gruppe Heeresstreifendenst zbV—Occupied Territories

HQ

3 officers, 6 NCOs and 18 enlisted ranks.
5 × pistols.
22 × carbines.
4 × medium field cars.
1 × heavy field car.
1 × 3 ton truck.

Officer Patrols

15 officers, 15 NCOs and 15 enlisted ranks.
30 × pistols
15 × carbines.
15 × machine pistols.
15 × medium field cars.

NCO Patrols

20 NCOs and 10 enlisted ranks.

20 × pistols.
10 × carbines.
10 × machine pistols.
10 × medium field car.

Typically, Patrols or *Streifen* were carried out by groups of three soldiers. Generally this would be one officer, one NCO and one enlisted rank, or by one senior NCO, one junior NCO and one enlisted rank. It is quite clear from studying the above equipment scales that patrol units in occupied areas were far more powerful than those on the home front where miscreant soldiers were unlikely to offer armed resistance!

What is also clear is that *Streifendienst* patrols were far more heavily armed than those of the *Feldgendarmerie* or *Feldjäger* as the issue level of machine pistols shows. The *Feldjäger* of course were entitled to call upon the *Streifendienst* to support them so probably did not require a heavier weapons load in their own right.

Bahnhofswache

During the war, at any time vast numbers of military personnel were in transit through all parts of Germany. Almost from the beginning of the war, the *Wehrmacht* faced difficulties in properly controlling discipline with large troop movements through major rail centres.

Bahnhofswache units were formed in order to maintain order and discipline at railway stations, checking travel papers and movement orders, not only to ensure smooth troop movements, but also to detain those without valid papers, such as deserters etc.

Uniforms and Insignia

As with the *Streifendienst*, members of the *Bahnhofswache* did not have a special uniform, or a particular specific colour of *Waffenfarbe*. Personnel from virtually any branch of the armed services could be temporarily attached to a *Bahnhofswache* unit. Special insignia however were introduced to identify troops acting as *Bahnhofswache* personnel. These included:

Armband

A yellow armband with the legend *Bahnhofswache* machine woven or printed in black Gothic style script.

Gorget

A gorget similar in general style to that worn by the *Feldgendarmerie* was produced for *Bahnhofswache* personnel. The neck chain and basic half moon shaped plate were identical to those of the *Feldgendarmerie*, bit where the *Feldgendarmerie* gorget featured stippled buttons to the left and right ends of the plate, the *Bahnhofswache* gorget had *Wehrmacht* pattern national

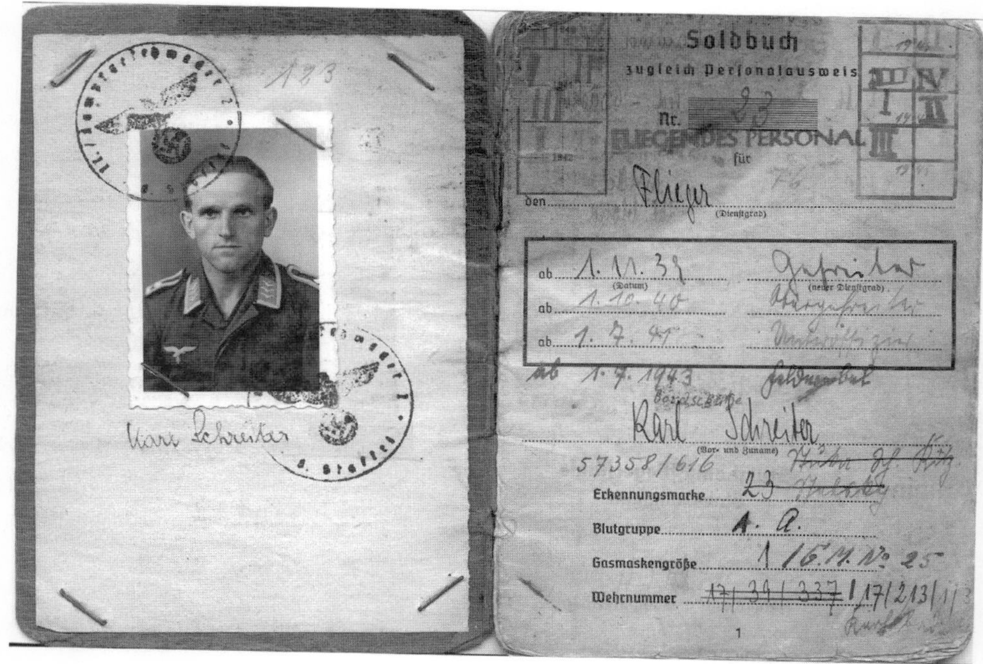

Soldbuch
zugleich Personalausweis
Nr. 23
FLIEGENDES PERSONAL
für
den Flieger
(Dienstgrad)
ab 1.11.39 (Datum) Gefreiter (neuer Dienstgrad)
ab 1.10.40
ab 1.7.41
ab 1.7.1943 Feldwebel
Karl Schreiter
(Vor- und Zuname)
57358/616
Erkennungsmarke 23
Blutgruppe A. A.
Gasmaskengröße 1
Wehrnummer
1

Soldbuch to *Feldwebel* Karl Schreiter a *Luftwaffe* member of the *Streifendienst*. (*Ian Jewison*)

A. Zuletzt zuständige Wehrersatzdienststelle: Karlsbad

B. Truppenteil bzw. Dienststelle:¹)

von	bis	Truppenteil bzw. Dienststelle	Staffel usw.	Nr. der Stammrolle
1.6.39				23
26.8.41		II./St.G.1	6 Staffel	143
4.5.43		3./Bordschützenschule		
		Kampfgeschwader 66	1. Staffel	
22.11.43	17.1.44			
		6./Kampfgeschwader 2		
31.10.44		I Frontflieger Sammelgruppe		2235/44
				75/44
15.12.44				463/44

C. Jetzt zuständiger Ersatztruppenteil	Standort
Flg. Ausb. Rgt. 10	
	Straubing

(Meldung dortselbst nach Rückkehr vom Truppenteil bzw. Dienststelle oder Lazarett, zuständig für Ersatz an Bekleidung und Ausrüstung)

¹) Vom Truppenteil bzw. Dienststelle einzutragen und bei Versetzungen von einem zum anderen Truppenteil bzw. Dienststelle derart abzuändern, daß die alten Angaben nur durchstrichen werden, also leserlich bleiben.

Weiterer Raum für Eintragungen auf Seite 17.

4

Fortsetzung zu Seite 4

B. Truppenteil bzw. Dienststelle:¹)

von	bis	Truppenteil bzw. Dienststelle	Staffel usw.	Nr. der Stammrolle
			1. Komp.	5994

C. Jetzt zuständiger Ersatztruppenteil	Standort
Flg. Ers. Bat. I	
-"-	-"-

(Meldung dortselbst nach Rückkehr vom Truppenteil bzw. Dienststelle oder Lazarett, zuständig für Ersatz an Bekleidung und Ausrüstung)

Wehrmachtstreifenlehrabteilung

¹) Vom Truppenteil bzw. Dienststelle einzutragen und bei Versetzungen von einem zum anderen Truppenteil bzw. Dienststelle derart abzuändern, daß die alten Angaben nur durchstrichen werden, also leserlich bleiben.

17

Schreiter had an interesting career, first in aircrew as an air gunner, then with the elite *Fallschirmpanzerkorps* Hermann Göring before ending the war in the *Streifendienst*. See the final entry at the bottom of the right hand page for '*Wehrmachtstreifenlehrabteilung*'. (*Ian Jewison*)

Above left: A *Streifendienst* unit. Note that all are combat veterans with at least the Iron Cross 2nd Class and most have been wounded in action. (*Ian Jewison*)

Above right: *Bahnhofswache* checking papers at a major railway station in Germany.

Above: A fine study of an enlisted rank on duty with the *Bahnhofswache*.

Right: *Luftwaffe* member of the *Bahnhofswache* posing with an NCO in the role of *Bahnhofs Offizier*.

emblems (the eagle and swastika with folded wings). The scroll had a dark grey painted finish with the legend *Bahnhofswache* in Gothic characters.

The central motif of the gorget was the number of the wearer's *Abteilung*. These numerals, plus the national emblems and the lettering on the scroll, were all finished in luminous paint.

Bahnhofs-Wach u Streifen Abt 101
Active in the northern sector of the Eastern Front and in Latvia.

Bahnhofs-Wach u Streifen Abt 102
Active in the Brandenburg region of Germany.

Bahnhofs-Wach u Streifen Abt 103
Active in the southern sector of the Eastern Front and Czechoslovakia.

Bahnhofs-Wach u Streifen Abt 104
Active in the Ukraine and in Hungary.

Bahnhofs-Wach u Streifen Abt 105
Active in the southern sector of the Eastern Front.

Bahnhofs-Wach u Streifen Abt 106
Active in the southern sector of the Eastern Front.

Bahnhofs-Wach u Streifen Abt 108
Active in the Hamburg area.

Bahnhofs-Wach u Streifen Abt 109
Active in the area along the upper Rhine.

Bahnhofs-Wach u Streifen Abt 110
Active in the Netherlands.

Bahnhofs-Wach-Kompanie Italien
Operated in Italy.

Bahnhofs-Wach u Streifen Abt beim Armeeoberkommando Norwegen
Operated in occupied Norway.

Bahnhofs-Wach u Streifen Abt Nordrussland
Active in the norther sector of the Eastern Front.

Above left: Oberfeldwebel of *Bahnhofswache* on duty. This was not a specific military career but simply a duty to which any soldier could be temporarily assigned.

Above right: This *Bahnhofswache* soldier may look very young, but wears the Wound Badge verifying that he has seen combat.

Below left: Bahnhofswache Unteroffizier wearing a pistol—the typical armament for this duty.

Below right: A variant of the *Bahnhofswache* armband being worn, with italic script lettering.

Soldbuch
zugleich Personalausweis

Nr. 150

für

den Oblt. d. R.
(Dienstgrad)

ab 1.2.1942 (Datum) Hauptm. d. R. (neuer Dienstgrad)
ab
ab

Erich Marquardt
(Vor- und Zuname)

Beschriftung und Nummer der Erkennungsmarke
Blutgruppe B
Gasmaskengröße 2
Wehrnummer Breslau 97/28/1

1

Soldbuch of *Hauptmann* Erich Marquardt who commanded a *Bahnhofswache* detachment.

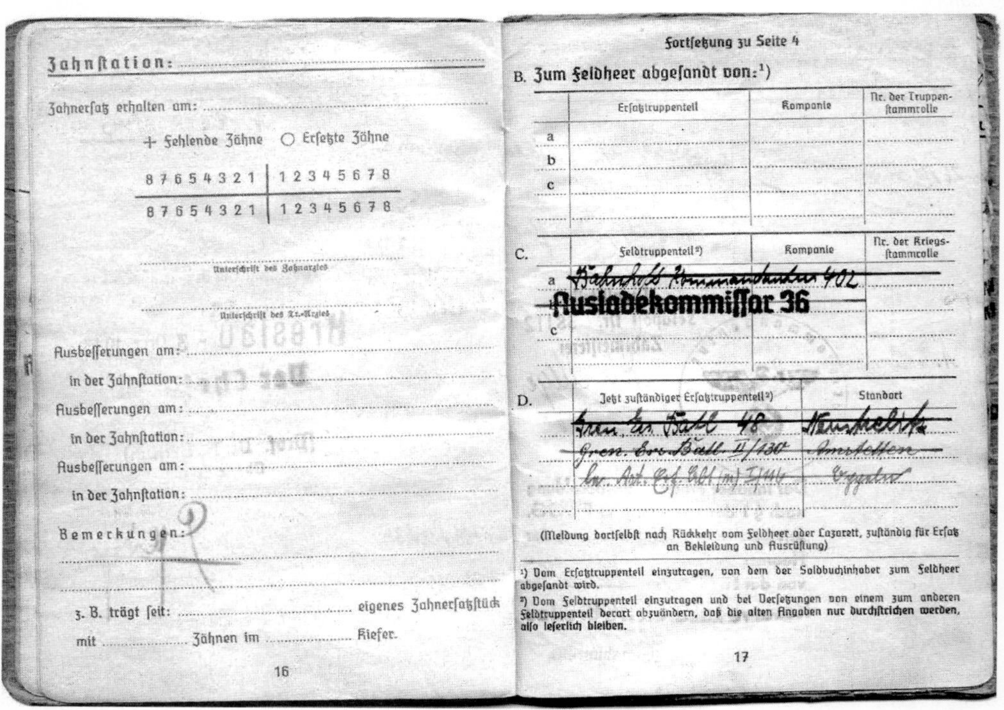

Zahnstation:

Zahnersatz erhalten am:

+ Fehlende Zähne ○ Ersetzte Zähne

8 7 6 5 4 3 2 1 | 1 2 3 4 5 6 7 8
8 7 6 5 4 3 2 1 | 1 2 3 4 5 6 7 8

Unterschrift des Zahnarztes

Unterschrift des Tr.-Arztes

Ausbesserungen am:
in der Zahnstation:
Ausbesserungen am:
in der Zahnstation:
Ausbesserungen am:
in der Zahnstation:

Bemerkungen:

z. B. trägt seit: ... eigenes Zahnersatzstück
mit ... Zähnen im ... Kiefer.

16

Fortsetzung zu Seite 4

B. Zum Feldheer abgesandt von:[1])

	Ersatztruppenteil	Kompanie	Nr. der Truppenstammrolle
a			
b			
c			

C.

	Feldtruppenteil[2])	Kompanie	Nr. der Kriegsstammrolle
a	~~Bahnhofs Kommandantur 402~~		
b	Ausladekommissar 36		
c			

D.

Jetzt zuständiger Ersatztruppenteil[2])	Standort
~~Gren. Er. Batl. 48~~	~~Neuhof~~
~~Gren. Ers. Batl. II/130~~	~~Amstetten~~

(Meldung dortselbst nach Rückkehr vom Feldheer oder Lazarett, zuständig für Ersatz an Bekleidung und Ausrüstung)

[1]) Vom Ersatztruppenteil einzutragen, von dem der Soldbuchinhaber zum Feldheer abgesandt wird.

[2]) Vom Feldtruppenteil einzutragen und bei Versetzungen von einem zum anderen Feldtruppenteil derart abzuändern, daß die alten Angaben nur durchstrichen werden, also leserlich bleiben.

17

Entry in the Marquardt *Soldbuch* showing an entry for *Bahnhofskommandantur* 402.

The *Bahnhofswache* armband was replaced by the gorget but in this interesting shot the soldier second from right wears both the armband and the gorget.

Another NCO of *Bahnhofswache* with combat experience as evidenced by the Wound Badge on his pocket.

Above left: Combat infantry veteran on duty with the *Bahnhofswache*.

Above right: *Bahnhofswache* on duty at a rural railway station, in the occupied Eastern territories.

Typical mixed *Luftwaffe*/Army *Bahnhofswache* group, some wearing decorations from previous combat duties.

Zugwache

The *Zugwache* were somewhat analogous to the *Bahnhofswache*, but whereas the former were responsible for policing railway stations, the latter were responsible for the trains themselves. Each train would have its own designated carriage for the *Zugwache,* who would ensure the travel papers of those travelling on the train were in order, apprehend any deserters or soldiers without proper paperwork, etc. In addition, the *Zugwache* would provide an instant armed response to any attacks on trains by partisans etc. when passing through dangerous areas.

Soldiers from any branch could be assigned to service in the *Zugwache*, and as this service did not have its own specific *Waffenfarbe* colour, would continue to wear the *Waffenfarbe* of their parent branch.

Examination of *Soldbücher* and *Wehrpässe* of soldiers with *Zugwache* experience indicate that, as opposed to being a career choice this was often a temporary assignment with soldiers passing from a particular branch of service or unit, experiencing a period of time in a *Zugwache* unit, and then moving on to a new assignment.

Special Insignia

The Gorget

In order to identify themselves as members of the *Zugwache*, members of these units wore a gorget when on duty. The gorget was of a similar style to that of the *Feldgendarmerie* being in typical crescent shape, stamped from thin sheet metal and with a plain undecorated chain. Replacing the buttons found on the *Feldgendarmerie* gorget were *Wehrmacht* pattern national emblems, each facing inwards towards the centre of the gorget. In the lower part of the gorget was a dark grey painted scroll bearing the legend '*Zugwachabteilung*' in Gothic characters. The centre field of the gorget bore three metal numerals representing the *Abteilung* number.

A variant of the gorget also exists with the word '*Zugwache*' rather than '*Zugwachabteilung*' on the scroll. It may be that the change from *Zugwache* to *Zugwachabteilung* came when the basic unit formation size was upgraded from *Kompanie* to *Abteilung* strength.

At least two sizes of metal numerals have been noted on genuine examples indicating perhaps more than one manufacturer of these gorgets. A further variant has been noted which is identical to the *Feldgendarmerie* gorget with only the wording on the scroll being altered to '*Zugwachabteilung*'.

Ausweis

To back up the gorget as a sign of their authority, members of the *Zugwache* also carried a special Ausweis. The example shown here carries the following text:

> Er hat die Berechtigung, gegebenfalls die Verpflichtung, allen Angehörigen der Wehrmacht und des Wehrmachtgefolges—mit Ausnahme von Generalen und im Generalsrang stehenden Wehrmachtbeamten in bezug auf seinen Aufgabenkreis Befehle zu erteilen.
>
> Gegenüber Offizieren und Wehrmachtbeamten im Offizierrang haben nur Offizier Befehlsgewalt und Prüfungsrecht.

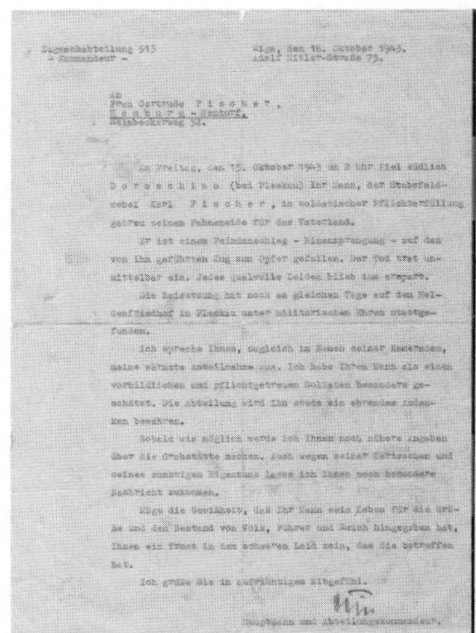

Zugwachabteilung 513
- Kommandeur -

Riga, den 16. Oktober 1943.
Adolf Hitler-Straße 73.

An
Frau Gertrude F i s c h e r ,
H a m b u r g - [illegible],
[illegible]weg 52.

Am Freitag, den 15. Oktober 1943 um 2 Uhr fiel südlich D o r o s c h i n o (bei Pleskau) Ihr Mann, der Stabsfeldwebel Karl F i s c h e r , in soldatischer Pflichterfüllung getreu seinem Fahneneide für das Vaterland.

Er ist einem Feindanschlag - Minensprengung - auf den von ihm geführten Zug zum Opfer gefallen. Der Tod trat unmittelbar ein. Jedes qualvolle Leiden blieb ihm erspart.

Die Beisetzung hat noch am gleichen Tage auf dem Heldenfriedhof in Pleskau unter militärischen Ehren stattgefunden.

Ich spreche Ihnen, zugleich im Namen seiner Kameraden, meine wärmste Anteilnahme aus. Ich habe Ihren Mann als einen vorbildlichen und pflichtgetreuen Soldaten besonders geschätzt. Die Abteilung wird ihm stets ein ehrendes Andenken bewahren.

Sobald wie möglich werde ich Ihnen noch nähere Angaben über die Grabstätte machen. Auch wegen seiner Wertsachen und seines sonstigen Eigentums lasse ich Ihnen noch besondere Nachricht zukommen.

Möge die Gewißheit, daß Ihr Mann sein Leben für die Größe und den Bestand von Volk, Führer und Reich hingegeben hat, Ihnen ein Trost in dem schweren Leid sein, das Sie betroffen hat.

Ich grüße Sie in aufrichtigem Mitgefühl.

[signature]

Hauptmann und Abteilungskommandeur.

Above left: Railway carriage designated for use of the escorting *Zugwache* troops.

Above right: Condolence letter from the unit commander to Fischer's wife explaining that he was killed in action when the train he was guarding was blown up after running over a mine.

2

Karl Fischer

(Eigenhändige Unterschrift des Inhabers — Rufname, Familienname)

3

I. Angaben zur Person

1	Familienname	Fischer
2	Vornamen (Rufname unterstreichen)	Karl Paul
3	Geburtstag, -monat, -jahr	2. Dezember 1907.
4	Geburtsort Verwaltungsbezirk (z. B. Kreis, Reg. Bezirk)	Flensburg
5	Staatsangehörigkeit	Deutsches
6	Religion	ev. luth.
7	Familienstand	geschieden verh.
8	Beruf (nach Berufsverzeichnis)	erlernter: Lehrant ausgeübter:
9	Eltern	Vater: Gustav Fischer (Rufname, Familienname); Konditor, Beruf (nach Berufsverzeichnis); † 1933 (wenn verstorben: † und Sterbejahr) Mutter: Magda Fischer (Rufname, Familienname); Jensen, Mädchenname (wenn verstorben: † und Sterbejahr)

Wehrpass for *Stabsfeldwebel* Karl Fischer of *Zugwachabteilung* 513.

12

noch IV. Aktiver

Zugehörigkeit zu Dienststellen des Heeres

von	bis	Dienststelle (Truppenteil usw.)	Stammrollen-Nr. Ranglisten-Nr.
[illegible] 1935	11.10. 1937	[illegible]	159
12.10. 1937	23.5. 1941	[illegible]	[illegible]
24.5. 41.	18.6. 41	Inf. Nachr. Ers. Kp. 20	37/28
[illegible]	4.1. 1943	Kommandeur des Streifendienstes beim Wehrkreiskommando X	14
4.1. 43	25.10. 43	Zugwachabteilung z. b. V. 513	[illegible]
—	—	Gen.-Kp./Ldesh.Ers.u.Ausb.Btl. 7	2528

13

Wehrdienst

oder der Luftwaffe (auch im Kriege)

von	bis	Dienststelle (Truppenteil usw.)	Stammrollen-Nr. Ranglisten-Nr.

Detail from the Fischer *Wehrpass* showing the entry for *Zugwachabteilung* 513.

Above left: Zugwache NCO with a comrade from the Reichsarbeitsdienst.

Above right: A superb portrait study of an enlisted rank serving with *Zugwachabteilung* 507.

Alle truppenteile und Dienststellen sowie jeder Wehrmachtangehörige sind verpflichtet, die Transportführer und Zugwachen auf Anforderung mit allen erforderlichen Mitteln zu unterstützen.

In relation to the bearer, this indicates that:

He has authorization, even the obligation, to give orders to all members of the armed forces and armed forces followers—with exception of generals and officials with equivalent general rank—related to the execution of his duties.

Only officers have authority over and rights to check officers and armed forces officials in officer rank.

All military units and agencies as well as each member of the armed forces is obliged to support the Transport leaders and *Zugwache* by all necessary means whenever required.

Clearly, when operating in the execution of their duties, members of the *Zugwache*, like their cousins in the *Feldgendarmerie*, also had wide ranging power and authority. The *Ausweis* goes on to clarify further details of the *Zugwache* soldier's status:

Dem Inhaber dieses Ausweises obliegt die Kontrolle aller Wehrmachtreisenden—einschl. Angehörigen des Wehrmachtgefolges—in den Zügen.

Er hat in Ausübung seines Dienstes die Eigenschaft einer militärischen Wache im Sinne des sIII Abs.2 MstGB.

Er ist berechtigt in und ausser Dienst Pistole zu tragen.

Soweit dienstliche Notwendigkeit vorliegt, ist er bei Flakbeschuss und Luftalarm von luftschutzmässigem Verhalten und vom Aufsuchen von Luftschutzräumen befreit.

The holder of this certificate is responsible for the control of all armed forces passengers—including members of the military retinue—on trains.

He has, in exercising his duties, the capacity of a military guard as defined in Section 2 sIII MstGB.

He is entitled to carry a pistol both on and off duty.

In as far as required by his duties, he is exempt from flak fire alarm and air from air-raid precaution measures and taking cover in air raid shelters.

And finally, an extract from the Military Penal Code reinforces his position and authority, indicating that any action or opposition to the orders of a member of the *Zugwache* would be treated as if they had been committed against the individual's own superiors.

Auszug aus MStGB III (H.Dv.275)

Wer eine militärische Wache im Dienste oder in Beziehung auf eine Diensthandlung mit der Begehung eines Verbrechens oder Vergehens bedroht oder wer sich ihr gegenüber einer Beleidigung, eines Ungehorsams, einer Widersetzung oder einer Tätlichkeit schuldig macht, wird ebenso bestraft, als wenn er die Handlung gegen einen Vorgesetzten begangen hätte.

This translates as:

> Extract from Military Penal Code Para III (Heeresdienstvorschrift 275)
>
> Whoever threatens a military guard on duty or in engaged on an official matters with the commission of a crime, or an offense, or who is guilty of an insult, of disobedience, of offering resistance or an assault, is just as punishable as if the action had been committed against a superior.

Order of Battle

Zugwache units were allocated '500' series numbers. The basic unit of the *Zugwache* was initially the *Kompanie*. However in 1942, the Company level units were upgraded to battalion strength and each *Kompanie*, whilst retaining its number, was renamed as an *Abteilung*.

Zugwach Units

The majority of *Zugwache* units began their life at *Kompanie* strength. They were initially classed as 'special purpose' units and carried the 'z.b.V.' (*zur besondere Verwendung*) suffix before this was dropped and from May 1942 onwards units were either upgraded to *Abteilung* or created at this level.

Zugwach-Abt. 502

Formed on 11 May 1942 from *Zugwach-Kompanie 502* which had originally been formed on 26 November 1941 in Freiberg in Saxony. It served with *Kommandeur des Heeresstreifendienstes für Reiseverkehr West* in Paris,

Zugwach-Abt. 503

Formed on 11 May 1942 from *Zugwach-Kompanie 503*, which had originally been formed on 29 November 1941 in *Wehrkreis VI*. Ultimately employed in *Wehrkreis III*.

An interesting shot of a *Zugwache* soldier from *Zugwachabteilung* 509 in mountain cap and boots on board a ferry which was transferring a train to Norway.

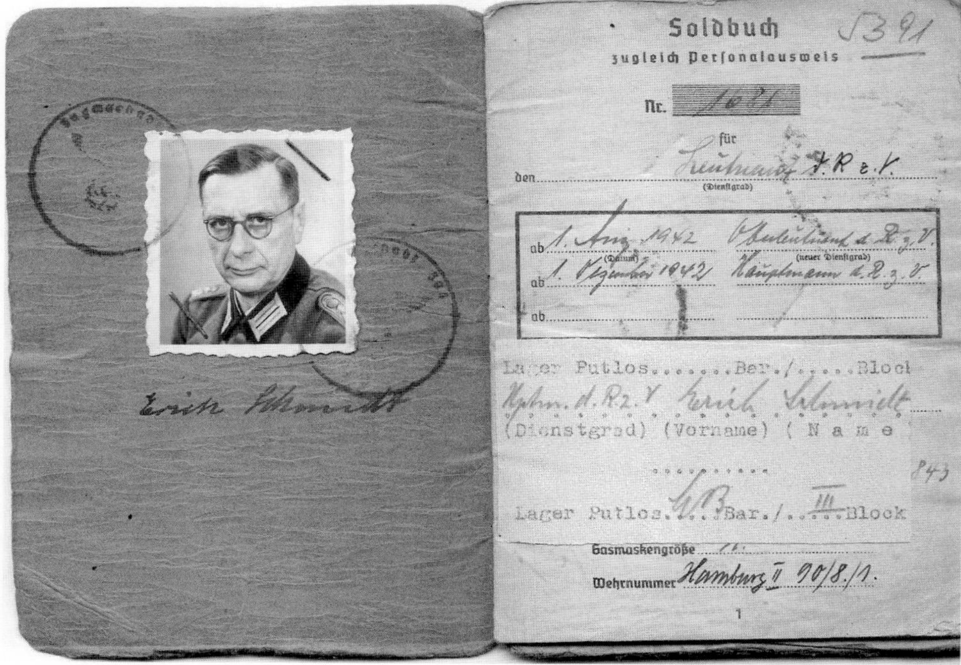

Soldbuch

zugleich Personalausweis

Nr. ...

für

den Leutnant d.R. z.V.
(Dienstgrad)

ab 1. Aug. 1942 Oberleutnant d.R. z.V.
(Datum) (neuer Dienstgrad)

ab 1. Dezember 1942 Hauptmann d.R. z.V.

ab ...

Lager Putlos ...... Bar. / .... Block

Hptm. d.R.z.V. Erich Schmidt
(Dienstgrad) (Vorname) (Name)

Lager Putlos ... Bar. / ... Block

Gasmaskengröße ...

Wehrnummer Hamburg II 90/8/1.

1

Soldbuch for *Hauptmann* Erich Schmidt, a unit commander with the *Zugwache*.

A. Zuletzt zuständige Wehrersatzdienststelle:

B. Zum Feldheer abgesandt von:[1])

	Ersatztruppenteil	Kompanie	Nr. der Truppen-stammrolle
a			
b			
c			

C.

	Feldtruppenteil[2])	Kompanie	Nr. der Kriegs-stammrolle
a	~~Zugwachkomp. z. b. V. 504~~		
b	~~Zugwachabteilung 504~~		1036
c	Zg. Wachabteilung 503		219

D.

	Jetzt zuständiger Ersatztruppenteil[2])	Standort
a		
b		
c		

(Meldung dortselbst nach Rückkehr vom Feldheer oder Lazarett, zuständig für Ersatz an Bekleidung und Ausrüstung)

[1]) Vom Ersatztruppenteil einzutragen, von dem der Soldbuchinhaber zum Feldheer abgesandt wird.
[2]) Vom Feldtruppenteil einzutragen und bei Versetzungen von einem zum anderen Feldtruppenteil derart abzuändern, daß die alten Angaben nur durchstrichen werden, also leserlich bleiben.

Weiterer Raum für Eintragungen auf Seite 17.

4

Anschriften der nächsten lebenden Angehörigen

des ...
(Vor- und Zuname)

1. Ehefrau: Vor- und Mädchenname ...
(ggf. Vermerk „ledig")
Wohnort (Kreis) ...
Straße, Haus-Nr. ...

2. Eltern: des Vaters, Vor- und Zuname ...
Stand oder Gewerbe ...
der Mutter, Vor- u. Mädchenname ...
Wohnort (Kreis) ...
Straße, Haus-Nr. ...

3. Verwandte oder Braut:*)
Vor- und Zuname ...
Stand oder Gewerbe ...
Wohnort (Kreis) ...
Straße, Haus-Nr. ...

*) Ausfüllung nur, wenn weder 1. noch 2. ausgefüllt sind.

5

The Schmidt *Soldbuch* shows service with *Zugwachkompanie/Abteilung* 504 and *Zugwachabteilung* 503.

A. Zuletzt zuständige Wehrersatzdienststelle: W. Bz. Kdo Reichenberg

B. Zum Feldheer abgesandt von:¹)

	Ersatztruppenteil	Kompanie	Nr. der Truppenstammrolle
a	Land. Schütz. Ers. Batl. 4		—
b			
c			

C.

	Feldtruppenteil²)	Kompanie	Nr. der Kriegsstammrolle
a	~~Zug-Wach-Kp. z. b. V. 502~~		
b	Zug-Wach-Abt. z. b. V. 502		52/4
c			

D.

Jetzt zuständiger Ersatztruppenteil²)	Standort
~~Land. Schütz. Ers. Batl. 4~~	~~Glauchau/Sa.~~
~~Lans. Sch. Ers. Batl. 24~~	~~Freiberg Sa.~~ / ~~Meißen / Sa.~~
	Leipzig Wurzk

(Meldung dortselbst nach Rückkehr vom Feldheer oder Lazarett, zuständig für Ersatz an Bekleidung und Ausrüstung)

¹) Vom Ersatztruppenteil einzutragen, von dem der Soldbuchinhaber zum Feldheer abgesandt wird.
²) Vom Feldtruppenteil einzutragen und bei Versetzungen von einem zum anderen Feldtruppenteil derart abzuändern, daß die alten Angaben nur durchstrichen werden, also leserlich bleiben.

Weiterer Raum für Eintragungen auf Seite 17.

4

Anschriften der nächsten lebenden Angehörigen

des Lt. Karl Schreier (Vor- und Zuname)

1. Ehefrau: Vor- und Mädchenname Elfriede geb. Jäckel (ggf. Vermerk „ledig")
Wohnort (Kreis) Wiesenthal a. N.
Straße, Haus-Nr. 455

2. Eltern: des Vaters, Vor- und Zuname
Stand oder Gewerbe
der Mutter, Vor- u. Mädchenname Pauline geb. Zwirschke
Wohnort (Kreis) Wiesenthal a. N.
Straße, Haus-Nr. 77

3. Verwandte oder Braut:*)
Vor- und Zuname
Stand oder Gewerbe
Wohnort (Kreis)
Straße, Haus-Nr.

*) Ausfüllung nur, wenn weder 1. noch 2. ausgefüllt sind.

5

The Schreier *Soldbuch* shows a change in the unit designation when it was upgraded from a *Leutnant* to an *Abteilung*.

Soldbuch
zugleich Personalausweis

Nr. 15

für

den Leutnant
(Dienstgrad)

ab 1. 3. 43 (Datum) Oberleutnant d.R. z.V. (neuer Dienstgrad)
ab
ab

Karl Schreier
(Vor- und Zuname)

Beschriftung und Nummer der Erkennungsmarke Stabskp. Inf.-Ers.-Btl. 102 Nr. 15

Blutgruppe A

Gasmaskengröße 2

Wehrnummer Reichenberg

1

Soldbuch for *Oberleutnant* Karl Schreier from *Zugwachabteilung* z.b.V. 502.

Zugwach-Abt. 504

Formed on 4 May 1942 from *Zugwach-Kompanie 504*, which had originally been formed on 1 December 1941 in *Wehrkreis X*. Disbanded on 15 November 1944.
Served with *Kommandeur der Heeresstreifendienst für Reiseverkehr West.*

Zugwach-Abt. 505

Formed on 11 May 1942 from *Zugwach-Kompanie z.b.V. 505*, which had originally been formed on 1 December 1941 in *Wehrkreis XII*. It served for some time in Berlin, and with *Kommandeur der Heeresstreifendienst für Reiseverkehr West*, then ultimately with *Heeresgruppe B*.

Zugwach-Abt 506

No information, but gorgets to this formation exist.

Zugwach-Abt. 507

Formed on 12 May 1942 from *Zugwach-Kompanie 507*, which had originally been formed on 8 May 1942 in *Wehrkreis XVII*. It served with *Kommandeur der Heeresstreifendienst für Reiseverkehr West* but was ultimately dispersed with *Stab/507* being located in *Wehrkreis V*, 1, 2 and 3. *Kompanien* with *Heeresgruppe Mitte* in Silesia and *4. Kompanie* in *Wehrkreis III*.

Zugwach-Abt. 508

Formed on 7 May 1942 from *Zugwach-Kompanie 508* originally formed on 1 May 1942 in Aachen in *Wehrkreis VI*. It served with *Kommandeur der Heeresstreifendienst für Reiseverkehr West* ultimately being located in Oberkotzau in northern Bavaria.

Zugwach-Abt. 509

Formed on 13 June 1942 in *Wehrkreis III*. Served under *Kommandeur der Heeresstreifendienst für Reiseverkehr Nord* and with *Armeeoberkommando Norwegen*.

Zugwach-Abt. 510

Formed on 14 October 1942 in *Wehrkreis I*. It served under *Kommandeur der Heeresstreifendienst für Reiseverkehr Nordrußland*, ultimately being dispersed with *1. Staffel* allocated to *Heeresgruppe C* in Italy and *2. Staffel* serving in North Norway.

Zugwach-Abt. z.b.V. 511

Formed on 10 October 1942 in *Wehrkreis II*, and later renamed as *Bahnhofs-Wach- u. Streifen-Abt. 109* during the Winter of 1944–45. It served with *Heeresstreifendienst beim Reiseverkehr* on the Eastern Front and from August 1944 in Paris.

Zugwach-Abt. 512

Formed on 8 October 1942 in *Wehrkreis IX*. It served with *Streifendienst beim Reiseverkehr*, by 1945 in Erfurt.

Zugwach-Abt. 513

Formed on 6 January 1943 in *Wehrkreis VII*, Munich *aus Abgaben der Wehrkreise I, III, IX und X*. Served with *Streifendienst beim Reiseverkehr Rußland -Nord*, and ultimately in the area around Neufahrwasser.

Zugwach-Abt. 514

Formed on 3 January 1943 in Köln, *Wehrkreis VI*. Operational with *Kommandeur der Heeresstreifendienst für Reiseverkehr* in central Russia and lastly with *Heeresgruppe Nord* in East Prussia.

Zugwach-Abt. 515

Formed 1943 in *Wehrkreis III*. Operational 1943 with *General z. b. V. IV* in Berlin, later with *Kdr. d. Heeresstreifendienst f. Reiseverkehr (Balkan—Marburg/Maribor)* and lastly in *Wehrkreis XVII* (Wien).

Zugwach-Abt. 516

A Staffel from this unit is known to have served in Italy.

Zugwach-Abt. 520

Formed on 26 August 1943 in *Wehrkreis III*. It served with *Kommandeur der Heeresstreifendienst für Reiseverkehr Rußland-Mitte* and ultimately with *Herresgruppe Nord* in East Prussia.

Zugwache relaxing with a glass of Schnapps.

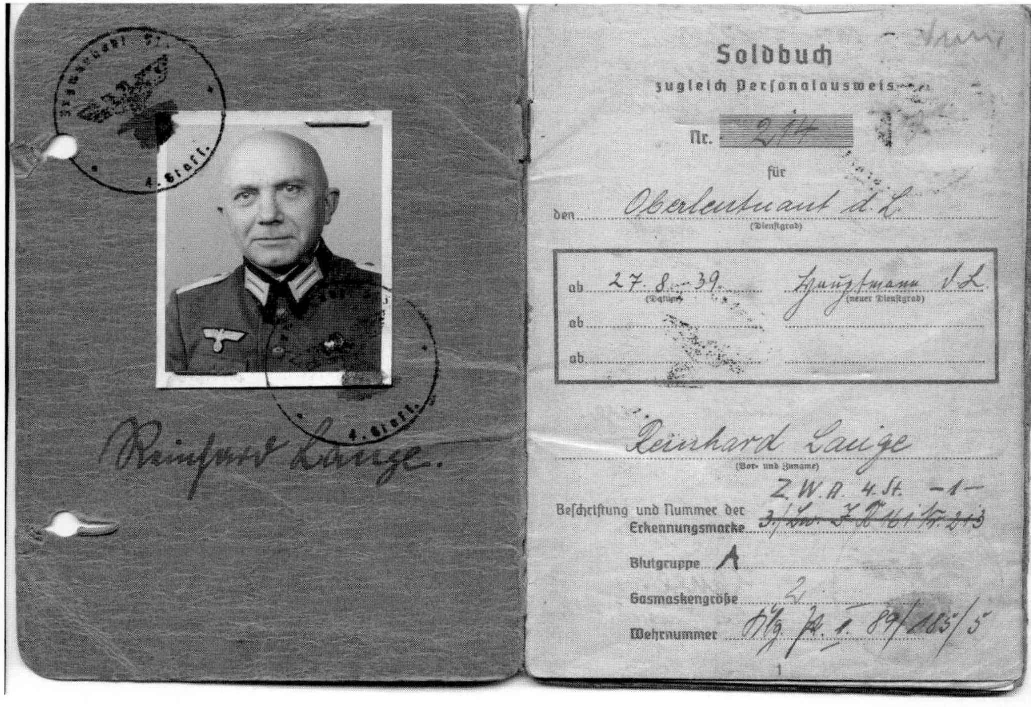

Reinhard Lange.

Soldbuch
zugleich Personalausweis
Nr. 214
für
den Oberleutnant d.L.
(Dienstgrad)

ab	27.8.39. (Datum)	Hauptmann d.L. (neuer Dienstgrad)
ab		
ab		

Reinhard Lange
(Vor- und Zuname)

Beschriftung und Nummer der Erkennungsmarke Z.W.A. 4.St. -1-

Blutgruppe A

Gasmaskengröße 2

Wehrnummer

1

Soldbuch for *Hauptmann* Reinhard Lange from *Zugwachabteilung* 503.

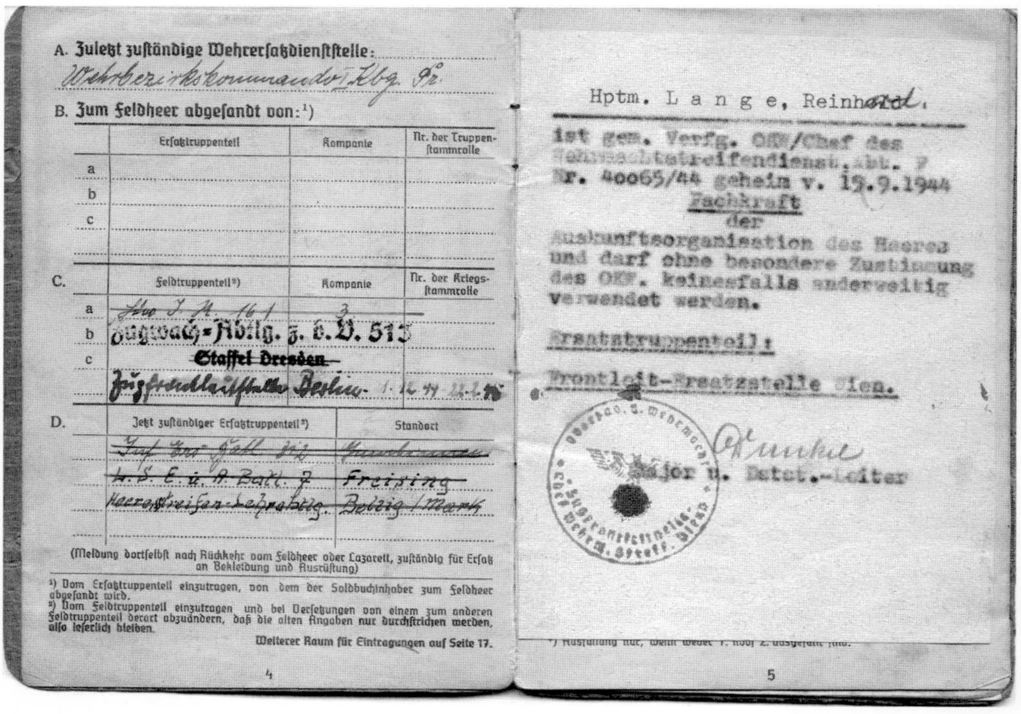

A. Zuletzt zuständige Wehrersatzdienststelle:

Wehrbezirkskommando I Kbg. Pr.

B. Zum Feldheer abgesandt von:[1])

	Ersatztruppenteil	Kompanie	Nr. der Truppenstammrolle
a			
b			
c			

C.

	Feldtruppenteil[2])	Kompanie	Nr. der Kriegsstammrolle
a	~~Arb. I.R. 161~~	3	
b	Zugwach-Abtlg. z. b. V. 513 Staffel Dresden		
c	Zugstreifendienst Berlin	1.12.44	

D.

Jetzt zuständiger Ersatztruppenteil[2])	Standort
~~Inf. Ers. Batl.~~	
~~L.S.E.u.A. Batl. 7~~	~~Freising~~
Heeresstreifen-Lehrabtlg.	Belzig/Mark

(Meldung dortselbst nach Rückkehr vom Feldheer oder Lazarett, zuständig für Ersatz an Bekleidung und Ausrüstung)

[1]) Vom Ersatztruppenteil einzutragen, von dem der Soldbuchinhaber zum Feldheer abgesandt wird.

[2]) Vom Feldtruppenteil einzutragen und bei Versetzungen von einem zum anderen Feldtruppenteil derart abzuändern, daß die alten Angaben nur durchstrichen werden, also leserlich bleiben.

Weiterer Raum für Eintragungen auf Seite 17.

4

Hptm. L a n g e, Reinhard,

ist gem. Verfg. OKW/Chef des Wehrmachtstreifendienst. Abt. 7 Nr. 40065/44 geheim v. 19.9.1944 Fachkraft der Auskunftsorganisation des Heeres und darf ohne besondere Zustimmung des OKW. keinesfalls anderweitig verwendet werden.

Ersatztruppenteil:

Frontleit-Ersatzstelle Wien.

Major u. Dstst.-Leiter

5

The *Soldbuch* reveals that Lange first served in Dresden before being transferred to Berlin

Equipment Levels

Zugwach Kompanie

Command Unit

I officer, 7 NCOs and 7 enlisted ranks.

3 × pistols.

12 × carbines.

1 × automobile.

Platoons

22 officers, 22 NCOs and 22 enlisted ranks.

66 × pistols.

A *Zugwachkompanie* consisted of a command element and 4 platoons, therefore the total *Kompanie* strength would be 89 officers, 95 NCOs and 95 enlisted ranks .

Zugwachabteilung zbV

Command

3 officers, 1 admin official, 3 NCOs and 6 enlisted ranks.

4 × carbines.

5 × pistols.

Zugwach Staffel

37 officers and 37 NCOs.

74 × pistols.

A *Zugwachabteilung* consisted of a command group plus 3 *Staffeln* giving a total manpower count of 114 officers, 1 admin official, 114 NCOs and 6 enlisted ranks.

The Kommandanturen

Each *Kommandantur* or local military headquarters in the *Reich* organised its own foot patrols to ensure discipline was maintained by soldiers in public view. Service with such patrols was not a 'career' as such but a simple duty to which soldiers serving at the *Kommandantur* could be assigned. There was no special uniform insignia or *Waffenfarbe*, but soldiers on patrol duty wore a special gorget bearing a scroll with the legend '*Kommandantur*' flanked each side by a *Wehrmacht* eagle. Above the scroll was an Arabic numeral. Photographs of the gorget being worn are extremely rare. From the outbreak of war, *Feldgendarmerie* were the primary organ for maintaining discipline.

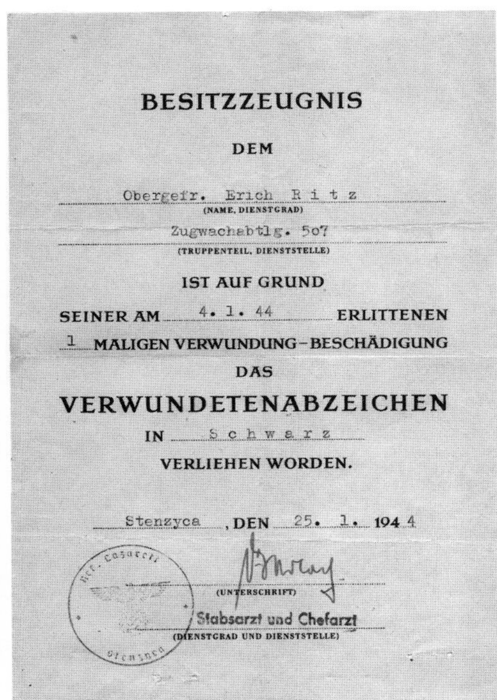

BESITZZEUGNIS

DEM

Obergefr. Erich R i t z
(NAME, DIENSTGRAD)

Zugwachabtlg. 507
(TRUPPENTEIL, DIENSTSTELLE)

IST AUF GRUND

SEINER AM 4. 1. 44 ERLITTENEN

1 MALIGEN VERWUNDUNG-BESCHÄDIGUNG

DAS

VERWUNDETENABZEICHEN

IN Schwarz

VERLIEHEN WORDEN.

Stenzyca, DEN 25. 1. 1944

(UNTERSCHRIFT)

Stabsarzt und Chefarzt
(DIENSTGRAD UND DIENSTSTELLE)

BESITZZEUGNIS

DEM

Gefr. Georg R e i d i n g e r
(NAME, DIENSTGRAD)

Zugwache 513 Staffel 4
(TRUPPENTEIL, DIENSTSTELLE)

IST AUF GRUND

SEINER AM 17. Januar 1944 ERLITTENEN

ein MALIGEN VERWUNDUNG-BESCHÄDIGUNG

DAS

VERWUNDETENABZEICHEN

IN "Schwarz"

VERLIEHEN WORDEN.

R a d o m, DEN 19. Februar 1944

(UNTERSCHRIFT)

Oberstabsarzt u. Chefarzt i.V.
(DIENSTGRAD UND DIENSTSTELLE)

Above left: Award Document for the Wound Badge in Black to *Obergefreiter* Erich Ritz of *Zugwachabteilung* 507.

Above right: Award Document for the Wound Badge in Black to *Gefreiter* Georg Reidinger of I *Staffel/ Zugwachabteilung* 513.

Above left: Zugwache Gefreiter about to board the train he is to guard.

Above right: This extremely rare shot shows the *Kommandantur* gorget being worn by a two- man foot-patrol.

The German Military Justice System

The German military justice system was rather complex and would require far more space than is available here to cover in detail. What is provided here is an overview to illustrate the fate awaiting some of those who may have fallen foul of the *Feldgendarmerie* and related units covered in this book.

After the end of the First World War and the creation of the Weimar Republic, the military lost all jurisdictions over the punishment of German soldiers. Thereafter any charges against a soldier would be processed through the civil courts.

The situation swiftly changed however, when the Nazis came to power. Hitler, along with many of his senior military officers, believed that Germany had been far too lenient with any soldiers who had contravened military regulations and that this had contributed to the rapid breakdown of order and discipline in the closing weeks or the First World War. It seems in fact that they may have had a point. It may surprise many to know that during the First World War the Germans had executed a total of 48 soldiers on various charges, whilst Great Britain had executed 346, figures which suggest that the German courts martial system was indeed lenient.

The Military Penal Code was reintroduced by a special decree of 12 May 1933, and a further decree on 5 September 1936 created the *Reichskriegsgericht*. This was to be Germany's highest military court. In the event this military court would also be responsible for the punishment of civilians as well as soldiers.

The military courts would prosecute charges in five basic areas:

(i) Treason.
(ii) High treason.
(iii) Undermining military morale.
(iv) Conscientious objection.
(v) Assisting the enemy.

The *Reichskriegsgericht* was based initially in Berlin but due to the bombing, was moved first to Potsdam and eventually to Torgau. Having reintroduced the Military Penal Code, the Nazis set about removing any clauses which they considered too lenient, desirous of a draconian set of rules by which miscreant German soldiers would be harshly dealt. In the event, a formal new code was never completed and published, but continued to be worked on throughout the period of the Third *Reich*.

The next most significant step was the creation of a special Wartime Military Penal Code, the

Kriegssonderstrafrechtsverordnung (KSSVO), on 17 August 1938. At the same time a new order, the *Kriegsstrafverfahrensordnung (KstVO)* was signed outlying the procedures to be carried out under this new code.

This new code was indeed draconian, with the rights of the accused reduced to a bare minimum and all rights of appeal abolished. Deserters in particular were to suffer the harshest of punishments. Hitler himself stated in Mein Kampf:

> At the front one <u>might</u> die, as a deserter one <u>must</u> die.

The new attitude towards accused soldiers was apparent in a comment made by the *Oberbefehlshaber des Heeres* just after the outbreak of war. Despite being considered by history an anti-Nazi and opponent to Hitler, *Generaloberst* Walther von Brauchitsch eagerly supported the harsh new system. His attitude towards errant soldiers is clearly reflected in a statement he made in December 1939.

> The more quickly a military parasite receives his just punishment, the easier it will be to deter other soldiers from committing the same or similar acts and to maintain military discipline among the troops…

This attitude towards those soldiers convicted by the military courts resulted in a massive increase in death sentences. In comparison with the 48 German soldiers executed during the First World War, during the Second World War, *at least* 33,000 German soldiers were put to death and this number is almost certainly well below the true figure as no accurate records exist of those executed on the orders of the notorious *fliegende Standgerichte,* or 'flying courts martial' which roamed Germany dealing out swift summary 'justice' in the closing stages of the war. Estimates of as many as 50,000 German soldiers being executed on the orders of the military courts is probably not far from the true figure.

One of the most heinous crimes in the eyes of the *Wehrmacht* was of course desertion or *Fahnenflucht*. It is interesting to note that even the harsh new penal code allowed for a jail sentence of up to 15 years for this crime—i.e. non-capital punishment. In reality however, such sentences were rare and only tended to occur in the early part of the war. From 1941 onwards such a crime almost invariably resulted in the accused being executed by beheading if tried in the *Reich*, or execution by firing squad if tried in the field.

At lower levels, the court through which many errant soldiers found themselves processed was the *Feldgericht* (field court martial) or *Standgericht* (summary court martial).

Summary courts martial were authorised in circumstances where:

a) For sound military reasons, the trial cannot be delayed.
b) A military judge is not immediately available.
c) Witnesses and evidence are available.

In these circumstances a regimental commander or officer with equivalent status could act as proxy for the Judge. Military Justice personnel were considered army officials rather than regular soldiers. They were effectively civil servants (*Reichsbeamte*) attached to the armed forces and

Soldbuch
zugleich Personalausweis
Nr. 1
für
Feldjustizinspektor
(Dienstgrad)
ab 1. 9. 1943
(Datum)
(neuer Dienstgrad)
ab
ab
Adolf Will
(Vor- und Zuname)
Beschriftung und Nummer der Erkennungsmarke St./Kf. Ers. Abt. 2 – 135 –
Blutgruppe 0
Gasmaskengröße 3
Wehrnummer
1

Soldbuch for *Feldjustizinspektor* Adolf Will. (*Ian Jewison*)

Soldbuch
zugleich Personalausweis
Nr. 1
für
den Kriegsrichter
(Dienstgrad)
ab 26. 3. 1941 Kriegsgerichtsrat
(Datum) (neuer Dienstgrad)
ab 1. 5. 1944 Oberstabsrichter
ab
Dr. Erich Block
(Vor- und Zuname)
Beschriftung und Nummer der Erkennungsmarke
Blutgruppe 0
Gasmaskengröße 2
Wehrnummer
1

Soldbuch of *Oberstabsrichter* Erich Block. (*Ian Jewison*)

A. Zuletzt zuständige Wehrersatzdienststelle: Allenstein (Ostpr.)

B. Zum Feldheer abgesandt von:¹)

	Ersatztruppenteil	Kompanie	Nr. der Truppenstammrolle
a			
b			
c			

C.

	Feldtruppenteil²)	Kompanie	Nr. der Kriegsstammrolle
a	~~Kommandant der Stadt Paris~~		~~49~~
b	~~169. Inf. Div.~~		~~60~~
c	~~(Geb.) AOK 20 [illegible]~~		~~Kr. 71~~
	~~Sonderstab O.K.H. II~~		~~Kr. 6~~

D.

Jetzt zuständiger Ersatztruppenteil²)	Standort
[illegible]	~~Königsberg~~ Berlin
	5 Danzig

(Meldung dortselbst nach Rückkehr vom Feldheer oder Lazarett, zuständig für Ersatz an Bekleidung und Ausrüstung)

¹) Vom Ersatztruppenteil einzutragen, von dem der Soldbuchinhaber zum Feldheer abgesandt wird.
²) Vom Feldtruppenteil einzutragen und bei Versetzungen von einem zum anderen Feldtruppenteil derart abzuändern, daß die alten Angaben **nur durchstrichen werden, also leserlich bleiben.**

Weiterer Raum für Eintragungen auf Seite 17.

4

Fortsetzung zu Seite 4

B. Zum Feldheer abgesandt von:¹)

	Ersatztruppenteil	Kompanie	Nr. der Truppenstammrolle
a			
b			
c			

C.

	Feldtruppenteil²)	Kompanie	Nr. der Kriegsstammrolle
a	Armeeoberkdo. 19	Stab	Kr. 219
b			
c			

D.

Jetzt zuständiger Ersatztruppenteil²)	Standort

(Meldung dortselbst nach Rückkehr vom Feldheer oder Lazarett, zuständig für Ersatz an Bekleidung und Ausrüstung)

¹) Vom Ersatztruppenteil einzutragen, von dem der Soldbuchinhaber zum Feldheer abgesandt wird.
²) Vom Feldtruppenteil einzutragen und bei Versetzungen von einem zum anderen Feldtruppenteil derart abzuändern, daß die alten Angaben **nur durchstrichen werden, also leserlich bleiben.**

17

The entry in Section D shows Block in the position of Oberkriegsgerichtsrat (Senior Court Martial Councillor). (*Ian Jewison*)

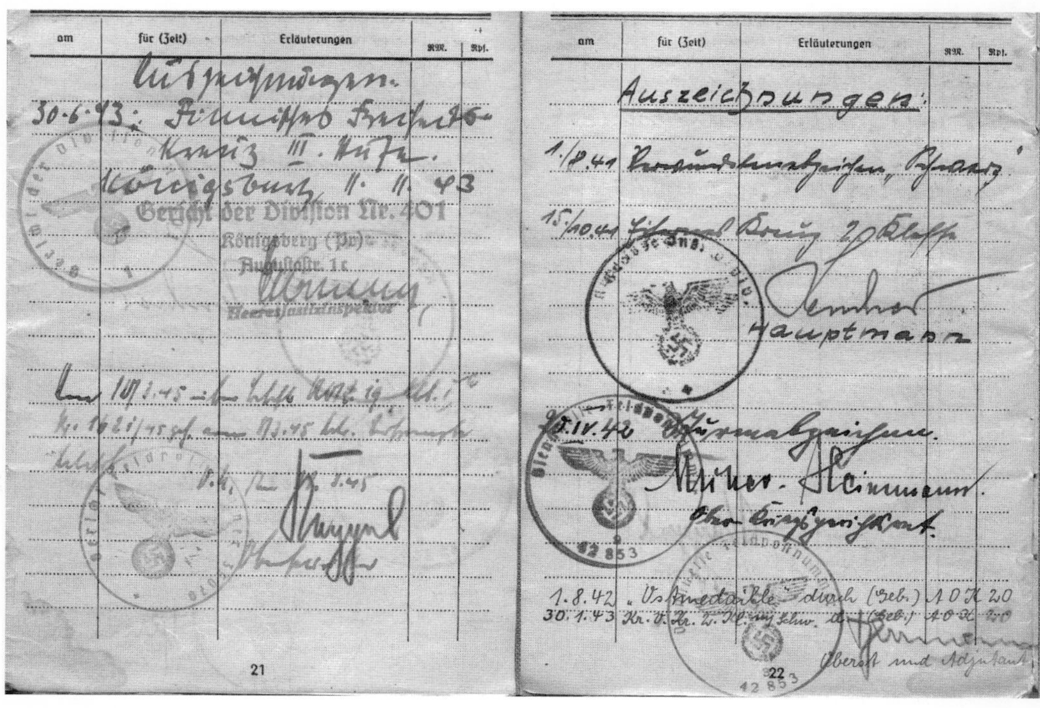

am	für (Zeit)	Erläuterungen	RM.	Rpf.

Gericht der Division Nr. 401
Königsberg (Pr.)
Auguststr. 1c
Heeresjustizinspektor

21

am	für (Zeit)	Erläuterungen	RM.	Rpf.

Auszeichnungen:
Hauptmann
1.8.42 Ostmedaille
Oberst und Adjutant

22

Note the ink stamp in the Block *Soldbuch* for the 'Gericht der Division 401'. (*Ian Jewison*)

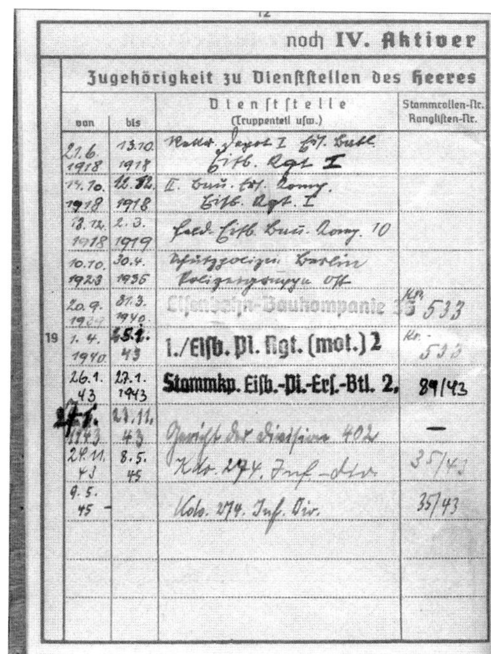

noch IV. Aktiver

Zugehörigkeit zu Dienststellen des Heeres

von	bis	Dienststelle (Truppenteil usw.)	Stammrollen-Nr. Ranglisten-Nr.
21.6. 1918	13.10. 1918	[illegible] Rgt. I	
14.10. 1918	12.12. 1918	II. [illegible] Rgt. I	
18.12. 1918	2.3. 1919	[illegible] 10	
10.10. 1923	30.4. 1936	[illegible] Berlin [illegible]	
20.9. [illegible]	31.3. 1940	Eisenbahn-Baukompanie [illegible]	Kr. 533
19 1.4. 1940	[illegible] 43	1./Eisb. Pi. Rgt. (mot.) 2	Kr. 533
26.1. 43	27.1. 1943	Stammkp. Eisb.-Pi.-Ers.-Btl. 2.	89/43
[illegible] 1943	23.11. 43	Gericht der Division 402	—
24.11. 43	8.5. 45	[illegible] 274. Inf.-Div.	35/43
9.5. 45 –		[illegible] 274. Inf. Div.	35/43

Entry from the *Wehrpass* of Adolf Will showing as third from last entry '*Gericht der Division* 402', the divisional Court. (*Ian Jewison*)

thus classed as *Wehrmachtbeamte*.

Justice personnel fell into three different career bands:

höherer Dienst: for which a university education with an appropriate degree was required. This band contained ranks from the equivalent of *Leutnant* up to *Generalleutnant*.

gehobener mittlerer Dienst: for which an educational level equivalent to somewhere between high school and college level was required, plus a further two or three years of training. This band contained ranks from the equivalent of *Leutnant* up to *Oberstleutnant*.

einfacher mittlerer Dienst: for which a high school level qualification was required plus having completed an apprenticeship or some form of trade training. This band contained ranks from the equivalent of *Feldwebel* up to *Oberleutnant*.

The overlap in ranks between these bands means that the relevant shoulder straps indicated rank, whilst the undermentioned special collar tabs indicated the career band. This means that the same shoulder straps may be seen with different collar tabs. The actual rank titles and equivalents were as follows

Generalleutnant = *Senatspräsident beim Reichskriegsgericht*
Generalmajor = *Reichskriegsgerichtsrat*
Oberst = *Oberstjustizrat; Oberstkriegssgerichtsrat*
Oberstleutnant = *Oberheeresjustizrat; Oberkriegsgerichtsrat*
Major = *Heeresjustizamtmann; Kriegsgerichtsrat*

Hauptmann	= *Heeresjustizoberinspektor; Reichskriegsgerichtoberinspektor*
Oberleutnant	= *Heeresjustizinspektor; Reichskriegsgerichtinspektor*
Leutnant	= *Heeresjustizsekretär; Reichskriegsgerichtsekretär;*
Oberfeldwebel	= *Heeresjustizoberwachtmeister; Reichsgerichtoberwachtmeister*
Feldwebel	= *Heeresjustizwachtmeister; Reichskriegsgerichtswachtmeister*

The uniform worn by these officials was identical to that worn by regular soldiers. Only their distinctive insignia set them apart. The *Waffenfarbe* of the *Beamte* was dark green, worn as piping top the visor cap and as underlay to the shoulder straps. The straps featured the same light blue *Nebenfarbe* as the GFP until March 1940 at which point a pale grey *Nebenfarbe* became standard for all branches. In place of the GFP cipher worn by the *Geheime Feldpolizei*, a white metal HV cipher was worn on the centre of the strap. Prior to the outbreak of war, officer grade equivalents wore a gilt cipher comprising the letters 'HV' (for *Heeresverwaltung*) on the shoulder strap whilst NCO grade equivalents wore a white metal cipher. From the outbreak of war, the cipher was in light grey metal for all ranks.

Further changes came in January 1944 when a new Branch of service was created for some of the officials of the *Wehrmacht*. According to *Heeresmitteilungsblatt* 44, Nr 263 of 3 May 1944, this new branch, the *Truppensonderdienst* (TSD) would absorb the justice officials and would introduce a new shoulder strap for justice officers. It would have the normal grey aluminium braid cords as used by regular branches, but on a wine red base. In place of the old 'HV' cypher, the strap now featured a bronzed sword emblem mounted with the point towards the buttonhole.
Standard officers collar *litzen* were used with a wine red *Waffenfarbe* strip down the centre of each bar.

All those serving as officials in the judicial branch (*Heeresjustizbeamte*) were transferred to the TSD into the following rank equivalents:

Above: The Administrative style shoulder straps were later replaced by a regular army style strap on a Bordeaux red base with a metal Sword of Justice emblem. (Ian Jewison)

Left: A fine portrait study of Block. The Administrative style shoulder straps for court martial officials lack the normal 'HV' (Heeresverwaltung) cipher of regular admin officials. (*Ian Jewison*)

Generalleutnant	=	*Generaloberstabsrichter*
Generalmajor	=	*Generalstabsrichter*
Oberst	=	*Oberstrichter*
Oberstleutnant	=	*Oberfeldrichter*
Major	=	*Oberstabsrichter*
Hauptmann	=	*Stabsrichter*

An additional grade, of *Generalrichter* fell somewhere between *Oberst* and *Generalmajor* in the same manner as the *SS* rank of *Oberführer*, effectively a senior full colonel.

Collar Patches

Collar patches were the standard *Beamte* pattern as worn by the GFP, with the same light blue piping to the top, rear and lower edges. The *Luftwaffe* had its own corps of administrative officials, the career bandings and qualifications etc for which, were identical to those for the army.

Shoulder straps for officer grade *Luftwaffe* administrative officials used identical bright silver braid as their regular *Luftwaffe* counterparts. Their status as officials was indicated by the use of a dark green base to the strap with an intermediate layer (*Nebenfarbe*) showing their specialisation. Both court martial and judicial officials used *Nebenfarbe* of wine red (*weinrot*) and Bordeaux red (*Bordeauxrot*) depending on their career band.

Justizwachtmeister	=	*Feldwebel—Weinrot*
Justizoberwachtmeister	=	*Oberfeldwebel—Weinrot*
Reichskriegsgerichtsekretär	=	*Leutnant—Bordeauxrot*
Kriegsgerichtinspektor	=	*Leutnant—Weinrot*
Reichskriegsgerichtobersekretär/ Reichskriegsgerichtsinspektor	=	*Oberleutnant—Bordeauxrot*
Reichskriegsgerichtsoberinspektor	=	*Hauptmann—Weinrot*
Kriegsrichter	=	*Hauptmann—Weinrot*
Amtsrat beim Luftwaffengericht	=	*Major—Weinrot*
Amtsrat beim Reichskriegsgericht	=	*Major—Weinrot*
Bürodirektor beim Reichskriegsgericht	=	*Oberstleutnant—Bordeauxrot*
Oberkriegsgerichtsrat	=	*Oberstleutnant—Weinrot*
Oberkreigsgerichtsrat beim Reichskriegsgericht	=	*Oberstleutnant—Weinrot*
Oberstkriegsgerichtsrat der Luftwaffe	=	*Oberst—Weinrot*
Oberstkriegsgerichtsrat beim Reichskriegsgericht	=	*Oberst—Bordeauxrot*
Ministerialdirigent	=	*Generalmajor—Weinrot*
Reichskriegsgerichtsrat	=	*Generalmajor—Bordeauxrot*
Senätspräsident beim Reichskriegsgericht	=	*Generalleutnant—Bordeauxrot.*

Collar patches followed the normal *Luftwaffe* format, but with small triangular embroidered pips in place of the normal wings. A base colour of dark green was used as standard in collar patches for *Luftwaffe* officials with the following exceptions in the legal branch.

Weinrot –
Kriegsrichter
Kriegsgerichtsrat der Luftwaffe
Oberkriegsgerichtsrat
Oberstkriegsgerichtsrat der Luftwaffe
Ministerialdirigent

Bordeauxrot-
Oberkriegsgerichtsrat beim Reichskriegsgericht
Oberstkriegsgerichtsrat beim Reickskriegsgericht
Reichskriegsgerichtsrat
Senätspräsident beim Reichskriegsgericht

The *Luftwaffe* differed from the *Heer* in that both the collar tabs and shoulder straps indicated specific rank. In order to reflect the careers banding therefore, different cord piping colours were used for the collar tab edging. For *höherer Dienst* , gold twist cord piping was used, for *gehobener mittlerer Dienst*, silver twist cord piping and for *einfacher mittlerer Dienst* silver and green twist cord piping. As with the other *Wehrmacht* branches, judicial officials from the *Luftwaffe* were absorbed into the *Truppensonderdienst* in 1944. The new branch utilised the regular design of collar tabs and shoulder strap but in the case of judicial officials, with *Weinrot* underlay to the collar tabs and shoulder straps.

The following ranks existed in the new judicial branch of the *Truppensonderdienst* in the *Luftwaffe*.

Stabsrichter	=	*Hauptmann*
Oberstabsrichter	=	*Major*
Oberfeldrichter	=	*Oberstleutnant*
Oberstrichter	=	*Oberst*
Generalrichter	=	*Generalmajor*
Generalstabsrichter	=	*Generalleutnant*

Naval Officials wore a uniform virtually identical to that used by their regular naval compatriots but for the fact that all insignia, buttons and trim were in silver rather than gold colour. This led to them being referred to by regular naval personnel as '*Silberlings*'

As with the regular navy, rank was indicated by a system of rings around the lower sleeve. Career banding was indicated by a hand embroidered silver wire motif worn above these rings. In the case of justice officials, the insignia consisted of a *Wehrmacht* pattern eagle and swastika with folded wings over a depiction of the scales of justice. For officials in the *höherer Dienst* career band three swords were positioned over the scales, for those in the *gehobener mittlerer Dienst* band, two swords and for those in the *einfacher mittlerer Dienst* band a single vertical sword. Rank titles were similar to those of the army but with the prefix 'Marine', thus an army *Kriegsgerichtsrat* would have as his naval equivalent a *Marinekriegsgerischtsrat*.

With the creation of the *Truppensonderdienst* in 1944, naval judges were transferred to this new branch.

Penal and Probationary Units

The unfortunate German soldier convicted of a military crime during the period of the Third Reich, but not sentenced to death, could still expect an extremely harsh fate. Any sentence handed down by the court was expected to be served *after* the end of hostilities. For the remaining duration of the war, the convicted soldier would be interred in one of the notorious *Strafgefangenelager* or punishment camps. The conditions in such camps were scarcely better than in some concentration camps.

As the war progressed however, the desperate need for manpower at the front saw soldiers incarcerated in such camps on sentences of three months or more transferred to penal battalions, or *Feldstrafgefangenenabteilungen.* In such units, convicted soldiers were kept on much reduced rations, and employed- unarmed -on the most dangerous of tasks. Mine clearing, bunker building and road construction were the tasks most likely to be imposed on them and often in areas heavily infested with enemy partisans. Casualty rates, as can be imagined, were extremely high.

Those who, by hard work and brave actions for between three and nine months were considered as having redeemed themselves could be transferred to a probationary unit, where though conditions were still harsh, it was possible for the soldier to regain his freedom in time. These *Feldstrafgefangenenabteilungen*, all of which were used on the Eastern Front, each consisted of a headquarters element and five companies as follows.

1 (Gefängnis) Kompanie
2 (Gefängnis) Kompanie
3 (Gefängnis) Kompanie
4 (Straflager) Kompanie
5 (Zuchthaus) Kompanie

A total of 22 such units were eventually created numbered between *Feldstrafgefangenenabteilung 1* and *Feldstrafgefangenenabteilung 22*, being formed between April 1942 and March 1945.

As well as *Feldstrafgefangenenabteilungen*, other units also existed which were used to both punish and/or rehabilitate convicted soldiers. For those convicted of lesser crimes, usually some minor disciplinary offences, and who were still considered worthy of wearing uniform and bearing arms, a number of *Bewährungsbataillonen* or probationary battalions were created. Initially, the opportunity for rehabilitation in one of these units was open to soldiers who fulfilled certain conditions, namely.

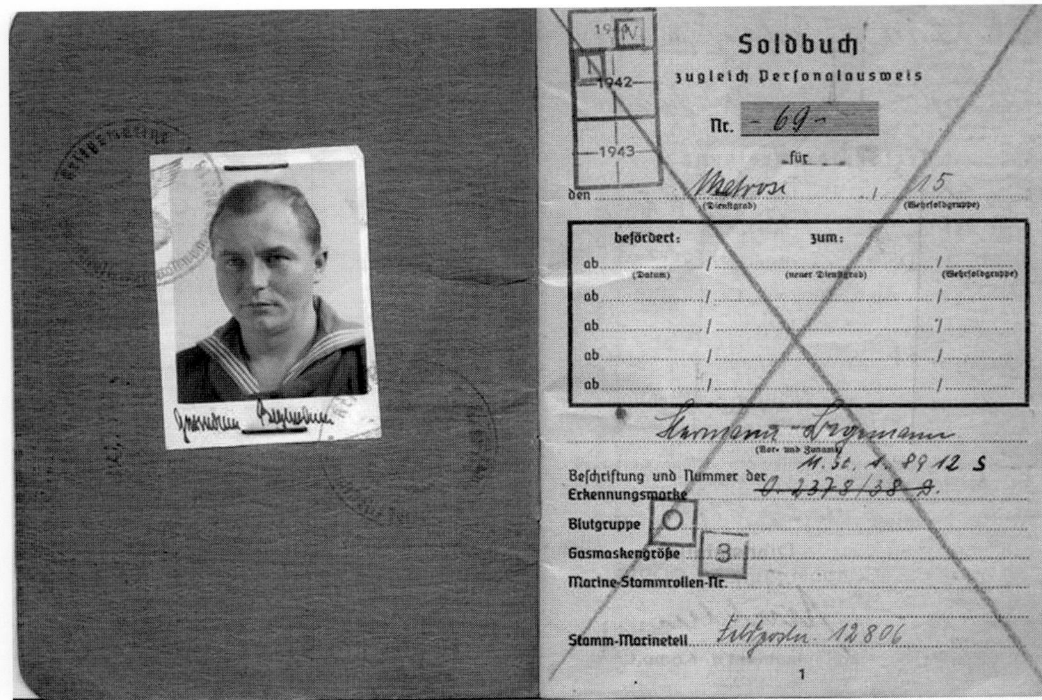

Soldbuch
zugleich Personalausweis
Nr. -69-
für
den Matrose (Dienstgrad) / 15 (Gebührnisgruppe)

befördert:	zum:	
ab .... (Datum)	/ .... (neuer Dienstgrad)	/ .... (Besoldungsgruppe)
ab	/	/ ....
ab	/	/ ....
ab	/	/ ....
ab	/	/ ....

Hermann Bergmann (Vor- und Zuname)

Beschriftung und Nummer der Erkennungsmarke M. St. A. 8912 S ~~0 2378/38 S.~~

Blutgruppe O

Gasmaskengröße 3

Marine-Stammrollen-Nr.

Stamm-Marineteil 12806

1

Soldbuch to Matrose Hermann Bergmann who was convicted and sentenced to serve in a Penal unit. (*Ian Jewison*)

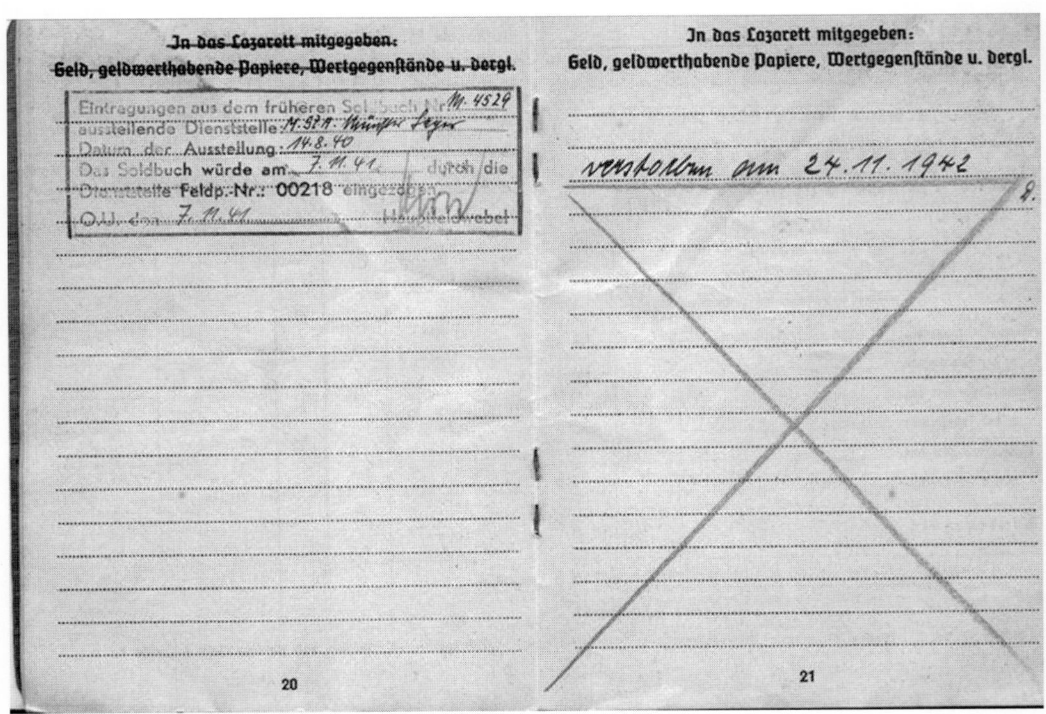

~~In das Lazarett mitgegeben:~~
~~Geld, geldwerthabende Papiere, Wertgegenstände u. dergl.~~

Eintragungen aus dem früheren Soldbuch Nr. M. 4529
ausstellende Dienststelle M.St.A. ....
Datum der Ausstellung 14.8.40
Das Soldbuch würde am 7.11.41 durch die
Dienststelle Feldp.-Nr.: 00218 eingezogen
O.U., den 7.11.41 Hauptfeldwebel

20

In das Lazarett mitgegeben:
Geld, geldwerthabende Papiere, Wertgegenstände u. dergl.

verstorben am 24.11.1942

21

Soldbuch entry showing that Begemann was killed on 24 November 1942. (*Ian Jewison*)

Inhaber wird überwiesen:

am (Tag der Inmarschsetzung)	an (neue Dienststelle, Feldpost-Nr.)	Gezahlter [1] Reisevorschuß RM		Bescheinigung der abgebenden Dienststelle (Feldpost-Nr.) – Verwaltung durch Stempel und Unterschrift
28.5.42	Strafgefängnis Germersheim	–		Dienststelle Feldpostnummer 00218A
	Wehrmachtgefängnis Torgau Fort Zinna			

[1]) Der Vorschuß ist von der zahlenden Dienststelle zunächst im Vorschußbuch zu buchen und von der neuen Dienststelle in der Reisekostenrechnung von den zuständigen Reisekosten abzusetzen, sodaß hier nur der verbleibende Reisekostenrest als Haushaltsausgabe gebucht wird. Der alten Dienststelle ist über die erfolgte Einziehung des Reisevorschusses kurze Mitteilung zu machen; sie bucht darauf den Reisevorschuß unter Vereinnahmung im Vorschußbuch endgültig als Haushaltsausgabe. (M.V.Bl. 1940, S. 908, Nr. 847).

23

Entries showing that Begemann was held first in *Strafgefängnis* (Military Prison) Gemersheim, then at the notorious Torgau prison. (*Ian Jewison*)

–1000	1–2000	2–3000	3–4000	4–5000	5–6000	6–7000	7–8000

Stammr. Nr.	Zu- und Vorname des Eingelieferten 57/2 303
4227/42	Begemann, Hermann kath.

Dienstgrad	Eingeliefert am:	Eintritt in Wehrmacht:	Geboren am:
Matr. Verw.Geh.	5.6.42	1.4.39	Wolfskirch 5.7.17

Truppenteil: 00 218 RS

Abt.	A	B	C	D	E	F	G	H
Dat.								

Gericht: Admiral der Seebefehlsstellen
J I 17/42
fortgesetzter Betrug — 1 Jahr 3 Mon. Straflager v. Germersheim

KENNKARTE

Entlassen am:	Entlassen zum (zur)
10. Juli 1942	

L/0883

Index card for Begemann showing that he was sentenced to 1 Year and 3 Months imprisonment.

The individual before being convicted had previously conducted themselves well, with no more than insignificant issues.

The offence for which the individual was convicted could be considered as a 'one-of' incident and out of character.

The individual must have shown a genuine desire to prove himself against the enemy and have expressed this in writing.

The individual had to be a member of the armed forces or at least liable for military service.

The sentence received must have been at least 6 months imprisonment.

The individual had to be capable of serving in an Infantry unit.

Prisoners serving sentences in civil or military prisons must serve at least one month of their sentence before being accepted. Service in a *Bewährungsbataillon* was considered honourable service and it was made clear that these were probationary, not punishment units though promotions were intentionally harder to achieve and the only awards which could be earned were combat awards such as the Infantry Assault Badge and Wound Badge.

The following Infantry Probationary Battalions were formed:

Infanterie-Bataillon z.b.V. 491	*Formed November 1944*
Infanterie-Bataillon z.b.V. 500	*Formed April 1941*
Infanterie-Bataillon z.b.V. 540	*Formed December 1941*
Infanterie-Bataillon z.b.V. 550	*Formed November 1941*
Infanterie-Bataillon z.b.V. 560	*Formed August 1942*
Infanterie-Bataillon z.b.V. 561	*Formed January 1943*

The Luftwaffe also maintained a small number of probationary units within which those convicted of lesser offences could redeem themselves. Most of these eventually came under army control around the time the *Luftwaffe's* field divisions were absorbed into the *Heer.*

Battalions 1–3 in the following list were subsequently renamed as *Jäger* battalions. Unlike their army counterparts, several of these *Luftwaffe* probationary units served on the Western Front, and in Italy in particular:

Luftwaffen-Feld-Bataillon z.b.V. 1-2	*Formed November 1942*
Luftwaffen-Feld-Bataillon z.b.V. 3	*Formed March 1943*
Luftwaffen-Feld-Bataillon z.b.V. 4-5	*Formed April 1944*
Luftwaffen-Feld-Bataillon z.b.V. 6	*Formed June 1944*
Luftwaffen-Feld-Bataillon z.b.V. 7	*Formed October 1943*
Luftwaffen-Feld-Bataillon z.b.V. 8-9	*Formed March 1944*
Luftwaffen-Feld-Bataillon z.b.V. 10	*Formed April 1944*

2

(Eigenhändige Unterschrift des Inhabers — Rufname, Familienname)

3

I. Angaben zur Person

1	Familienname	Reddin
2	Vornamen (Rufname unterstreichen)	
3	Geburtstag, -monat, -jahr	3. 10. 02.
4	Geburtsort Verwaltungsbezirk (z. B. Kreis, Reg. Bezirk)	
5	Staatsangehörigkeit (auch frühere)	
6	Religion	
7	Familienstand	
8	Beruf (nach Berufsverzeichnis)	erlernter / ausgeübter
9	Eltern	Vater (Rufname, Familienname) / Beruf (nach Berufsverzeichnis) / (wenn verstorben: † und Sterbejahr) † 1931 — Mutter (Rufname, Familienname) / Mädchenname / (wenn verstorben: † und Sterbejahr)

Wehrpass of *Gefreiter* Paul Reddin who served as a guard with a penal unit.

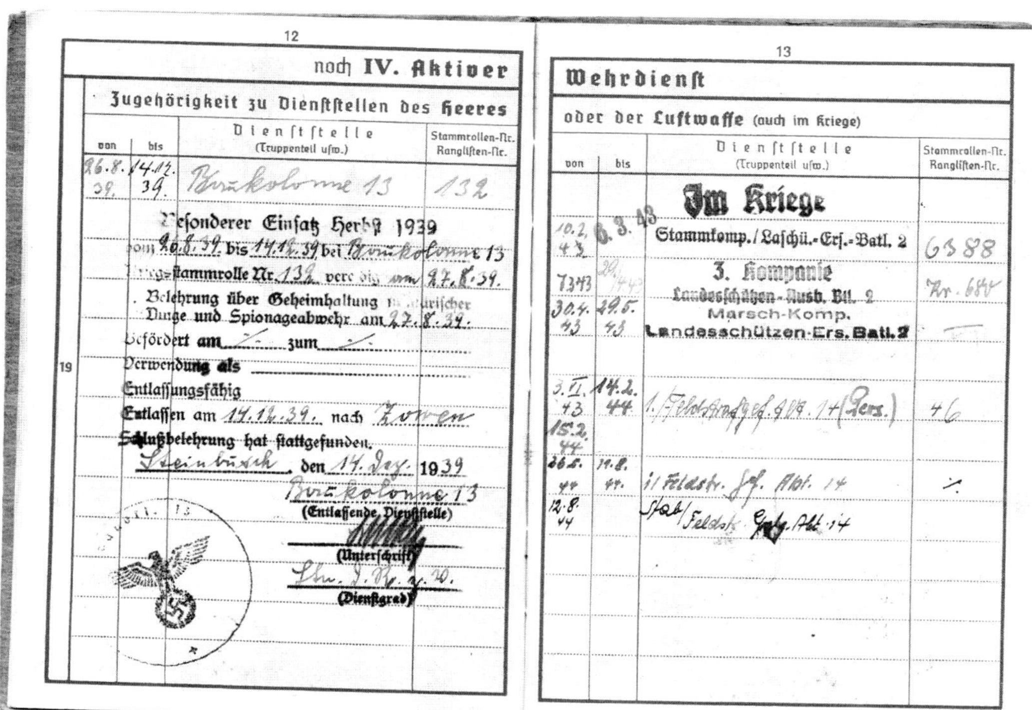

12

noch **IV. Aktiver**

Zugehörigkeit zu Dienststellen des Heeres

von	bis	Dienststelle (Truppenteil usw.)	Stammrollen-Nr. Ranglisten-Nr.
26.8. 39.	14.12. 39.	Baukolonne 13	132
		Besonderer Einsatz Herbst 1939	
		vom 26.8.39 bis 14.12.39 bei Baukolonne 13	
		Kriegsstammrolle Nr. 132 verpflichtet am 27.8.39.	
		Belehrung über Geheimhaltung militärischer Dinge und Spionageabwehr am 27.8.39.	
		Befördert am — zum —	
		Verwendung als	
		Entlassungsfähig	
		Entlassen am 14.12.39. nach	
		Schlußbelehrung hat stattgefunden.	
		den 14. Dez. 1939	
		Baukolonne 13	
		(Entlassende Dienststelle)	
		(Unterschrift)	
		(Dienstgrad)	

19

13

Wehrdienst

oder der Luftwaffe (auch im Kriege)

von	bis	Dienststelle (Truppenteil usw.)	Stammrollen-Nr. Ranglisten-Nr.
		Im Kriege	
10.2. 43	6.3.43	Stammkomp./Laschü.-Ers.-Batl. 2	6388
7.3.43	29.4.43	3. Kompanie Landesschützen-Ausb. Btl. 2	
30.4. 43	29.5. 43	Marsch-Komp. Landesschützen-Ers. Batl. 2	
3.VI. 43	14.2. 44	1./Feldstrafgef. Abt. 14 (Pers.)	46
15.2. 44			
26.5. 44	11.8. 44		
12.8. 44			

Entries from the Reddin *Wehrpass*. Note that he served with *Feldstrafgefangenen Abteilung* 14.

Luftwaffen-Feld-Bataillon z.b.V. 100	*Formed December 1942*
Luftwaffen-Feld-Bataillon z.b.V. Finland	*Formed 1942*

Unsurprisingly the navy, as the smallest branch of the services, had the fewest of this type of unit, with just three known to have existed. These were probationary rather than penal units with the normal length of stay for errant sailors around three months or so. Prior to the outbreak of war, the Navy's disciplinary unit, formed in 1936, was known as the *Sonderabteilung der Kriegsmarine*, but on the outbreak of war was renamed as the *Kriegssonderabteilung*. At some later date, exactly when is not known, a second unit was formed, known as *Kriegssonderabteilung Ost*. It is believed that the original *Kriegssonderabteilung* was responsible to the North Sea (*Nordsee*) command and the *Kriegssonderabteilung Ost* to the Baltic (*Ostsee*) Command.

In July 1942, both of these units were disbanded and replaced by the newly formed 30 and 31 *Schiffstammabteilungen* with the former responsible to *Nordsee* command and the latter to the *Ostsee* command. Later in the war, serious disciplinary problem cases would be sent to designated naval companies within the *Feldstrafgefangenenabteilungen* of the army.

Both the staff elements and those serving sentences wore field grey naval uniform, but staff were also provided with regular blue naval uniforms for off-duty and walking out wear. Initially, staff wore the cap ribbon of the ship or establishment they were seconded from but from September 1938, were ordered to wear the ribbon '*Kommandantur Kiel*'. On the outbreak of war, the standard '*Kriegsmarine*' ribbon was used. The shoulder straps worn featured crossed un-fouled anchors with the letter S (for *Sonderabteilung*) above.

A number of units with numbers in the 900 series were also created, but are outwith the scope of this book as rather than being filled by soldiers who were being punished due to having fallen foul of the *Feldgendarmerie* and the military justice system, these units were created from those who previously been classed as *Wehrunwürdig* or unworthy of military service for various reasons.

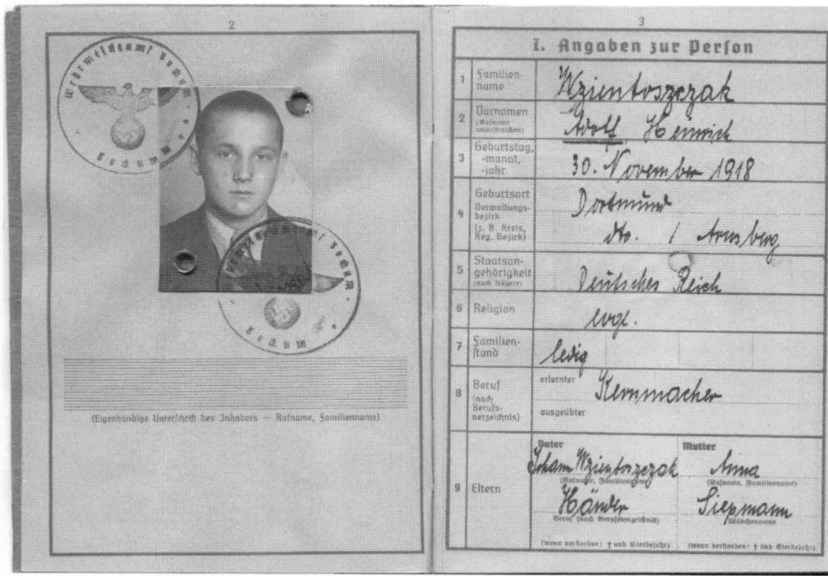

2

(Eigenhändige Unterschrift des Inhabers — Rufname, Familienname)

3

I. Angaben zur Person

1	Familienname	Wzientoszczak
2	Vornamen (Rufname unterstreichen)	Adolf Heinrich
3	Geburtstag, -monat, -jahr	30. November 1918
4	Geburtsort, Verwaltungsbezirk (z. B. Kreis, Reg. Bezirk)	Dortmund do. / Arnsberg
5	Staatsangehörigkeit (auch frühere)	Deutsches Reich
6	Religion	evgl.
7	Familienstand	ledig
8	Beruf (nach Berufsverzeichnis)	erlernter ausgeübter
9	Eltern	Vater: Johann Wzientoszczak (Rufname, Familienname); Händler (Beruf (nach Berufsverzeichnis)); (wenn verstorben: † und Sterbejahr) Mutter: Anna (Rufname, Familienname); Siepmann (Mädchenname); (wenn verstorben: † und Sterbejahr)

Wehrpass to Adolf Wzientoszczak, of *Feldgendarmerie Trupp* 336.

12 | 13

noch IV. Aktiver Wehrdienst

Zugehörigkeit zu Dienststellen des Heeres oder der Luftwaffe (auch im Kriege)

von	bis	Dienststelle (Truppenteil usw.)	Stammrollen-Nr. Ranglisten-Nr.
31/8. 39	30.10. 39	Kraftf. Ers. Komp. 69	364/39
30.10. 1939	30.4. 1942	1. Kompanie Verkehrs-Regl. Btl. 752	Kr 153/39
1.5.42	25.5. 42	Feldgend.-Abtlg. (mot.) 551	–"–
26.5. 1942	7.10. 1942	2./Feldgend. Ers. Abt. 3	478/42
8.10. 42	7.11. 42	1./Feldgend. Ers. Abt. 3	545/42
8.11. 42	5.12. 42	1. Feldgend. Ausb. Abt. I	Kr. 56
6.12. 42	12.1. 43	Feldgend.-Trupp 336 I.D.	Kr. 35
13.1. 43	23.2. 44	Feldgend.-Trupp 336	Kr. 35a

At first a fairly unremarkable document, showing him serving first with a Traffic Control unit and ultimately with the *Feldgendarmerie Trupp* of 336 *Infanterie* Division, with service throughout the campaign in the West and on the Eastern Front.

Nachweisung über etwaige Aufnahme in ein Standort-, Feld-, Kriegs- oder Reservelazarett

Lazarett	Tag und Monat der Laz.-Aufnahme	Jahr	Krankheit	Unterschrift des absendenden Truppenteils (Hauptmann usw. Hauptfeldwebel)	Tag und Monat der Entlassung aus dem Lazarett	Jahr	Etwaige Bemerkung in Bezug auf die Entlassung aus dem Lazarett (übergeführt nach Nr. als geheilt zum Truppenteil usw.)	Unterschrift des die Entlassung bewirkenden Lazarettbeamten
Leichtkr. Kriegslaz. 4/[illegible]	[illegible]	43	-13-		24.8.	43	[illegible]	[illegible]
Leichtkr. Kriegslaz. 4/[illegible]	31.8.	43	-13-	Ortslazarett (mot) 3/562	14.11.	43	[illegible]	[illegible]
Feldlazarett 2/542	13.11.	43						
Feldlazarett (mot.) 614	16. Okt.	1943			29. Okt.	1943		
Kriegslazarett 1/606	11.11.	43	-36-		15.11.	43	Truppe	Oberzahlmeister [illegible]

Mitgegebene Wertsachen und Papiere siehe folgende Seiten!

12 | 13

The Wzientoszczak *Soldbuch* also still exists however and as well as showing the medical code 13 for Venereal Disease (considered a self-inflicted illness) it also shows 36, a code used for faking illness.

Bescheinigungen
über die Richtigkeit der Zusätze und Berichtigungen auf Seiten 1 und 2

Lfd. Nr.	Art der Änderung	auf Seite	Datum	Truppenteil	Unterschrift	Dienstgrad und Dienststellung
1	Rangverlust	1	8.1.44	Fg.Kpp. 336		Leutnant d. Feldgend. u. Führer d. Feldg.-Trupps
	Gem. Urteil					
	Gericht d. 336. I.D.					
	St.L. 11/44					
	v. 25.1.44					

Leutnant d. Feldgend. u.
Führer d. Feldg.-Trupps

This behaviour earned Wzientoszczak a demotion (*Rangverlust*) from a junior NCO (*Unteroffizier*) to private with the resultant loss of pay and status.

22. Gesucht.

Gesucht wird Unteroffizier (tatsächlich nur Obergefreiter) Reinhold Lechler (nachstehendes Lichtbild), geb. am 13. 1. 1924 in Hassloch (Westmark). L. treibt sich zwischen Ost- und Westfront angeblich auf der Suche nach seiner Truppe herum.

Trägt EK. I. und II., Ostmedaille, Krimschild, Verwundetenabzeichen in Silber, Infanteriesturmabzeichen und rum. Medaille »Kreuzzug gegen den Bolschewismus«. Festnehmen und nächstem Kriegsgericht zuführen unter gleichzeitiger Mitteilung an Dienststelle Feldpostnr. 14 777 zu St. L. 423/44.

A 1945 dated 'Wanted' notice stating that if the suspect is apprehended he is to be handed over to the nearest Court Martial.

Axis Military Police

Japan

Japan's military police force, the *Kempeitai* (literally 'Corps of Law Soldiers') was founded in 1881. It initially consisted of just 349 men, but by the end of the Second World War had expanded to at least 36,000 plus several thousand auxiliaries.

Although the Imperial Japanese Navy maintained its own very small police branch, known as the *Tokkeitai*, a reciprocal arrangement between the various braches of the armed forces allowed the *Kempeitai* authority over all military personnel. The *Tokkeitai* seems to have been used by the navy principally to prevent the army interfering in matters the navy considered its own.

Organisation

Area Headquarters

A *Kempeitai* headquarters, commanded by a Major-General (*Shosho*) with a full Colonel (*Taisa*) as his second in command, was co-located with each army which was nominally in control of a specific area. Each area headquarters was then in charge of three field offices.

Field Office

The Kempeitai field office was commanded by a Lieutenant-Colonel (*Chusa*), with a Major (*Shosa*) as his second in command. Each field office controlled approximately 375 *Kempei*. The field offices were in turn sub-divided into sections.

Sections

The *Kempeitai* section (*Buntai*) was commanded by a captain (*Tai-i*) with a first- lieutenant (*Chu-i*) as second in command. Each section fielded around 65 *Kempei*. The Sections were further sub-divided into detachments.

Detachments

The *Kempeitai* detachment (*Bunkentai*) was normally commanded by a second- lieutenant (*Sho-i*) with a warrant officer (*Junshikan*) as second in command. Each detachment consisted of around 20 *Kempei* divided between three squads.

Above: Japanese *Kempei Tai* armband, the Kanji represent the words 'Law Soldier'

Left: Kempei Tai troops, all wearing the distinctive armband.

Squads

Three types of squad were to be found in each detachment, the police squad *(keimu han)*, the admin squad *(naikin han)* and a special duties squad *(Tokumu han)*. Auxiliaries were not permitted to rise above the rank of sergeant-major (*Shocho*).

Duties

The principal duties of the *Kempeitai* were as follows:

a) Issuing and controlling travel passes
b) Recruitment of local labour.
c) Counter Intelligence
d) Propaganda and counter-propaganda
e) Security in rear areas
f) Psychological warfare

Uniforms

Members of the *Kempeitai* most commonly wore the standard M1930 (M90) or M1938 (M98) uniform in the field, although civilian clothing was also authorized for wear in certain circumstances. On the earlier M1930 uniforms, branch of service was shown by the colour of the swallow-tail shaped collar tabs, black in the case of the *Kempeitai*, with ranks bars being worn on the shoulder.

On the M1938 uniform jacket the Kempeitai wore a branch of service insignia in the form of a inverted black double chevron above the breast pocket of the tunic. In both cases a white armband with Japanese '*Kanji*' characters for '*Ken*' (Law) and '*Hei*' (Soldier) was worn by non-commissioned ranks.

A small gilt metal eight-pointed sunburst was also introduced to be worn just behind the collar rank by officers on the M1938 tunic.
Generic badges of rank were worn on the collar.

Armament

Typical weapons carried by Officers were the *Katana* sword as well as a pistol, and a pistol with bayonet for junior ranks. In addition, NCOs often carried a wooden *Kendo* sword (*Shinai*), this being used as a form of club to administer beatings to prisoners.

Italy

The military police function for the Italian armed forces was performed by the Corps of Royal *Carabinieri*, a formation which had been created in July 1814 by Royal Patent. In somewhat similar fashion to the *Gendarmerie* in France, the *Carabinieri* had wide ranging powers and operated in both civil and military matters. During the Second World War, *Carabinieri* were active in the military police role in all areas where the Italian Army was engaged. Like their German counterparts in the *Feldgendarmerie*, the *Carabinieri* were involved both in the purely military support role, but also in the war against the partisans, most prominently during the occupation of the Balkans.

Special uniform distinctions included an old Napolenic style bicorn hat known as the *Lucerna* which carried a large vertical plume. On operational duties the plume was removed and the hat normally covered with a grey-green cloth cover. The *Carabinieri* badge consisted of a large silvered metal flaming grenade emblem bearing the initials 'VE' for King Victor Emmanuel.

Carabinieri also wore distinctive collar patches but the basic field service uniform was the same as worn by other Italian army troops.

Following the armistice with the Allies, both the new Government forces in the south and the fascist regime in the north fielded *Carabinieri* units, the latter being used in anti-partisan operations. In October 1943, the Germans attempted to disband these units, having no trust in them, and deport their members to German as forced labour. This simply resulted in thousands of *Carabinieri* deserting to the resistance. Over 9,000 *Carabinieri* were either killed or wounded fighting alongside the partisans against the Germans.

Hungary

As a member of the Axis since aligning itself with Germany and Italy in November 1940, Hungary fielded considerable numbers of troops on the Eastern Front following the German invasion of the Soviet Union. Along with their regular formations, the Hungarian army fielded units of the *Csendőrség* or *Gendarmerie*. These troops were recruited directly from the army (*Honvédség*) into the *Gendarmerie* in the first place so when the Field *Gendarmerie* was created and troops assigned back for service with the army, they were already trained soldiers who were then given the additional training required to perform their military police duties.

Normal *Gendarmerie* wore a gorget with the Hungarian coat of arms over a banner with the legend '*Csendor*' whilst the field security troops wore a similar gorget with the banner bearing the legend '*Tabori Biztonsag*'

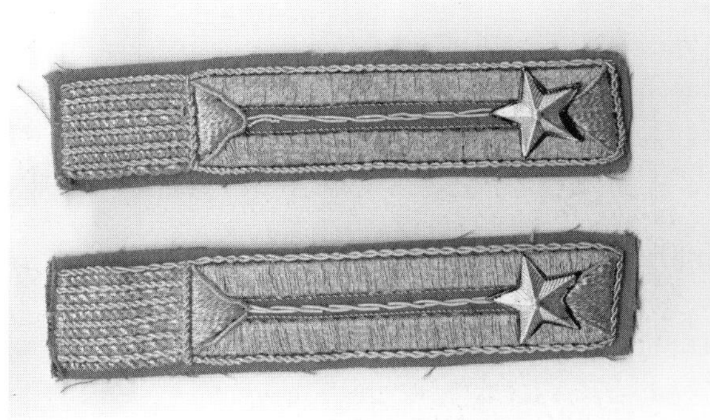

Above left: *Carabinieri* Cap Badge, the Second World War period with 'VE' (Victor Emmanuel) cipher.

Above right: Collar badges for *Carabinieri* NCO for the grey green service tunic.

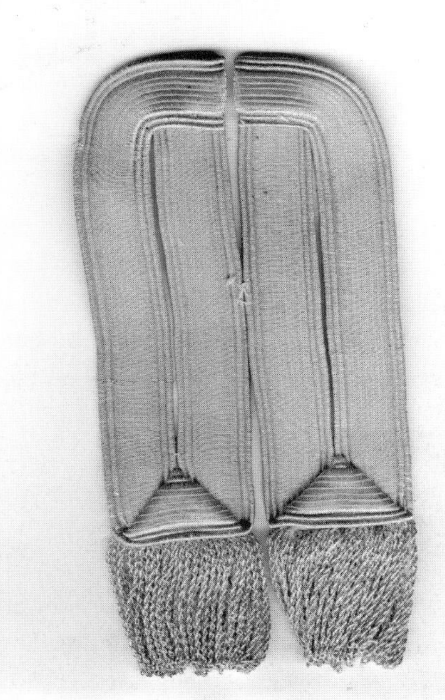

Above left: Collar badges for senior *Carabinieri* ranks for the double breasted dress blue uniform.

Above right: Hungarian *Gendarmerie*, with their distinctive headgear. Note the circular patrol Leader's badge just at the point of the coat collar of the *Gendarme* in the centre.

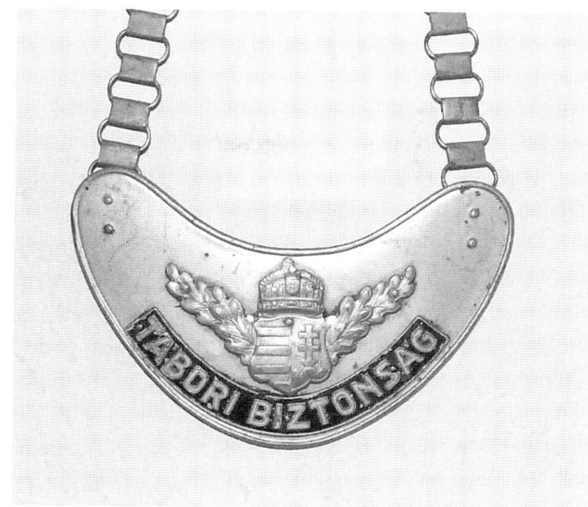

Above left: Breast badge for a patrol leader of the Hungarian Field Police. The reverse has a clip fitting to allow it to be clipped to the right breast pocket.

Above right: Hungarian Field Police gorget.

A member of the Hungarian Field Police operating with the German *Feldjägerkorps*. Note the Hungarian gorget being worn. (*Otto Spronk Photo Files*)

Romania

Romanian forces fighting alongside their German allies on the Eastern Front from June 1941 included units of the *Gendarmerie*/military police who performed following main activities:

a) Preventing partisan activities;
b) guarding civilian and military installations;
c) maintaining law and order;
d) repel attacks by enemy airborne and paratroopers;
e) monitoring of political opponents/resistance.

The Romanian *Gendarmerie* was declared a military corps by a law passed in April 1943 which stipulated that it would perform the function of both civilian and military police and was subordinated directly to the war ministry though its services could also be called upon by the interior ministry.

On 23 August 1944, Romania changed sides, and from then on the functions of its MPs included:

a) to locate and neutralise enemy soldiers as well as their ammunition and weapons depots;
b) to block enemy movement along supply routes;
c) to disarm small groups of enemy soldiers;
d) to arrest or eliminate enemy airborne troops;
e) to secure captured enemy depots;
f) to arrests of enemy troops and pro Nazi elements;
g) to arrest and eliminate pro-Nazi partisans in Transylvania;
h) to find and destroy pro-Nazi propaganda; Gendarmerie units also acted in an infantry role when required.

Bulgaria

A grey- green four patch-pocket tunic with high collar not dissimilar to those worn by German troops but with extremely long 'points' to the scallops on the pocket flaps was used, generally with six button fastening to the front. Collar patches were German style '*Litzen*' but with wide Imperial Russian style shoulder straps.

For military police personnel, a heavy metal shield shaped Gorget bearing a rampant lion under the legend '*Voenna Politsiya*' (military police) , all topped by the Royal Crown was worn. The Gorget was silvered finish for lower ranks and gilt for officers.

Above left: Very rare gorget as worn by Bulgarian Military Police. (*Peter Groch*)

Above right: A *Feldgendarmerie-Trupp* assembled for a wreath laying ceremony at the funeral of a comrade.

Geliebt, beweint und unvergessen.
Ruhe sanft, lb. Matthias!

Fern der Heimat ruht in fremder Erde mein geliebter Lebenskamerad, unser bester Vati, unser lieber Sohn, Bruder, Schwager und Schwiegersohn

Matthias Schiller

Gefreiter bei einer Feldgendarmerie-Einheit.

Im Alter von 33 Jahren gab er am 26. Dez, 1941 im Kampf gegen den Bolschewismus sein Leben für Führer, Volk u. Vaterland.

Ehre seinem Andenken!

Obituary card for *Gefreiter* Matthias Schiller, klilled in action on the Eastern Front on 26 December 1941 in the 'battle against Bolshevism'!

Zur frommen Erinnerung
an meinen lieben Gatten, Vater, Sohn
und Bruder

Alois Wieland

Obergefreiter der Feldgendarmerie
geb. 19. Sept. 1907 in Schemmerberg
gefallen am 6. Juni 1944 im Westen

In fremder Erde schlummerst Du.
Von fremder Hand gebracht zur Ruh.
Bitter ach ist unser Schmerz,
Doch unser Aug schaut himmelwärts,
Wo Du nun weilst in ewger Wonne,
Geschmückt mit einer Heldenkrone.
Denn die für Herd und Heimat sterben.
Vom Herrn als Lohn die Krone erben.
Vater unser. Ave Maria.

A. Berger, Laupheim

Obituary card for *Obergefreiter* Alois Wieland, killed in action on the Western Front on D-Day, 6 June 1944.

Zum Andenken
an meinen guten Mann
und treubesorgten Vater

Jakob Hunglinger

Gefreiter in einer
Feldgendarmerieabteilung
Vermessungstechniker

welcher am 26. Dezember 1941
im Alter von 29 Jahren ostwärts
der Linie Orel-Kursk (Rußland)
den Heldentod fand.

Er kämpfte bereits in Frankreich.

Wenn Liebe könnte Wunder tun
Und Tränen Tote wecken,
Dann würde dich wohl ganz gewiß
Nicht fremde Erde decken.

Er ruhe in Frieden!

Obituary card for *Gefreiter* Jakob Hunglinger, surveyor with a *Feldgendarmerie Abteilung*, killed in action in Russia 26 December 1941.

Wir bitten um das Gebet für

Herrn

Karl Lehr

Feldgendarm

Buchdruckereibesitzer in Passau

welcher nach schwerer Verwundung bei Nowka am 29. März 1942 im Kriegslazarett zu Witebsk im Alter von 31 Jahren den Heldentod gestorben ist.

Er ruhe in Frieden!

Du hast ihn uns geliehen, o Herr,
Und er war unser Glück.
Du hast ihn zurückgefordert,
Und wir geben ihn dir ohne Murren.
Aber das Herz ist voll Wehmut.

St. Hieronymus

Buchdruckerei Lehr, Passau

Obituary card for *Feldgendarm* Karl Lehr, who died on 29 March 1942 of wounds received in battle near Nowka.

This was the fate that many *Feldgendarmen* would share with their counterparts in the combat arms.

Bibliography and Recommended Reading

Böckle, Karl-Heinz, *Feldgendarmen, Feldjäger, Militärpolizisten*, Motorbuch-Verlag, Stuttgart, 1987

Gessner, Klaus, *Geheime Feldpolizei*, Militär Verlag der DDR, Berlin 1986

Hispan, José Garcia, *La Guardia Civil en la Division Azul*, José Garcia, Garcia Hispán Edition, Alicante, 1992

Krichbaum, Wilhelm and Munoz, Antonio, *Secret Field Police*, Europa Books, Bayside, USA, 2008

Lamont-Brown, Raymond, *Kempeitai*, Sutton Publishing, Stroud, 1998

Pasnay, Charles, *Rapporten van de GFP 1940–44*, Pasnay, Charles, Uitgeveridje Nederlansche Boekhandel, Antwerp

Williamson, Gordon, *German Military Police Units 1939-45*, Osprey Publishing, Oxford.

Witter, Robert, *Chain Dogs*, Pictorial Histories Publishing, Montana, 1994

Witter, Robert, *Chain Dogs Vol. 2*, Pictorial Histories Publishing, Montana, 1994

Period Publications

Allgemeine-Heeresmitteilungen—Various, Oberkommando des Heeres, Berlin

Deutsche Uniformen Zeitschrift, Otto Dietrich Verlag, Berlin

Feldgendarmerie Vorschrift, Oberkommando der Wehrmacht, Berlin 1940

Heeresdienstvorschrift—Various, Oberkommando des Heeres, Berlin

Heersverordungsblatt—Various, Oberkommando des Heeres, Berlin

Luftwaffenverordhunsblatt—Various, Reichsluftfahrtministerium, Berlin

Marineverordnungsblatt—Various, Oberkommando der Kriegsmarine, Berlin

Uniformen Markt, Otto Dietrich Verlag, Berlin

On-Line Sources

Lexicon der Wehrmacht—at www.lexikon-der-wehrmacht.de

Probably the single best source for research into the German armed forces in the Second World War.

Feldpost Number Database—at www.axishistory.com